The First Tank War

Doctrines and Battles of World War I

Bruce Oliver Newsome, Ph.D.

The First Tank War: Doctrines and Battles of World War I

by Bruce Oliver Newsome, Ph.D.
www.BruceNewsome.com

Sign up for bonus content and news: https://www.patreon.com/c/bruceolivernewsome

Published by: Perseublishing,
PO Box 181802, Coronado, California 92178, United States of America

Copyright © 2025 Bruce Oliver Newsome, Ph.D

All rights reserved. No part of this publication may be reproduced or stored in a retrieval system or transmitted, in any form or by any means, electronic, mechanical, photocopying, recording or otherwise, without prior permission in writing from Tank Archives Press.

HIS027090	HISTORY / Military / World War I	
HIS027240	HISTORY / Military / Vehicles	
HIS027060	HISTORY / Military / Strategy	
NHWR5	First World War	
NHWL	Modern warfare	
JWMV	Military vehicles	

ISBN: 978-1-951171-24-7

Cover design by Bruce Oliver Newsome, Ph.D., image by Google Gemini.

Acknowledgements

The author wishes to thank:
- David Fletcher, Historian, The Tank Museum
- Andrew Hart, patron
- Gemma Hollman, Senior Archives Assistant, Libraries & Collections, Kings College London, for permission to quote from Liddell Hart's papers
- Jonathan Holt, Archives Assistant, The Tank Museum
- Bryn Loyd, Archives Assistant, The Tank Museum
- Scott Meyer, patron
- Midland County, Texas, libraries
- The National Archives, Kew, UK
- Michelle Pfalzgraf, Librarian, University of Texas Permian Basin
- Sheldon Rogers, Archives Assistant, The Tank Museum
- Katie Thompson, Archives Assistant, The Tank Museum
- Marjolijn Verbrugge, Archive and Supporting Collections Manager, The Tank Museum, for permission to quote from the archives
- David Willey, Curator, The Tank Museum

Contents

Acknowledgements	2
Contents	3
Maps	4
Tables	4
Photographs	5
Abbreviations	6
Introduction	7
1: Doctrine, 1914-1916	13
2. Flers, Courcelette, and Thiepval, September 1916	23
3. Ancre, November 1916	49
4. Doctrine, 1916-1917	53
5. Arras, April 1917	71
6. Messines Ridge, June 1917	77
7. Passchendaele, July 1917	83
8. Plan 1918 and Tank Raids 1917	89
9. Cambrai, November 1917	99
10. Fuller's First Plan 1919	123
11. Fuller's Tank Raids, January to June 1918	137
12. Foot's Plan 1919	141
13. Fuller's Second Plan 1919	145
14. Hamel, July 1918	167
15. Sauvillers, July 1918	177
16. Amiens, August 1918	181
17. Albert and Bapaume, August 1918	197
18. Arras, August 1918	201
19. Épehy, September 1918	205
20. Canal du Nord, September 1918	207
21. Saint-Quentin Canal, September 1918	211
22. River Selle, October 1918	217
23. Mormal Forest, October 1918	221
24. River Sambre, November 1918	225
25. Findings	229
References	242
Index	246
About the author	254

Maps

1. Flers, Courcelette, and Martinpuich, September 1916 — 22
2. The mock battlefield at Elveden, Norfolk, 1916 — 40
3. The Somme campaign, July to November 1916 — 48
4. Fuller's assault waves, February 1917 — 65
5. Fuller's tank tactics, February 1917 — 66
6. Arras, April 1917 — 70
7. Messines Ridge, June 1917 — 78
8. Passchendaele, July 1917 — 82
9. The Cambrai plan, 4 August 1917 — 94
10. The Cambrai plan, 29 October 1917 — 98
11. Fuller's suggested formation of a section of tanks and two platoons of infantry — 107
12. Fuller's suggested formation of two sections of tanks and a battalion of infantry — 108
13. Fuller's tactics for a section of tanks employing fascines — 109
14. The Cambrai offensive, November 1917 — 119
15. Fuller's formation of a company of tanks and two battalions of infantry, 27 January — 132
16. Fuller's tactics for cleaning and stopping trenches, 27 January 1918 — 133
17. Fuller's formation for a frontal attack on a village, 27 January 1918 — 134
18. Fuller's morcellated front, 27 January 1918 — 144
19. Hamel, July 1918 — 166
20. Sauvillers, July 1918 — 176
21. Amiens, August 1918 — 180
22. German anti-tank minefields, 1918 — 196
23. Operations from 17 October 1918 — 224

Tables

1. Force structure at Flers, Courcelette, and Martinpuich, 15 September 1916 — 27
2. Martel's required classes of "tank," November 1916 — 55
3. Force structure at Passchendaele, 31 July 1917 — 85
4. Issues and solutions for an offensive in Spring 1918, according to Fuller, June 1917 — 90
5. Force structure and objectives for Fuller's "Tank Raids," 8 August 1917 — 96
6. Force structure for the offensive at Cambrai, as of 28 October 1917 — 103
7. Force structure for the offensive at Cambrai, as of 20 November 1917 — 103
8. Fuller's expectations for "tank raids," 28 January 1918 — 137
9. Future deliveries of tracked vehicles, as estimated in April 1918 — 152
10. Fuller's force requirements, missions, concentrations for Plan 1919, in May 1918 — 153
11. Future deliveries of tracked vehicles, as estimated in June 1918 — 154
12. Future deliveries of tracked vehicles, as estimated in September 1918 — 157
13. Force structure at Hamel, 4 July 1918 — 168
14. Force structure at Sauvillers, 23 July 1918 — 178
15. Tank units in France, as of 8 August 1918 — 184
16. Tank formation structure from 30 July to 8 August 1918 — 185
17. Allocations and missions, as of 24 July, 26 July, 30 July, and 8 August 1918 — 186
18. Allocations of supply companies, by August 1918 — 191
19. Forces and objectives at Bapaume, 21 August, and Albert, 22 August 1918 — 199
20. British-administered tank formations and units in France, early September 1918 — 203
21. BEF-administered formations and units in France, 27 September 1918 — 204
22. The BEF's allocations for the offensive at River Sambre on 4 November 1918 — 226
23. British doctrines and operations of the Great War, by geography, inputs, outputs — 240

Photographs

1. Holt 75 Tractor, 1914	12
2. Pushable shield, 1915	14
3. California Giants, 1915	15
4. Killen-Strait Tractor takes on barbed wire, 1915	17
5. The pilot Heavy Tank, 14 January 1916	19
6. Ernest Swinton in 1918	21
7. Giffard le Quesne Martel in 1925	21
8. D17 or Dinnaken, on 17 September 1916	47
9. The tank staff in Bermicourt, mid-1917	52
10. Stephen Foot in 1918	58
11, The front page of The Daily Mirror, 22 November 1916	63
12. Infantry cross Messines Ridge, 7 June 1917	81
13. Mark IV tanks knocked out at "Clapham Junction" on 31 July 1917	84
14. The Tank Corps intelligence staff's panoramas of the ridge before Cambrai	100
15. A surviving copy of Hugh Elles' Special Order Number 6, November 1917	115
16. Marcoing bridge	117
17. The bridge at Masnières, and the Mark V that caused its collapse on 20 November	118
18. Renault FT light tank	122
19. One of the first nine A7Vs tanks, in March 1918	179
20. Mark V* tanks, circa 9 August 1918	190
21. The road from Albert to Bapaume, at Pozières, and a knocked out Mark I	198
22. Medium A tank	200
23. The Saint-Quentin Canal at Bellenglise	209
24. The Saint-Quentin Canal south of Riqueval Bridge, and the infantry who crossed it	210
25. The Saint-Quentin Canal at Bellicourt	211
26. The Mak IX Tank (carrier)	223

Abbreviations

AEF	American Expeditionary Force
AFV	armoured fighting vehicle
AP	armour-piercing
Aus.	Australian
BEF	British Expeditionary Force
BGGS	Brigadier-General, General Staff (corps echelon)
Cdn.	Canadian
CGS	Chief of the General Staff
CIGS	Chief of the Imperial General Staff
DAA&QMG	Deputy Assistant Adjutant and Quartermaster General
DCGS	Deputy Chief of the General Staff
DGMWS	Director-General Mechanical Warfare Supply
DGTC	Director-General Tank Corps, War Department
DMO(&I)	Director of Military Operations (and Intelligence)
DoD	Department of Defense
DSD	Director of Staff Duties
FOO	Forward Observation Officer
Fr.	France or French
FSR	Field Service Regulations
GHQ	General Headquarters (usually field army or regional echelon)
GS	General Staff
GSO	General Staff Officer
HE	high-explosive
hp	horse-power
HQ	headquarters
in.	inch
IWM	Imperial War Museum, London
km	kilometers
kmh or kph	kilometers per hour
LHCMA	Liddell Hart Centre for Military Archives
m	meters
MG	machine-gun
MGGS	Major-General, General Staff (regional echelon HQ)
mm	millimetres
MoD	Ministry of Defence
MP	Member of Parliament
mph	miles per hour
MS	manuscript
MW(S)D	Mechanical Warfare (Supply) Department, Ministry of Munitions
NZ	New Zealand
Panzer	Panzerkampfwagen (armored fighting vehicle)
pdr	pounder (a gun; numerical prefix is nominal weight of projectile)
RA	Royal Artillery
RACTM	Royal Armoured Corps Tank Museum, Bovington, Dorset
RAF	Royal Air Force
RE	Royal Engineers
RFC	Royal Flying Corps
RHA	rolled homogenous armour; Royal Horse Artillery
RNAS	Royal Naval Air Service
RTC	Royal Tank Corps
RTR	Royal Tank Regiment
TS	Tank Supply Department, Ministry of Munitions (later: MWSD)
UK	United Kingdom
US(A)	United States (of America)
WD	War Department
WO	War Office
yds.	yards

Introduction

During the Great War (1914-1918), the proposed mechanical solutions to the stalemate included big-wheel landships, wheeled bridge-pushers, trench-straddling personnel carriers, self-propelled artillery, and machine-gun carriers. The preferred acquisition was named tank, but even tanks remained contested, between different weight classes, armaments, types of mobility, and protection levels.

The doctrine too remained contested. Indeed, many of the same questions are asked today. Should tanks surprise the enemy or be preceded by bombardment? Should tanks assault by day or night? Should they be concentrated or distributed? Should they be combined with all arms, some arms, or no other arm? Should they lead or follow other arms? Should they sustain a penetration or hit and run? Should they hold objectives or rally to the rear? Should they aim at enemy fortifications, or infantry, or artillery, or supplies, or headquarters?

The term "**tank**" is often used loosely for any armoured or fighting vehicle, but is best operationalized as a tracked, armoured, fighting vehicle (AFV) whose armaments are designed to fire anywhere on its circumference. Not all AFVs are tanks. Some are optimized for carrying personnel or supplies, for instance, even though they might also be tracked and turreted. During the Great War, British authorities categorized all variants as "tanks," although later they sensibly differentiated tanks from carriers (Newsome 2021a).

Doctrine is any set of official guidelines. By 1916, tanks were in use, but the doctrine for their use remained unsettled. British doctrine was subject to users in France, users at home, politicians, staff in the War Office, staff in the Admiralty (which used AFVs of its own), higher echelon commanders, the commander-in-chief of the combatant command in France (British Expeditionary Force; BEF), and the staff at the BEF's General Headquarters (GHQ). That year, tank operations were small and distributed, and mostly frustrating, but sometimes spectacular. By 1917, the value of tanks was proven. In 1918, they necessarily contributed to the defeat of Germany, without need for the decisive offensive planned for Spring 1919.

The Neglected Principles

This book reviews the doctrines and battles involving British tanks during the Great War. The book rediscovers seven principles of mechanized warfare: **terrain**, **concentration**, **surprise**, **combined arms**, **speed**, **sustainment**, and **exploitation**. These principles are not obvious. No formal principles of mechanized warfare or even manoeuvre warfare were articulated at the time. The British Army's eight "principles of war" (objective; offensive; security; mass or concentration; economy of force; movement; surprise; cooperation), as articulated by the War Office's Field Service Regulations (FSR) (as re-editioned in 1909 and re-issued in 1913), were not formally applied to mechanized or manoeuvre warfare until the 1920s, although some appear in the tank arm's doctrine in 1918 (see Chapters 10 onwards).

Furthermore, some principles were subordinated or conflated with others. The principle of mobility is most conflated.* **Mobility** is the ability to move. It is

---

* None of the terms in this paragraph is defined by the US DoD's dictionary (2021) or the UK MoD's glossaries (2025).

routinely conflated with manoeuvre, but they are not the same, although they are related. **Manoeuvre** is movement with intent to reach an advantageous position or to prevent the enemy's movement into an advantageous position. Both mobility and manoeuvre are conflated with their means. Pedestrians, equines, and bovines are the traditional self-moving means of war. **Mechanization** is the substitution of machines for bio-locomotion. **Vehicles** are means for moving things. Some vehicles are capable of moving themselves, so are known as **automobiles**. **Armour** is a protective material. Although "armour" is often used as a shorthand for armoured vehicles or even mechanized forces, manoeuvre does not need to be achieved with either vehicles or armour. Mobility is still achieved mostly in unarmoured vehicles. Manoeuvring on foot continues to be trained, despite mechanization. (In English, carried troops are conventionally known as **"mounted,"** and moving on foot is known as **"dismounted."**)

The principle of appropriate terrain implies mobility: the principle of mobility is dependent on the selection of appropriate terrain. Over time, the requirement for easier terrain was rebutted by the requirement for more mobile machines. The elevation of a principle of mobility to the same level as the principle of appropriate terrain was tempting, but never formally articulated in any doctrine written by or for the tank arm, until the 1920s.

The Seven Principles of Mechanized Warfare

Terrain is the scope, topography, and morphology of an area of land. The principle of terrain expects forces to be used where the terrain is conducive. Artillery prefer to fire from behind cover. Cavalry prefer open terrain where they can exploit their speed. Infantry prefer woods and buildings, which cover them from enemy observation and fire. Even before tanks deployed to France, doctrinists realized that tanks should attack where the terrain is dry, open, and undamaged or has been improved by engineers. None of these qualities was true of the first operations involving tanks. Doctrinists continued to specify appropriate terrain, and to require more mobile vehicles, until the principle was routinely fulfilled in 1918.

The **concentration** of forces is the quantity of forces per area. The principle of concentration expects friendly forces to concentrate against the enemy, ideally where the enemy is weakest, in order to achieve a local superiority. The principle of concentration is often attached to a caveat about the advantages of distribution, wherever one is trying to avoid enemy forces, or to move quicker on multiple routes than one could move on one route. Offensively, the principle of concentration was already one of the eight principles of war before tanks were ever mooted. Nevertheless, when tanks were first deployed their concentration was much weaker than their prior doctrinists had wished. Users continued to specify their wish, until it was routinely fulfilled in 1918.

Surprise is an affect in reaction to something unexpected. The principle of surprise expects friendly forces to surprise enemy forces so that the enemy forces are less capable than otherwise they would be. The enemy forces might be unready in that particular space and time. They might be caught in transit before they can optimize for combat. They might be facing away from the attackers. They might be cognitively incapacitated by the psychological shock of the unexpected. Surprise is conventionally subcategorized in space and time, such that a force might be surprised in only space, or only time, or both. Before tanks were introduced, higher echelons routinely gave up surprise in hope that days of preliminary bombardment would disable enemy defences. The tank doctrinists usually preferred surprise over preliminary bombardment. They got their way by late 1917.

To **combine arms** means that at least two arms cooperate. During the Great War, Anglophones did not talk of "combined arms," rather of "cooperation." The Tank Corps' final wartime note on tank-infantry doctrine defines **cooperation** as "the act of working together to one end, namely, to clinch with the enemy and destroy him" ("Infantry and Tank Cooperation and Training," 27 January 1918: 1, RACTM E19149.127). The principle of combined arms expects the advantages of one arm to compensate for the disadvantages of another, or the advantages of both arms to synergize. For instance, artillery bombard enemy artillery indirectly (without direct line of sight), until other arms can directly neutralize enemy artillery, after which friendly artillery can safely move forward. Artillery usually cooperated indirectly, rarely in direct sight of other arms. Tank doctrinists expected infantry and tanks to cooperate directly (although disputes remained about which arm should lead, how close they should be, and how they should behave towards different targets). However, the first use of tanks was rushed, such that at least some infantry had no experience with tanks, and some tank crews struggled with identifying friend or foe. Over time, doctrinists perfected the combination of tanks, infantry, indirect-fire artillery and machine-guns, direct-fire artillery, aircraft, Royal Engineers acting as combat engineers, and tanks adapted for engineering.

Speed is the rate of movement. As typically used, the term implies quickness relative to normal. The principle of speed expects you to act quicker than enemies react. The principle is applied to: **command**[*] (make decisions quicker than the enemy, although decision-making faces a trade-off between speed and accuracy or correctness); **control**[**] (make subordinates execute your intent quicker); **communications**[***] (get information about the enemy quicker; and communicate your intent to the executors quicker); and movement over terrain (reach objectives quicker).

Clearly, the principle of speed overlaps the principles of terrain and mobility. Speed has never been an official British principle of war, although many doctrinists have emphasized speed of advance, from Sun Tzu to the first tank doctrinists. As Chapter 1 shows, urgency is explicit in Ernest Swinton's doctrine of February 1916, lest enemy artillery fire hits assaulters on their objectives, or counter-attackers get organized before assaulters consolidate. The deployed tankies agreed. However, the first operations were slowed by a creeping barrage, to a speed less than half the maximum speed of the first tanks – a fact ignored by commanders of the time and historians later, who complained about the slow speed of tanks.

---

[*] The US DoD (2021: 40) defines "command" as "1. the authority that a commander in the armed forces lawfully exercises over subordinates by virtue of rank or assignment," and "2. an order given by a commander; that is, the will of the commander expressed." The UK MoD glossary does not define it.
[**] The US DoD (2021: 48) defines "control" as "authority that may be less than full command exercised by a commander over part of the activities of subordinate or other organizations." The UK MoD glossary does not define it.
[***] I define communications as the movement or the means of movement of information. The US DoD's dictionary (2021) and UK MoD's glossaries do not define it.

In August 1917, the Tank Corps chief of staff (J.F.C. Fuller) developed a raiding strategy that expects an advance into the enemy's rear, and a return to friendly lines, within hours, before the enemy can intercept. By 1918, JFC Fuller was pondering medium tanks that could strike enemy headquarters before the enemy could counter the offensive. Still, he did not separate a principle of speed, although he listed it under the principle of mobility (as a principle of war). In the 1920s, Basil Liddell Hart conflated the two, a conflation that usefully draws attention to speed, but neglects other aspects of mobility (such as agility and obstacle-crossing), other capabilities (especially lethality), and other principles (especially sustainment) (Newsome 2024 and 2025).

Sustainment is the enablement of forces to keep operating.[*] Before tanks were deployed, the British Army already struggled to replenish the assaulters with their consumables (such as ammunition and water) and with materials (such as barbed wire) and tools to fortify captured objectives against counter-attackers. A solution is to reserve infantry with loads of consumables and defensive equipment, ready to fortify the objectives after the assaulters have captured them. Another solution is to send a fresh wave of assaulters to each objective line. When tanks were introduced, no resources were provided for sustaining them during operations. Instead, they were supposed to rally to the rear within hours. Even there, service and support were inadequate. (Conventionally, the arms are differentiated from their services and supports, such as mechanics, armourers, medics, and veterinarians. At the time of the Great War, the British Army tended to refer to service and support as "trades.") Poor sustainment, terrain, and mechanical reliability contributed to a perception that tanks are useless beyond hundreds of yards of assault (a perception that some historians continue to perpetuate). However, the tank arm's acquisition of supply tanks, mechanical reserves, and fighting reserves helped to establish a reputation, by 1918, for tanks to penetrate miles into enemy territory, even though mechanically their reliability had not improved much.

Exploitation is the pursuit of enemies in retreat and/or the interdiction of enemy command, control, communications, or logistics.[**] JFC Fuller wrote: "Exploitation is pursuit – the annihilation of a broken enemy by every available means" ("Tank Operations Decisive and Preparatory, 1918-1919," 28 January 1918: 2, appended to his journal as "A8," RACTM E1980.18). However, he also wanted exploiters to target enemy command, control, communications, logistics, and particularly artillery. The principle of exploitation expects provision of some type of force that is optimized for pursuing and interdicting. In the Great War, the arm optimized for these things was the cavalry, mainly on promise of speed. However, speed is only part of mobility, and horses are less mobile than pedestrians in certain terrain. At first, tanks were expected to break through the defensive lines, before cavalry

---

[*] The US DoD (2021: 132, 206) defines sustainment as "the provision of logistics and personnel services required to maintain and prolong operations until successful mission accomplishment," and defines logistics as "planning and executing the movement and support of forces." The MoD glossary defines neither.

[**] The US DoD (2021: 78) defines exploitation, in general, as "taking full advantage of success in military operations, following up initial gains, and making permanent the temporary effects already created," and, in particular, "an offensive operation that usually follows a successful attack and is designed to disorganize the enemy in depth."

exploit into the rear, but, in their first operations, tanks failed to break through, and the cavalry was not any quicker on the battlefield anyway. Over time, the tank arm planned on achieving more exploitation for itself, and required medium tanks as specialized tanks for exploitation. The tank doctrinists usually allowed for cooperation with cavalry, but mostly out of deference to GHQ. As soon as 1917, they were prospecting attacks by light or medium tanks on artillery, logistics, command, control, and communications, simultaneous with the main assault. By 1918, Fuller prospected such attacks before the main assault, on promise that defenders at the front would be incapacitated by confusion and scarcity.

The Tension Between Raids and Penetrations

Months after tanks were first used, a headquarters was established for the new arm. This HQ gathered meritorious staff, including Hugh Elles, Giffard Martel, Stephen Foot, F.H.E. Townshend, and eventually J.F.C. Fuller. By 1917, Fuller was writing doctrine that was authoritative for subordinate users, but still subject to higher echelons, and still restrained by inadequate resourcing. Within months, he suggested combined-arms "tank raids" to fill the gaps between offensives. Months later, in November 1917, elements from his proposals for raids and offensives came together in a satisfying offensive at Cambrai – on good terrain, where and when the enemy did not expect, with concentrated, combined arms, at unprecedented speed, with unprecedented sustainment of the assaulters, and some capacity to exploit.

In 1918, Fuller developed a technically ambitious proposal for a decisive offensive in 1919, best known as "Plan 1919." As Chapter 13 explains, it is often touted as the inspiration for Germany's *Blitzkrieg* in 1939. Yet Plan 1919 contains a dilemma between combined-arms offensives and independent tank raids. Indeed, Plan 1919 vaguely expects future medium tanks, without other arms, to surprise the enemy's headquarters, before a general assault by combined arms. Fuller himself never resolved this dilemma. By 1923, he erred towards independent raids on enemy socio-economics by submarine-launched amphibious tanks. He soon refocused on sustained offensives by combined arms, although he remained over-confident that smaller all-mechanized armies, supported by their own aircraft, could occupy the enemy's capital within days. He ignored the dilemma in later years, which helps to explain why historians have missed it.

Historians have missed too the fact that the conventionally identified Plan 1919 of May 1918 was actually Fuller's second Plan 1919, and that both are developments from a Plan 1918 that he wrote in 1917, as this book reveals for the first time.

Preview

The first chapter of this book compares the doctrines for mechanized warfare proposed from 1914, even before tanks were first used in 1916. The second chapter discovers how tanks were used in their first battles in September 1916, at Flers, Courcelette, and Thiepval. Chapter 3 moves on to the battles of Ancre in November.

The next chapter traces the development of doctrine by the headquarters of what would become the Tank Corps, from late 1916 to 1917.

Chapters 5 to 7 review the role of tanks in the first great battles of 1917: Arras, Messines Ridge, Passchendaele. Chapter 5 includes the first French-British conference on tank doctrine. Chapters 5 to 7 include the first experiences of Canadian and

Australian formations with tanks.

Chapter 8 reveals Fuller's creative proposals for envelopment and raiding by tanks, during the Summer of 1917. Chapter 9 explains how a proposal for a tank raid became a satisfying combined-arms offensive at Cambrai in November, and how it was undermined by under-provision for sustainment and exploitation.

Chapter 10 describes Fuller's proposal of January 1918 for a decisive offensive in Spring 1919 (effectively the first "Plan 1919," although he never dated Plan 1919 back to January).

Chapter 11 reviews Fuller's simultaneous proposals for combined-arms raids in 1918, pending the resourcing for a decisive offensive.

Chapter 12 introduces a little-known alternative Plan 1919, by Stephen Foot, then working on the tank staff in the War Office, after serving in France with the Tank Corps. Chapter 13 transitions to Fuller's subsequent Plan 1919, which Fuller dated to May, although without admitting any influence from Foot.

Chapters 14 to 24 explain the great combined-arms offensives of 1918: Hamel, Sauvillers, Amiens, Bapaume and Albert, Arras, Epehy, the Canal du Nord, the St. Quentin Canal, River Selle, Mormal Forest, and River Sambre.

Chapter 25 reviews the doctrinal and operational findings from the Great War, synthesizes the quantitative data from the chapters, compares the conventional wisdom in the historiography, and establishes the tank's real contributions to victory in 1918, and the lessons for the principles of mechanized warfare today.

A Holt 75 tractor, as received by the British in October 1914.

1
Doctrine, 1914-1916

The Great War broke out in August 1914. For months, operations stayed mobile, although by October the front around the port of Antwerp, Belgium, was starting to look like a siege. Since the forces there were largely British naval forces, including Royal Marines and the Royal Navy Air Service, both of which were unusually well mechanized for the time, the Admiralty was quicker than the War Department to realize requirements for mechanized solutions to the gathering stagnation.

However, the Admiralty's requirements were not for what we now know as tanks. From October 1914 to June 1915, Winston Churchill (1874-1965), as First Lord (the highest political appointee) of the Admiralty, wasted colossal resources on the wrong requirements, including a wheeled bridge-layer, various designs of wheeled trench-straddling personnel carrier, various designs of big-wheel landship, a push-able tracked shield, and an evolutionary series of articulated, wheeled, half-tracked, and tracked machine-gun carriers. So far as Churchill could be said to have a preferred doctrine, he argued for night-time advances by trench-straddling infantry carriers, as this chapter's first section explains.

Ernest Swinton, a soldier, had most influence on tanks as developed and used. In the second section, you will read Swinton's doctrine for combined-arms attacks at dawn. Churchill, after leaving the Admiralty accepted combined arms, but stuck with his insistence that vehicles could survive only at night, as this chapter's third section explains. Thereafter, Swinton got to his most realistic doctrine, for a "great combined offensive," which you will read in the fourth section. This is what the doctrinal staff at BEF GHQ effectively standardized, just before tanks were first used operationally, as I reveal in the chapter's fifth section.

Churchill's Night-time Infantry Carriers

In October 1914, Churchill proposed that an unarmoured, unarmed tractor (of which many types were already in use, mostly to pull artillery) should be used to push bridges across trenches. In his first letter to the Prime Minister on the requirement (January 1915), Churchill advocated a night attack, so that enemy artillery could not target the machines. He added a requirement for armoured personnel carriers, from which friendly infantry could lob grenades and fire machine-guns into trenches. This requirement was technically accessible and doctrinally valid: the use-case survives today. However, Churchill imagined only wheeled platforms. Tracked platforms had been available in Britain for years, but largely ignored by its government. In Autumn 1914, the Army acquired half-tracked tractors by Holt Manufacturing of California, but the Admiralty acquired wheeled tractors. Tracked running gear would prove to be necessary to automotive travel across damaged, excavated, or fortified terrain.

Worse, within days he focused on a ridiculous idea that tandem steam rollers could flatten trenches. (He likely imagined revetments of the type he had seen during the Boer War, rather than the trenches being excavated in France.) Quick

13

A standard pushable Pedrail carriage is demonstrated with a mock shield in June 1915.

tests proved that steam rollers could not mount a couple sandbags, let alone crush trenches. In the same month, he authorized designs of big wheel landships (potentially weighing hundreds of tons) and hand-pushed (unmotorized) tracked shields.

In February, he formed the Landships Committee to focus on (motorized) trench-enfilading personnel carriers, which had been suggested to him in October as alternatives to bridge-pushers. To straddle a trench, the designers regrettably chose two articulated, wheeled platforms, although they later switched to half-tracked platforms imported from Bullock of Chicago. They did not bring any expertise in tracked platforms, and not much expertise in automobiles (they specialized in roadways and electrics).

None of Churchill's requirements necessarily contributed to the tank. The decisive period for the requirement was the month from late May 1915, when Churchill was demoted (as a condition of the Conservatives joining the Liberals in a coalition government). In the same month, the Admiralty revealed its Landships program to the War Office. In late June, the War Office appointed its own representatives to the Committee, of whom the most influential was Swinton. The soldiers redirected the requirement away from a personnel carrier, with little armament or battlefield mobility, to an artillery-armed, trench-crossing "machine-gun destroyer." Churchill continued to expect any vehicles to operate at night, and specified spotlights or a searchlight on each vehicle, which somewhat contradict his contention that vehicles would not survive in daylight (Newsome 2021a: 17-18, 22-23, 28-29, 48-49).

Churchill was practically and justifiably kept out of the requirements, specifications, design, and development of tanks, but would still have opportunities to influence the doctrine for use of tanks, after Swinton had his say.

Swinton's Dawn-time Tanks

The most useful person appointed to the Landships Committee in June 1915 was Swinton – a Royal Engineer, official historian, and the Cabinet's official correspondent to GHQ. Swinton had first suggested the requirement, was most consistent in its vision, authored the final specifications for what was eventually accepted as the Mark I Tank, and would write the first official doctrine for tanks.

Swinton first escalated a requirement for an AFV in October 1914, when he heard of the demonstration of Holt half-tracked tractors as potential gun tractors. He suggested that an armoured body could accommodate a machine-gun team. He attended trials of loaded Holt tractors on mock battlefields, through February 1915, but thereafter lost touch. On 1 June, Swinton (1932: 131-132) sent a memorandum to BEF GHQ, essentially a requirement for what we know as a tank, with doctrinal justifications. This was before the use of the word "tank" to mean a vehicle. The memorandum requires "Armoured Machine-Gun Destroyers," which suggest more about their targets than their capabilities. He prescribed a "surprise...assault...on a large scale," which implies an offensive along dozens of miles of front, although he confused the implication by imagining a notional "attack" (presumably one of many attacks in any offensive), in which he assumes 50 vehicles, and recommends one vehicle every 100 yards (91 m), i.e., an assault front of 5,000 yards (4,572 m).

Swinton wanted a preliminary artillery bombardment, to break enemy wire. (He did not envision tracked vehicles that could defeat current German wire obstacles. Certainly the Holt could not.) Still, he limited the preliminary bombardment to a few hours of nighttime, in hope that the Germans would not have time to concentrate reserves. He advocated an attack at dawn. During the assault, British artillery would bombard German artillery guns, which were the main threats to vehicles. The vehicles would neutralize machine-gun nests by driving over or bombarding them. Once the vehicles enfilade the German trenches, the British infantry should advance. Once the infantry neutralize the trenches, the vehicles should keep going, followed by the infantry.

Swinton's doctrine foreshadows most of the doctrine that would be normalized by late 1917, except his perpetuation of preliminary bombardment. His foresight is remarkable: he had not yet seen any fully-tracked, unarticulated, armoured or fighting vehicle. Still, from June 1915 he was the leading specifier of the first proper tank. By July, the War Department specified (to William Foster & Company) a fully tracked AFV, with an armed turret, using tracks of unprecedented length, which had just arrived from Bullock of Chicago. The product ("Little Willie") was the first effective tank, although Foster and public-sector partners (led by Walter Gordon Wilson of the RNAS) would need to develop new tracks and running gear before producing what would be accepted in February 1916 as the Tank Mark I.

In June 1915, the two California Giants from Bullock of Chicago are displayed for the first time with their mirrored gear for articulating, steering, and winching up the fronts. Wilson stands at right.

BEF GHQ effectively accepted Swinton's doctrine for a tank "attack" but not an offensive, by sending to the War Office a requirement for just 50 tanks, dated 11 September. At this date, Foster was still modifying Little Willie before its first demonstration, and assembling the wooden mock-up of the eventual Tank Mark I, and developing the latter's tracks (Williams-Ellis 1920: 12; Newsome 2021a: 42-47).

Churchill's Caterpillars

In November 1915, Winston Churchill resigned from his remaining governmental appointments, after the government's decision to withdraw all operations in Turkey, which he had initiated. He travelled to France to command an infantry unit, at unwarranted rank and with the Parliamentarian's privilege of returning to London whenever he wanted.

To his credit, he was humble enough to spend a few months with a unit and to adjust to what he had learned from the soldiers on the Landships Committee. (He had continued to chair it for most meetings since June.) On 3 December, upon arrival at GHQ, he wrote for the BEF's commander-in-chief an unsolicited doctrinal suggestion ("Variants of the Offensive").[*] Here he rejects a preliminary bombardment, which would ruin surprise. Perhaps he had heard of Swinton's doctrine, or had realized what the soldiers preferred, now that he was one of them. In order to maintain surprise, he prescribed a secret assembly, and an assault in darkness.

Rather than rely on one type of vehicle both to enfilade enemy trenches and to carry infantry to clear the trenches, the new document combines enfilading-vehicles with pedestrian infantry. The document starts with his year-old proposal for pedestrians to carry and to push armoured shields.[**] He intends the pushable shields to be dropped 40 to 50 yards (37 to 46 m) from enemy machine-guns, in the mistaken belief that a shield just 15 feet (4.6 meters) wide would "mask" a machine-gun's fire at that range. More usefully, he proposes that a pushable shield should be dropped wherever the enemy wire needs to be cut by hand. In any case, he wishes both types of shield to be discarded at the first enemy trench. Even where he combines pedestrians with vehicles, he is ambiguous about how far they should advance beyond the first line. He allows the vehicles to be abandoned in daylight, which implies that both the crews and the infantry would take cover in captured enemy trenches by dawn.

The document is unclear whether it is proposing the shields as alternatives or complements to tanks. The title ("Variants of the Offensive") suggests that the shields are alternatives, but the document describes them first, as if they are preferred. His image of what later would be termed tanks is anchored in his own earlier requirements. The document talks frequently of "caterpillars," and once of "movable machine-gun cupolas," which paraphrases a term for a tandem tracked vehicle that had been proposed to, and authorized by, the Admiralty since March.

---

[*] A copy that Churchill submitted to the post-war Commission on Awards to Inventors can be viewed at the Churchill Archives Centre, Churchill College, University of Cambridge (CHAR 2/109/136).

[**] Churchill specified a personal shield, "hang[ing] on the left shoulder, giving protection from just below the rim of the helmet to the hips," and a row of shields, covering 5 to 15 men, pushed on a wheel or track.

The First Tank War

The document does not mention "landships" or "land cruisers" (the current official term for the future tanks). He claims that each is armed with only two or three machine-guns, and has capacity for a flame-thrower, but these were always his preferred specifications, and survived only as potential armament for the eventual tandem tracked vehicle (which predictably failed). He wrote of about 70 vehicles "nearing completion," perhaps betraying his wish that the two "California Giant" half-tracks (which had arrived from Bullock of Chicago in June, and been tied together in tandem soon after) had earned a production order. He promised that "caterpillars" could cross "any ordinary obstacle," and that "nothing but a direct hit from a field gun will stop them."* In fact, the half-tracks never successfully crossed a mock battlefield, and were never armoured or armed. A competitor, with tandem tracks by Pedrail, could not climb a step of 4 inches when completed months later. He had not specified or seen the pilot tank, even though its assembly had started more than a month earlier. Yet he was now aware of the difficulties of crossing muddy battlefields, as betrayed by one admission that any attack by "caterpillars…requires, at the present season, frost, darkness, and surprise." This is fair, but incongruous, given the document's confidence elsewhere that "caterpillars" can win the war (Newsome 2021a: 39-43).

Churchill was perhaps trying to revive his own failed projects. The section on "caterpillars" begins with an airy claim that the "cutting of the enemy's wire and

---

* When republishing an edited version of this document, he claims to have "underrated their immunity" (1923: 80)!

On 30 June 1915, the Killen-Strait tri-tracked tractor is driven into into some barbed wire. Standing right to left are David Lloyd George (Minister of Munitions), Major-General George Scott-Moncrieff (Director, Fortifications and Works, War Office), Winston Churchill (Landships Committee), and Colonel Wilkinson D. Bird (Director of Staff Duties, War Office).

the general decimation of his firing-line can be effected by" the "caterpillars" that he thought were "nearing completion." The method is unclear until later in the document, when he urges the reader to ask the Admiralty for a demonstration of the "naval torpedo-net-cutter." He claims that this "proved absolutely successful" when pushed by "them" (caterpillars), and "has only to be witnessed to carry conviction." In fact, the only demonstration he had seen (30 June 1915) was of a small unarmed and unarmoured tri-tracked tractor, by Killen-Strait of Appleton, Wisconsin, with an attachment shaped like open scissors, which failed to breach a few strands of barbed wire, staked and tensioned. (Later, the preferred attachment for proper tanks was a grapnel, by which tanks could pull wire out of the way.) The tri-track was never tried against the coils of tougher wire of the type that the Germans stacked and staked in front of tensioned wire. Churchill had not yet seen current German fortifications with his own eyes. So far as he had seen photographs, they had not overcome his over-optimism for Admiralty projects.

In January 1915, Churchill had specified that vehicles should proceed to the second defensive line, once friendly infantry occupy the first line, but his paper of December is ambiguous. It states that "caterpillars" are "capable of actually crossing the enemy's trench and advancing to cut his communication trenches, but into this aspect it is not necessary to go now." Later in the document, he declares that "caterpillars" could help infantry to capture "several successive lines of trenches" in darkness, but in daylight should be abandoned to enemy artillery fire.

In sum, Churchill's document is foresightful of pre-dawn surprise attacks without preliminary bombardment, but over-optimistic for crossing battlefields and cutting wire with half-tracked and articulated vehicles, and under-ambitious for sustaining mechanized advances in daylight (although this under-ambition likely betrays his awareness that the equipment he had sponsored had failed).

This is the document that General Douglas Haig received days after taking over the BEF on 19 December. Haig directed it to his staff, with a handwritten query, "Is anything known about the Caterpillar referred to in para. 4, page 3?" It prompted also Haig's agreement to Churchill's request for command of a unit.

Swinton's "Great Combined Operation"

The pilot tank ("Big Willie"; later known as "Mother") was demonstrated up to 8 February 1916. Within days, Swinton (1932: 198-214) developed his doctrine of 1 June 1915 from two pages to eight pages of foolscap paper.[*] His new doctrine:
- maintains a short preliminary bombardment, measured in hours, to cut wire;
- hopes for surprise by eschewing the days of preliminary bombardment that both sides had normalized;
- wants tanks to move forward at night, without alerting the enemy;
- schedules the assault just before dawn, so that their start is invisible to the enemy, but the terrain is soon visible to the driver;

---

[*] The document is titled "Notes on the Employment of Tanks." Swinton sent copies to the War Office and GHQ in March, which do not survive. He lodged a copy with the Ministry of Munitions in April (LHCMA Stern 1/6/78), and later reproduced most of the text in memoirs (1932: 198-214). No copy ever reached the Tank Museum.

- wants artillery to drop smoke in front of the defensive line;
- escalates the counter-battery fire, given his realization of the tank's vulnerability to even "glancing hits" from artillery: he wants aircraft and heavy artillery to drop high-explosive, gas, and smoke shells on artillery positions;
- escalates the force, given the current order (100 tanks), although he assumes a 10 percent unreadiness rate, and thus assigns 90 tanks to the attack;
- widens the attack to 9,000 yards (calculated from the prior rate of one tank per 100 yards);
- maintains that tanks should crush machine-guns as first choice, and should fire on them only where closing with machine-guns would be inconvenient;
- suggests fire-and-movement: tanks should close on machine-guns, or use their six-pounder guns to suppress the most distant enemy fire, while other tanks use their machine-guns to suppress the infantry;
- reduces the tank-infantry gap, by specifying that infantry should advance when the tanks are three-quarters of the way across no-man's land, with expectation that tanks and infantry would hit the enemy line at the same time;
- emphasizes combined arms, what he calls "coordination action of all arms," and "one great combined operation," by aircraft, artillery, infantry, and tanks;
- specifies tank communications: radios in one-tenth of tanks (with a range of 5 miles (8 km) using morse code), cable-burying equipment in another one-tenth, and signal balloons and rockets in some or all tanks;
- deepens the objectives from the third defensive line to the artillery line;
- urges tanks and grenadiers to advance along the sides of the enemy's communication trenches, to each line of defensive trenches, and ultimately the enemy's artillery line;
- expects tanks to counter artillery directly, at an effective range of 2,000 yards (1,829 m), with telescopic sights.

While Swinton under-estimated the tank's capability to crush wire, he over-estimated both the tank's mobility on cratered ground and the sustainability of the tank. To be fair, Swinton's involvement was limited to command of the nascent tank force in England, which did not yet exist. The immediate solution was a much larger force, so that the British could sustain the advance despite the high failure rate. Indeed, Swinton always urged that the force should not be deployed until it had filled with tanks of the first batch (in April the order was extended from 100 to 150 tanks) (Williams-Ellis 1920: 19-20; Fuller 1920: 162).

Swinton's document expects the crews to train on a mock battlefield in England.

Big Willie is proven in Lincoln, circa 14 January 1916.

The British tank arm was authorized on 14 February. The next day, Swinton was appointed as the doctrinal and training commander at home, pending an operational commander overseas. In March, Swinton, at the rank of temporary colonel, took command of a Tank Detachment. It was soon redesignated as the Special Armoured Car Section, Motor Machine-Gun Service, Machine-Gun Corps. Effective in May, it became the Heavy Section, Machine Gun Corps (HSMGC). It would not become the Tank Corps until June 1917.

For months, the nascent force lacked a sufficient training area. It lacked tanks for experiment, except the pilot tank, and lacked a range on which to fire six-pounder guns. It was currently accommodated at the Machine-Gun Service's depot at Bisley, whose ranges were not rated beyond small arms. Swinton spent most of his time in London, focused on the acquisition of tanks and personnel.

In March, Swinton (1932: 236, 243-245) recruited an engineer officer (Major M. O'C. Tandy), then convalescing in England, to find a sufficient training area. In the first week of April, Tandy reported plenty of compliant space near Thetford, Norfolk – in total, 15 square miles (39 square km) of flat, sandy heath-, wood-, and farm-land (including tracts owned by the agreeable Lord Iveagh, at Elveden). The inhabitants were removed, while the area was fenced and gated and restricted to authorized personnel. One tract (1.5 miles or 2.4 km wide) was converted into a mock battlefield, by three pioneer battalions, under the advice of Tandy, Brevet Major Giffard le Quesne Martel (who had commanded a company of engineers in France, recently near the Somme River, where GHQ planned a decisive offensive for July), and four engineer subalterns detached from the War Office.

From June, individual tanks were tried against mock obstacles (including exploded craters). Section exercises were not possible until July. At this time, staff were still considering whether to split the section (six tanks) into subsections of two or three tanks. Tandy had recommended three to five. The answer seemed to depend on the target. When a pair of tanks attacked a mock redoubt, one tank was ruled disabled before it could open fire, and the other failed to spot two enemy machine-guns that decimated the infantry. In two other cases of pairs attacking, the tanks in each pair lost each other. Given three tanks, the centre tank could take the lead and set direction, while the other tanks protect respective flanks (Major A. Holford Walker, "Tactical handling of tanks in action," 21 July 1916, UKNA WO 158/834).

The first company-echelon exercise was demonstrated on 21 July, just before GHQ insisted on deployment by August. Thus, doctrine remained largely theoretical and untested before the first tank operation, in September. Swinton (1932: 197-198) himself assessed that his doctrine was not fulfilled until the offensive at Cambrai in November 1917. He clearly blamed the delay on GHQ.

GHQ

GHQ was in a hurry to use tanks to restart the failed and unprecedently costly offensive around the River Somme, which had started on 1 July (see Map 3). GHQ decided to turn Swinton's memorandum of February into a manual, titled "Preliminary Notes on Tactical Employment of Tanks," dated 16 August.* However, the

---

* The original is held by UKNA (WO 158/834). A copy is held by RACTM (E2021.1963.14).

manual reduces Swinton's eight pages to four, misses many of Swinton's emphases and caveats, and downplays the tank's capabilities.

Worse, GHQ retained two habits against which Swinton and Churchill had aligned. First, GHQ retained days of preliminary bombardment, thus foregoing surprise as to location, if not timing. Second, GHQ took no notice of Swinton's and Churchill's prescriptions for tanks to lead. The document begins: "The object of the tank is to help the infantry forward, and especially to deal with the enemy machine guns." The manual specifies a creeping artillery bombardment, to be followed by infantry, and lastly tanks, until enemy machine-guns open up on the infantry. The manual allows for many possibilities but few preferences for what should happen once enemy machine-guns open up.

Worst, GHQ downplays the tank. The first paragraph warns of "a difficult operation." The second paragraph warns of the risks from enemy artillery. The final paragraph re-emphasizes the risks and uncertainties:

> The tank is a novel engine of war, and untried. Its use will require careful study and preparation on each separate occasion. Special care must be taken that the tanks do not fall into the enemy's hands.

Not surprisingly, this short and conflicted document is not of much practical use. Consequently, tankies, infantry formation commanders, Army commanders, and GHQ spent a lot of time in conferences in September trying to reconcile their respective doctrines. Since almost all the tankies in France were serving at company echelon or below, most of their inputs went unrecorded and unreconciled.

Ernest Dunlop Swinton (1868-1951) was photographed at the end of 1918 wearing the rank of a Major-General, before retirement into academic history. He signed this copy for publication by Albert Stern (1919: 80-81). Giffard le Quesne Martel (1889-1958) preferred to be publicized as the inventor of tankettes in 1925.

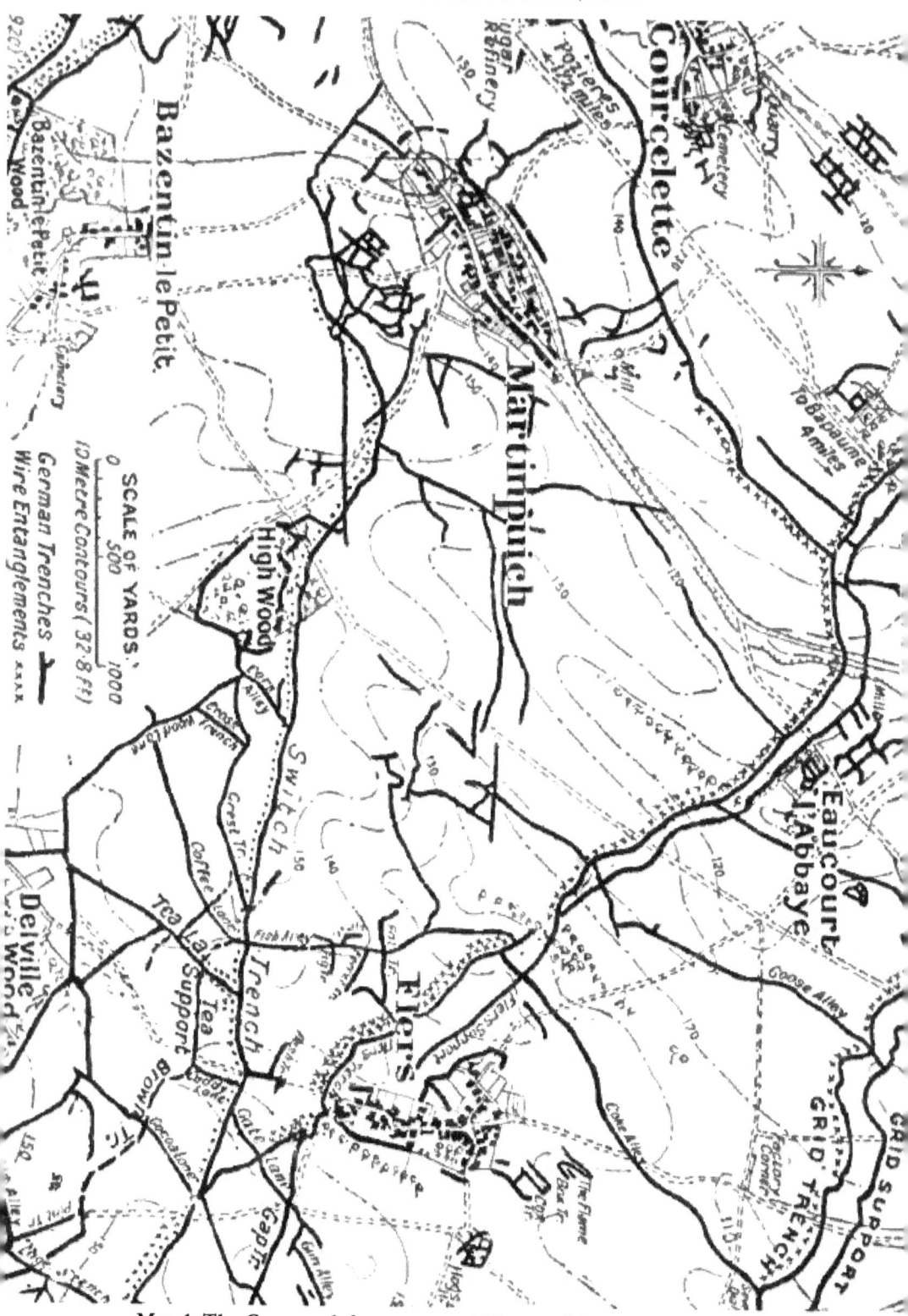

Map 1: The German defences around Flers and Courcelette (*The Times History of the W* written and published by *The Times* newspaper, 1920: XI, 389).

2
Flers, Courcelette, and Thiepval

The first operation to involve tanks conformed more to legacy practices than to any tank doctrine. Three corps of 4th Army were supposed to capture Martinpuich, Flers, and Combles (from left to right, west to east), and thence the narrower ridge from Gueudecourt through Les Boeufs to Morval, with the hope that the cavalry could exploit a breakthrough to the north-east. On the left, the Reserve Army, with some tanks, aimed at Courcelette (3.5 miles or 5.6 km west of Flers), just to protect 4th Army's flank (see Map 1).

The first operation to involve tanks started on 15 September. It was as disappointing as all others on the Somme, except for some spectacular advances by tanks towards Flers and Courcelette. The second operation occurred on 25 September, at Thiepval, just 2.5 miles (4 km) west of Courcelette, so is considered in this chapter.

The sections below examine the terrain, concentration, surprise, combined arms, speed, sustainment, exploitation, and outcomes.

Terrain

Swinton's (1932: 131, 201-203) paper of 1 June 1915 does not mention terrain, except to promise that tracked technologies would enable the vehicle to climb a "ditch" and a "parapet." In December, Churchill promised that "caterpillars...are capable of traversing any ordinary obstacle, ditch, breastwork, or trench," and "can climb any slope." By February 1916, Swinton had spent three months observing the pilot Mark I and its ancestors, so his second doctrine notes that tanks cannot cross water much deeper than 1 foot (0.3 m), steps higher than 3 feet (0.9 m), slopes of more than 45 degrees, or normal bridges. He warns that "[al]though the tanks can cross soft soil and muddy ground they will travel better in dry weather," and should not be deployed against "canals, rivers, deep railway cuttings with steep sides, or woods and orchards."

However, in August, GHQ required tanks to attack "villages, woods, strong points[,] and hidden machine gun positions," which indirect fire struggles to neutralize. Worse, GHQ expected tanks to "find sufficient cover" in villages and woods while helping the infantry to consolidate the objectives. GHQ adds caveats, in a separate note on force structure, of all things: here, GHQ admits that tanks might lose their sponsons or guns in collisions with trees. These caveats would fall on deaf ears if users read the doctrinal manual without the note on force structure. Even if users read both documents, they would not come away with much clarity. GHQ was somewhat schizophrenic about the mobility of tanks: GHQ warned that tanks could easily fall into enemy hands, but also admitted the latest specifications: steps of 5 feet, trenches of 10 feet,* all "wire entanglements, hedges, walls, etc.,"

---

* The Tank Corps' "training note" on "Infantry and Tank Cooperation and Training" (27 January 1918: 2) agrees with steps of 5 feet, trenches of 10 feet, and slopes of 45 degrees, although official papers of 1920 specify a step of 4.5 feet.

trees 18-inches [457 mm] in diameter,* and "an ordinary fir plantation or coppice of young trees."

Yet GHQ chose an area for the assault that was already muddy, damaged by shell fire, and well fortified. Swinton did not know of the intended area until Haig pointed it out on a map, on 19 August, during Swinton's visit to Advanced GHQ. Swinton (1932: 261, 277) remembers that Haig "did not enter into any discussions of his reasons for using them at this time." Elsewhere, Swinton admits regret that he did not protest their premature use. Presumably, he regretted not protesting the area too.

GHQ selected the area partly because it is flat, although Haig was thinking of the cavalry's chances on the relatively undamaged terrain behind the defended lines more than the tank's chances in front. In England, tanks had trained on well-drained heathland, in imitation of the sector around Loos, but in the meantime (July) GHQ had launched a larger offensive on the Somme, which churned vegetated soils into mud, ruined the drainage, cratered the ground, and mangled the wire and posts. The journalist Philip Gibbs (1919: 2) watched the tanks struggling to negotiate a mock battlefield in France, from 6 September. He later wrote that "in the mud-swamps of Flanders they had had no chance at all."

The preliminary bombardment started on 12 September, which further damaged no-man's land to little effect on the defences. Rain on 13 September restored the mud. The photographs of the battlefield suggest that even the best tanks in use today would struggle. Indeed, tanks today are not optimized for the mud and obstacles for which the first tanks were specified, and usually offer inferior step-climbing, trench-crossing, track-to-ground contact, ground pressure, and mean maximum pressures, although they are more powerful (Newsome 2021a: 65-67; 2021b: 131).

Concentration

GHQ's urgency reduced the number of tanks available. On 1 June 1915, Swinton (1932: 131) had required that they "should be employed as a surprise in an assault on the German position to be carried out on a large scale...[T]heir existence should not be known until all are ready," after "no preliminary efforts made with a few machines, the result of which would give the scheme away."

On 3 December, Churchill urged use of the first batch of tanks when ready, although he also stated that none should be used until the batch is complete.

Swinton's (1932: 203) doctrine of February warns that tanks "should not be used in driblets," but "be kept as secret as possible until the whole are ready to be launched, together with the infantry assault, in one great combined operation."

GHQ was disengaged and ultimately dismissive of these warnings, although the warners did not help themselves by hypothesizing attacks by a few dozen vehicles. On 1 June, Swinton had imagined a surprise attack by 50 armoured, armed, tracked vehicles, although his notional attack is part of a larger offensive. In September, GHQ informed the War Office it could use 50, in a brief reply that does not indicate any larger use or any rate of concentration. By December, Churchill mistakenly

---

* In September, one tank was required to demonstrate against a tree 26-inches (660 mm) in diameter, but the challenge was not considered safe.

thought that 70 "caterpillars" were "nearing completion." He did not specify any rate of concentration, other than 5 pushable shields per battalion. At some point, Churchill copied this document to the Cabinet's Committee of Imperial Defence (CID). Its date of receipt and impact remain unclear. On 24 December, an inter-ministerial conference discussed acquisition of "land cruisers," without mentioning Churchill or his paper. Deferential to GHQ, the attendees agreed the budgeting for 50 "land cruisers," and the raising of a Tank Detachment, Machine-Gun Corps, to man them, at a generous rate* that actually produces enough recruits to crew 100 tanks (CID, "The question of the provision of caterpillar machine-gun destroyers or `land cruisers', their equipment, manning, and cognate subjects," minutes approved 13 January 1916, UKNA CAB 42/7/7).

On 2 February, the pilot tank was demonstrated to ministers for the first time. On the day, Commodore Murray Sueter, in charge of the Royal Naval Air Service's earlier experiments with the Admiralty's fighting vehicles, suggested that 3,000 tanks should be ordered, although by the time of the final demonstration, on 8 February, he talked of hundreds. He sent this requirement to the CID, whose chief civil servant (Secretary), Maurice Hankey, agreed. However, on 11 February, the War Office received from GHQ a requirement for only 40 – a number GHQ never justified. Swinton urged at least 100, which were approved on 14 February. Writing around the same time, Swinton assumed a readiness rate of 90 percent, so assumed 90 crossing the start line. In March, Swinton proposed that each tank should be protected against infantry by two variants armed with only machine-guns. (He called the variant a "man-killing tank"; he later chose the term "Female," leaving the pilot tank, which he had called a "machine-gun destroyer," as a "Male."**) This proposal was resolved in the first week of April, as one Female per Male. In the last week of April, the production order was extended to 75 Males and 75 Females.

On 14 April, Haig visited the War Office, when he asked for some tanks in France by 1 June, ready to join the BEF's great summer offensive on the Somme. This might begin in June, depending on the success of coordinated offensives on Allied fronts. Swinton took his time to investigate, before writing on 26 April that some could be shipped by 1 August, and 75 crews could be ready by the end of

---

* One officer and 10 other ranks were authorized for each of the 50 tanks. Half as many were authorized as reserves. The total works out at 75 officers and 750 other ranks. Insisting on a commissioned officer in each tank would allow for only 75 tanks to be crewed, but a crew of the time is equivalent in size to an infantry section, which is routinely commanded by a non-commissioned officer.

** The Male mounted two six-pounder guns and four machine-guns (one six-pounder at the front of each side sponson, one machine-gun in the rear of each sponson, one for firing to front or rear, and one spare). Females mounted six machine-guns (two on each side, one at front or rear, one spare). The six-pounder fired high-explosive shells of more use against targets behind cover, but machine-guns could be stowed with more ammunition. Also, the mountings allowed for two machine-guns to sweep 180 degrees each side (with an overlap of 60 degrees), while one six pounder swept 121 degrees (the two six-pounder lines of fire converged 60 yards or 55 m in front of the tank). Six-pounders are not portable, but machine-guns were supposed to be dismounted and carried forward when the tank bogs down, breaks down, runs up against an impassable obstacle, or runs out of fuel. Indeed, Males were more likely to get stuck because of the larger barrel. Thus, both Males and Females continued to be acquired throughout the war (Newsome 2021a: 68)

August. At the time, he believed that Haig had accepted what he had written in February about tanks not being used prematurely in "driblets." Haig's CGS gave Swinton the same impression in May (Swinton 1932: 204, 214, 226-227, 234-235; Liddell Hart 1959: I, 49-53, 60).

Recruiting of soldiers across the Army as a whole did not start until April, after disappointing efforts to recruit from the RNAS (naval ratings were paid better) and the Motor Machine-Gun Service (medium machine-gunners did not expect to assault). Six companies and a battalion HQ were planned from the start. At some point the structure was changed to 15 smaller companies and three battalion HQs. However, GHQ would not allow tanks to be organized above the company echelon. The force structure was fixed at six companies, each with 25 tanks (four sections, each with six tanks, plus one spare tank). By early June, enough personnel had been trained for two companies to move into the field at Elveden. Enough other personnel had been recruited to fill the six companies (a total authorization of 184 officers and 1,610 other ranks), so recruiting was stopped. At the time, the Heavy Section was training with the pilot tank alone (now known as "Mother"). By the end of June each of the first two companies held just six tanks (Swinton 1932: 221-222, 226, 257).

The pair of companies at Elveden attracted GHQ's attention, because, at current structure, each pair was serviced and supported by quartermaster and workshop detachments. GHQ was in a hurry to salvage some honour from the offensive that had started on 1 July. This became clear to Swinton (1932: 261, 267) only later in July. Swinton repeated that he preferred to keep all six companies together. However, GHQ hurried a follow-on offensive before the weather could worsen. Eventually they reached an agreement for one company to enship in the first half of August, the second by the end of August. The first company exercise, with all 25 authorized tanks, was scheduled to coincide with a visit by the CIGS and War Secretary[*] on 21 July. GHQ's representatives did not arrive until just before its end. They joined a conference the next day, when they pressed for enshipment of six tanks and a workshop in the first week of August, and 12 tanks in each subsequent week, so that six tanks could be committed to action at a time.

The CIGS (Field-Marshal William Robertson) wrote to Haig to suggest that the BEF should wait until January, when 500 tanks could be ready. On 29 July, Haig replied with a "good hope" that a few tanks could destabilize the Germans on the Somme "before the Autumn," and a promise that he would not use them unless he expects good results. On 19 August, he told Swinton he would commit them to an offensive in mid-September at Flers and Courcelette, without justifying his timing. GHQ's "Preliminary Notes on the Employment" also do not justify the timing.

> As probably only small numbers will be available in the first instance, and as it may be required to use them as they arrive, it is necessary to consider how they can be employed under these conditions.

Company C enshipped in the second half of August, Company D in the first week of September, a third company in subsequent weeks. The latter's first ten

---

[*] David Lloyd George transferred from the Ministry of Munitions to the War Department earlier in July, in succession to Lord Kitchener, who had drowned on a mined warship.

Army	Corps	Divisions	Tank units	Tanks allocated	Tanks assembled	Tanks reached start line	Tanks crossed started line	Tanks engaging enemy	Urban Objectives
Reserve	Canadian	3rd Cdn.	One section from C Company	3	3	3	1 (+2)	1	Courcelette
		2nd Cdn.		3	3	1	1	1	
4th	III	15th	One section from D Company, plus an improvised section	4	2	1	1	1	Martinpuich
		47th		4	4	4	4	2	
		50th		4	2	2	2	1	
4th	XV	NZ	Three sections from D Company	4	4	4	4	4	Flers and Gueudecourt
		41st		10	10	8	4	4	
		14th		4	4	3	3	1	
4th	XIV	Guards	Three sections from C Company	10	10	8	6	4	Morval and Les Boeufs
		6th		4	3	3	1 (+2)	3	
		56th		4	3	3	3	1	
TOTAL: 2	4	11	9 sections from 2 companies	54[1]	48[2]	40[3]	28 (+4 late)[4]	23[5]	6

Table 1: force structure for the offensive on 15 September 1916 (see the memoirs and war diaries held by RACTM and the publications cited in the notes below).

---

[1] In Fuller's (1920: 54) history of the arm, the distributions are 8, 17, 17, 7 per corps respectively, for a total of 49 (excluding 10 unfit). In his memoirs (1936: 81), the distributions become 5, 12, 18, 18, for a total of 53, but Fuller did not realize that Canadian Corps received 6, not 5. Thus, the total is 54.

[2] Tanks allocated and tanks assembled tend to be confused. A larger number of tanks were allocated days before the attack, than managed to assemble two days before the attack. The first British-French conference on tank tactics was given a report of 49 tanks allocated (4 March 1917, UKNA WO 158/841). The arm's first history reports an allocation of both 49 tanks and 48 tanks, of which the latter is the number assembled (Williams-Ellis 1920: 27-29). Fuller (1920: 54; 1936: 81) initially reported 49 allocated, but later changed this to 53 allocated, and 49 assembled, i.e., he must have transposed the initial misreport of allocations (49) as the number assembled (48). Liddell Hart (1959: I, 67) reported 49 "available." T.L.H. Butterfield (1966: 159) reproduced Fuller's later figures. David Fletcher (1994: 2), Trevor Pidgeon (1995), J.P. Harris (1995: 64-67), and Richard Faulkner (1995: 37) induced from the official histories 48 "assigned" or "allotted."

[3] This number is normally undercounted because of the lateness of some tanks arriving at or crossing the start line. Few timings were recorded in the moment. Liddell Hart (1959: I, 67, 70), Harris (1995: 64-67), and Faulkner (1995: 37) induced from official histories 36 on the start line. Churchill (1927: 171) and David Cavaleri (1995: 26) reported 35 on the start line. These authors seem to confuse the number that reached the start line with the lower number that crossed it.

[4] Swinton (1932: 282) reported 32 "sallied forth." Churchill (1927: 171), Fuller (1936: 81), and Cavaleri (1995: 26) report 31 crossing the start line. Harris (1995: 64-67) and Faulkner (1995: 37) report 30 crossing the front line. These lower numbers ignore some of the tanks that started late. In most cases, tanks started minutes late (the latest starters did not join the infantry of 6th Division until a newly organized attack in the afternoon), but I still count them as crossing the start line.

[5] Lower counts tend to be reported, since some tanks received enemy fire but did not necessarily return fire, while some opened fire on friendly troops but not necessarily enemy troops. Officially, 23 tanks advanced successfully, as reported to the first British-French conference on tank tactics (4 March 1917, UKNA WO 158/841). Harris (1995: 64-67) and Faulkner (1995: 37) induced from the official histories 21 in combat on 15 September, and 3 in combat on 16 September.

tanks were used to supplement Companies C and D for their first operation.

Training in France started on 6 September. Frequent demonstrations (including unnecessary stunts, such as knocking down trees) and changes to the plan wore down the tanks and crews. Even at full strength, service and support assets were thinly spread: one officer and four other ranks supplied the two companies; three officers and 50 other ranks maintained the tanks. The personnel readiness rate was not recorded before the first operation; memoirs suggest that the crews were undersupplied. The Ordnance Department was still forming a detachment to handle tank stores at the nearest port (Havre). The paired-company assets were immobile, and thus stayed at the railhead, although the nearest Corps Ammunition Park could provide lorries for dumping ammunition. Once the tanks moved towards an operational area, the crews administered themselves, unless mechanics came to them. The crews received timetables, aerial photographs, and annotated maps, but some were invalidated by changes, as late as the day before assault (Williams-Ellis 1920: 25-26; Swinton 1932: 278-279).

Still, of the 60 tanks in France, 54 tanks were allocated (enough to fill the first two companies and an improvised section), of which 48 reached the assembly area on 13 September, 40 reached their starting points by the morning of 15 September, 34 crossed the start line (although two were delayed for hours), and 25 engaged or were engaged by the enemy. Historians have tended to under-count, given their uncertainties or high standards for what counts as crossing the start line or reaching the enemy (see Table 1).

In December 1915, Churchill had proposed that "caterpillars" should take starting positions 200 to 300 yards (183 to 274 m) apart. Given his imagination of 70 "caterpillars" nearing completion, he implies a front of 14,000 to 21,000 yards (8 to 12 miles; 12,802 to 19,202 m). In February, Swinton (1932: 209-210) repeated his prior specification of 100 yards between tanks, with a maximum of 150. Swinton assumed 90 tanks would be available, so prescribed a front of 9,000 yards (5 miles; 8,230 m). In April, the production order was extended to 150 tanks, which suggests a front of 13,500 yards (7.7 miles; 12,344 m), at Swinton's rate. In June 1916, Tandy suggested a minimum interval of 100 yards between tanks, and a maximum of 250 yards. In August, GHQ acknowledged an "original conception" of tanks every 100 to 150 yards. Since it wanted to use the first two companies immediately, it implies a front from 5,000 yards (2.8 miles; 4,572 m) to 7,500 yards (4.3 miles; 6.858 m).

The front for the formations involved on 15 September measured about 7 miles (12,320 yards; 11,265 m). The assault front measured about 3.5 miles (6,160 yards; 5,633 m).* Thus, one tank was allocated for every 228 yards of offensive front, or 114 yards of assault front. One artillery piece was available for every 5 yards of assault front. These rates appear to fall within the range allowed by Churchill and Tandy, but do not comply with Swinton's "original conception," as GHQ paraphrased it.

The tanks were not concentrated in a coherent line, as Swinton, Churchill, and Tandy had intended. If the tanks had been kept together in support to successive brigades, one company of tanks could support a division on to three successive defensive lines (one brigade per defensive line), one section (six tanks) per infantry

---

* Liddell Hart (1959: I, 69, 71) reported the 4th Army's front as 5 miles long, and "the main weight" on a 3-mile front, towards the right flank of the 4th Army's area.

battalion. At this rate, the two companies should have been distributed across two divisions.

Instead, they were distributed across two armies, four corps, and 11 divisions, for an average of 13.5 tanks per corps (a maximum of 18), less than five tanks per division, i.e., a concentration per formation more than 12 times thinner than ideal.

Tanks were distributed at the rate of one subsection (one Male, one Female) per infantry platoon, to attack particular objectives.* In August, GHQ had prescribed this rate "in certain cases," but, by September, GHQ effectively normalized the rate in most cases. The ideal rate (six tanks per unit in the assault, excluding reserves) was not normalized until August 1918.

Churchill, David Lloyd George (then Secretary of State for War), and Edwin Montagu (who had succeeded Lloyd George as Minister of Munitions) complained later that GHQ employed tanks prematurely in insufficient numbers (Churchill 1923: 80; Lloyd George 1938: I, 385, II, 1334; Owen 1955: 322). However, none of these men formally objected at the time. As shown above, in December Churchill had urged GHQ to use the first 70 (CHAR 2/109/136).

The first official historian of the tank arm, Basil Liddell Hart, admitted (1959: I, 67) "disadvantages" in the "petty scale," and objected to the rush and inadequate preparation, but considered it "understandable" given the stagnation on the front. Further, Liddell Hart claimed that "[s]ome of the most senior officers of the wartime Tank Corps considered, in retrospect, that on balance the benefit outweighed the forfeit." He did not name or cite any officers. Robin Prior (2014: 105) praises the early use of "the tank in small numbers," as it was "untried" and unreliable, so any "large scale" use would have been "a fiasco," but this argument contradicts the wish for large scale to maximize surprise and to compensate for unreliability. Gordon Corrigan (2003: 291) conceded that "Haig may have been wrong, but... anything that might help was better than nothing." Adam Hochschild (2011: 214) judged that the secret had been "squandered."

Surprise

The choices affecting surprise include preliminary bombardment, assembly, start time, smoke, and operational security.

Preliminary Bombardment

Churchill wished for vehicles to operate only at night, when enemy artillery could not target tanks directly, so he saw no need for a preliminary bombardment. Swinton wanted a preliminary bombardment to break enemy wire and to cover the noise of the tanks moving forward, but he also wanted it reduced from days to hours. In June, Tandy confirmed this choice, and suggested that the few hours of bombardment should be spread over several days, to confuse the Germans as to the intended day of assault (although only if machine-gun bombardment at night could prevent German repair parties). To confuse the enemy in space as well as time, Tandy suggested that the bombardment should be spread across different parts of the front than just the assault front (Major Tandy to Colonel Swinton, 21 June 1916, UKNA WO 158/834).

---

* At current force structure, each section was supposed to hold three Male and three Female tanks, and each subsection held one Male and one Female.

GHQ chose three days of continuous bombardment, without spreading the bombardment over other days or other fronts. The Germans certainly realized the assault front, and had time to prepare their reserves, although they did not know exactly the day of assault.

Assembly

Back on 1 June 1915, Swinton (1932: 132) had suggested that tanks should be assembled at night and hidden in pits, until twilight, when they could drive up ramps over the parapet.

In December, Churchill expected tanks to be assembled and launched within the same night, without material cover.

In February, Swinton (1932: 202) wrote into his second doctrine a warning that "the chance of success of an attack by tanks lies almost entirely in its novelty and in the element of surprise." Swinton confirmed that tanks should entrain under tarpaulins (marked "drinking water only" or suchlike) and assemble at irregular intervals under the cover of trees or villages, about two miles (3,219 m) from the leading trench. He wanted them to be assembled overnight, some days before the attack, so crews would have time to reconnoitre the approaches to the front, and to gather intelligence on objectives. The tanks should move forward to the starting line on the night of assault, or (if the terrain is open) into pits days earlier.

In Norfolk, from June, the nascent companies practiced assembling overnight, following a tape, dipped in luminous paint, and the tail lamp of the tank ahead. On 21 June, Major Tandy suggested that tanks could move, during successive nights, into starting positions, each hidden by canvas screens, within 300 yards of the friendly support line, without attracting enemy attention (Major Tandy to Colonel Swinton, 21 June 1916, UKNA WO 158/834).

GHQ's "Preliminary Notes" of August acknowledge that the tank's "safety lies in surprise, in rapid movement, and in getting to close quarters," emerging from "material cover," smoke, or darkness. The "Notes" acknowledge that pedestrian guides can use "a small light or luminous disc" and that "tanks can move across country by night, but over unknown country it must be light enough for the driver to see where he is going."

Indeed, moves and assemblies are riskier for tanks and pedestrians, especially the guides, who were usually tank commanders, each holding an electric torch, since white tape was practically invisible at night, even with luminous paint. One account suggests, in the context of the offensive at Cambrai in November 1917, that "5 or 6" tank commanders (at least 1 percent) were run over during "approach marches," while stuck in mud in front of a sleepy driver (Captain H.B.M. Groves, "Precis," 18 December 1934, Cambrai Battlefield Tour 1935, RACTM Hotblack 2).

Start time

Churchill's prescription for assault in darkness is ambitious; he did not admit the difficulties of navigating in darkness. He specified 10 to 15 minutes driving before crossing the leading trench, which implies a distance of 600 to 900 yards (549 to 823 m), if he knew the cross-country speed of tanks. He estimated another 300 yards (274 m) before reaching the first enemy trench. Churchill specified electric lights on each vehicle, to help with identifying targets and to scare the enemy, but he did not specify the same for navigation. Likely he wished to preserve surprise until the vehicles cross friendly lines, before they switch on lights.

In February, Swinton (1932: 202) acknowledged that an assault in darkness would reduce exposure to the enemy, but worried about navigating obstacles and distinguishing friend from foe. He suggested an assault "just before dawn, so soon as there is sufficient light to distinguish objects to some extent," i.e., in twilight.

On 21 June, Tandy confirmed Swinton's wish to assault just before dawn. Tandy suggested that the tanks would not be distinct to the enemy in twilight until they cross friendly lines – a journey of 4 minutes. Another 400 yards (5 miunes) would get the tanks to the first German defensive line.

GHQ's short doctrine of August acknowledges the advantage of assaulting in darkness, but does not specify when.

On 15 September, the assault started in twilight, although at different times for different assaulters: 0515 hours (more than one hour before sunrise) for the three tanks tasked with clearing a salient between Ginchy and Delville Wood; 0530 hours for the two companies of infantry following these three tanks; 0600 hours for the other tanks; and 0620 hours for the other infantry. This choice of twilight would be normal in subsequent operations, although some commanders preferred to attack in the afternoon, so that counter-attackers would have little time before dark.

Smoke

Swinton wanted smoke mixed with the high-explosive falling on the enemy's forward line, and smoke and toxic gas mixed with the high-explosive falling on positions not under assault (to mislead the enemy as to the location of assault).

GHQ's "Preliminary Notes" acknowledge the advantages of "material cover," smoke, or darkness before the assault, but ruled on none of these things. Thus, smoke would not be utilized until later operations.

Operational Security

The secret leaked before even the Mark I was accepted for mass production. Churchill was likely one of the leakers, as he promiscuously distributed, and talked up, his paper of 3 December 1915. On 8 December, a Scottish Radical Member of Parliament asked the War Secretary whether the Ministry of Munitions had shared a paper "on the use of mobile forts propelled by caterpillar tractors for use in traversing ground honeycombed by trenches; and if so, has he reported favourably on their utility?" The reply was negative. Journalists were warned not to report the discussion, but they were asking the same question (Glanfield 2001: 123).

Production orders were distributed in February 1916, covered by stories that the parts were for mobile water tanks, snow-ploughs, or pumps. Nobody involved in the final assembly could have believed these stories, although perhaps most of those involved in the supply of sub-assemblies believed them.

By August, tanks were in France, being demonstrated on and around a mock battlefield, without any perimeter security. Rumours attracted observers. Formation commanders sent their officers and eventually whole units. Civilians worked or passed through the area, some of whom were spies.

On the enemy side, Leutnant Otto Schulz "heard rumours about a new Allied weapon, and our intelligence had sent us notes about a vehicle which they believed was being built in certain French factories. But when we saw the first real tank it was like nothing we had ever imagined" (Foley 1963: 15).

Combined Arms

The traditional arms are artillery, infantry, and cavalry. Tanks offer a new arm in effect, and are treated as an arm in this analysis, although they were organized as a section of the Machine-Gun Corps until July 1917, and would not be authorized as a permanent arm until 1923.

The Machine-Gun Corps' viability as an arm was ambiguous. The infantry too used machine-guns. The Machine-Gun Corps mostly supported infantry attacks by indirect fire. This is why operational orders usually conflated machine-gun and artillery units together in a section titled "bombardment."

The Royal Engineers were not considered an arm; the British Army, unlike some armies, did not separate combat engineers for the assault; nevertheless, the Royal Engineers often were tasked with clearing obstacles in the assault, and thus could be found cooperating with arms under enemy fire.

In this book, combined arms will be analysed as: preliminary bombardment by artillery and machine-guns (before the other arms assault); creeping bombardment (during the assaults by other arms); aircraft (which might contribute to any of the bombardments, combine with the assaulters, or range independently); tanks and infantry together; and tanks and engineers together – or at least tanks with engineering attachments. Cavalry are considered under the principle of "exploitation."

Artillery bombardment: Preliminary

Since June 1915, Swinton (1932: 212-213) had wanted scout aircraft to plot the enemy's artillery before the assault, and bombers and heavy artillery to neutralize these guns, with explosives and toxic gas, during a short preliminary bombardment, and during a shorter but more focused bombardment during the assault itself. Each bombardment would be measured in hours.

In December, Churchill suggested no preliminary bombardment, given his confidence that "caterpillars could "crush and cut" enemy wire, but he had never seen any vehicle crush wire.

In February 1916, Swinton confirmed his wish for a short preliminary bombardment to cut the wire, after seeing demonstrations of the pilot tank, and confirmed his prior requirement for bombers and "heavy artillery" to attack enemy artillery. He acknowledged that some readers might view these requirements as excessive, but re-justified the investment, given the acute risks posed by artillery to tanks, and the necessity of tanks to a breakthrough.

On 21 June, Tandy reported that a tank could not crush wire sufficient for infantry to follow. Tandy required some artillery fire to cut the wire sufficiently for the tank to get in. Still, he suggested that the preliminary bombardment "should be the minimum required to make passable the wire of the first German firing line; no attempt need be made to destroy the German trenches and dugouts" (Major Tandy to Colonel Swinton, 21 June 1916, UKNA WO 158/834).

GHQ stuck with its habit of a preparatory bombardment lasting days, targeting primarily trenches and bunkers, secondarily the wire. Days of bombardment were justified to be certain that the wire was cut. (The wire tends to blow around in the blasts, without breaking, until repeated stresses to the same wire.) GHQ chose a bombardment that is not short by Swinton's or Tandy's specification, although at 3 days it is short compared to the preliminary bombardment before the first battle of the Somme (7 days).

GHQ's targeting of trenches and bunkers was less justified. Shrapnel was useless against personnel in their bunkers, although it might catch enemies outside. High-explosive shells (unless categorized as heavy) could not collapse the bunkers (10 meters or 33 feet deep) or even the trenches (at least 1 meter or 3.3 feet deep). Still, the blasts were powerful enough to leave craters that offered cover for pedestrians. However, these same craters increase the chance of a tank bogging or breaking down, particularly given the soil, season, and weather. The 4th Army gathered 1,258 artillery pieces, including 338 heavies, and fired 828,000 rounds (30,000,000 pounds; 13,607,771 kg) of shells over the three days. The damage to the strongpoints was trivial, but to the ground was considerable.

On 25 September, the day of the second offensive with tanks (at Thiepval), GHQ repeated a preliminary bombardment. However, on 26 September, tanks attacked without preliminary bombardment for the first time, on assumption that prior bombardment had already cut the wire. To forego any preliminary bombardment conforms with Churchill's memorandum of December 1915, except he had specified an attack at night. Otherwise, the choice is closest to Swinton's doctrine of June 1915 – a twilight attack, with no more bombardment than necessary to cut wire.

Artillery bombardment: Creeping

The first tank attack occurred about a year before the Royal Artillery's forward observers pre-registered enemy artillery "silently" (by triangulating their noise or flash) or responded on call to assaulting troops. Instead of on-call fire, artillery support during the assault came entirely as a creeping barrage: a scheduled series of bombardments, falling in a line ahead of the assaulters, and jumping forward every several minutes.

In February, Swinton prescribed a creeping barrage, falling first on the wire in front of the enemy's first trench, and jumping onto enemy artillery.

> The principal objective of our guns should not be to endeavour to damage the German machine-guns, earthworks, and wire behind the enemy's first line [but] to help the infantry helping the tanks, i.e., by concentrating as heavy a counter-fire as possible on the enemy's main artillery position.

GHQ's doctrine of August conforms with Swinton's, but is less categorical.

> Whenever tanks are employed, special attention must be paid to counter battery work, and the tank should move under cover of a close barrage, which should not lift from the objective until the tanks are close to it.

Previous barrages had proven insufficient to suppress defenders, particularly when they crept forward quicker than the infantry. For 15 September, the 4th Army slowed the rate of advance to 50 yards (46 m) per minute, and increased the rate of fire to 3 rounds per gun per minute. This was good for the infantry, but not for the urgency of advance.

One innovation of more use to the tanks was the introduction of bombardment by medium machine-guns. So long as their fire was accurate on enemy trenches, they could suppress enemy infantry, without damaging the ground. Their role is often ignored, because assaulters usually could not hear or see their bullets during an artillery bombardment.

Aircraft

From 30 January 1916, each field army held a brigade of the Royal Flying Corps (RFC). Each brigade held a "Corps Wing," for scouting and observing for ground artillery, and an "Army Wing," for long-range reconnaissance and bombing. Each wing held about three squadrons: the count was meant to match the number of field corps. Each squadron held about as many aircraft as a tank company held tanks. Most of these planes were configured with a rear-facing machine-gun for defence. In 1917, the RFC received specialized fighter planes to prevent German planes from operating over the battle area, although they never quite succeeded.

At the time, aircraft operated independently of ground forces, except to observe friendly artillery fire and to report friendly and enemy movements. In March, Swinton (1932: 212, 235, 251) sent to CID his doctrine of February, which contains a request for aircraft to scout for enemy artillery before the assault, and to drop bombs on enemy artillery during the assault. In April, Hankey responded that surplus aircraft should be reconfigured with machine-guns and bomb racks, and armour plates under the pilot's seat, to attack enemy artillery at low level. (Hankey termed such aircraft "grasshoppers.") Swinton agreed. The idea was submitted to the RFC's commander (General Sir David Henderson), who rejected it as infeasible. History proves that Henderson was wrong, technologically and doctrinally.

Over the summer, Swinton's nascent tank force cooperated with the RFC's local squadron in signalling, using the RFC's signalling lamps. However, "[w]hat could be conveyed by code was very limited in extent, and the chain of transmission was so cumbrous and slow as to be almost useless" (1932: 251).

GHQ assigned two squadrons to bomb enemy communications during the three days of preliminary bombardment, from 12 September. On the day of assault, three squadrons flew over 3rd Army, although mainly to counter German aircraft, and to report progress on the ground, rather than to attack targets on the ground.

Tanks and Infantry

In December 1915, Churchill had proposed that "caterpillars" should lead through the wire, then let the infantry pass through. He did not specify any interval between vehicles and infantry, or any use of vehicles to shield infantry. Rather, his infantrymen were supposed to carry their own shields.

In February, Swinton (1932: 209-210) recommended that tanks should lead, so that tanks attract the fire that would otherwise decimate the infantry. Swinton wanted infantry to wait until the tanks get three-quarters of the way to the enemy line, so that both arms hit the enemy parapet at the same time. He suggested an increased proportion of grenadiers ("bombers"), to clear the enemy's trenches and bunkers. He wants the tanks and infantry to keep going, before enemy artillery fires on the captured line. He suggests that tanks and grenadiers should advance alongside the communication trenches, ready to intercept any enemy reinforcements coming forward, and any defenders fleeing rearward.

Swinton stressed the role of the Females in protecting the Males, and of infantry in protecting both types.

> The necessity for the co-ordination of all arms to work together in the offensive generally requires no remarks here, but the desirability of the specially careful consideration of the subject in the case of an operation

by tanks, requires some emphasis, since the orchestration of the attack will be complicated by the introduction of a new instrument and one which somewhat alters the chain of interdependence of all. A recapitulation of this chain will make the matter clear. The tanks cannot win battles by themselves. They are purely auxiliary to the infantry, and are intended to sweep away the obstructions which have hitherto stopped the advance of our infantry beyond the German first line, and cannot with certainty be disposed of by shell fire. It follows, therefore, that the progress of the attack, which depends on the advance of the infantry, depends on the activity and preservation in action of the tanks (1932: 211).

In June, Tandy confirmed "that the infantry attack should follow the tank advance at as close an interval as possible, that is to say, that the infantry advance should be timed so that the infantry may reach the German first line on the heels of the tanks." The tanks should probably keep going through the first enemy line to the next, without waiting for the infantry to consolidate anything, in order to minimise the time in which the defenders of the next line could make ready. This distance could be covered in six or seven minutes (assuming 300 yards between the two lines, and an interval of 150 yards between tanks). Tandy applied the same principle to subsequent defensive lines, all the way to the reserve line.

The first exercises by tanks against the mock battlefield in Norfolk validated Swinton's and Tandy's doctrine.

> Probably the tank attack would draw the fire of the machine guns, and provided that the infantry did not leave their trenches till the tanks had nearly reached the enemy lines. The attention of hostile machine gunners would be fully occupied with their own precarious position, and the attacking infantry would be able to advance through the gap in the wire with little loss (Major A. Holford Walker, "Tactical handling of tanks in action," 21 July 1916, UKNA WO 158/834).

However, in August, GHQ set down that the infantry should lead, to protect tanks from direct artillery fire. Yet GHQ expected the tanks to take the lead to attack machine-guns that survive the bombardment – which, GHQ predicted, would be most likely in "villages, woods, strong points[,] and hidden machine-gun positions." Swinton's doctrine of February had spent many pages explaining how time and coordination would be lost if tanks were expected to wait for infantry to point out targets. In contrast to Swinton's clarity, GHQ's "Preliminary Notes" under-specify what the tanks are supposed to do once they take the lead.

> Within the limits of the objective given to an attack it is generally possible to pick out the points from which the greatest resistance is to be expected. An allotted number of tanks should be told off to deal with each of these pivots of defence. They should be closely supported by bodies of infantry told off for the purpose, who will advance under cover of the tanks, clear up behind them, and eventually consolidate the locality when taken…

> Whether the tanks should deal only with the perimeter of the objectives, or penetrate into it, depends on circumstances, but their primary task

will consist in preventing the locality with which they have to deal from interfering with the progress of the main infantry attack...

Finally, occasions may arise when the 6-pdr. tanks could be used as light mobile artillery in close support of the infantry during the final stages of a successful advance, until such time as field artillery can be brought up.

There are, therefore, 4 ways in which tanks may be employed:

a. The advance in line in large numbers;

b. The attack in groups, or pairs, against selected objectives;

c, Employment single, or in pairs, for special purposes;

d. Employment as mobile light artillery.

This is hardly prescriptive enough to help the arms to agree on how they should combine. Most usefully, the manual's final paragraph reiterates that "every attack by tanks must be combined with an infantry attack, and it will be the special duty of that infantry to co-operate closely with the tanks and to take special care that the tanks do not fall into the enemy's hands."

In February, Swinton had suggested that tanks could signal with flags, coloured balloons, and rockets. In June, Major Tandy had suggested that an officer or NCO should be detailed at the rear of each tank in case the infantry come under fire that requires the tank's attention. He suggested also a "red disc" to indicate to infantry that a tank is cutting wire or receiving fire, a "white disc" to indicate no danger. By 21 July, the nascent tank force in Norfolk was already testing some means by which the infantry could attract the attention of a tank's crew. In practice, the crews soon got in the habit of sending a runner to communicate with another tank. The runner would attract a crew's attention by banging a shovel or crowbar on the rear door, where it was helpfully stowed for this purpose. Presumably some infantrymen saw or were shown this practice, but probably most of the assaulters were never so trained before 15 September.

In August, GHQ did not mention how tank crewmen and infantry were supposed to communicate, except to imply that an enemy machine-gun would be obvious once it opens fire. In fact, even from inside the best of tanks in use today, an entrenched machine-gun is practically invisible from inside the tank, although muzzle flash and smoke eventually give it away. GHQ's subsequent note on force structure acknowledges that the Tank Companies are installing signalling equipment, "but it is doubtful how far these will prove efficient." Swinton had expressed this doubt, but at least he had ideas for tank-infantry communication. GHQ had none.

Most infantry involved on 15 September had watched tanks demonstrating during the prior nine days. The proportion that trained with tanks is unclear. The demonstrations themselves were not necessarily realistic, since higher commanders often wanted tanks to crush trees and race around, in order to impress and bolster infantry as to the capabilities of these novel weapons. At least one brigade rotated each platoon with the tank companies, to practice walking in single file behind a single tank, "because we knew it had to make gaps in enemy barbed wire, and a little column of infantry had to follow through the gap" (Philip Neame, interview, 26 January 1976, Reel 11, IWM 48).

The doctrine was still being negotiated with formation commanders on 13 September. At some point, GHQ's prescription for infantry to lead was turned around. Nevertheless, GHQ did not embrace Swinton's prescription that infantry and tanks should hit the first defensive line at the same time. Instead, it scheduled the tanks to reach the line five minutes ahead of the infantry.

Tanks and Engineers

The Germans routinely staked barbed wire in front of their fire trenches. To date, wire obstacles had been cleared by artillery fire, explosives placed by hand, or hand tools.

Personnel on foot could manually cut their way through, lift the supporting stakes, and drag the materials away. The process is slow and laborious, and practically suicidal under enemy fire. Quicker results could be achieved with explosives, although the blast sometimes dislodges stakes without breaking the wire, depending on the tension in the wire. Engineers liked to tension the wire enough to keep it at some height above the ground (waist-high was default; ideally, different wires were strung at ankle-, waist-, and neck-height), but this tension is not sufficient to break under blast, unless sufficient stakes are blown in opposing directions.

In June 1915, the War Office gained control of the Admiralty's landship projects, and specified more realistic obstacle-crossing capabilities – beyond the width of current German trenches, and above the height of current German parapets. The capability to cross German wire obstacles was specified qualitatively, without any specifications of the depth, height, density, or tension, although the specifications for climbing steps and crossing trenches imply that the tank could mount wire obstacles. Still, wire-crossing capability was not easy to test, given the risks to the tank's moving parts, the slow supply of tanks, and their rushed deployment.

Also in June 1915, the War Office's Department of Chemical Warfare transferred to the Ministry of Munitions, as the Directorate of Trench Warfare Supply, and started development of a self-propelled flamethrower. The first proposal describes an "egg-shaped armoured car or land cruiser," weighing 35 tons. "The front and rear of the car should be fitted with heavy steel cow-catchers for cutting away, tearing down and crushing barbed wire entanglements" ("Suggestions for Armoured Land Cruiser," UKNA MUN 5/210/1940/13). No such fitting was developed. The tandem Pedrail chassis, which the Directorate inherited from the Admiralty in 1915 and tested in 1917, could not mount parapets, and was never tested against wires.

In December 1915, Churchill misinformed GHQ that the Admiralty had already proven that a "caterpillar" could push a naval torpedo-net cutter through German barbed wire obstacles. In fact, no tracked vehicle ever pushed a naval torpedo-net cutter. (It weighed half-a-ton, and would need to be pushed along the ground or held off the ground with some equally heavy mounting.) Rather, in June 1915, the Killen-Strait tri-track tractor had pushed a pincer-shaped device into some strands of wire that had been staked under tension. The device was too small and fragile to gather and cut all the wire. It was never tried against any of the heavier, stiffer, harder wires (actually strips cut from sheets of steel).* The Germans liked to stack coils of such wire in front of the tensioned wire, although not if under enemy observation or short of time.

Churchill's self-promotion of the Admiralty's projects helps to explain his expectation, as of 3 December, that "caterpillars" could steer into the length of the obstacle – automatically cutting wires, while simultaneously engaging the enemy's trench.

> On reaching the enemy's wire they turn to the left or right and run down parallel to the enemy's trench sweeping his parapet with their fire, and crushing and cutting the barbed wire in lanes and in a slightly serpentine course. While doing this the Caterpillars will be so close to the enemy's line that they will be immune from his artillery. Through the gaps thus made the shield[-]bearing infantry will advance.

Swinton was better qualified to judge, being a Royal Engineer by commission. In February, Swinton prescribed that each assault "tank will clear only its own width" in wire, in contrast to Churchill's prescription to turn into the length of the wire. Swinton specified no method by which an assault tank would "clear" wire, except implicitly to rely on weight to crush wire, as he explicitly relied on "weight" to crush machine-guns. After the first tanks and infantry pass a defensive line, Swinton (1932: 213) expects the following tanks to clear wider gaps for cavalry or infantry to exploit. "[E]xperiments are being made in trawling along the entanglements laterally by pairs of machines connected by a wire hawser." Whatever these experiments were, they did not involve pairs of tanks, because only one tank existed. The experiments and demonstrations with the pilot tank in January and February had involved trenches, craters, and steps, but no wire. Swinton (1932: 253) remembered experiments with grapnels in the summer, but does not explain where they went. His training officer reported experiments with some sort of attachment for pulling wire, which proved that the wire was more of a hazard once uprooted than when staked (Major A. Holford Walker, "Tactical handling of tanks in action," 21 July 1916, UKNA WO 158/834). Grapnels would not be used operationally until November 1917.

The nascent tank arm's mock battlefield in Norfolk was not completed until May, and it did not have enough tanks to allow for experiments against the worst of mock German obstacles until June. The tank's mobility over craters, trenches, and revetments did not concern anybody much, but enemy wire entanglements did. The Germans staked wires 40 yards (37 m) deep, as modelled in Norfolk. Even if tanks passed through, some wire would remain entangled in moving parts, which might seize. On 21 June, Tandy reported to Swinton that, although he was still experimenting, he thought the passage of one tank would be insufficient to crush wire to allow infantry to follow. He suggested that the tank driver should aim at wire already cut by artillery fire, and turn into it to widen the gap (but not to keep going down the length of it, as Churchill had suggested) (Major Tandy to Colonel Swinton, 21 June 1916, UKNA WO 158/834). At some point, Martel found

---

* The preferred "wire" was later named after the German who perfected it (Horst Dannert or Donaert). It is self-supporting, rated for loads up to 82 imperial tons (83 metric; 92 short), and impossible to cut mechanically, except with the aid of oxy-acetylene flame.

no need for a tank to turn into the wire, although he accepted the narrowness of the resulting passages.

> The path left by a tank after passing through a wire entanglement was quite passable to infantry and required no improvement; the only point to watch was that a second tank should not attempt to make a second path less than 30 yards to a flank; if it did so the effect of pressing down the wires in this second path often caused sufficient tension in them to raise the wires in the first path (Martel 1931: 47).

On 21 July, Swinton's training officer reported on section-echelon exercises against the mock enemy defences in Norfolk. Swinton's allowance for a short preliminary bombardment to cut enemy wire seemed to be borne out by the pilot tank's difficulties in crossing wire entanglements, without itself getting entangled. The training officer assumed a preliminary bombardment to cut the wire, and suggested that tanks should rush the wire where it is not cut, "with no pause and at top speed…and crush it into the ground preparatory to the next infantry advance." He went on to suggest that the leftmost tank in a section should race into the wire, before turning to its right to crush the wire, while the other tanks are engaging the enemy. However, the officer admits that the tank would present a flank-on target to any artillery in line of sight (Major A. Holford Walker, "Tactical handling of tanks in action," 21 July 1916, UKNA WO 158/834).

On 15 September, tanks endeavoured to find gaps blown by the preliminary bombardment, but their difficulties navigating the broken terrain, and even distinguishing friendly from enemy trenches, suggest that if they did find any gaps, they stumbled upon them.

Speed

On 15 September, the creeping barrage slowed the advance to 1.7 mph (50 yards or 46 m per minute), even without the effects of the cratering. On 26 September, the Reserve Army's creeping barrage was slower still: 100 yards (91 m) per 3 minutes, until after the first defensive line, when it accelerated to 50 yards per minute.

On good ground, the first tanks move more than twice as quick. In February, Swinton had reported the tank's speed as 4 mph (117 yards or 107 m per minute) "on the level," and 2 mph (59 yards or 54 m per minute) "on rough ground and when climbing." In June, Swinton received Tandy's estimate that tanks could probably average 2 mph across enemy trenches, and 3 mph (88 yards or 80 m per minute) between trenches.* GHQ's doctrine of August, based on Swinton's input rather than Tandy's, specifies that tanks move at "2 miles per hour when climbing or on very rough ground," and 4 to 5 mph "on the level."

Swinton had some effect on Haig verbally during visits to GHQ from 19 August. On 11 September, Haig suggested to Henry Rawlinson (4th Army's commander-in-chief) the "necessity for advancing quickly so as to take full advantage" of tanks. However, GHQ and 4th Army HQ slowed the creeping barrage to less than half the

---

* The Tank Corps' "training note" on "Infantry and Tank Cooperation and Training" (of 27 January 1918) repeats these specifications, except that the speed across trenches falls to 1.0-1.4 mph (30-40 yards per minute).

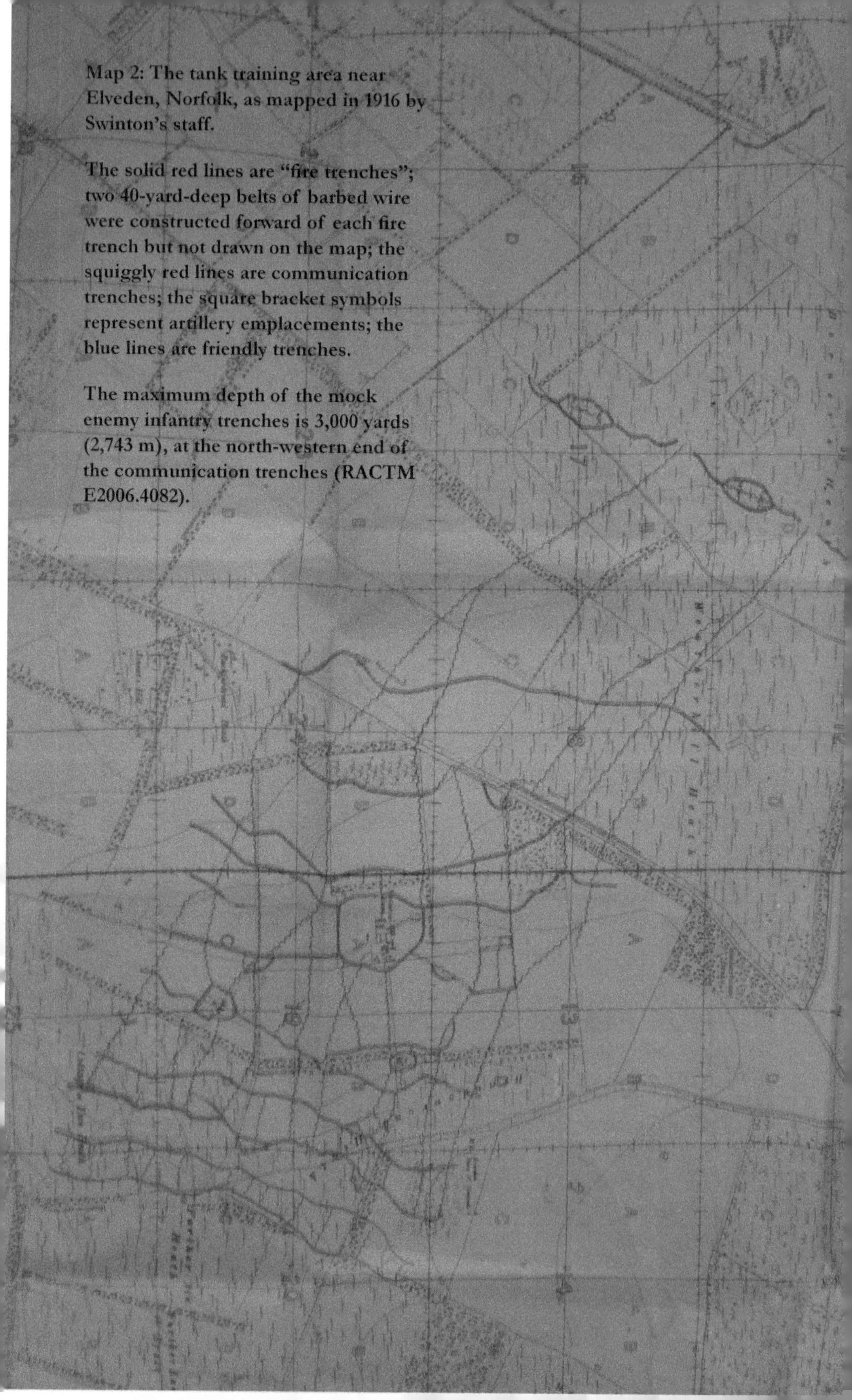

Map 2: The tank training area near Elveden, Norfolk, as mapped in 1916 by Swinton's staff.

The solid red lines are "fire trenches"; two 40-yard-deep belts of barbed wire were constructed forward of each fire trench but not drawn on the map; the squiggly red lines are communication trenches; the square bracket symbols represent artillery emplacements; the blue lines are friendly trenches.

The maximum depth of the mock enemy infantry trenches is 3,000 yards (2,743 m), at the north-western end of the communication trenches (RACTM E2006.4082).

tank's maximum speed. When they and sympathetic historians complained later of the slow speed of tanks, they ignored the impediments. Swinton (1932: 211) blamed the preliminary bombardment most. Remember, he had wanted only a few hours of overnight bombardment to break the wire. Having seen tanks training over the mock battlefield in England, he estimated their rate of opposed advance at 1 mph, but still expected them to cover 12 miles in the available hours of daylight.

On 15 September, the tanks were slowed by craters, the creeping barrage, and the packaging of at least a pair of tanks and an infantry platoon per objective (4th Army HQ's decision). Elsewhere, sections were split into packages of three tanks each, or combined, in packages of eight or ten tanks. These packagings curbed the crew's ability to choose the most navigable route, and help to explain why some tanks lost coordination with each other, erred rearwards, or fired upon friendly infantry (Williams-Ellis 1920: 25; Cavaleri 1995: 26).

Sustainment

To explain the complicated options for sustainment, the sub-sections below address the depth of advance, infantry waves, reserves, tank waves, supplies, and communications.

Depth

Churchill's doctrine is ambiguous about depth of advance. Swinton's (1932: 207) doctrine of February acknowledges that the enemy's "defensive zone" might be "3 or 4 miles" (5,280 to 7,040 yards; 4,828 to 6,437 m) deep, but promises that tanks could advance 12 miles (21,120 yards; 19,312 m) in one day – if they keep going before the enemy pins them down, and if the terrain is "level" enough. GHQ's doctrine of August does not specify any depth of advance. GHQ's plan for the 15th of September expects the tanks to break through all the German defensive lines, despite the broken terrain.

Current German doctrine specified:

1. a *Vorfeldzone* ("forward field zone"; normally translated by the British as "outpost line"), normally 500 to 1,000 meters (547 to 1,094 yards) deep, 8,000 meters (8,749 yards) at deepest;

2. a *Kampffeld* ("fighting field"; normally translated as "resistance line," which was actually the German term – *Hauptwiderstandslinie* – for the first of the three defensive lines), 2,000 meters (2,187 yards) in depth; and

3. a *Hinterzone* ("rearward zone"; normally translated as "support line"), for the reserves and artillery, 1,000 meters (1,094 yards) in depth (Zabecki 2018: 45).

These estimates suggest a total depth from 3,500 meters (3,800 yards; 2.2 miles) to 11,000 meters (12,000 yards; 6.8 miles).* The defences on the Somme were at least 4,000 yards (3,658 m) deep. However, in England, the tank crews trained on mock German fortifications just 3,000 yards (2,743 m) deep (see Map 2). Martel was most to blame, since he was the only engineer involved who had served on the Somme. In June, Tandy warned Swinton that "the German defended zone never presents uniformity over any great length of front," with two to four lines of trenches in the "first position" alone. Scattered strongpoints make the lines look even less regular.

---

* Separate estimates include a maximum of 8,000 m (8,750 yards; 5 miles) (Short 2004: 21).

In September, the tanks would need to cover 4 miles (6,437 m) of cratered ground just to get from the assembly area to the enemy's front line – equivalent to the depth of enemy defences that Swinton had expected in February. Thus, to achieve Swinton's doctrinal expectation of reaching the enemy's artillery, the tanks would need to traverse at least 11,000 yards (6.25 miles; 10,058 m) in daylight.

They would not reach that far, but that is GHQ's fault more than Swinton's, given that GHQ rejected his insistence on passable terrain. At deepest, the advance reached 3,500 yards (3,200 m). In general, the advance measured 2,500 yards (2,300 m) (Williams-Ellis 1920: 23; Swinton 1932: 207).

Infantry Waves

To sustain an advance, the main options are either to refill assaulters with their consumables, such as ammunition, food, and water – or to send forward fresh forces to take the lead from the assaulters. A third option, somewhat of a hybrid of the other two options, is to send forces forward just to consolidate objectives, so that assaulters can keep going without worrying about defending what they have captured. The consolidation forces can be optimized for defence with heavier weapons (such as mortars), equipment for digging (such as spades and picks), and equipment for constructing (such as sandbags for restoring revetments, wooden boards for use as retaining walls, corrugated iron for roofing, and armoured shields for observation posts).

To date, the British sustained attacks in two main ways, First, they allocated at least one following wave to overtake the leading wave if stuck. The leading wave would then become a consolidating wave, awaiting horse-drawn supply wagons, with heavy equipment and extra supplies. Only in 1918 did the BEF normalize different waves for assaulting and consolidating each line.

Second, the British reserved infantry for use contingently, according to opportunities or emergencies.

Reserves

Reserves are useful for reinforcing successful penetrations and meeting counter-attacks. Allied strategy and tactics tended to under-allocate reserves, due to over-estimation of the attacker's impetus, under-estimation of the depth of enemy defences, and under-estimation of German capacity for counter-attack. German doctrine emphasized depth, reserves, and counter-attacks, at every echelon. A new edition of the main German manual, issued nominally on 1 December, emphasized deeper defences, larger reserves, and quicker counter-attacks.

Counter-attacks are supposed to catch the attackers before they can catch their breath, manage their stress, and improve whatever defences they have captured. The captured firing positions are facing the wrong direction, the fortifications are likely damaged, the attackers are carrying light weapons for assault rather than defence, and the attackers might have exhausted their consumables already. Counter-attacks ideally force the attackers into flight, during which they are most exposed. However, counter-attackers expose themselves when moving forward, at worst after the attackers have optimized for defence. For some historians, German propensity to counter-attack "helped [to] make the Somme almost as costly in lives for the Germans as it was for the Allies" (Hochschild 2011: 214).

In German doctrine, the regiment (equivalent to a British infantry brigade) was deployed with one battalion forward, the other two units behind, ready to advance, on the authority of the leading unit's commander. If the regiment's counter-push (*Gegenstoss*) fails, higher echelons might commit reserves to a formal counter-attack (*Gegenangriff*) (Zabecki 2018: 44-45). To overwhelm such a regiment, the attacker needs at least one brigade, with one unit forward and three units following. (In 1918, the British brigade was reduced to three units.) However, following units might struggle to squeeze into the space available, particularly if defenders keep the area under fire. Often, the leading unit left the other units far behind. The units might be reserved too far back (even behind brigade HQ) to exploit a penetration or meet a counterattack. Thus, the leading unit was usually expected to keep going through successive defensive lines until it ran out of initiative, at which point a reserved unit might be ordered to take over.

No tanks were reserved on 15 September. Their allocation averaged fewer than 5 tanks per division, fewer than 2 tanks per brigade, fewer than 1 tank per unit. The advance of the tank "Dinnaken," ahead of infantry, into Flers, within the second line, and of tanks into Gueudecourt, within the third line, suggest that a reserve of tanks could have penetrated further.

Tank Waves

At this time, tanks were expected to keep going without follow-on waves or reserves. In January 1915, Churchill had expected "caterpillars" to cross "several" enemy trenches, although by December he thought this was only possible in darkness, due to the threat of enemy artillery in daylight. Indeed, he allowed for tanks to be abandoned upon daylight. He never mentioned any possibility of countering artillery in daylight, rallying vehicles, withdrawing vehicles, or supplying them.

In February 1916, Swinton intended "the assault to maintain most of its starting momentum and break through the German position quickly," i.e., through three infantry lines and the artillery line. Swinton expected assaulting infantry to follow tanks without consolidating each captured line. Rather, "reinforcements" would consolidate. His hybrid solution is not obvious to the hasty reader, due to the scattered structure of his paper, although the following section is clearest.

> [T]he tanks will halt at the enemy's frontline, keeping it under enfilade, only until our assaulting infantry have reached it, when they will proceed straight ahead at full speed for the German second line, as far as possible following up alongside the hostile communication trenches, which they will sweep, thus dealing with any German reinforcements or bombing parties coming up...[A] step-by-step advance – which has the drawback of giving the enemy time to reinforce the sector threatened – is not a course to be recommended for any positive advantages...[T]he more speedy and uninterrupted their advance the greater the chance of their surviving sufficiently long to do this. It is possible, therefore, that an effort to break through the enemy's defensive zone in one day may now be contemplated as a feasible proposition...[A]n advance of 12 miles [19.3 km] forward could be carried out during the daylight hours...past the enemy's main artillery positions (Swinton 1932: 209-210).

To clarify, Swinton wants the assaulters to keep advancing until the end of the day. He specifies a second wave of tanks and infantry, but as "reinforcements," of which the tanks' role is apparently limited to widening the gaps in the wire for the cavalry, while the infantry's role is to consolidate the gains.

In June, Tandy validated Swinton theoretically, by estimating that infantry could consolidate one line within five minutes, and reach the next line on "the heels" of the tanks, and that tanks could advance between enemy defensive lines in 6 to 7 minutes. However, events would prove them over-ambitious. Tandy acknowledged that tanks might need to turn around to deal with machine-guns that open up on the infantry. He ruled that tanks should "never pass far beyond a line of trenches (say 50 yards) until they have seen that our infantry have taken the trench."

GHQ's doctrine of August is short and unclear about whether the assaulters or following forces should keep going. It has less confidence in tanks than infantry, although it aims for a breakthrough. It warns that the risks from enemy artillery to the tank "limit its employment, unless we are prepared to risk the loss of all the tanks by pushing them as far forward as they can go." GHQ wants tanks to follow infantry, until machine-guns open up on the infantry, and to return to the follower position after the resistance has been neutralized. GHQ does not want tanks to consolidate objectives, except where tanks can hide in villages or woods. GHQ allows for tanks to continue on to the next objective or to return to their assembly area, "according to their original orders," without indicating a preference.

Supplies

In February, Swinton urged "preparation to send forward reinforcements, guns, supplies[,] and ammunition," and planned to replenish the tanks "with fresh crews and ammunition" by "the end of the first day," although he admitted that "schemes have yet to be worked out." Implicitly, he relied on replenishment by the horse-drawn wagons issued to infantry formations, although he might have expected the corps to allocate transport. Like Swinton, Tandy failed to specify any way to supply the assaulters.

GHQ suggests that "tanks may prove useful for taking up stores, hauling guns over trenches, for clearing up behind the leading lines of infantry, for removing captured guns, for destroying obstacles, and possibly for reconnaissance," particularly in close country. Specialized supply carriers and tractors were not developed from tanks until 1917, although on 15 September 1916 at least one tank carried ammunition forward to the infantry after rallying to the rear.

No assets were provided for sustaining the tanks, except whatever horse-drawn wagons might be released by infantry division HQs. These were not scheduled to move forward until after the cavalry would go forward to exploit any breakthrough, and thus sustained only the first two objective lines on the day (Fuller 1936: 80).

Communications

A complementary action is to send forward signallers with wireless radios, followed by signallers to lay telephones cable (ideally buried, as protection against blast and sabotage), so that the assaulting and consolidating forces can report status and call for reinforcements or supporting fire if the enemy were to counter-attack. A final complementary action is to send forward indirect-fire artillery that otherwise would not be able to fire beyond the most advanced troops from pre-assault firing positions.

Otherwise, communication with reinforcements and suppliers was by runners. Assaulters did not carry radios at this time. Some aircraft carried radios, but were not yet committed to support of the assault. Runners could bear written messages to rear battalion HQs (behind the starting line), which could telephone messages back to brigade HQs, if the cable survived.

The tanks, as yet, carried no radios or cable-burying equipment. At the time, these equipments were so heavy that they needed to be transported on carts. In March, Swinton (1932: 248-249, 270-271) had asked the RE Experimental Wireless Establishment to develop a reduced radio to fit the tank. By the end of July, one was available for each company. However, the type had proved inaudible against the tank's noise in June, although the operator (the RE provided the operator) could still send morse code. Yet just before enshipment in August, GHQ banned them, for fear of interference with other signals.

GHQ ruled against the hydrogen-filled balloons that Swinton had planned since February, lest they draw enemy fire.

Tanks were carrying pigeons already, but these returned to lofts controlled by infantry division HQs – if they returned at all. Most signals were carried by runners on paper or in memory, which implies greater delay, although more reliability.

Exploitation

During the Great War, the main arm of exploitation was the cavalry, but in France it spent most of the war behind the lines waiting for an opportunity that never came. Swinton's (1932: 213) doctrine expects tanks and infantry to sustain the advance through the artillery line, without mentioning cavalry, until, as an apparent afterthought or sop, he justifies the widening of the gaps in the wire, by a second wave of tanks, to allow a "subsequent advance of reinforcements, or a burst through of a mass of cavalry."

The Cavalry Corps (then three divisions) was on standby to exploit any breakthrough in the Somme campaign. Similarly, the Corps was warned to be ready to exploit a breakthrough at Flers or Courcelette. The Cavalry Corps' first objective line was the high ground from Rocquigny to Bapaume. From there, it was supposed to attack the artillery line, from Le Sars to Warlencourt and Thilloy.

GHQ allocated the Corps to 4th Army. Separately, GHQ reserved two cavalry divisions (nominally Indian divisions, although they held British units), ready to exploit a breakthrough by the Cavalry Corps. No cavalry were called forward, as the assaulters did not capture a sufficiently wide or deep channel for exploitation. Even if cavalry had been called forward, they would have struggled in conditions that had defeated most of the tanks. No other arms were allocated for exploitation.

Outcomes

The advances were deepest wherever tanks advanced – up to 3,500 yards (3,200 m) deep (at Flers). The captures included part of the third defensive line, but did not reach the artillery line. The operation captured twice as much ground for half the casualties as experienced on 1 July (see Table 1).

On the left, Canadian Corps captured Courcelette and neutralized the strongpoint known as "Sugar Factory," with four of the six tanks allocated, or really the two that kept up with the assault wave. Two arrived to mop up, after being dug out of the mud on the start line.

In the centre, the XV Corps advanced deepest, through Flers to Gueudecourt. Of 18 tanks allocated, 14 reached the start line, of which 9 crossed the start line and the German trenches. Three tanks had been scheduled to advance at 0515 hours, followed by infantry from 14th Division, to clear Delville Wood, although only D1 engaged the first defensive line, and was knocked out by indirect fire shortly after clearing the trench. Eight tanks advanced ahead of the infantry of the New Zealand Division and 41st Division, of which at least 7 helped to neutralize the strongpoint before Flers. At 0845 hours, an airman reported "tank seen in main street Flers going on with large number of troops following" (changed in the press to "tank walking up the high street of Flers with the British Army cheering behind"). This tank (designated "D17," named "Dinnaken") was one of the four tanks that crossed the start line in support of 41st Division. However, the infantry became disorganized or cautious inside Flers, and failed to advance further. Four other tanks bypassed Flers and reached the third defensive line, on the outskirts of Gueudecourt. One tank took the lead, enfiladed and traversed the last enemy trench, and caused the surrender of 300 Germans. A separate tank entered Gueudecourt, where it destroyed a field gun. However, other artillery knocked out this tank and two other tanks by direct fire; the fourth turned back.

The III Corps captured most of Martinpuich. The most direct route was taken on the left by 15th Division, with one tank. It supported the infantry from behind, until the infantry were held up, to the south-west of the village. The tank went forward to destroy some machine-guns, before it withdrew for want of fuel. Once refueled, it returned with ammunition for the infantry to consolidate the village.

To the right of 15th Division, between Martinpuich and High Wood, two tanks supported 50th Division into the first line. One enfiladed the trench before being knocked out by artillery fire. The other carried on to the east of the village, through the second defensive line, where it knocked out three machine-guns, but ran out of fuel and received a bullet in its engine oil cylinder. The four tanks supporting 47th Division could not make headway across the broken stumps of High Wood. (The division committed most of its reserves, before taking the strongpoint therein.)

On the right of III Corps, where the terrain was worst for tanks, the IV Corps never got close to Morval or Les Boeufs. Eighteen tanks were allocated, of which 10 crossed the start line on time. Ten had been allocated to the Guards Division, of which six crossed the start line: one ditched, one broke its tail, and four proceeded to the first objective (a strongpoint known as the Quadrilateral). Coordination with the infantry was poor, in part because the enemy sensibly did not fire on the tanks. On the right, two tanks enfiladed the wrong enemy trench, before returning. On the left, two tanks also strayed towards the wrong targets, until one bogged down.

To their right, four tanks were allocated to 6th Division, of which one crossed the start line on time, got lost, turned back towards a friendly trench, opened fire, was corrected, and fired on the forward enemy trench, but had no effect on the Quadrilateral. It rallied to replenish fuel and to plug holes in its sponsons. Two tanks started late, in time to join an improvised attack at 1300 hours, except this was cancelled, although not before these two tanks received fire. Furthest right, three tanks crossed the start line with 56th Division, but one lost a track, and one ditched.

The third helped the infantry to capture the first German trench, before Combles (Williams-Ellis 1920: 28; Fuller 1920: 56).

Of the 34 tanks that crossed the start line, 23 engaged or were engaged by the enemy, although 4 of these were late (see Table 1). Fuller (1936: 81) reports 18 reaching enemy trenches, of which 6 bogged, 8 were knocked out by artillery, 2 caught fire for internal reasons, and 2 remained operational through the first day. Only nine crewmen had been killed. Churchill (1927: 171) and Cavaleri (1995: 26) report 9 tanks crossing the German "outpost" area, and thus being in position to engage the enemy's second line. Four crossed the third line. Twelve tanks rallied.

On 25 September, 13 tanks were committed to an attack on Thiepval, 2.5 miles (4 km) west of Flers, of which nine bogged in craters before reaching the enemy, two supported the infantry into Thiepval before getting stuck, and two remained available. One of the two tanks was allocated to attack a 1,500-yard length of trench (known as the Gird Trench), where protective wire had survived the bombardment. This tank reached the friendly infantry's north-western lodgement around 0630 hours. Around 0730 hours, it started moving south-eastwards. Using only machine-guns (it was a Female variant), it killed countless defenders, without damage to itself, and forced 370 Germans to surrender to the south-eastern lodgement, which suffered only 5 friendly casualties. Once the captured trench was occupied by the brigade's third battalion, the tank supported the fourth battalion into the village, although the tank itself ran out of fuel. Eight tanks were committed the next day, without preliminary bombardment, to capture Thiepval Chateau and Schwaben Redoubt (Fuller 1920: 57).

D17 ("Dinnaken") and some of the infantry from 122nd Brigade, 41st Division, who entered Flers on 15 September, are reunited two days later (IWM Q5578).

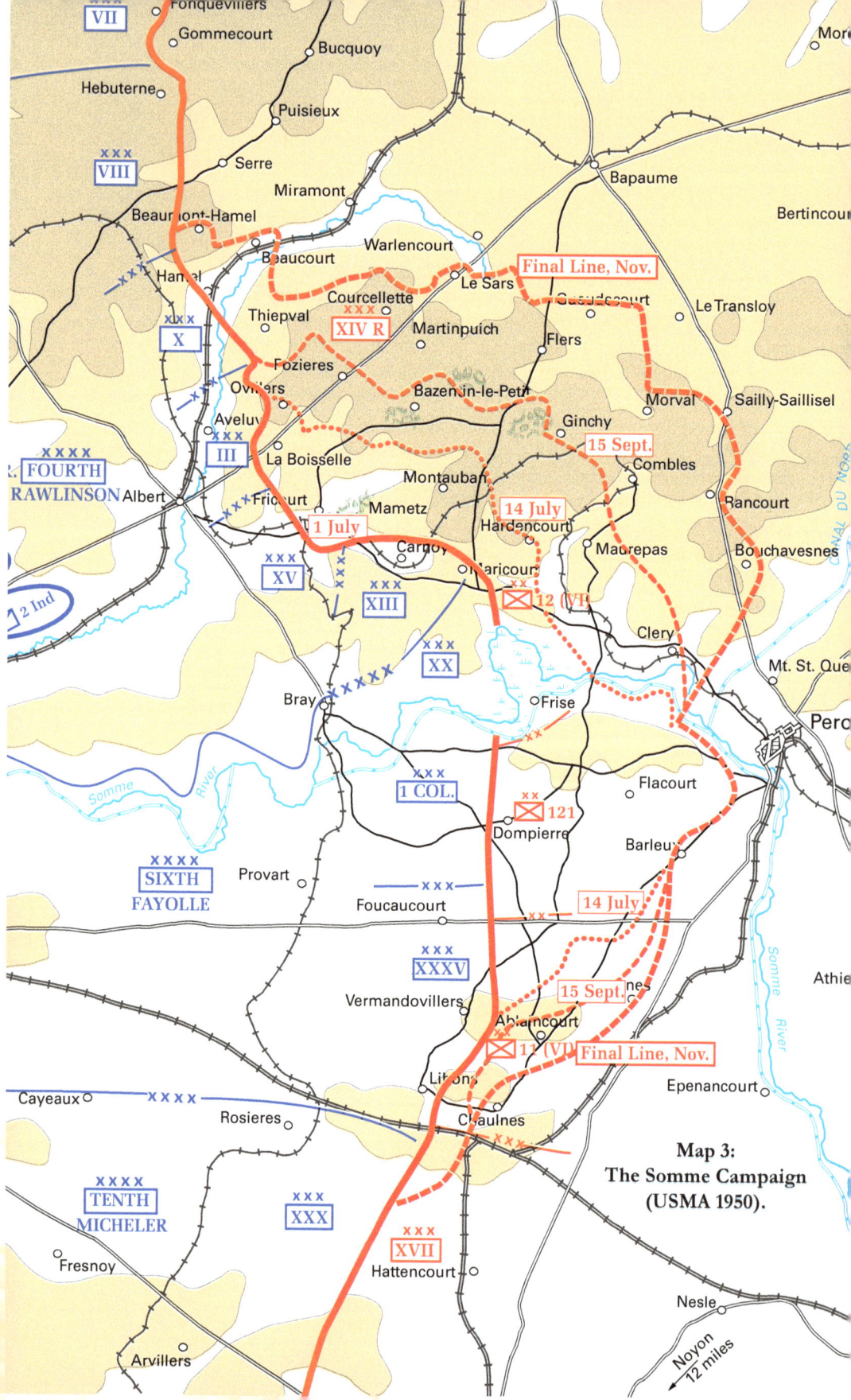

Map 3: The Somme Campaign (USMA 1950).

3

Ancre, November 1916

While a tank HQ was developing in France (see Chapter 4), tanks were involved in attacks from 17 October to 18 November, including a nominal offensive on 13 November, astride the Ancre river, to the west of Thiepval (see Map 3). The offensive was intended to reduce the German salient between Thiepval (just 2.5 miles or 4 km east of Courcelette) and Serre-lès-Puisieux (4.5 miles or 7.2 km north-west of Courcelette). These actions went ahead without any written changes to doctrine, although some precedents and improvements were normalized during the actions themselves. As in the previous chapter, this chapter analyzes the operations by the principles of terrain, concentration, surprise, combined arms, speed, sustainment, and exploitation, and by the outcomes.

Terrain

The most obvious lesson in all tank operations to date is the desirability of dry, level, unbroken ground, although GHQ did not care, so long as it was trying to rescue some honour out of the offensive it had launched on 1 July. (The River Ancre was part of the Somme front, being a tributary, flowing south-eastwards through Albert to Corbie.) All of the actions in October and November were on wet and damaged ground. The ground is level in the floodplain, but soon rolls into shallow hills and valleys, through many small villages and woods.

The terrain is more difficult in that season and weather, although the distances are not great. On 13 November, the assault front was no more than 4,000 yards (3,658 m) long. The final objective line was between 2,050 yards (1,875 m) and 3,500 yards (3,200 meters) from the start line. The attackers would need to cross: 800 yards (732 m) of damaged, rolling ground, and three to four German trenches, to reach the first objective line (from Beaucourt Station up a valley to the eastern outskirts of Beaumont Hamel, and northwards along the Redan Ridge, to west of Serre; another 600 yards (549 m) to 1,000 yards (914 m) to the second objective line (west of Beaucourt, along the east slope of Redan Ridge and east of Serre, to the boundary of V and XIII Corps); and another 650 yards (594 m) to 1,700 yards (1,554 m) to the final objective line (from Beaucourt northwards along the valley and road that leads to Puisieux).

The difficulties of the terrain are epitomized by operations on 13 November alone, when both tanks sent against Beaumont Hamel, and all three tanks sent against St. Pierre Divon (1.5 miles or 2.4 km south-east of Beaumont Hamel), bogged down without crossing the first defensive line. The Army needed many times more tanks to sustain the attack.

Concentration

The Reserve Army (Hubert Gough) planned to attack with eight divisions, from II and V Corps. The main effort was assigned to V Corps, with four divisions (2nd,

3rd, 51st, 63rd). These were supposed to secure Beaumont Hamel and Beaucourt. The II Corps, with four divisions (4th Canadian, 18th, 19th, 39th), was to advance from Stuff Trench and Schwaben Redoubt to the Hansa defensive line, securing the road bridges by Beaucourt station and Beaucourt Mill.

Only 15 tanks were committed. On average, 1.9 tanks were available for each division, about 1 tank per seven battalions, and 1 tank per 267 yards of front. With 1,389 artillery pieces, the attacking formations boasted 1 piece per 2.9 yards of front.

Surprise

GHQ intended to exhaust enemy morale and deplete enemy reserves with frequent attacks. GHQ hoped that the enemy would not have time between attacks to confirm any attack in advance.

GHQ persisted with a preliminary bombardment, over days, except that the daily bombardment was reduced to one hour each morning, for seven days, with hope that the Germans would not realize which day would be assault day. Indeed, the Germans were surprised in time and (to less extent) space.

The bombardment started at 0545. The assault started at 0645 (zero hour), in twilight, about 75 minutes before sunrise. The attack by the 63rd Division, on Beaucourt, was to begin 200 minutes after zero hour, so as to benefit from daylight, given the navigational issues. Mist obscured the assaults.

Combined Arms

Artillery

The preliminary bombardment lasted one hour on each of seven days, and focused on the wire, trenches, and bunkers of the first defensive line. In the hour before assault, a machine-gun barrage was added, this time aimed at the German machine-guns on the ridge behind Beaumont Hamel.

The creeping barrage started upon assault, targeting the enemy's first (nearest) trench. After six minutes, the bombardment would creep 100 yards (91 m) in five minutes (0.7 mph), with a pause on the rearward zone.

Tanks and Infantry

No change was made to the norm established in September that tanks should lead, although the infantry got ahead whenever the tanks bogged. Once tanks were dug out, they were usually directed to help infantry that were pinned down, and soon re-took the lead.

Tank crews had been trained since the summer to dismount their machine-guns if their tanks were incapacitated. Dismounted guns are useful to provide covering fire for the advancing infantry, and to defend the tank, so long as they could be placed behind some sort of cover before the enemy gets line of fire on the gunners. The viability of an immobile Male tank's six-pounder guns was ambiguous, until 14 November. Three tanks were sent against a strongpoint to the south of Beaumont-Hamel, of which one was knocked out by an enemy shell, and two bogged down, within sight of the strongpoint. Their fire persuaded 400 Germans to surrender. This action normalized an expectation that Male tank crews should man their guns even if immobilized (Fuller 1920: 58).

One tactical innovation can be dated to 17 November, when the only tank available locally was allocated to outflank a particularly strong defensive position, known as the Triangle, atop high ground, 1,200 yards (1,100 m) east of Beaumont Hamel (midway in the advance from Beaumont to Beaucourt). A frontal approach had been churned by so many artillery bombardments that local commanders agreed that the tank should attack from the flank, the infantry from the front. Fix-and-flank tactics were already conventional for the infantry, and are apparent in some pre-deployment doctrine for tanks (such as Swinton's wish for Males to fire on distant guns while Females manoeuvre on closer targets). Tanks and infantry fixed and flanked targets for each other expediently, but had not trained to do so, although the doctrinal emphasis on cooperation suggests they should. Navigationally, a flanking attack is more difficult than a frontal approach, particularly for a tank crew peering through slits in armour plates, in misty conditions, during shortening days, on broken ground. Overnight, the nascent tank arm's intelligence officer (Captain F. Elliot "Boots" Hotblack, on which more in the next chapter), taped a route slightly beyond the British front. However, just before dawn, snow obscured the white tape. Hotblack volunteered to walk in front of the tank. Helped by the frozen ground, he continued almost to the German position, without being hit, then returned to HQ. The tank advanced alongside the German trench, firing (with machine-guns only, being a Female) at infantry inside the trench and at the horsed transport beyond. Friendly infantry went to ground short of their objective, and planned a second attack, for the morrow. Hotblack led the tank behind British lines for replenishment and maintenance, although a change of wind caused the ground to thaw and soften, so the second attack was called off. As he recalled later, "the margin between the possible and the impossible was very narrow…[A]s the day temperature rose, the conditions had become impossible." He was awarded a Distinguished Service Order for his actions that day, and set the standard for tank commanders to follow (Williams-Ellis 1920: 37; Liddell Hart 1959: I, 88n-89n).

Speed

The infantry were given 56 minutes to reach the first objective line, equivalent to a speed of just 0.5 mph, or 15 yards (13 m) per minute. They were given an hour to consolidate the first objective, before advancing on the second. These speeds and delays do not fulfil the urgency of Swinton's doctrine.

Sustainment

As in September, no tanks or units were reserved, and no provision was made to sustain the assaulters, except to use the infantry divisions' horse-drawn carts to sustain the infantry on the objective lines. Since this sustainment was scheduled for after the cavalry were supposed to exploit the breakthrough, the wagons did not advance before the tanks rallied to the rear.

Exploitation

As in September, the three cavalry divisions of the Cavalry Corps were allotted to exploit any breakthrough, but they were never called forward, and probably could not have traversed the battlefield if they had been called forward.

Outcomes

None of the battles of September, October, or November broke through the defences entirely, although in places tanks had been necessary to local penetrations beyond the enemy's third defensive line, up to 3,500 yards (3,200 m) from the start line (15 September). The advances of October measured in hundreds of yards. The offensive of 13 November aimed only 2,050 yards (1,900 m) from the start line, at shallowest, but the deepest advance of the day fell short of the final objective line by about 300 yards (274 m). That line would not be secured for another two years.

Unfortunately, the low number of tanks involved, their high failure rate in the waterlogged, cratered, and excavated terrain, and the high failure rate of the different offensives that made up the misnamed "Battle of the Somme," allowed for polarized interpretations, which would plague the tank arm for the rest of the war, and continue to plague the historiography today.

On 24 November 1916, the tank staff moved from Beauquesne to Bermicourt – half-a-mile north of the road between Hesdin and St. Pol. By then, Elles was complaining of too many responsibilities, too little support from BEF GHQ and home authorities, and too few staff. He rapidly gained more staff and promotions for the original staff. This photograph was taken outside the HQ's mess, in Chateau de Bermicourt, in mid-1917. The officers are (from left to right) Lieutenant-Colonel J.F.C. Fuller (chief of staff), Major S.G. Brockbank (Central Workshops), Brigadier-General Hugh Jamieson Elles (commander), Major R.P. Butler (Salvage Company), Lieutenant-Colonel T.J. Uzielli (DAA&QMG), Major H.C. Atkin-Berry ("A" Branch or personnel branch), and Captain R.W. Dundas ("Q" Branch or logistics and supply branch).

4

Doctrine, 1916-1917

Although GHQ had sabotaged the debut of tanks in many ways, the offensive towards Flers and Courcelette persuaded GHQ of their value. On 19 September, it required 1,000 tanks with thicker armour, and an administrative HQ for them in France. The HQ's convoluted development of doctrine is explained below through sections on its commander (Hugh Elles), its first effective chief of staff (Giffard le Quesne Martel), the most published doctrinist of their peer group (JFC Fuller), two other external staff officers with doctrinal input (Stephen Foot; F.H.E. Townshend), its first formal chief of staff (Fuller), and his first "training notes" for the tank arm.

Elles

GHQ appointed Hugh Elles (pronounced "Ellis") (1880-1945) as the new HQ's commander.* Elles was a Royal Engineer by commission, which lent mechanical ethos, although most of the engineering taught to and performed by the Royal Engineers is not mechanical. He was certainly an experienced staff officer. He had served as a staff captain in 1914, a Brigade Major (a brigade's chief of staff) from February 1915 until being wounded in April, and a staff officer at GHQ since his convalescence. In August, GHQ appointed him as one of its liaisons to the front. In January 1916, Haig sent Elles to London to investigate tanks. He stayed there as a liaison to the Tank Supply Committee, through which he met Swinton. From May, he often visited Swinton's nascent force in Norfolk. In September, Swinton recommended Elles to command the tanks now in France. The appointment was effective on 29 September.

Elles had not commanded higher than a platoon, but the new HQ was meant to be administrative. His immediate priorities were to organize the tanks and crews arriving in France with those returning from petty actions on the Somme front, to stand up a Central Workshops, a Salvage Company, and quartermaster staff, and to liaise with GHQ and the formations in the planning of future operations with tanks. He reviewed and escalated doctrine, but does not seem to have authored any on his own. He seems to have relied on Swinton initially.

> It is remarkable that one of the first official papers on the tactical use of tanks, written by General Swinton early in 1915, should have been almost literally translated into action in 1918. To General Swinton, too, is due the implanting into all ranks of the fundamental idea of the tank as a weapon for saving the lives of infantry (Elles, in Williams-Ellis 1920: v).

Swinton (1932: 198n) admits that his influence on the tank arm in France was verbal. His doctrinal paper of February 1916 did not reach Tank Corps HQ until January 1918. Before the end of October 1916, Swinton was released back to the War Cabinet as its correspondent. In November, his role in England was taken over

---

* He was then ranked Colonel. He was not gazetted as Brigadier-General until 1 May 1917.

by Brigadier-General F. Gore Anley, who focused on discipline and training. His HQ was disrupted for months by the home force's move, by road and rail, for at least 230 miles, from Thetford to Bovington Camp and nearby Wareham (while the Camp was being expanded), in Dorset.

On 8 October, GHQ approved a Heavy Section HQ at brigade echelon. The next day, GHQ recommended its redesignation as the Tank Corps, but for now the War Office refused to separate a new arm. In November, the War Department upgraded it to Heavy Branch, but did not separate it as the Tank Corps until June 1917.

GHQ's approvals of 8 October include Elles' first four staff appointments:

1. Giffard le Quesne Martel (RE) was the Brigade Major – effectively the first chief of staff.
2. Captain Michael J. Tapper (London Regiment) was appointed as the Staff Captain – effectively the deputy chief of staff.
3. Captain T.J. Uzielli (Royal Lancashire Regiment) was the DAA&QMG (Deputy Assistant Adjutant and Quartermaster General);
4. Captain F. Elliot "Boots" Hotblack (Norfolk Regiment) was the intelligence officer, which meant he was also the chief reconnaissance and mapping officer.

Martel

In April 1916, GHQ sent Martel to Thetford to advise on the mock battlefield that Swinton had required since February. Elles and Martel met there in May. In October, Elles invited Martel to join his staff. Martel was a fellow engineer, and more experienced with both engineering in France and tank training in England. However, Martel had no experience as a staff officer or doctrinist. His first doctrinal inspirations were naval, like those of Churchill and most of the subordinates who had worked on landships for the Admiralty in 1915. By November, Martel escalated a paper entitled "A Tank Army." In his first published account, he wrote that "we [the staff] prepared a paper…to clear our minds as to the possible eventual future of tanks," "suggesting the employment of an army consisting entirely of fighting vehicles" (1931: 15; 1949: 14). In a memoir, Martel (1945: 38) replaces "our minds" with "my mind" – a selfish change that indicates the risks of relying on Martel as a source, and foreshadows his misrepresentation of Fuller's doctrine.

The "Tank Army" paper does not survive, but Martel archived a shorter derivative within days ("The Transition from Present Day Warfare to Tank Warfare"), which is often conflated with "A Tank Army." Both documents were inspired by naval warfare, and assumed fantastical technologies, so they were more useful to future requirements than current doctrine (see Table 2).

The second paper foresees an army operating entirely with tracked vehicles, except in wooded, mountainous, or fortified areas, where normal lorries and foot traffic would predominate. The paper imagines nine classes of tracked vehicle, of which at least seven are meant to be armoured. (He failed to specify any armour on the "Signals Tank" and "Ambulance Tank," although armour is implicit.) Some are variants of each other, although some are sufficiently different in size or weight that they must be base models. Each would be naturally buoyant, water-tight, and propelled in the water by a screw at the back. Smaller vehicles would be powered by internal combustion engines, larger ones by steam engines.

The fast, light "destroyer tanks" would be most numerous, in place of infantry and cavalry. The "torpedo tanks" are anti-tank vehicles, which the US Army would categorize as "tank destroyers" by the Second World War, with tactics they would call "shoot-and-scoot." Martel expected "torpedo tanks" to approach at speed and launch fantastical "torpedoes" at enemy vehicles, before making smoke in order to escape. The "battle tanks" are optimized for defeating other tanks, except the "Heavy Battle Tank," which is a self-propelled howitzer for indirect fire.

Martel's paper foresees variants for supplying tanks during offensives, for carrying stretchered casualties, for carrying signals, and for engineering. All these variants would be developed during the Great War, although not necessarily deployed.

The self-propelled howitzer is the least fantastical requirement in the paper, and the quickest to be fulfilled. In June, the developers of the Mark I Tank had already started a program to spin off a carrier for a medium artillery piece. In January 1917, someone at the Ministry of Munitions sent an internal memo promising a trial, within a week, of "a gun-carrying tank carrying either a 60-pounder or 6-inch howitzer." Fifty were on order. The pilot was demonstrated in March. At least 48 were delivered from June through July, although within a year they were converted into supply carriers (Fuller 1920: 167-169; Fuller 1921: 107; White 1970: 171, 240).

Table 2: Martel's required classes of tank, November 1916 (Martel 1945: Appendix H).

Tank class	Role	Armour	Armament	Speed (mph)
Destroyer	Direct short-range anti-tank and anti-infantry fire; scouting; raiding	½ inch (12.7 mm)	Automatic one-pounder at the front; Lewis gun each side	20
Torpedo	Direct anti-tank fire at about 500 yards	½ inch (12.7 mm)	Five torpedoes, each weighing 100 pounds, "similar to the present big trench mortars"	30
Light Battle	Direct long-range anti-tank fire	1.5 inches (38.1 mm)	3-inch gun at the front; automatic one-pounder each side	8
Medium Battle	Direct long-range anti-tank fire	6-8 inches (152.4-203.2 mm)	6-inch gun at the front; automatic one-pounder each side	4-5
Heavy Battle	Indirect fire	½ inch (12.7 mm)	12-inch howitzer	2
Royal Engineers	Destroy and construct obstacles	½ inch (12.7 mm)	Lewis gun at front	20
Signals	Wireless communications (squadron HQ to division HQ; lower echelons would signal with lamps and written messages)	?	none	?
Supplies	Carriage of supplies to other tanks	Splinter-proof	none	15 (with a 5-ton load)
Ambulance	Carriage of wounded	?	none	?

Fuller Before the Tank Corps

Martel did not satisfy Elles as chief of staff. In mid-December, GHQ authorized Elles to hire a GSO2 (General Staff Officer, second class), i.e., someone certified as a chief of staff at brigade echelon. Although Martel held the requisite rank, he did not hold the certification or equivalent experience. Also, GHQ already wanted the War Office to authorize escalation of the arm from brigade echelon to a Tank Corps.

Uzielli suggested JFC Fuller (1878-1966), who brought years of experience as a staff officer and years more as a developer of doctrine. Back in July, Uzielli had been serving on the Quartermaster staff at 3rd Army HQ, when Fuller arrived as deputy chief of staff.

In 1914, Elles and Fuller had coincided at the Staff College. Elles was in the Senior Division (second year), Fuller in the Junior, even though Elles was more than two years younger. (By the end of 1916, Elles was aged 36 years, while Fuller was 38.) Elles' seniority by rank is best explained by Fuller's self-admitted lateness in taking his profession seriously, and the poor reception towards his aggressive and introverted intellectualism. His intellectualism complemented the extroversion and practicalism of the officers already serving tank HQ. Without Fuller, tank HQ would have got to the same doctrinal principles, but not as quickly or forthrightly.

In memoirs, Fuller claimed to realize at the age of 5 years that God and everlasting damnation are logically incompatible, and to realize soon afterwards that adults are normatively hypocritical about sin and charity. He "was an exceptionally truthful child" and adult, on which he blamed a lifetime of social difficulties. He read "rationalist" philosophical books that helped him become "anti-religious" and "agnostic." He described his personal "philosophy" as "synthetic-iconoclastic" – meaning a mix of constructive and destructive critical thinking (1936: 2, 458-460, 471). He described himself also a "heretic" (1923: xii; 1926: 31; 1936: 391, 478), a "skeptic" and contrarian (1936: 465), and an "unconventional soldier" (1936: 463).

As a teenager, he was disinterested in social norms, formal instruction, higher discipline, sports, or killing things, but chose to join the Army. He never explained his reasons, except to write flippantly that his maternal grandmother wished him to join the Army Class in secondary school, and that the class allowed him to read novels at the back. Perhaps equally flippantly, he claimed to pass the Army's examinations by memorizing answers to questions his tutor had predicted. His performance was bifurcated: top in history, geography, and drawing, but bottom in Latin (1936: 3-4).

Fuller entered Sandhurst on 1 September 1897. After the conventional year, he was commissioned, into a minor infantry regiment. For regimental officer training, he was posted to Mullingar in Ireland, to where his unit (1st Battalion, Oxfordshire Light Infantry) was due to transfer from Curragh. At this point, he started reading philosophy. In September 1899, they moved to Plymouth in England, but five weeks later war broke out with the Boers in South Africa. From November 1900 until December 1901, his duties consisted of consolidating different positions, without fighting. For the last six months of the war (6 December 1901 to 31 May 1902) he was detached as an intelligence officer in command of two white agents and about 70 black scouts. In this role, he rode more than 3,000 miles (4,828 km), half at night – 40 to 50 miles per night, for at least 50 nights, in search of the enemy. After returning to base, he sometimes led infantry detachments to find the enemy (1931: 137-138). He did not report to any unit, but directly to a regional intelligence officer (Major-General William G. Knox), who would continue to mentor him. In memoirs, he admits to being sorry to return to peacetime and his regiment (1936: 9-16).

In Autumn 1903, the 1st Battalion sailed for India, where he picked up new philosophies, some of them regrettable, such as Aleister Crowley's (1875-1947) various magical cults. He continued to fall out with his regimental superiors. For 1907, he chose to serve in England as adjutant (administrator) of a reserve unit (2nd Battalion, South Middlesex Volunteers). Fuller's archives* do not contain any artifacts from his time with the reserves. His memoirs make clear that he "enjoyed immensely" the period, until Summer 1911, when the sight of sweating men in full kit made him realize his own privileges. He undertook to apply to study at the Staff

---

* In the 1960s, Fuller sent his archives to Rutgers University, New Brunswick, New Jersey.

College. He dated a personal change "between the years 1910 and 1912," when he "turned from destructive to constructive criticism," having "taken no interest whatever in things military" and found soldiering "intensely boring" (1936: 20-22, 460).

In 1912, he applied for the Staff College, but failed. Meanwhile, he turned his newfound professional interests into two books (*Hints on Training Territorial Infantry*; *Training Soldiers for War*), although these were not published until 1914. In those years, "training" documents could be as much doctrinal as pedagogical, and certainly these books are mostly doctrinal.

That same year, Fuller's time as a Territorial adjutant expired, so he rejoined his regiment, now in Aldershot, as a company commander. His archives prove diverse roles in the following year: battalion trainer, battalion intelligence officer, brigade machine-gun officer, railway transport officer. His regimental achievements justify his application to the Staff College of 1913. Meanwhile, he wrote several articles on training and entrainment for professional journals. In January 1914, he entered the course, where he wrote more articles for publication (1936: 21-23, 459).

That course was cut short by the crises preceding the Great War. On 5 August, the students dispersed. While awaiting orders in Southampton, he was identified as an author of an article on entraining soldiers, so was invited to serve locally as Deputy Assistant Director of Railway Transport. He did not enjoy it much, but could not see how he could escape. On 1 June 1915 (the same day when Swinton was writing his first doctrine for AFVs), Fuller received notice to join the VII Corps (3rd Army) as GSO3; the movement orders arrived on 18 July; he embarked on 19 July (1936: 44-50). He was assigned as the deputy operations officer, although for months the only operations were defensive. His stay was comfortable and sociable, although his privileges rankled. On 4 February 1916, he took a promotion to GSO2 at 37th Division, in the same corps. He participated in the planning – from May – of the great Somme offensive. This destroyed the division within two weeks, so, on 17 July, he transferred to 3rd Army HQ, as its deputy chief of staff. This is where he would first hear of tanks.

Foot

Fuller shared an office within the 3rd Army's HQ with an engineer staff officer (Captain F.H.E. Townshend), to whom a fellow engineer (Captain Stephen Foot) sent a paper entitled "Strategy and Invention," soon after Foot's division came out of the line (15 July). Foot's temperament was similar to Fuller's. The paper criticizes current tactics and urges higher staff to call for ideas and inventions from the rank and file, and to sponsor the best ideas for development in England.

Short of effect, Foot started work on a different paper, which he passed through a different channel to BEF GHQ, again without effect. His division was committed to the offensive towards Flers and Courcelette in September, when he saw tanks for the first time. His division was withdrawn at the end of September. Stimulated by a discussion in the mess, he wrote a letter directly to the War Secretary (Lloyd George), proposing reforms of the Army. Two weeks later, in October, he received reprimands from the Adjutant-General downwards, and cancellation of a recommendation for promotion to GSO3 on the divisional staff.

When he saw a circular inviting applicants to join a new arm, he applied. On the application form, he asked for command of a company of tanks. In response to a question about why he wanted to join, he wrote: "Because I believe that the tanks will win the war." In his memoir, he added desires to assuage guilt about serving largely without direct danger, and to earn quicker promotion. He was not accepted until December – until Martel, a friend from training in 1910, noticed his name on the list of applicants. He was assigned to D Battalion, but 12 hours later Elles sent for him, to inform him of appointment as Adjutant of Central Workshops (Foot 1934: 168-171).

Foot and Townshend remained friendly, but Foot's memoir (1934: 159) seems unaware that Townshend soon produced his own paper.

Townshend

Early in August 1916, Townshend asked Fuller to read a paper written in red ink, which they came to know as "The MS in Red Ink." Townshend noted that the enemy line was about 500 miles (805 km) long but only 5 miles (8,800 yards; 8,047 m) deep, so they needed to fight only 5 miles, before an almost unopposed advance through enemy territory to victory. In mid-August, they learned of tanks.

> Under obligations of the profoundest secrecy, Townshend and I obtained permission to visit Yvrench, and off we went by car on, if I remember rightly, the afternoon of August 20. As we approached the area, more and more did it assume the aspect of Epsom Downs on a Derby morning. There were scores and scores of cars there and hundreds and hundreds of spectators, both English [including Haig] and French [including Joseph Joffre, commander-in-chief, French Army]. Everyone was talking and chatting, when slowly came into sight the first tank I ever saw. Not a monster, but a very graceful machine, with beautiful lines, lozenge-shaped, but with two clumsy-looking wheels behind it…As the tank approached us, Townshend and I simultaneously looked at each other and exclaimed: "What price 'The MS in Red Ink'?" Here was the unknown x in the equation of victory (1936: 78-79).*

Fuller and Townshend returned to 3rd Army HQ, which was not directly involved in the first offensive with tanks. Nevertheless, the HQ received reports from the day of assault.

In December, Townshend received a request from Foot to meet with the Chief Engineer of 3rd Army, in pursuit of timber for building the Central Workshops.

Fuller at Tank HQ

Fuller was thus primed for the request from Uzielli and Elles to join the tank staff. Fuller's appointment was approved on 26 December:

Foot, as a Major, in 1918 (Foot 1933).

---

* A differently worded and informative version of this quote was published as: "September 15 is Tank Day," *Evening Standard*, 15 September 1943: 6.

he left 3rd Army HQ around lunchtime, and arrived at the Chateau of Bermicourt around tea-time.

> There I found Elles standing by a Canada wood-stove, home-made, and giving forth a terrific heat…After a preliminary greeting, he said to me: "This show badly wants pulling together; it is all so new that one hardly knows which way to turn. I want you to do this: to put some discipline, some esprit de corps into the men; then we shall have a wonderful show" (1936: 87).

Elles is talking here about using recreation, entertainment, and training to improve compliance, morale, and cohesion. The next day, Fuller toured the four battalions, and was appalled by their slovenly appearance and conditions.

Fuller returned to tell Uzielli to take responsibility for discipline, until the DAA&QMG would deliver improved accommodation, ablutions, clothing, and food. In January, a new shower facility opened, some new clothing was issued, and dining, recreation, and rest facilities were developed (Fuller 1936: 90).

Thereafter, Fuller focused on training. As noted earlier, "training" was then a term that captured doctrine, not just pedagogy.[*] Implicitly, Fuller was selected as the lead doctrinist. He was the only man at tank HQ who had published doctrine. He was also the most experienced staff officer in the HQ, more experienced than even Elles. The HQ produced doctrinal papers in the name of the commander or the chief of staff, but even those under the name of commander tend to be signed by Fuller "for" Elles. Fuller's diary often betrays frustration with Elles. For instance, on 13 June 1918, he complains that "it has taken Elles 10 months to make up his mind" about how to reorganize tank units. On 19 July, Fuller urged Elles to appoint the next chief of staff, while Fuller was transitioning to a full-time staff position in London. "He won't make up his mind and will regret the delay before long."

Fuller's memoir (published when Elles was Master-General Ordnance – a non-doctrinal position, except through requirements and acquisitions) implies that Elles focused on morale while Fuller focused on doctrine.

> To both officers and men he was what Henry IV of France had been to his soldiers: boyish and reckless in danger; perhaps a better soldier than a strategist, yet one who could profit from the co-operation of his advisers and who was universally loved and trusted by his followers (1936: 88).

Fuller was still ranked Major, while Elles was still a Colonel, until bumped to Brigadier-General a few days after Fuller's arrival. Given the hundreds of tanks now in France, the Heavy Branch was overdue for separation from the Machine-Gun Corps as a Corps in its own right. Normally the staff of a fighting division or an administrative arm would be led by a GSO1 – at Colonel rank. Effective 1 April, Fuller was clarified as the Tank Corps' first GSO1 and operations officer, responsible for training, doctrine, and planning for operations, at the rank of temporary (wartime) Lieutenant-Colonel.[**] Publicly, Fuller (1920: xi; 1936: 192) described himself as "the Chief General Staff Officer of the Tank Corps, for a period extending from December 1916 to August 1918."

---

[*] Readers might be misled by Liddell Hart's (1959: I, 91) history of the arm, which reports that "Fuller's immediate concern was to improve and systematize the training."
[**] He was promoted to substantive Colonel in 1919.

Training Notes

Fuller later claimed that when he and Townshend first saw a tank in August, they "visualized its proper use as identical with my original Cambrai project of a year later" (executed on 20 November 1917). Hotblack confirms that Fuller's talks the personnel that winter "foretold most of what happened at Cambrai." In 1916, "these ideas seemed very futuristic even to officers of the Tank Corps" ("The Battle of Cambrai," circa December 1934, RACTM Hotblack Box 2).

Fuller developed a training schedule to last three months (January through March), but soon shortened it on orders to be ready for an offensive in the Spring. He issued the HQ's first "Instructions on Training" before the end of December. The instructions emphasize (in order) esprit de corps, discipline, physical fitness, and trade skills. The training is categorized almost by echelon: Depot, Lectures, Camps of Instruction, Courses of Instruction, Schools, Battalions, and Brigades. The Battalions and Brigades were responsible for individual training (to be completed by 15 February) and collective trainning. Fuller ordered individual training with two objectives: "first, to impart technical knowledge and skill; secondly, to cultivate general knowledge so as to enable all ranks to obtain the highest benefit from the schemes set in collective training." He ordered collective training to comprise three doctrinal skills: "close co-operation with the other arms; rapidity of movement across ground in fighting formations; selection of objectives with reference to the plan of operation."

Meanwhile, Fuller delivered four lectures to each company, on (respectively) discipline, morale, esprit de corps, and leadership.

> These were quite unconventional and referred to no published regulations, and I felt they appealed to the men...Most of these lectures were given in barns lit by a few candles. One I remember giving in the schoolroom at Blangy, lit by a solitary oil lamp, which went out shortly after I began. The rest of this talk took place in pitch darkness, and I still believe it was the best I have ever given (Fuller 1936: 91).

Fuller put all officers of Captain and higher rank through an exercise, based on the attack on Beaumont Hamel. The exercise was essentially by correspondence. He issued the first pages of the instructions on 10 January, the final pages about one month later, for a total of 34 foolscap pages. He compiled consensual solutions, which he returned as the agreed solutions, and which influenced the doctrine that he issued in early February.

Fuller (1936: 111-112) later characterized the arm's legacy papers as "nothing more than a few platitudinous notes," although he was likely being as egocentric as Martel. Fuller recalled Martel's "A Tank Army" as "a longish paper" that "visualised the employment of a force of 1,864 machines." Fuller recalled Martel's second paper ("The Transition from Present Day Warfare to Tank Warfare") as a requirement for "mortar and torpedo tanks to drive an enemy out of houses and villages – a most valuable suggestion and one which was later on experimented with." Fuller here is referring to a Mark IV demonstrated with a 3-inch (76-mm) Stokes mortar on 5 February 1918, although Martel had analogized "torpedoes" to 100-pound trench mortar shells – apparently thinking of the 8-inch (203-mm) Livens trench mortar. The Stokes was an anti-personnel mortar, valued for the tube's portability and the "bomb's" plunging trajectory into trenches and behind the enemy's cover. Martel had prospected "torpedoes" as anti-tank, not anti-personnel weapons.

Most of the papers that Fuller inherited are training notes, each a few pages long, and specific to a particular task or skill. On 17 February, he issued "Tank Training Note No. 16," which he later described it as "the first training manual of its kind." It covers force structure, force employment, logistics, discipline, morale, welfare, rest, and recreation (LHCMA Fuller 1/1/6; 1936: 96).*

The tank arm's papers mostly specify requirements. They rarely refer to any principles of war or operations. Fuller continued to support and apply the British Army's official "principles of war," from before to after the war. However, he rarely applied any to tank doctrine. The only principle of war that consistently appears in his doctrine for tanks is surprise. Later, when justifying tanks to the Ministry of Munitions, he lists the eight principles of war in one column, next to a column titled "effect on tanks." However, he writes little in the second column: "The great offensive and protective powers of the tank combined with its mobility enable all these principles to be more easily applied." This statement refers to "all" the principles, but appears to privilege three principles of war: offensive, security, and mobility. (Surprise and economy of force appear elsewhere in the document.)

Fuller follows with 10 "chief conditions of war" (time, space, ground, supply, communications, numbers, armament, moral[e], weather, obstacles), which get closer to the principles of tank doctrine. These "conditions" map on to my earlier identified principles of mechanized warfare as follows: "ground," "weather," and preparations for avoiding or crossing "obstacles" fall under the principle of suitable terrain; "numbers" (of forces and yards of front) compute as concentration; matters of "time" and "space" affect both terrain and surprise; "armament," "moral[e]," and "obstacle"-crossing affect combined-arms, but do not capture all the options, issues, training instructions, or plans that go into combining arms; "supply" and "communications" fall under sustainment. None of Fuller's "conditions of war" speaks to "exploitation" (Fuller to the Minister of Munitions, "Tanks as Time and Man[-]Savers," 12 December 1917, Appendix 2, RACTM E1980.18).

Fuller was not too attached to his "conditions of war." He rarely mentioned them again. In the next month, Fuller identifies three "principles" of "an infantry and tank operation": "mobility," "security," and "offensive power." These three are also principles of war, although he does not describe them so ("Infantry and Tank Cooperation and Training," 27 January 1918: 5, RACTM E1980.18).

"Principles of war" rarely appear in any document produced or received by the tank arm during the Great War. We know that Fuller regarded most of his doctrinal papers as practical, tactical, and operational, to which the principles of war might seem too abstract. This is best illustrated by his dispute with GHQ's staff officer for tanks, on 2 March 1918. The officer complained that Fuller's current draft manual on "Infantry and Tank Cooperation" should reflect "General Staff language. "I informed him that our intention was to instruct men and not to spend our time

---

* It contains fourteen sections: Tank Organization; Tank Operations; Tank Tactics; Tank Co-operation with Other Arms; Preparations for Offensive; System of Supply; System of Communication; Reinforcements; Methods of Camouflaging; Battle History Sheet (Appendix 1); Loads and Stores (Appendix 2); Disc and Light Codes (Appendix 3); Lamp and Shutter Letter Code (Appendix 4); Station Calls (Appendix 5).

producing polished platitudes." The officer replied that the principles of war, as articulated in the FSR, should be the standard. Fuller agreed, except to point out that "men fight with weapons not principles, and that the FSR does not mention 50 percent of the weapons we are now using in this war."

The tank arm's priority was always the next operation, not universal principles. Thus, readers are left to realize the principles of mechanized warfare for themselves. As described in sections below, Fuller's Tank Training Note Number 16 maps on to seven principles of mechanized warfare. (The section on combined arms includes a review of the false accusation that Fuller wanted all-tank forces.)

Terrain

Fuller's mindfulness of suitable terrain is expressed as reminders about how easily tanks could break down while struggling to cross craters, trenches, and other obstacles. Fuller had seen tanks demonstrating on cratered ground in August, and read the battle reports in September. More importantly, once he arrived at Elles' HQ in December, he heard first-hand of the difficulties of the battles of September, October, and November. He still had not seen Swinton's paper of February 1916, which had made the point most strongly, although he had inherited GHQ's paper of August 1916, which paraphrases some of Swinton's reminders.

Concentration

A tank concentration of the scale Swinton had proposed seemed feasible by Spring 1917, given GHQ's request, on 19 September, for 1,000 tanks with thicker armour. The first 100 of this requirement would be fulfilled by an extension order for Mark Is, pending improved marks, of which Marks II and III would be available for use in April 1917, the Mark IV in June. In November, Martel speculated about a "Tank Army" of nearly 2,000 tanks, although he, unlike Swinton, was uninvolved in the tortuous negotiations for orders, schedules, and specifications.

A question remained as to whether GHQ would use as few as six tanks at a time, as it had demanded in July 1916, or would allow for all available tanks to be concentrated for its next offensive. Before the war, Fuller had repeatedly stressed the principle of concentration, against "any moderately weak point," and stressed it particularly in any future war with Germany, whose army would outnumber the British Army. Concentration aims for local material preponderance, even despite general inferiority. He recognizes the value of distributed approaches, to confuse the enemy about the ultimate objective, but recognizes also that such approaches must concentrate at the enemy's weak point before the enemy intercepts any approach. "In other words, strike in mass and strike all together" (1914c: 380, 389). Before and after discovering tanks, he intended to concentrate all arms for a direct, narrow penetration wherever the enemy is weakest; to withdraw before the enemy could counter; and to re-concentrate to strike wherever the enemy is denuded (1928: vi; to Jay Luvaas, 1 May 1964, Fuller papers, Box 1).

Surprise

The tank was no longer secret by the time the 16th Tank Training Note was ready. British journalists started reporting on the tanks at Flers and Courcelette on 25 September. Journalists were not permitted to publish any photographs or drawings, until *The Daily Mirror* printed photographs of tanks in France on 22 November (right). Other newspapers printed the same on the next day. In January 1917, the War Office released into public cinemas a film about the Battle of Ancre (13-18 November), which features moving pictures of tanks. In the same battle, German soldiers had captured tanks.

Although the Germans were no longer surprised by the existence of tanks, they still could be surprised by tanks in space and time. Sometime in January 1917, GHQ proposed a massed tank attack on Gheluvelt plateau, Flanders, without a preliminary bombardment. Haig might have recalled Churchill's similar prescription of December 1915. His staff were surely mindful of tank HQ's wish for less damaged ground and more surprise. Haig's planning staff wrote the idea into an effective addendum (dated 14 February 1917) to the proposed offensive at Arras for April. Towards the end of February, the Germans withdrew from their salient at Gommecourt to a new defensive line between Arras and Craonne (known to the British incorrectly as the Hindenburg Line; termed *Siegfriedstellung* by the Germans). Given ongoing failures in tank supply, and other issues, the attack across Gheluvelt plateau (but not the offensive at Arras) was postponed, as explained in the next chapter.

GHQ's belated allowance for abandonment of preliminary bombardment was perhaps known to Fuller while he was writing Tank Training Note Number 16. (Fuller was not keeping a diary at this time.) GHQ dated its addendum three days before Fuller dated the Note, although the Tank Corps was not necessarily privy to GHQ's planning.

Fuller was not yet ready to rule out the use of preliminary bombardment to cut enemy barbed wire. As in peacetime, Fuller's first principle of war is "surprise." His "Tank Training Note" is conflicted about preliminary bombardment. He wants to keep it short, but allows for a preliminary bombardment of up to 48 hours, as had been specified by 3rd Army's artillery officer (S.E. "Tom" Hollond) for the 3rd Army's offensive in Spring 1917. Nevertheless, he also allows for any preliminary bombardment to be cancelled, given compromised defences, as had been decided for the attack on 26 September.

His "Tank Training Note" is clear about the dangers of careless talk and noisy assemblies, and specifies camouflage during assemblies.

Combined Arms

Artillery

Fuller's papers of 1914 focus on training methods, the employment of weapons, and strategic lessons from military history. Only three survived his relocations, by the time he reviewed them for his memoirs, in 1935, although some had been published in 1914. As he lectured from April 1914, machine-guns and quick-firing artillery had revolutionized tactics (1914c: 380). He predicts that "battles will become more static, i.e., entrenched...because freedom of manoeuvre will be limited by wire and field works" and because "quick-firing artillery" will catch pedestrians before they can take cover. He expects a preliminary bombardment to break the enemy's fortifications eventually, if the artillery is concentrated and supplied with enough ammunition. By May, he urges a more "cooperative" method: infantry should threaten the enemy enough "to force the enemy to unmask so that the artillery may bring a breaching fire to bear against him."

> I, at present, disagree with the seemingly growing idea of firing for moral effect alone – such as "walls of fire" and the plastering of localities with shrapnel. Morale effect soon loses its sting if material effect is wanting; and I think it should be reserved for the last stages of the attack, when nerve-power is beginning to fail ("Lessons Learnt at Artillery Practice Camp, Larkhill, May 2nd-9th 1914," no date, Fuller papers, Box 1).

Fuller's first doctrine for the tank arm follows his pre-war doctrine by requiring the artillery's Forward Observation Officers (FOOs) to catch up with the assaulters during their consolidation of the objective, in order to correct indirect fire on the next defensive line, and particularly on any enemy artillery guns there.

Aircraft

Since before the war, Fuller had wanted aircraft to mark enemy artillery guns with smoke, as a warning to infantry and as a marker for any FOO keeping up with the infantry ("Lessons Learnt at Artillery Practice Camp, Larkhill, May 2nd-9th 1914," no date, Fuller papers, Box 1). At the time, communications between infantry and aircraft were visual, while communications between assault infantry and artillery were by runner, until signals detachments could catch up, with their radios and cables. Similarly, his *Tank Training Note No. 16* expects scout aircraft to range ahead, marking enemy artillery for attack by bombers and tanks.

Tanks and Infantry

After the first day of the Somme campaign, in July 1916, Fuller (1936: 82) had written against the infantry advancing in extended lines. He favoured distributed columns, at the rate of about ten men per column. *Tank Training Note Number 16* expects a platoon of infantry to follow each tank, except in open warfare (i.e., without barbed wire), where Fuller allows for the infantry to shift from column to line, between the tanks.

He wants at least two waves of infantry: the first wave ("moppers up," mostly grenadiers) captures the enemy's fortifications; the second wave ("supports") holds the captured fortifications against any enemy counter-attack. He prefers to reserve a third wave of infantry, in case of some additional threat (see Map 4).

Ideally four tanks (a section) should take on each enemy position, certainly not fewer than two, due to their unreliability (see Map 5). Each pair should advance in column, so that the rear tank is ready to take over from a disabled leader, or to meet any resistance bypassed by the leader. Once across the enemy trench, the pair would turn, in order to drive along the length of the defensive line, attacking its defenders from the rear (less risky for the tanks, but riskier for friendly infantry). Given four tanks, each pair could turn in opposite directions. Given friendly forces on the flanks, each pair could turn towards respective flanks before crossing the trench, then turn towards each other, to envelop the enemy.

Given friendly consolidation of just one flank, the pair closest to that flank could keep going towards the next defensive line, as could a third pair in all scenarios.

Once the infantry consolidate the captured positions, the tanks should be released to advance on the next line of defences. The tanks and infantry should be organized in as many echelons as the enemy has defensive lines (Fuller assumed three). Each echelon would advance in two sequential lines – the second to react to any unexpected defences on the way.

The *Training Note* characterizes the tank as "a mobile fortress," which reminds readers of crews fighting from within or without immobilized tanks (as on 14 November). In early March, Fuller issued a pamphlet ("Formation of Emergency Lewis Gun Units") that allows for units short of tanks to be re-roled as pedestrian light machine-gun units, in attack and defence. This would be executed during the

Map 4: Fuller's depiction of assault waves and objectives. The lines A-B, C-D, E-F, and G-H are objective lines. The assaulters are arranged as tanks (I), infantry (L), tanks (J), infantry, and cavalry (K). The black boxes represent tanks tasked with protecting and expanding the flanks (Fuller 1936: Diagram 6).

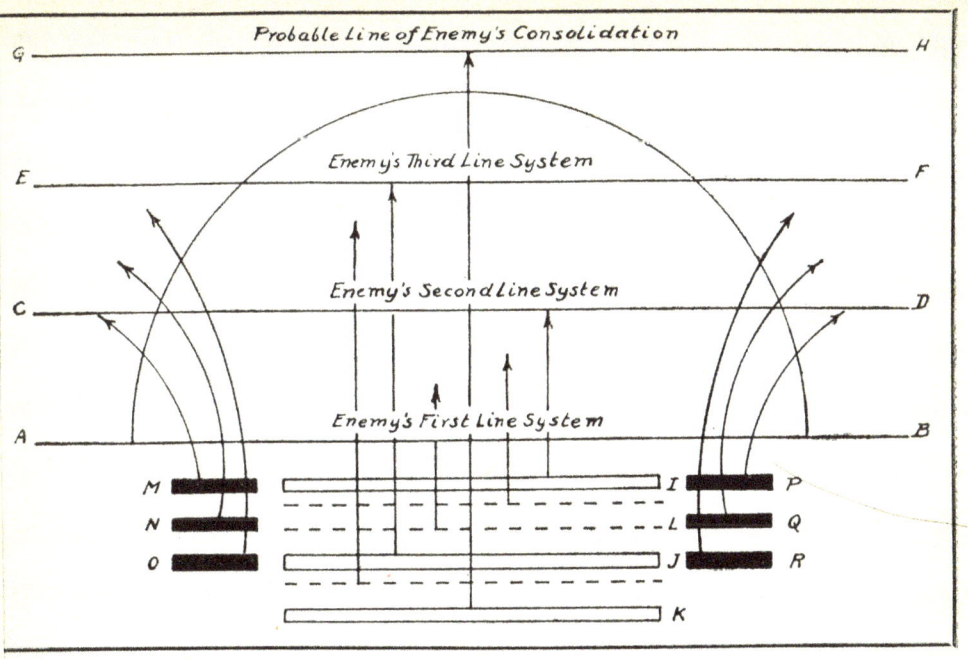

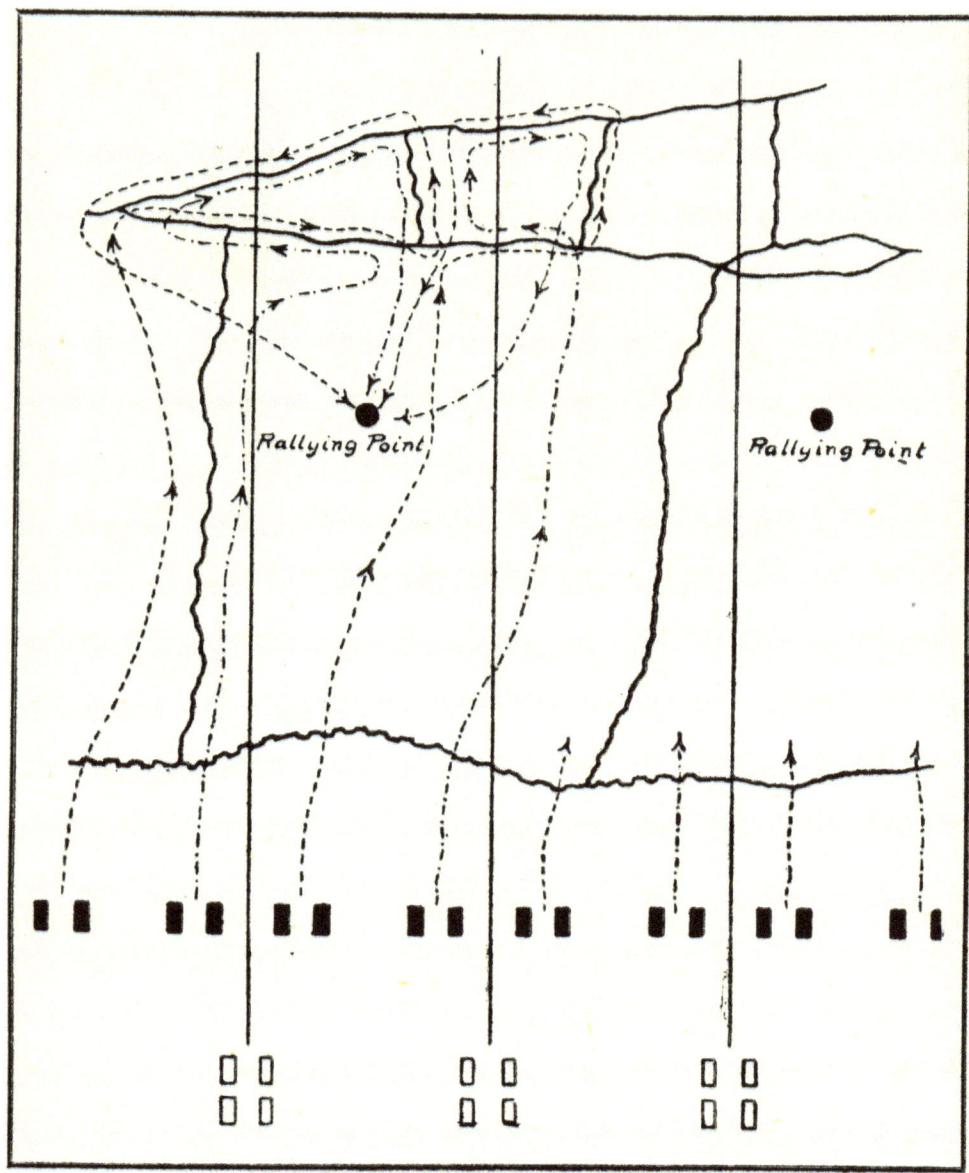

Map 5: Fuller's depiction of tank tactics, by subsections (pairs of tanks) and sections (four tanks each section). The white squares represent reserves (1936: Diagram 7).

German counter-offensive of March 1918. In the meantime, it surely reminded tank crews of their secondary role as pedestrian fighters.

Fuller's *Training Note* of February contains three sequential sections, titled "Tank Operations," "Tank Tactics," and "Tank Co-operation with Other Arms," each of which specify tanks cooperating with other arms. None allows for operations by tanks alone.

In March, Martel returned from a brief posting outside the Heavy Branch, and showed to Fuller his paper from November on "A Tank Army."

> It was a crude paper, and after a short time Colonel Fuller relieved me of any work of this nature by writing about the great future possibilities of tanks in a manner which eventually raised the widest interest (1931: 16).

Fuller certainly rejected Martel's idea that twelve imaginary categories of tanks and variants could operate independently of other arms. Martel's first memoir reverses his own error by suggesting that Fuller could not imagine tanks except as infantry-support weapons.

> I showed him the paper. He read it with interest and then told me that he doubted if it was on the right lines, because he thought that tanks would always be an adjunct to the infantry and not an arm of their own. However, a few months later he was writing and preaching a doctrine about the future of tanks in a convincing manner which I could never have equalled (Martel 1945: 38).

In fact, Fuller made combined arms a core principle. Fuller followed Swinton's (1932: 198) acknowledgement since February 1916 that any doctrines for "tanks are not intended to imply that the whole of our offensive operations are to be subordinated to their action." Rather, tanks are "auxiliary to the infantry," in that the tank "is primarily a machine-gun destroyer." Swinton made clear that tanks support infantry on to objectives, and cannot consolidate objectives on their own. Fuller repeated this observation. Nobody in the Tank Corps disagreed.

This consensus would not be overturned until Martel and Liddell Hart agreed (in 1925) that tankettes could replace all the arms. After the Second World War they covered up their reductionism to a single arm by blaming Fuller for what they termed an "all-tank army." Liddell Hart, citing Martel, put about that Fuller was "strongly anti-tank" (note on talk with Charles Broad, 22 May 1946, LHCMA) and "thought the tanks would always be an adjunct to the infantry" (1959: I, 94; II, 87, 90, 102, 164, 247). When Liddell Hart's disciple Jay Luvaas queried Fuller about Martel's account, Fuller replied: "At the time what I held was: with a tank which could only move at about 3 mph on the battlefield and had to be re-fueled and overhauled after each 15 miles, it had to cooperate with infantry, as it did at Cambrai" (to Luvaas, 1 May 1964, Fuller papers, Box 1). Nevertheless, Luvaas (1964: 342) published that Fuller was "skeptical about the possibilities of tanks." Azar Gat (1998: 29) perpetuated Luvaas' version. Neither man offered any evidence, other than Martel's and Liddell Hart's hearsay, that Fuller ever doubted tanks or wished to amalgamate arms.

Tanks and Engineers

In November 1916, Martel had written at length about the fortifications that engineers should construct around the tank "base," including a trench, land mines, and concrete or wooden pillars to prevent enemy tanks from following, except through well-defended gaps. Offensively, he requires a "Royal Engineers Tank" to destroy and construct obstacles, although this is not really a tank, being armed with just one machine-gun (for self-defence).

Martel's paper specifies amphibiousness for all vehicles, which helps the assaulters to overcome obstacles that otherwise the engineers would be asked to bridge, and to evade other obstacles.

In the next months, Fuller realized the need for cooperation from engineers in the breaching of enemy fortifications, but did not specify amphibiousness until January 1918.

Tanks versus Tanks

In November 1916, Martel foresaw future armies meeting with tanks alone. Most of the tank types in his paper are optimized to fight other tanks. The main anti-tank weapon ("torpedo") is futuristic, under-specified, and invalid. He expects torpedo tanks to race up to enemy tanks, and to open fire at a range of about 500 yards (457 m), with any of five "torpedoes," each weighing 100 pounds, "similar to the present big trench mortars." Here, Martel is likely thinking of the 8-inch (203-mm) Livens trench mortar that was first deployed in July, on the Somme front, after Martel had left for Norfolk. It propelled a drum containing three imperial gallons (14 liters; 3.6 US gallons) of oil, with an igniter triggered on impact with the target. Martel presumably hoped that burning liquid would penetrate the joints between armour plates. However, he does not acknowledge that the torpedo tank is hardly survivable at 500 yards. He specifies it with plates only 0.5 inches (12.7 mm) thick, which could be perforated by a machine-gun firing armour-piercing bullets, at a much higher rate of fire than a mortar can fire drums. German 7.92-mm armour-piercing bullets could potentially perforate this thickness at the maximum range at which the Livens mortar could fire drums (200 yards). Perhaps Martel had these facts in mind when he specified a range for "torpedoes" of 500 yards.

Late in March, Fuller wrote a requirement for anti-tank weapons, in expectation of German tanks. He preferred tanks to counter tanks (implying a requirement for more Male tanks), but suggested that the infantry should be issued with 0.5-inch heavy machine-guns, whose armour-piercing bullets perforate 14 mm of armour at 500 yards – thicker than any current tank armour, body armour, or portable shield (Fuller 1936: 112).

Speed

Fuller does not see the need for a creeping barrage if tanks are available. He thus releases assaulters from the pace of a creeping barrage. On good terrain, the tanks could advance at their maximum speed of 4 mph (117 yards or 107 m per minute).

Like Swinton, Fuller urges the assaulters to advance as quickly as possible through the defensive lines into the artillery line. Effort to advance would save effort to fight, because the enemy would have less time to gather resistance.

Fuller clearly worries about resistance to the infantry more than the tanks, where he urges infantrymen to release the tanks as soon as the infantry are in the act of consolidating the captured positions.

Sustainment

Martel's paper of November requires variants of tanks to supply assaulters, so that the assaulters can defend their objectives from any counter-attackers, or keep penetrating. Martel required variants for evacuating stretchered casualties, who otherwise would distract the assaulters from defending and penetrating.

Fuller had seen the difficulties of sustainment at every echelon up to a field army HQ. *Training Note No. 16* prescribes a direct, narrow, sustained penetration.

He later emphasized the pamphlet's "insistence…on the employment of tanks in mass, in echelon[,] and with strong reserves" (1936: 110).

He was already mindful of the unreliability of tanks, which he attempts to solve with redundancy. This is why the *Note*'s section on "Tactics" specifies four tanks (one section) per enemy position, no fewer than two tanks. The *Note* addresses sustainment of the attack in three sequential sections: "System of Supply," "System of Communication," and "Reinforcements." Further, the second appendix lists the "Loads and Stores." The remaining three appendices concern signals.

The *Note* requires "Tank Tenders," mostly to supply the infantry with their entrenching tools and heavy equipment during the consolidation of the objective, and also to replenish both infantry and tanks with ammunition. (Four months later they would be used for the first time.) Yet some historians have perpetuated a myth that the Tank Corps neglected sustainment. For instance, J.P. Harris (1995: 86-90) misreported that Fuller imagined tanks as untroubled by terrain, enemy weapons, and wear and tear.

Exploitation

If the tanks were to break through the final enemy line, *Tank Training Note No. 16* allows for horse cavalry to exploit the breach, but not without tanks (given the threats to unarmoured flesh from machine-guns).

This suggests that he agreed with the requirement for faster tanks (medium tanks), which were already in development, but not used for more than a year. Since the development of new tanks was a higher secret, he would not wish to refer to them in a manual, which would be shared with the lowest ranks. We cannot know what he was thinking and saying at the time on the subject, because he was not yet keeping a diary, but his later publications suggest he was mindful of the requirement for specialized exploitation tanks from the start of his time with the tank arm (Fuller 1920: 73-79; 1936: 97, 110).

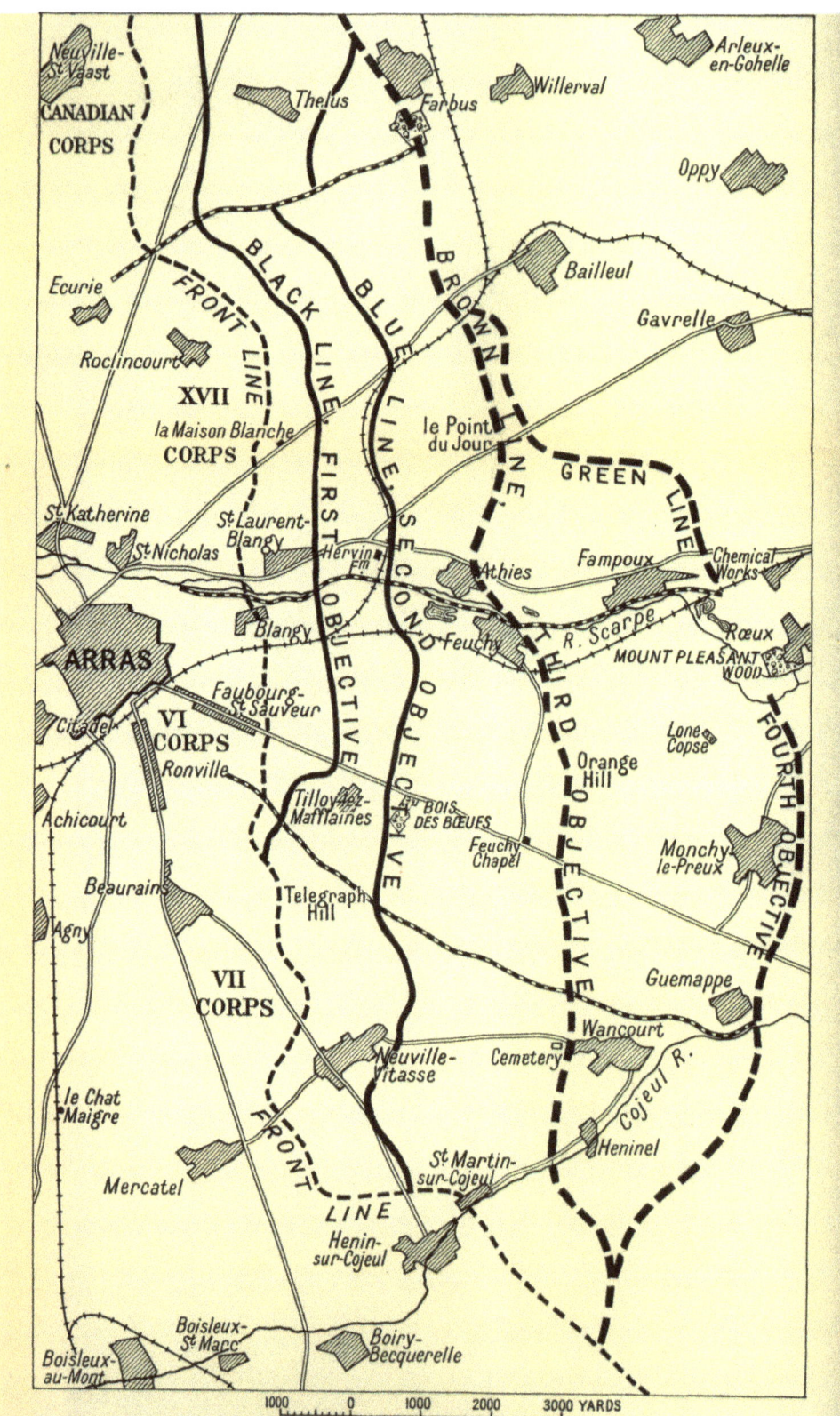

Map 6: Formation areas and objective lines for the offensive of 9 April (Fuller 1920).

5

Arras, April 1917

In June 1916, GHQ started planning an offensive east of Arras (see Map 6). The plan was revived in October, with two battalions of tanks, for launch in March. However, as tank supplies fell behind schedule, the launch was delayed until 9 April. The delay allowed for an unprecedented British-French conference on tank doctrine, held on 4 March in the War Office. The DCIGS (Major-General Robert D. Whigham) chaired seven other British officers* and eight French officers.** Elles was the only representative from the Tank Corps in France, and is not recorded as speaking in the minutes. His French equivalent (Jean Baptiste Eugène Estienne)*** is recorded most (UKNA WO 158/841).

Like previous chapters, this chapter analyses the thinking and operations of this period in terms of the principles of terrain, concentration, surprise, combined arms, speed, sustainment, and exploitation, before presenting the outcomes.

Terrain

The front of the offensive was long, taking in three British armies. In the north, the Canadian Corps (1st Army) would take Vimy ride – a gentle, dry escarpment, except that parts were waterlogged after damage to the drainage. Most of the tanks were allocated to the waterlogged lowland astride the Scarpe River, on the 3rd Army's front. In the south, the 5th Army (formerly Reserve Army) was on slightly elevated ground, although between the rises this ground too was waterlogged.

By now, the British principals realized suitable terrain for tanks, more so than the French. On 4 March, Estienne allowed for a surprise attack by tanks, ahead of infantry, on good terrain, but preferred preliminary bombardment. The Britons pointed out, according to the minutes, the "necessity of careful reconnaissance of the ground and the effect of such reconnaissance on the tactical role assigned to tanks in any particular operation." From the Ministry of Munitions, Sir E Tennyson d'Eyncourt (Chief Technial Adviser) and Albert Stern (Tank Supply Department)

---

* The DMO (Major-General Frederick Maurice), Director of Artillery (Major-General Sir. H.G. Smith), and the Administrative commander for the tank force (Major-General F. Gore Anley), from the General Staff; the DGMWS (Lieutenant-Colonel Albert Stern) and Chief Technial Adviser (Sir E Tennyson d'Eyncourt) from the Ministry of Munitions; DCGS (Major-General R.H.K. Butler) from BEF GHQ; and Elles from the Tank Corps.
** General Estienne, Commandant Doumenc, and Captain Henri Michel from the French tank force; Commandant Nogues (Ministry of War); Commandant Velpry (Grand Quartier General); Monsieur Breton (Under-Secretary for Inventions); Lieutenant-Colonel Challat and Lieutenant Hubert (Ministry of Armaments).
*** Probably Estienne would have had a harder time if Fuller had been present. When Fuller visited Estienne's HQ, he thought that Estienne and other officers were too interested in "putting a woman in every tank." On 20 June 1918, Fuller wrote in his diary of disappointing news from the French front. "The French Tank Corps did not distinguish itself. It never will under such a 'dud' as Genl. Estienne."

asked whether tanks should be restricted to ground undamaged by heavy guns. Presumably this was a question for GHQ, but no response is recorded from GHQ's representative (Major-General Richard H.K. Butler, DCGS).

Concentration

The four tank companies in France were authorized as battalions in December 1916. The 1st Brigade HQ was formed in January 1917, 2nd in February, 3rd in April – although the latter awaited battalions. The plan since October was to raise nine battalions (three per brigade), and to issue 72 tanks to each battalion. The arm would then be able to deploy 648 tanks at unit echelon alone.

However, the battalion and company echelons proved unwieldy, while tank supply fell behind schedule, so each battalion was cut from 72 tanks to 60, each company from 24 tanks to 20. The section too proved unwieldy, so was reduced from 5 tanks to 4. Consequently, the company (4 sections) fell from 20 tanks to 16, and the battalion to 48 tanks. The section fell to 3 tanks, when 12 of the 48 tanks in the battalion were nominally reserved as training tanks.

At the time, the arm held only 70 tanks. It had not received any new tanks since October. The promise was for 240 Mark IV tanks by March, but in November this promise was cut to 96 Mark IVs, enough for two battalions (48 tanks each). None arrived by March, when the arm recorded no tanks ready for battle. It suspended driver training and lodged a demand on the home base (Bovington), for every tank that could be spared. By 1 April, the arm in France gathered 60 reconditioned Mark Is and Mark IIs, including 26 Mark IIs from Bovington. Fuller estimated that four times as many (i.e., 240) would have been needed to achieve "a great victory" on 9 April. (The first Mark IVs did not arrive until late April.)

Fuller wanted to concentrate all 60 tanks on one sector. He aimed at Bullecourt, on chalk plains that had not been damaged significantly by artillery, in 5th Army's area. However, GHQ reiterated that the focus must be in 3rd Army's area. Fuller had studied that area as a staff officer at 3rd Army HQ the previous year. Within the area, he proposed to concentrate all 60 tanks south of the River Scarpe, where the flood plain rises slightly onto chalkland, with Monchy-le-Preux as the objective. Instead, the tanks were distributed across all three armies, and a front of 15 miles (26,400 yards; 24,140 m) (Fuller 1920: 82; 1936: 101, 103, 110).

The 1st Army was given 8 tanks to assault Vimy Ridge and the village of Thélus. The 3rd Army received 40 tanks: 8 to support XVII Corps north of the River Scarpe; 32 to support VI Corps and VII Corps south of the Scarpe. The 5th Army received 12 tanks.

A dozen tanks were reserved; 48 were allocated to the assault of 9 April – one tank per 550 yards (503 m). Given 14 divisions in the attack on 9 April, only 3.4 tanks were available for each division, 1 tank for every 3.5 battalions, on average.

By contrast, for the attacks organized for 10 April, the front was narrowed to 1,000 yards (914 m), with 12 tanks allocated, i.e., one tank per 83 yards. For 11 April, 22 tanks were allocated, to three separate attacks, of which the largest was on a front of 1,500 yards (1,372 m), again with 12 tanks allocated, i.e., 1 tank per 125 yards (114 m).

On 4 March, Estienne had stressed concentration, particularly in surprise attacks (absent a preliminary bombardment by indirect-fire weapons). He assumed 1,600 meters per division, two tank "groups" (16 tanks per group) per division, suggesting one tank every 50 meters (55 yards). However, British officers responded that tank units should be allotted to a corps for distribution to divisions. Estienne later commented on the minutes, to clarify that French groups are indeed distributed from higher echelons, but he still expected at least one group per division.

Surprise

Hollond had planned for a preliminary bombardment of two days. Indeed, that plan had inspired Fuller to write into his doctrine of February that a preliminary bombardment should last no longer than two days.

For some surprise in timing, Fuller wished to commit tanks after the culmination of 3rd Army's advance – two to three days after the initial assault, by his estimation. For some surprise in space, he wished to commit tanks outside of 3rd Army's area, wherever the Germans would withdraw forces to concentrate against 3rd Army. However, GHQ committed two-thirds to 3rd Army on the first day.

The French probably encouraged GHQ's choice for preliminary bombardment. Back in June 1916, Estienne had urged Swinton (1932: 255) not to use tanks until the French were ready; at the time, Swinton was unaware of GHQ's intent to rush the first batch of tanks into action in September. French tanks still had not been used in combat by 4 March. That day, Estienne acknowledged a choice between a surprise attack without preliminary bombardment and a deliberate attack with. Estienne and colleagues, as commissioned artillery officers, in charge of a new arm named *l'Artillerie d'Assaut*, were selection-biased towards preliminary bombardment.

Estienne acknowledged that tanks should be assembled in secrecy, moved forward at night or in fog, and otherwise hidden, but estimated surprise as improbable given the difficulties of concealing preparations for attack. Thus, he did not accept that a preliminary bombardment would make any difference to surprise.

Further, Estienne decided that the attackers would not be able to navigate the broken terrain until hours after dawn, which betrays disengagement from British experience. His preferences conformed with the only representative from GHQ (Butler).

Once Hollond left 3rd Army for another role, General Edmund Allenby, under GHQ's pressure, extended the preliminary bombardment to 21 days, of which the last four days were continuous.

Combined Arms

Artillery

The preliminary bombardment consumed 1,400,000 shells and lasted 21 days, of which the first 17 days focused on enemy wire, the final four days on enemy trenches and artillery. Some enemy guns had been pre-registered by bracketing.

Corps HQs continued to control the preliminary and creeping barrages, except that some batteries could be directed by division and brigade commanders.

The preliminary and creeping bombardments certainly neutralized enough wire and fire positions to give the first wave an easy advance to the first defensive line. However, beyond the first line the damage to the fortifications was mild, while the damage to the ground was as bad as before. This slowed up the following infantry, the tanks, and particularly the artillery, so that the leading infantry ran ahead of artillery support (Fuller 1920: 85-86; 1936: 99-107).

Tellingly, by the end of the first day, the 5th Army planned attacks over the next two days without preliminary bombardment.

Aircraft

Aircraft helped. Aircraft signalled to tanks by dropping smoke on artillery. They could drop written reports on friendly HQs, although such messages might not be relayed to assault troops until they rallied. Since 1916, aircraft had carried radios, by which scouts could signal by morse code the locations of enemy artillery, and adjust friendly artillery fire, but the targets were normally indirect-fire artillery rather than the direct-fire artillery that concerned tanks most. Further, British scout aircraft were still operating in airspace that German fighters tended to dominate.

Tanks and Infantry

At the British-French conference of 4 March, nobody disputed that the arms should be combined. The commander of the French tank force said that tanks were most valuable in assisting infantry to advance. Estienne added conditions for which arm should lead: without preliminary bombardment, tanks should lead; after preliminary bombardment, infantry should lead, given the broken ground.

Estienne specified a gap of up to 3 km (2 miles), so that the tanks are not spotted and thence bombarded in the first hours of daylight. (Estienne did not allow for an assault in darkness or twilight.) The minutes paraphrase him as saying that "tanks will not, under normal circumstance, come into action until the infantry advance is checked by the enemy's strongpoints." Tanks would follow in columns, overtake the infantry, deploy into lines conforming to the objectives, "and enable them [infantry] to carry the successive enemy lines of defence."

By April 1917, British infantry were better equipped and structured to cooperate with tanks, given new GHQ manuals on lower tactics, issued in February. Before February, each of the platoon's four rifle sections was supposed to advance in column behind a tank, or in line behind a creeping barrage. Now the sections were specialized: the rifle section would normally lead; the grenadier sections would take flanks (one section was equipped with hand grenades, one with rifle grenades); and the Lewis machine-gun section would follow, with the platoon HQ. The rifle-grenades and machine-gun were the main fire support weapons. The rifles and hand grenades were the main assault weapons. The new platoon was less exposed and more lethal. Platoons were trained to use the same tactics of fire-and-movement to support each other, and to take advantage of tank fire.

Speed

The tank arm continued to train for urgency of advance, but the damage to the terrain, and the pace of the creeping barrage, were no better than in previous assaults: 50 yards per minute (1.7 mph).

Sustainment

On 4 March, Estienne had unknowingly endorsed Fuller's ambition to advance tanks and infantry into the enemy's rear. The downside was that the assaulters would outrun supplies and the supporting fire from friendly field guns, until supplies and field guns could be pulled forward. Estienne had no solution, except to dump supplies and repair assets at the assembly area (5 to 6 km, or 5,468 to 6,562 yards, behind the start line), to which, presumably, the tanks would rally. The French tanks were much smaller, and thus offered less capacity for supplies.

Eyncourt pointed out that the Mark IV tanks could be expected to get ahead at a higher speed than previous marks. He wished to counter the infantry's impression, as reported earlier in the conference, that tanks are too unreliable. Eyncourt added that "to a great extent they can carry their own supplies, ammunition, food, water, etc., for a considerable period, and are therefore largely independent of supplies coming up from behind." Therefore, a surprise combined-arms attack can be made with less preparation, and to a greater depth.

Fuller was not present on 4 March. Back at tank HQ, he advocated for three assault waves (one for each of three defensive lines) and a reserve. "Waves of tanks succeeding one another in echelon with a strong reserve to draw on could hardly have failed to force a passage for the infantry, and so have compelled the Germans to fall back" (Fuller 1920: 82; 1936: 101, 103, 110).

For 9 April, the heavy tanks were supposed to rally to the rear before the end of daylight, and thus before any sustainment of the captured lines.

Exploitation

In November 1916, Martel had required categorically "light" and "medium tanks" for fighting other tanks, and an even lighter tank ("Destroyer Tank") for fighting, scouting, and raiding. Martel required no specialized tank for exploiting breakthroughs. By 1917, British home authorities were developing medium tanks for exploitation, but they were more than a year away from deployment.

On 4 March 1917, Estienne voiced requirements for medium and light tanks to exploit the breakthrough. Estienne required a heavy tank (15 to 30 tons) to cross the worst natural and man-made obstacles. He required a medium tank (6 to 15 tons) to cross temporary bridges over waterways that could not carry a heavy tank. And he required a light tank (4 to 6 tons) that could be carried on the back of a lorry for quick concentration at the assembly area. Estienne prospected a reserve, with three light tanks for every medium. The mediums were required to "crush" enemy wire and resistance that the lights could not handle. He required lights also as command tanks (one per "battery," in French parlance, equivalent to a British section). The British did not endorse a light class, although Stern "pointed out that light tanks might perform the role of cavalry in attacking the enemy's gun positions." The conference would conclude that all three classes should be developed. However, the French light tank was certainly not as fast as a horse, and probably Stern did not mean to suggest so. Further, the light tank accommodated the smallest 37-mm gun in inventory, and was preferred with a machine-gun, given the small turret (which accommodated only one man, who was tasked with command, gunnery, and loading). Machine-guns are not much use against artillery behind gun shields or fortifications. Estienne seems to suggest that light tanks should be armed with only machine-guns, when he specifies that half of tanks should be armed with machine-guns, the rest with 75-mm guns (which could not fit in the light tank). He was happy with the light tank, but considered France's nominal heavy tanks as medium-weight inferiorities compared to the British heavy tanks.

Eyncourt seems to have been happy with the British male heavy tank's armament, but wished for thicker armour, specifically to resist artillery guns. Most attendees agreed that tanks were not yet reliable or fast enough to act as cavalry.

On 9 April, 14 divisions faced 12 German divisions in the line. Nine British and Commonwealth divisions were reserved, against five reserved on the German side. No tanks were reserved. Again, the three cavalry divisions were allocated to exploit any breakthrough, but were not called forward until the third day, to little effect.

Outcomes

Six tanks bogged on their way to the startline on 8 April; 24 bogged down or broke down after the startline on 9 April. On the northern flank, all eight tanks crossed the German frontline but bogged down 500 yards beyond it, short of Vimy Ridge. Within 3rd Army, four of the eight tanks north of the River Scarpe bogged without reaching the objective, as did most of the tanks south of the Scarpe.

For the next day, Major WHL Watson, commanding D Battalion, persuaded 5th Army (Hubert Gough) to launch 11th Company (12 tanks) against Bullecourt, on a narrow front of just 1,000 yards. Watson argued against a preliminary bombardment, which would give up surprise for little material effect, due to the weakness of the 5th Army's artillery. Gough agreed to an attack at 0430 hours on 10 April, but the tanks got lost in a sudden snowstorm.

The 5th Army scheduled another attack for 0430 hours on 11 April, with a front of 1,500 yards, aiming between Bullecourt and Quéant, again without preliminary bombardment. Only 12 Marks I and II tanks were allocated, of which 11 started. Four would attack Bullecourt, two would attack the Hindenburg Line north-west of Bullecourt, three were to aim at Reincourt and Hendecourt, and two would move eastwards down the trenches. The tanks were soon disabled by artillery fire, except a pair that got into Reincourt and Hendecourt, followed by the infantry from 4th Australian Division. Fuller (1920: 87) considered this attack a success, and in conformity with his doctrine of February, except that counter-attackers captured the villages, the two tanks, and several hundred prisoners.

Six tanks were sent to attack Monchy. Three tanks bogged, but the other three continued across a depression from Freuchy Chapel into Monchy, through which the cavalry passed. On the right, four tanks were supposed to attack from Neuville Vitasse down the Hindenburg Line (two were tasked to consolidate the trenches, the other two to press on to Hendecourt), but all were knocked out.

Bullecourt remained in enemy hands until a third attack, which dragged from 3 to 17 May, and never secured all its approaches.

> I was convinced that had we engaged the whole of our 60 tanks on the 5th Army front, and had the attack been properly prepared, not only would a complete breakthrough have been effected, but that it would have been accomplished without destroying the forward communications. Before this attack my suggestions had been based on theory, now practice had borne them out, and though I realized that it would be extremely difficult to get GHQ to grasp this, seeing that the battle had ended disastrously, I considered it not to be impossible (Fuller 1936: 108-109).

6

Messines Ridge, June 1917

The Western Alliance was politically and materially stronger than Germany, but had not yet established an Allied command. In the meantime, the British generally operated when and where the French wanted. The British first attacked when and where they preferred in June 1917, at Messines Ridge (Ferguson 1998: 305).

The 2nd Army had been preparing to take Messines Ridge (see Map 7) for a year. On 20 March, Anthony Courage (2nd Tank Brigade) developed a plan for tanks to support the offensive. On 23 March, Elles forwarded it to 2nd Army HQ. On 29 March, the Brigade started reconnoitering the front. In April, Stephen Foot was appointed Brigade Major, after four months as Adjutant of Central Workshops.

> The 2nd Army, under General [Herbert] Plumer, was in charge of that attack, and every Wednesday morning the Chief of Staff, Major-General C.H. Harington (better known as "Tim"), held a conference at his Headquarters to hear how the preparations for the battle were getting on. The chief staff officers of the corps taking part in the attack (all brigadier-generals) used to attend these conferences, and I was there representing the tanks. At last I was really "in the know."
>
> As a battle, Messines was remarkable for its elaborate preparations; and the precision with which each step was executed, according to plans made beforehand, was largely responsible for our success (Foot 1934: 177).

Terrain

Fuller (1936: 121) agreed that the offensive "was well planned and carefully prepared by the 2nd Army," and that Messines Ridge offered good going for tanks, with slight rises and well-drained sandy soil, but complained that the long preliminary bombardment (28 May until 7 June) inundated the terrain.

Concentration

The front measured 9 miles (15,840 yards; 14,484 m). For the offensive, the 2nd Army gathered 1,510 field guns and 756 heavy guns and howitzers, against 344 field guns and 400 heavy pieces on the German side. The Allied concentration works out at one piece per 20 yards (18 m) of front (Neiberg 2005: 258).

Since April, two tank battalions had arrived from Britain, for a total of six in France. Fuller hoped that GHQ would learn from Arras that tanks should be concentrated against as few objectives as possible. However, the battalions were either incomplete or differently equipped. Only the 2nd Brigade was filled with the new Mark IV tanks – a total of 72. (Each battalion held 36 fighting tanks, two spare Mark IV tanks, and six Mark I tanks converted to carry supplies.) GHQ allocated only these 72 tanks to the new offensive, of which it reserved 24. Thus, only 48 were

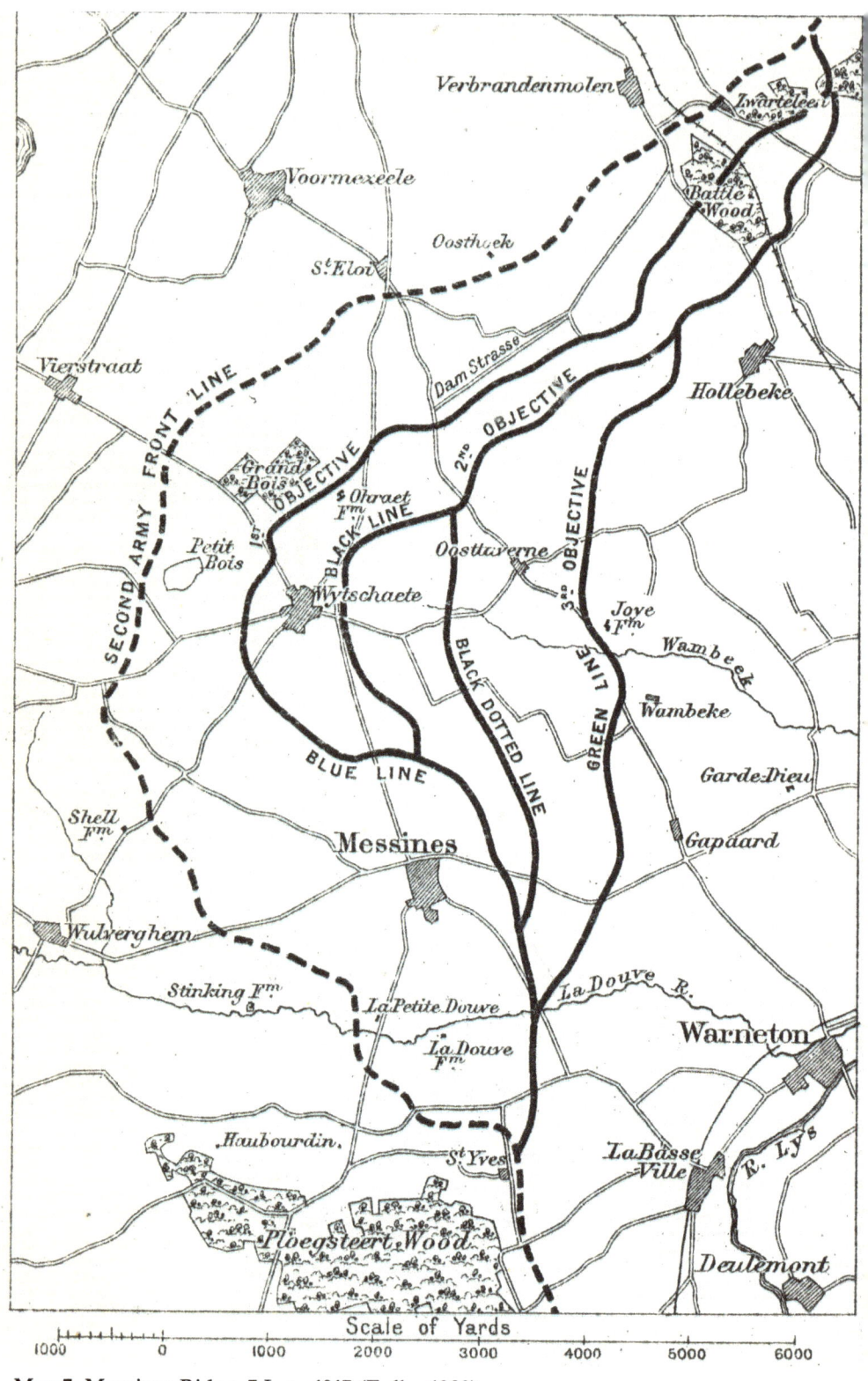

Map 7: Messines Ridge, 7 June 1917 (Fuller 1920).

allocated to the initial assault, and these were distributed across three corps. Fuller considered the total too small and the distribution too wide.

The 2nd Army allocated nine divisions to the assault on the Ridge. Thus, on average, only four tanks were available per division, one for every three battalions, one for every 330 yards (302 m) of front.

Ironically, although the tanks were few, they were not given as much to do as in previous operations. Of the 72 fighting tanks eventually committed, only 11 broke down or were knocked out. Fuller (1936: 121) concluded that the offensive "was essentially an artillery-infantry battle, the 88 tanks [including 16 supply tanks] taking part in it playing an entirely subsidiary role." Foot (1934: 177) agreed that "tanks did not play a very important part in the battle, but we learnt some valuable lessons, while it gave us chances of getting to know each other in the brigade."

Surprise

Fuller hoped that GHQ would follow his doctrine, from February, for a short preliminary bombardment, lasting no more than two days. Instead, GHQ chose ten days. Fuller repeatedly suggested cutting it short, and bombarding sectors that would not be assaulted, but GHQ never responded. The preliminary bombardment alerted the enemy to the place of assault, and gave plenty of time for the enemy to reinforce, although it certainly denuded enemy artillery (its main target).

GHQ tried to surprise the enemy as to the timing of the assault by ordering aircraft to cover the noise of tanks moving overnight to their starting positions.

The Germans were surprised by the particular day of assault, the involvement of tanks, and most of the mines, but were not surprised as to location in general or the inevitability of an offensive.

Combined Arms

Mines

The most dramatic effects were achieved by the nearly 500 tons of explosive carried by miners to the ends of 19 tunnels under the Messines Ridge, which killed or buried alive almost 10,000 Germans and shocked another 7,300 into surrender. The first 1,500 yards of the German defences fell into Allied hands without a fight, except for a stretch of the Ypres–Comines canal (Neiberg 2005: 259).

Artillery

GHQ chose a preliminary bombardment of ten days, focused on artillery. About 9 in 10 enemy guns had been pre-registered in previous weeks by bracketing the sound and flash of their fire, although some could have moved before the assault.

Since February, Fuller laid down that no creeping barrage is necessary where tanks are present. The barrage certainly suppressed defenders, but also damaged the terrain, and left the artillery unready and under-resourced to respond to targets of opportunity beyond the first defensive line.

Aircraft

More than 300 aircraft were committed to clearing the skies over the target area, attacking enemy artillery, and spotting for friendly artillery.

They succeeded: this offensive may be considered the first under Allied aerial dominance.

Tanks and Infantry

In May, GHQ expanded its "Preliminary Notes" of August 1916 from four to six pages ("Notes on the Use of Tanks and on the General Principles of their Employment as an Adjunct to the Infantry Attack," SS-164). Despite the new title, little had changed. Fuller described it as "insignificant" and internally "contradictory." He highlighted the following text as evidence that GHQ still undervalued tanks.

> It should seldom be necessary to employ tanks at the commencement of an offensive to assist the infantry assault…[where defences] can be adequately dealt with and destroyed by our own artillery bombardment [or where] ground that has been very heavily shelled, or is very sodden to a considerable depth, is unfavourable to its employment (in 1936: 111).

Speed

Fuller urged his superiors to rely on the lethality and mobility of tanks without a creeping barrage, but again they chose a creeping barrage, of 50 yards (46 m) per minute (1.7 mph).

Sustainment

In November, Martel had circulated requirements for several classes of tank, including supply tanks. Fuller advocated "tank tenders" in his "Training Note No. 16" of February. Such vehicles were used for the first time in the Battle of Messines Ridge, having been converted from old Mark I tanks. (The armoured gun sponsors were replaced with especially constructed "supply sponsons" of soft steel.) The delay in the arrival of Mark IV tanks had prevented the execution until May 1917.

The products were assigned to carry supplies from forward dumps to "rallying points," where fighting tanks could rest and replenish between attacks. Two supply tanks were allocated to each tank company. Each carried sufficient consumables (fuel, oil, grease, ammunition, and water) for five fighting tanks. The 16 tenders offered more than enough capacity to supply the 72 fighting tanks (Fuller 1920: 109, 166). Their use to sustain tanks contrasts to their subsequent use to sustain infantry.

Exploitation

For the first time, tanks were reserved. Ten hours after Zero Hour, 24 reserved tanks and all operational assault tanks were supposed to support three divisions (one in each of three assaulting corps) over the ridge, down to a defensive line that the Germans called *Sehnenstellung* (the Allies called it Oosttaverne). (Separately a corps was reserved, with four divisions, but had not been allocated to the move on the *Sehnenstellung*.) The three divisions captured their objectives on schedule, except for a 1,000-yard stretch of the line, at the junction of the II ANZAC Corps and IX Corps. Mistaken British artillery fire drove some of the Australians back, although other reserves moved in, after the repeated mistakes had been corrected.

Outcomes

In one day, the 2nd Army took the Messines Ridge and advanced 3 miles (5,280 yards; 4,828 m) deep on a front of 5 miles (8,800 yards; 8,047 m), thanks mainly to the mines. Of the 72 tanks, 11 were disabled by enemy artillery, and 48 bogged down or got stuck in trenches. The 2nd Army caused 23,000 casualties, but suffered 17,000, and was unable to exploit its gains. A German withdrawal on 11 June added another mile to Allied gains. By then, the BEF suffered 25,000 casualties (Ferguson 1998: 293; Corrigan 2003: 350-351; Neiberg 2005: 259).

British infantry advance through smashed German fortifications on Messines Ridge, 7 June 1917 (IWM Q5787).

Map 8: British formation areas and objective lines for the offensive towards Passchendaele (Third Battle of Ypres), July 1917 (Fuller 1920).

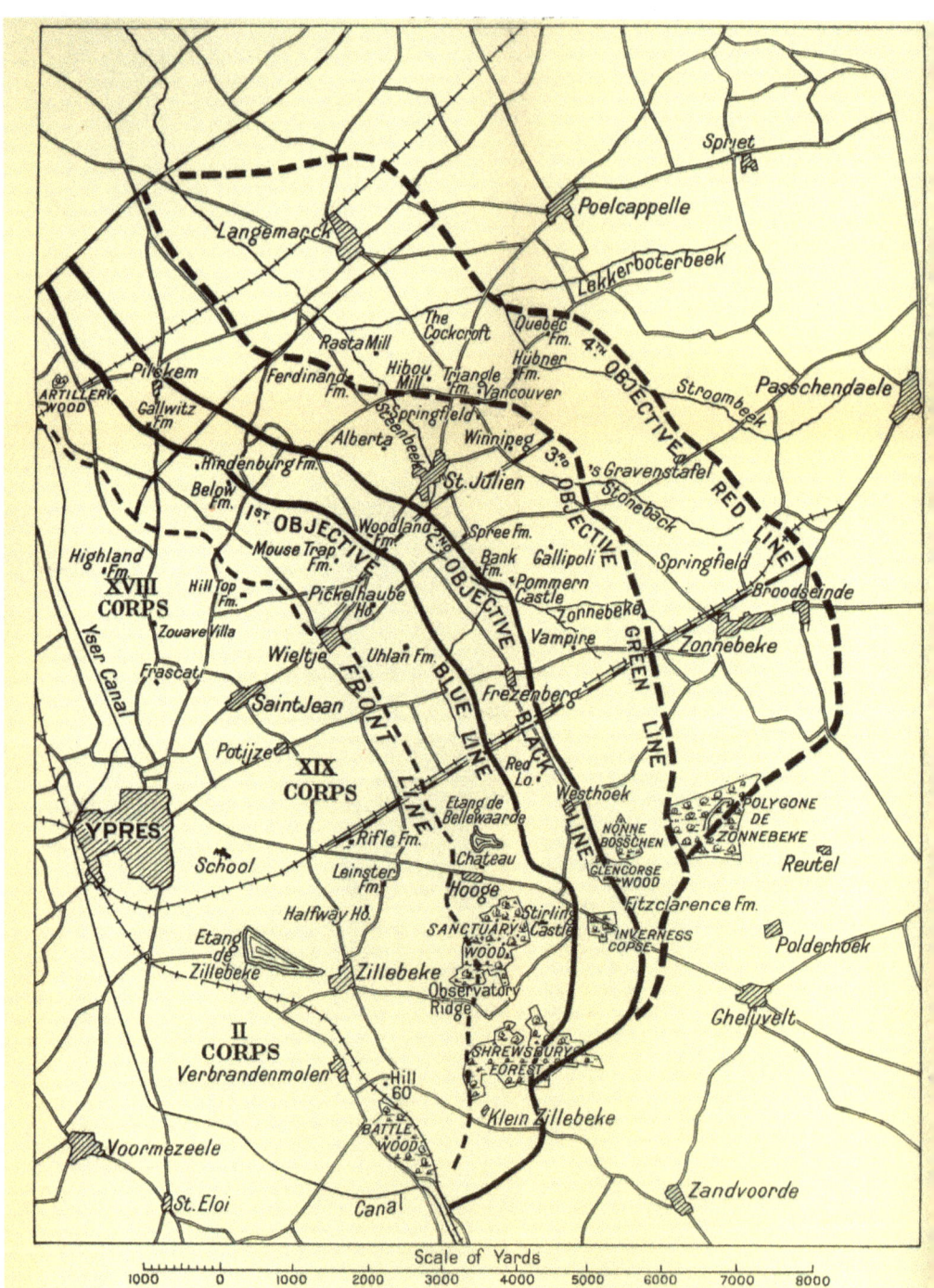

7

Passchendaele, July to November 1917

The offensive at Messines secured the southern flank of the BEF, which GHQ wanted for a potential drive out of the salient at Ypres. However, Haig waited almost seven weeks to launch the next offensive, and chose the most waterlogged area, which he exacerbated with a long preliminary bombardment.

Five British armies, three tank brigade HQs, and eight tank battalions were now in France. From May, GHQ warned them to prepare to advance north-eastwards, towards the Belgian coast, where a division would be landed amphibiously (see Map 23). Although the amphibious part was cancelled, the 5th Army (Hubert Gough) was left with orders to capture the ridge from Passchendaele (Passendale) through Staden to Klerken, and the railway from Roulers (Roeselare) to Torhout (Thourout). Since Passchendaele is barely beyond Ypres, and little ground was taken, the operation is known also as the Third Battle of Ypres (see Maps 8 and 23). It would start on 31 July, but would be extended several times, until it formally closed on 10 November.

Terrain

A sufficient cause of the operation's failure was the terrain. The assaulters would need to pass three defensive lines, and 6,000 to 7,000 yards (5,486 to 6,401 m) of defended ground. The reserves would need to advance 20 miles (32 km), over reclaimed marshland. The water table in most of Belgium is just 2 feet below the surface. The preliminary bombardment destroyed the drainage, and churned top soil, clay, and water into a mix that was analogized, at the time, to "porridge," "treacle," "swamp," and "morass."

> At Heavy Branch Headquarters what perplexed us was, how anyone realising that the initial stage of the battle was likely to last for weeks could be so optimistic as to suppose that the spires of Bruges would ever be seen except from the air, or that the condition of the ground after such prolonged fighting would admit of even pack animals crossing it, let alone cavalry (Fuller 1936: 143-144).

Hotblack toured the front most frequently. On 15 June, he reported that, given rain, the terrain would be unsuitable for tanks, except on the main ridge. He did not need to wait for the rainy season, because GHQ soon insisted on three-and-a-half weeks of preliminary bombardment. Hotblack and Fuller kept GHQ updated with maps showing the inundations. Foot was involved, at 2nd Brigade HQ.

> [T]here is no doubt that GHQ had ample warning from the higher command of the Tank Corps. It was perfectly true that tanks were capable of dealing with a German pill-box – that was proved on many occasions; but it was only true if the tank could reach the pill-box...
>
> I have seen a mule sunk in the ground until only its head was visible; I

> sank myself on one occasion nearly up to my armpits, and if I had been alone I could certainly not have extricated myself; hundreds of wounded men were drowned or suffocated in the mud (Foot 1934: 181-182).

The commander of 1st Tank Brigade (Christopher d'Arcy Baker-Carr) also failed to dissuade GHQ.

> After our preliminary bombardment, which lasted for sixteen days with ever-growing intensity, and the German retaliation thereto, the whole surface of the ground consisted of nothing but a series of overlapping shell craters, half-full of yellow, slimy water. Through falling into these ponds, hundreds upon hundreds of unwounded men, while advancing to the attack, lost their lives by drowning…The original roads had almost ceased to exist, and, in order to enable wheel traffic to move at all, even in the area behind the line, it was necessary to lay down corduroy tracks which were constantly destroyed by shell fire (Baker-Carr 1930: 229).

Sergeant J.C. Allnatt recalled that "every member of the Tank Corps, even those of the lowest rank, knew that they should not be there" (Forty 1989: 41-42).

Gough was late to disagree with Haig. Gough and his staff were experienced at army echelon since June 1916 (when the 5th Army had been formed as the Reserve Army), but insular and unfamiliar with the area. Haig rotated 5th Army in place of 2nd Army given dissatisfaction with Herbert Plumer's failure to exploit the capture of Messines Ridge. Gough realized he was supposed to be more compliant. His HQ assembled in Flanders on 1 June, six days before the attack at Messines. Both Gough and his staff had reputations for arrogance and disengagement from lower

These Mark IV tanks of 6th Company, B Battalion, 2nd Brigade, became bogged and damaged on the high ground around the junction (known to the British as "Clapham Junction") of Pappotstraat and the road to Menin on 31 July 1917. The photograph was taken on 20 September (RACTM).

echelons (Neiberg 2005: 261-262). Fuller recalled Gough as the most "bull-headed" of army commanders, and distrusted throughout Tank Corps HQ.

On 17 July, Fuller found the area around Gough's HQ sodden, suggesting that even personnel who never left the HQ could envision the terrain at the front.

The assault was postponed twice, first to 28 July, second (on 25 July) to 31 July. Rain fell heavily on the day of assault (31 July) and all but three days of August. August saw 1.8 times as much rain as average in previous years. GHQ's intelligence chief (Brigadier John Charteris) did not visit the front until 9 August. He blamed the rain for the assaulters' difficulties, but the rain had been normal in July.

Gough blamed the tanks most, when he reported to GHQ on 14 August. "They are slow, vulnerable and very susceptible to bad 'going'." On 22 August, Eyncourt (as Chief Technical Adviser to the Ministry of Munitions), probably prompted by Fuller, wrote to Haig to suggest "more suitable ground," rather than requiring "all sorts of arrangements for unditching, etc." On 27 August, Haig replied to admit the desirability of better terrain, but still required technologies that could cope with the given terrain. Yet Haig's final despatch to government on the offensive (December) admits that the terrain was impassable to pedestrians and equines, not just tanks (Charteris 1929: 272; Lloyd George 1938: 1306; Fuller 1936: 175-177).

Concentration

The 5th Army gathered about 3,200 artillery pieces and 121,000 artillerymen and Army Service Corpsmen to service them. The 5th Army started with a front about 10 miles (16 km) long, which suggests one artillery piece every 5.5 yards (5 m).

By July, the three tank brigades held eight battalions, but only six were ready. These six held 36 tanks per battalion, 216 tanks in total, and 2,500 men to crew and service them. For the first day, 120 tanks were distributed across 13 divisions (see Table 3), i.e., 9.2 tanks were available per division, 1.3 tanks per battalion, one tank per 147 yards (134 m) of front.

Even counting all 216 tanks, less than 17 tanks were available per division, 1.4 tanks per infantry battalion, one tank per 81.5 yards (74.5 m).

Even counting tanks on the first day overstates the concentration, given that the campaign was extended and expanded. Before its close in November, 50 British and

Higher formation		II Corps		XIX Corps		XVIII Corps		3rd Army
Tank Brigade		2nd		3rd		1st		-
1st wave, to Black Line	Division	24th	30th	15th	55th	39th	51st	-
	Tanks	4	12	12	12	8	4	-
2nd wave, to Green Line	Division	8th		15th	55th	39th	51st	-
	Tanks	24		12	12	8	4	-
3rd wave, to east of Green	Division	18th	25th	16th	36th	11th	48th	-
	Tanks	8	0	0	0	0	0	-
Reserves	Tanks	24		24		12		36
Main natural obstacles		Marshes and woods, with only three defiles suitable for tanks		Steenbeek valley and reclaimed marshes		Steenbeek valley and reclaimed marshes, with one defile suitable for tanks (at St. Julien)		-
Objectives		Broodseinde ridge; right flank		Gheluvelt to Langemarck		Over Steenbeek at Mon du Rasta and Military Rd		-
TOTAL	Divisions	5		4		4		up to 4
	Tanks	72		72		36		36

Table 3: Force structure for 31 July 1917 (Fuller 1920: 118-121; 1936: 247).

Commonwealth and 73 German divisions were committed.

Surprise

Counter-battery fire started on July 6, the bombardment of German frontlines on 19 July, for a total of 26 days of preliminary bombardment.

The assault started on 31 July, around dawn, in mist, which soon turned into rain. The obfuscation was welcome, but of no import to most tanks, which bogged down without reaching the enemy.

Combined Arms

Artillery

The 5th Army's artillery fired 4 million rounds, weighing 107,000 long tons (108,717 metric; 119,840 short), in the preliminary bombardment alone, without destroying the defences. Gough's only doctrinal contribution was an urging (sent to unit commanders in mid-June) to have confidence in the bombardment's effect on the enemy's "demoralization and confusion."

> 1. It has been conclusively proved that, with the artillery at our disposal, a carefully organized and thoroughly prepared attack can break through any defences which the enemy devise, and

> 2. It has also been proved that, after the initial attack has succeeded, the enemy is temporarily in a state of demoralization and confusion. His communications are disorganized, he may have lost a good many guns, his artillery is in doubt as to the position of the infantry, and the infantry are upset by want of artillery support.

The creeping barrage suppressed defenders, but the assaulters fell behind, so the defenders had time to man their defences before the assaulters arrived.

Aircraft

The Allied aircraft were tasked primarily with air supremacy, but failed, due to German aerial reinforcements in advance of the assault, and the rain on the day of assault and thereafter. The battle for air supremacy left few missions for attacking enemy artillery, which were the Tank Corps' main concern.

Tanks and Infantry

Since the offensive at Messines, nothing changed doctrinally for tank-infantry cooperation.

A bell pull was installed on the rear of some tanks, by which a pedestrian could attract the attention of the crew. The rate of distribution is unclear.

Tanks and Engineers

No innovations in engineering were introduced in July. The only innovation that might be considered helpful to engineers was the introduction of unditching gear, which helped tanks to escape terrain that otherwise engineers might be asked to improve by levelling (by excavation), filling (by hauling and dumping other materials), or surfacing (usually with a corduroy road).

The unditching gear was developed and produced by Central Workshops. An oak beam was stowed on two rails mounted on the roof of the tank. This beam could be slid by hand down the rails on to the tracks, and chained to the tracks. When the tracks were driven forward, the tracks would carry the beam underneath the tank to engage the ground, and hopefully to help the tank to escape the mud.

Speed

As in earlier operations, a creeping barrage started upon assault, at a rate of 50 yards (46 m) per minute (1.7 mph). Nevertheless, the assaulters could not keep up.

Sustainment

On 5 July, Haig issued to army commanders a more detailed plan. On 9 July, Tank Corps Advanced HQ hosted a conference with tank staff and commanders. By now, the doctrinal work was more technical than tactical. On 13 July, Fuller issued to the brigades a paper on the use of supply tanks and refilling points. On 15 July, he followed up with a paper on "Reorganization on the Battlefield." On 20 July, he sent three papers on subjects that remained outstanding since the conference of 9 July: "Recovery of Tanks Damaged in Action"; the use of the new unditching gear; and a list of 23 structural and tactical issues on which he wanted the units to collect lessons-learned during the operation.

GHQ and the 5th Army continued to change the allocations of the tanks until 28 July. The most significant concession to Fuller's doctrine of February was to allocate about one-third of tanks to each of three waves – one for each of the main defensive lines (see Table 3). However, this allocation was moot given that most tanks never reached the first defensive line. Only 8 tanks were in the third wave.

To reinforce any failing wave or to advance beyond the third line, 96 tanks and three divisions (one division per assaulting corps) were allocated, but these never got going, because of the disappointing advances of the first day.

Nominally, six supply tanks were issued to each tank battalion for sustainment, as in the offensive on Messines Ridges, which suggests a requirement for 36 supply tanks. The totals issued before the assault and used on the day remain unclear.

Exploitation

The only exploitation force was the Cavalry Corps, with three cavalry divisions. Even though the operation lasted months, the cavalry were never sent in. They could not have passed the battlefield without a lot of work by engineers to make ways. Even the ground behind the captured lines was too wet to allow galloping.

Outcomes

Of the 216 tanks allocated to the offensive, 120 were allocated to the assault on the first day (31 July), of which 52 were allocated to the first wave. Those that reached the German first line (codenamed "Black Line") were knocked out by enemy artillery. Another 19 managed to attack the second line ("Green Line"). By the end of the first day, 42 tanks were written off.

On II Corps front, the tanks arrived late, found the infantry held up by enemy fire, overtook them, and were caught in defiles by enemy artillery fire. Around Hooge, tanks suffered their highest rate of casualties of the day.

On XVIII Corps' front, the tanks were stopped by the mud and a sunken road (to St. Julien).

Tanks were most successful with XIX Corps. They contributed to the assaults on Frezenberg Redoubt, Spree Farm, Capricorn Keep, and Bank Farm, and to their defence against counter-attacks.

On 31 July, the advance was measured in hundreds of yards in most places. The longest advance went about 5,000 yards (4,500 m), on the left. The lines shifted little in succeeding days. Passchendaele was supposed to be captured on the fourth day, but on that day it was still about 7,000 yards (6,400 m) away.

The offensive continued for months. In contrast to normal force employment, Fuller liked to draw stakeholders' attention to the following minor action: On 19 August, 12 tanks supported 48th Division to attack nine strongpoints, at the cost of 15 infantry and 13 tank casualties. The division's commander (Major-General Robert Fanshawe) had estimated, before he was allocated tanks, 600 to 1,000 casualties.

During September, four tank battalions were withdrawn to refit for an alternative offensive (eventually aimed at Cambrai), leaving four battalions available for attacks every few days. Haig and his chief of staff (Launcelot Kiggell) continued to invest in further attacks, given their chief intelligence officer's (John Charteris') confidence that German morale was about to break (based on intuition more than material evidence). Their inexperience of intelligence analysis, self-isolation at GHQ, and dismissal of representations from lower echelons, contributed to their denialism. On 28 September, Haig issued a statement claiming that repeated attacks were using up the enemy's reserves and morale. He warned troops to prepare for a decisive operation, around 9 or 10 October.

The tanks dropped out after 9 October. Writing in 1919, Fuller summarized the lessons for tanks:

> The main lessons learnt from this day's fighting were: the unsuitability of the Mark IV tank to swamp warfare; the danger of attempting to move tanks through defiles which are swept by hostile artillery fire; the necessity for immediate infantry co-operation whenever the presence of a tank forced an opening; and the continued moral effect of the tank on both the enemy and our own troops (Fuller 1920: 122).

Attacks continued until 10 November, when the offensive officially ended, after 103 days. British and Commonwealth casualties numbered 27,000 on the first day, 86,000 after 7 weeks, more than 100,000 once 2nd Army captured Polygon Wood on 4 October, more than 275,000 once Passchendaele was captured on 4 November (three months late). The Germans suffered 200,000 casualties.

The capture of Passchendaele cost 15,000 Canadian casualties. The salient there was deepest, but still less than 5 miles (8,800 yards; 8,047 m) from the start line – still 22 miles (38,720 yards; 35,405 m) from central Bruges and Ostend, still exposed to German counter-attacks, still without potential for using the town as a node for communications (Neiberg 2005: 264-269).

8
Plan 1918 and Tank Raids 1917

In Summer 1917, during the long build-up and longer execution of what is known as the Battle of Passchendaele, Tank Corps HQ was sensibly working on doctrines and plans for more effective battles. This was the period in which Fuller first proposed a decisive offensive in Spring 1918 (which I have identified as "Plan 1918"), a surprise attack on Cambrai in 1917, and "tank raids" in 1917 – all of which would influence the offensive at Cambrai in November. The sections of this chapter focus on Fuller's Plan 1918, the proposals to attack somewhere around St. Quentin or Cambrai, and Fuller's paper on "tank raids" respectively. Chapter 9 will focus on the offensive at Cambrai as launched in November.

Plan 1918

On 10 June 1917, three days after the start of the offensive against Messines Ridge, Fuller started a new doctrinal paper: "Projected Bases for the Tactical Employment of Tanks in 1918." The first two words capture the paper's focus on sustainment, inspired by the use of supply tanks for the first time, three days earlier. He later repudiated its "hideous title," which under-estimates its scope. An addition, dated 8 August, is annotated as "The Tactical Employment of Tanks 1918" (LHCMA Fuller 1/2/2). It contains most of the estimates, ambitions, and requirements that made famous his plan for a decisive offensive in Spring 1919, which became known for short as "Plan 1919." Thus, the paper should be known for short as "Plan 1918."

Terrain

The paper does not specify any particular terrain, but eschews bombardment (except counter-battery fire), in order to "prevent the heavy shelling of the ground." "[I]t must be remembered that the future of tanks lies on unshelled ground."

The paper does not specify any particular area, but specifies a front of 20 miles (35,200 yards; 32,187 m). The longest British offensive front to date (at Arras in April) was officially reported as 15 miles (26,400 yards; 24,140 m).

Plan 1918 is not for assaults along a continuous front. A continuous front has no flanks that can be enveloped by indirect approaches. Instead, the defences must be penetrated directly. Fuller aims for "envelopment" of the enemy after penetrating a defensive line. Each "penetrating" approach creates a salient into the defended zone, from which attackers could turn laterally to meet each other, enveloping the defenders in between. Fuller had prescribed envelopment in general since before the war. Upon joining the tank arm, he prescribed envelopment at lowest echelon (usually by a section of tanks and a platoon of infantry). "Projected Bases" is the first of Fuller's papers to raise the prospect of envelopment by tanks and infantry to the highest echelon.

Fuller lists six "difficulties" and their technical and technological solutions (see Table 4). The first difficulty is "to draw in and exhaust the German reserves" where

Fuller's prospected "difficulties"	Fuller's solutions
To draw in and exhaust the German reserves	To select an area of attack from which the enemy cannot withdraw without acknowledging defeat, and of employing tanks in this area in order to economise infantry
To capture the German front line and the area up to their third-line system, in face of incessant machine-gun fire	To move forward tanks and infantry under a protective barrage, the tanks replacing the artillery barrage immediately this barrage reaches its limit of range, [followed by] echelons of medium tanks, field guns in tank transporters, armoured cars, cavalry[,] and tractor-drawn infantry
To hold this third line for several days without much artillery support and under every type of shell the enemy can fire at us	To attack at once the enemy's guns with light tanks and special parties of infantry directly the enemy's defences in front of these guns have been captured
To see the enemy slip away from our grasp, directly the approach of our guns makes a further advance possible	Directly this attack has succeeded, to launch every light tank available, independent of guns and infantry, into the destroyed area in rear of the enemy's gun positions, and clear this area of machine-guns in order to enable our armoured cars, cavalry[,] and tractor-drawn infantry to pursue
To move forward through a wilderness – roads destroyed, wells blown in, houses demolished, in face of swarms of guerrilla machine-gunners	
To begin the battle all over again	

Table 4: **Fuller's doctrinal problems and solutions, in his own words, for an offensive in Spring 1918, as written 10-11 June 1917 (LHCMA Fuller 1/2/2; 1936: 125-127).**

they can be enveloped. His solution has implications for terrain: "to select an area of attack from which the enemy cannot withdraw without acknowledging defeat, and of employing tanks in this area in order to economise infantry."

Concentration

Fuller requires 1,000 heavy tanks, 750 light tanks, 1,000 infantry carriers, 750 artillery transporters, 250 artillery ammunition carriers, 1,000 supply carriers, 200 bridging carriers, and 100 radio carriers. On a front of 20 miles, one heavy tank would be available for every 35 yards (32 m). Counting the light tanks (although he requires them mostly for exploitation), one tank would be available per 20 yards (18 m). One tracked armoured vehicle would be available for every 7 yards (6 m).

Given that he wished to concentrate on several parts of the front, in order to achieve penetrations that could meet as envelopments, the concentrations would be much denser locally, but Fuller does not indicate any width of penetration or any number of penetrations that would enable us to calculate the local concentration.

Surprise

Fuller followed his choice since the Spring to eschew preliminary bombardment, and to urge secrecy in assembly, in hope of surprise in both time and space.

For the first time, Fuller betrays a dilemma between surprising the enemy (for an easier assault) and attracting reserves to the point of assault (for a more decisive victory). Fuller estimates decisiveness within "a few thousand yards," although only "by hitting the enemy at a point which he dare not abandon, or at one at which he does not expect to be attacked." The dilemma is not explored in his "Plan 1918." By May 1918, in "Plan 1919," Fuller opts for attracting reserves to each point of assault, given his confidence in improved resourcing and higher receptivity.

Combined Arms

Artillery

Given surprise and mechanical wire-cutting, Fuller hopes that "all guns might be concentrated on counter-battery work," not a full preliminary bombardment.

However, he still wants a "protective barrage" throughout the advance, up to the third defensive line, "the tanks replacing the artillery barrage immediately this barrage reaches its limit of range."

Tanks and Infantry

As in previous doctrines, his paper requires Male heavy tanks to destroy the machine-guns, Females to enfilade enemy trenches, and infantry to clear trenches.

Tanks and Engineers

Plan 1918 requires some sort of "mechanical…wire cutting" capability, so that no preliminary bombardment of the enemy wire is necessary. Fuller's paper does not prejudge any option. Soon, Central Workshops would decide that a grapnel is the best solution.

Speed

Fuller's paper does not emphasize speed, although it is implicit. His explicit emphasis is on enveloping enemy forces. In previous papers, Fuller had followed Swinton's urging for rapidity of advance, before the enemy reacts. By contrast, in this paper he wants the enemy to be sucked into the envelopments. His emphasis here is on accuracy of decision-making more than speed, without denying speed.

Sustainment

By Fuller's own account, his paper of 10 June was his first to detail a sustained penetration by tanks and variants and other arms into the enemy's rear. In the rear, the arms could pursue combatants in flight, and disable the non-combatants on which the combatants depend. Penetrating the rearmost line would be indecisive if we were counter-attacked without the capabilities and intent to hold the ground. Fuller is not advocating here for a raid. His decisive penetration and his raid are two different proposals.

Fuller's paper carries forward Townshend's observation (in "MS in Red Ink," August 1916) that an attack would be decisive if it could be sustained beyond the last German line. Since then, by Fuller's understanding, the enemy had shifted a larger proportion of defenders from the first defensive line and from the reserves into the second and third defensive lines. These shifts keep more defenders out of range of British 18-pounder field guns (about 4,000 yards or 3,658 m beyond the British frontline), and put defenders in a better position to attrit advancing troops, after the first line has disrupted them. Also, more troops would be available in the third line to sabotage communications before any withdrawal. Nevertheless, Fuller estimates decisiveness within "a few thousand yards," although only if "hitting the enemy at a point which he dare not abandon, or at one at which he does not expect to be attacked." Such an offensive is urgent, given that he expects the Germans to construct new second and third lines outside the range of the 18-pounder, and to destroy forward communications (to slow the relocation of British artillery).

Supply tanks were proven in June, at Messines, and in July, at Passchendaele. They were few in number, and served the fighting tanks. By Fuller's own account, his paper of 10 June was his first to require carriers and tractors ("mechanical transporters") for the other arms. He required them for infantry, medium machine-gunners, artillery, consumables (such as ammunition), fortification materials, engineering equipment, bridging equipment, and wireless radios. For the infantry, he requires "bullet-proof motor transporters." To counter enemy artillery, he requires "mobile echelons of heavy and super-heavy guns and howitzers," and carriers for their ammunition.

> The tank today carries forward the riflemen of the future. These riflemen, or machine-gunners, must be supported by tank artillery and by tank bayonet-men, so as to occupy and make good what the tank riflemen render possible…[We must decide] the types of tanks and transporters we shall require to meet the probable eventualities of 1918 (1936: 128-130).

In August, Fuller updated his paper of June with requirements for 1,000 infantry carriers (each carrying either 20 infantrymen or four Vickers Medium Machine-Guns and 16 crewmen), 1,000 supply carriers (each carrying 5 long tons: the same rating as current carriers), 750 gun transporters (each carrying a 18-pounder gun, 4.5-inch howitzer, 6-inch howitzer, or 60-pounder gun), 250 artillery ammunition transporters, 200 bridging carriers, and 100 radio carriers. Ideally, all these carriers would be variants of a "Universal Transporter," rated for a load of 5 long tons, as per the extant carrier. The paper prospects "a great saving in manufacture if all transporters would be of one type."

In lieu of the automobiles above, Fuller requires towed armoured carriers of the same capacity. An appendix contains profile sketches of potential trailers, titled "Martel's Tender." Fuller adds that the towed carrier for infantry and machine-gunners should be cut with firing holes so that "it might be left out as a strong point."

Exploitation

Plan 1918 schedules (in order) penetrating approaches, envelopments behind the defensive lines, a consolidation of the third defensive line, the defence of this line against counter-attacks (potentially over days), an attack on the artillery line, and a pursuit.

In discussing the problem of reaching the third defensive line, Fuller places, behind the assaulters, "echelons of light tanks, field guns in tank transporters, armoured cars, cavalry[,] and tractor-drawn infantry." (He would change the light tanks to mediums, after seeing Renault's small, slow, two-man tank in February 1918.) Together, these elements should "hold this third line for several days without much artillery support and under every type of shell the enemy can fire at us."

Once "the enemy's defences in front of [the enemy's artillery] guns have been captured," those "guns [should be attacked] with light tanks and special parties of infantry directly." He requires 750 "light tanks," but is unclear how many infantry carriers would be involved. A thousand carriers could carry 20,000 infantrymen, i.e., the combatant parts of two divisions. Perhaps some infantry would be reserved for the next phase.

> Directly this attack [on the artillery] has succeeded, [we should] launch every light tank available, independent of guns and infantry, into the destroyed area in rear of the enemy's gun positions, and clear this area of machine-guns in order to enable our armoured cars, cavalry[,] and tractor-drawn infantry to pursue (in 1936: 128-130).

Plan 1918, unlike Plan 1919, does not aim the fast tanks at logistics and headquarters, although these targets are implicit in any pursuit. In any case, Plan 1919 idealizes independent tank attacks on logistics and headquarters before the main assault, which makes Plan 1919 more fantastic and risky, albeit more rewarding.

The Cambrai-St. Quentin Prospect

On 12 June 1917, Tank Corps HQ was visited by Major-General Sir John Capper, one month into his administration of the Heavy Branch and the Tank Committee, and one month away from promotion to Director-General Tanks (DGTC). Capper estimated that Britain would not be able to deliver the 5,050 tanks and carriers that Fuller wanted for a decisive offensive, even by Spring 1918.

The next day, they developed a scheme to attack with hundreds of tanks and thousands of infantrymen, without preliminary bombardment, on the good terrain between Cambrai and St. Quentin. On 14 June, Capper left for Britain with copies of both papers. From the War Office, he escalated the scheme to GHQ. On 14 July, GHQ hosted a discussion between Capper, Elles, the BEF's chief of staff (Launcelot Kiggell), his deputy (Richard Butler), the BEF's Director of Military Operations (John "Tavish" Davidson), and the BEF's lead officer for force structure (Kenneth Wigram). Capper reported that everyone except Kiggell agreed to consider the paper further (Fuller 1936: 131).

Kiggell was preoccupied with the ease with which German counter-attacks were pushing attackers out of defensive lines before they could consolidate. Some weeks later, Fuller suggested that while tanks assault, variants could deposit 20 men and five machine-guns (per variant) behind the enemy's defensive line, to hold up the reserves. Fuller expected the defenders, without reserves, to collapse within 24 hours. This requirement was one of the stimuli towards local development of a lengthened Mark IV tank, to carry machine-gun teams. (The other stimulus was wider anti-tank trenches.) Mark V* heavy tanks were the eventual fulfilments sent from home, although they were not ready for use until August 1918.

On 2 August 1917, Fuller toured the Passchendaele battlefield. The next day, he formally recommended to Elles the withdrawal of the Tank Corps, in preparation for the surprise capture of St. Quentin, on the boundary with the French front. This would divert German resources from Passchendaele, straighten the line, and prove the Tank Corps' doctrine. However, Elles predicted that Haig would never agree to such cooperation with the French.

Fuller reduced the scope to the area south of Cambrai, within 5th Army's front (see Map 9). Given the Tank Corps' disappointments with "bull-headed" Gough, before the offensive towards Passchendaele, Fuller and Elles agreed to escalate the new proposal directly to GHQ. Fuller finished the proposal on 4 August, for Elles to carry to GHQ that afternoon. The DMO (Davidson) was open to consideration, but said that the CGS (Kiggell) would not be.

That evening, Fuller dined with the commander of 3rd Tank Brigade (John Hardress-Lloyd), who suggested that the proposal would have more chance if it were to be seconded by the new commander of 3rd Army (General Sir Julian Byng), whom Hardress-Lloyd had known as commander of Canadian Corps during its victory at Vimy Ridge in April. Hardress-Lloyd visited Byng on 5 August, who went to see Haig the next day. Haig was keen. He called in Davidson, who agreed.

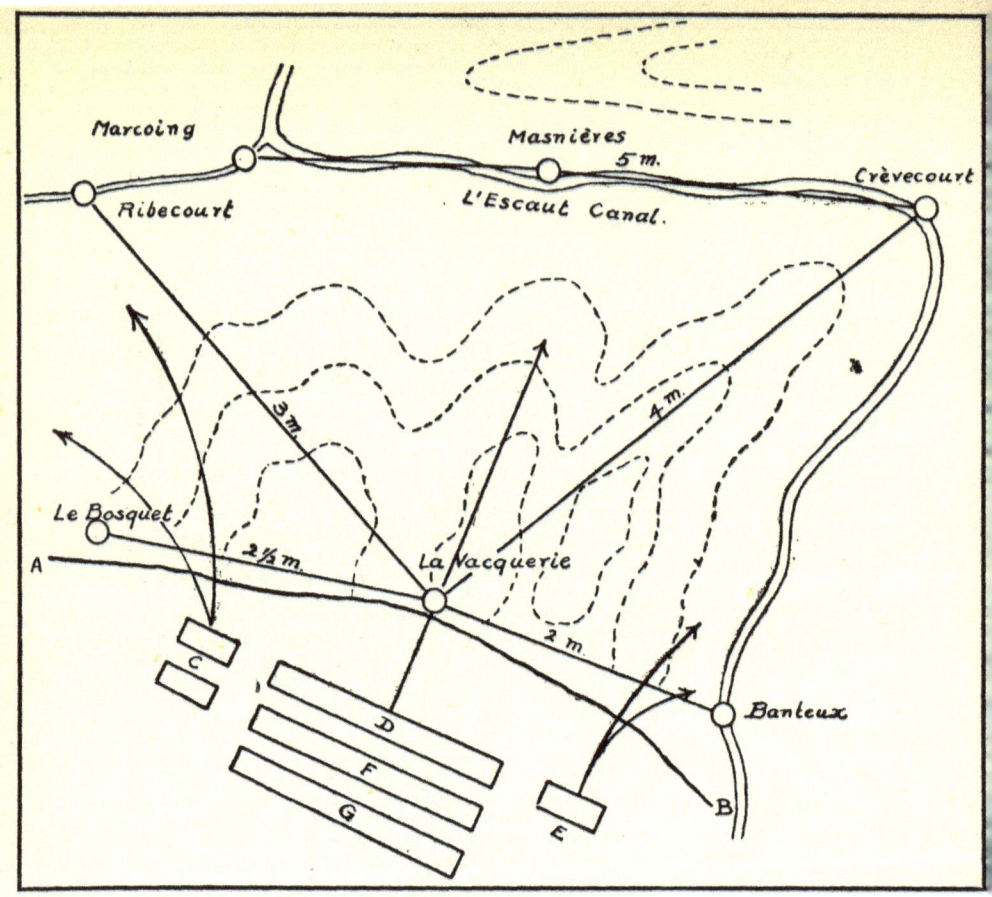

Map 9: Fuller's scheme of 4 August 1917 to advance towards Cambrai. The first echelon of tanks (D) targets artillery, the second (F) attacks infantry, the third (G) is in reserve, to mop up. Other tanks protect and expand the flanks (C, E). Cambrai is 5 miles (8 km) by road from Marcoing. The straight-line distance from the start line (A-B) to Marcoing is about 4 miles (6.4 km) (Fuller 1920).

Kiggell walked in, to insist that the BEF must focus on Passchendaele. The current offensive's retention of all three tank brigades prevented an attack at Cambrai on the date Byng had proposed (20 September), and for about a month after the last tanks were released (9 October). For now nobody knew if it would be executed at all (see Chapter 9), or whether it would be a raid or an offensive, or something in between.

Tank Raids I

Although the Tank Corps would lack the resources for a decisive offensive until 1918, GHQ still wanted frequent indecisive offensives in 1917, in hope that they would eventually break enemy morale. Elles suggested that "raids" would be more efficient, and better for Allied morale. Fuller liked the term because it helps the arguments for surprise and against preliminary bombardment.

On 8 August, Fuller developed a paper, entitled "Tank Raids," although it specifies all arms (see Table 5). Most operations of the Great War involved no tanks, so the use of "tank" as an adjective was meant to highlight the arm's inclusion, not the other arms' exclusion. Even the word "tank" implied other arms. By then, "tank" was used to mean fighting tanks and all variants, including carriers for artillery, infantry, and engineers. Only in the 1920s was "tank" categorically reduced to an AFV with all-round lethality, as I defined it in the introduction. We should not use later understanding of the word to interpret Fuller's "tank raids" as all-tank raids. Thence, we should not confuse them with the all-tank raids that Basil Liddell Hart proposed by 1929, and for which Percy Hobart over-optimized the 1st Tank Brigade in the 1930s (Newsome 2024).

By "raid," Fuller meant a "spoiling attack," not a hit-and-run raid (what Liddell Hart called an "in and out" approach). Fuller targeted combatants, not the socio-economic targets that Fuller briefly entertained in 1923, and which Liddell Hart took up by 1925. In 1917, Fuller summed up each raid as "advance, hit, and retire." Fuller wanted to attrit "personnel and guns," to "demoralize and disorganize" survivors, and to force the enemy to distribute resources that otherwise could be used in offensives or counter-offensives. These intents would be achieved best if an occasional raid were followed by an offensive. He wanted five or six such raids, each in a new surprise area, before a decisive offensive in Spring 1918.

Terrain

Fuller wanted raids to be launched on dry, undamaged terrain. He still focused on the area between Cambrai and St. Quentin (see Map 23), although his tank raid would be smaller in scope than the surprise offensive he had specified in June. He specified the raid with a front of 8,000 yards (7,315 m; 4.5 miles), and an objective line 4,000 yards (3,658 m) deep (to keep within range of friendly field guns).

Like his proposed surprise offensive, Fuller's proposed tank raid should be launched into an area whose exits are constrained and easily interdicted. He was concerned mostly to stop counter-attackers arriving, although he also wished to prevent the defenders from escaping. Thus, he specified an area bound by canals, whose bridges could be interdicted by artillery and aircraft during the assault. The area between Cambrai and St. Quentin is bound by canals and canalized rivers.

Concentration

Fuller specified a combined-arms divisional group, equivalent in scale and balance to what would be later termed, inaccurately, an "armoured division." He specified: all three tank brigades, with all six ready tank battalions (216 tanks); at least as many brigades of pedestrians (detached, without horses, from a division or two divisions of cavalry); four companies of machine-guns; one company of Royal Engineers; twenty 60-pounder gun carriers; twenty 6-inch howitzer carriers; and ground-attack aircraft.

With 216 tanks allocated, one tank would be available per 37 yards (34 m) of front. Two cavalry divisions could detach 88 field guns, ignoring any other artillery that might be committed from other echelons, i.e., one piece per 91 yards (83 m).

A combined-arms divisional group was never formed during the Great War, but the requirement was correct. The British Army experimented with such a force in

Attacking echelon or wave	Field artillery	Heavy artillery	Machine-guns	Tanks	Royal Engineers, riding in tanks	Dismounted cavalry	Aircraft
First	To throw smoke in advance of the attackers	To counter enemy artillery; to bombard enemy crossings of the canals	To bombard the flanks	To attack enemy guns	To attack enemy guns	-	To attack enemy guns and enemy communications to the rear
Second	-			To crush enemy wire and to attack enemy trenches	To cut wire and to throw grenades into dugouts	To attack enemy trenches	-
Third	-			To attack flanking positions and to mop-up enemy trenches		To attack flanking positions and to mop-up enemy trenches	Intercept counter-attackers

Table 5: Force structure and objectives for "Tank Raids," 8 August 1917 (1936: 172-173).

the 1920s, although it would not form permanent equivalent divisions until 1939. In between times, Liddell Hart specified a single brigade of light tanks, which makes a useful contrast. The 1st Tank Brigade held about as many tanks as Fuller specified in 1917, but they are less lethal and survivable, albeit faster. Liddell Hart specified two-man light tanks, each armed with a machine-gun, in order to maximize speed. He imagined that they would be so fast, small, and easily distributed that not even enemy aircraft could interdict their infiltration and exfiltration of the enemy rear. Liddell Hart expected them to be distributed across as broad front as possible. In 1934, the 1st Tank Brigade practised an infiltration on a front of 9 miles (14.5 km), with about 200 tanks, i.e., one tank every 79 yards. Its ambitions grew longer.

Fuller could not imagine in 1917 that all-tank raids would define the British Army's one and only tank brigade of the 1930s. If a tank raid had been launched in the Great War, as Fuller had specified it, the precedent should have prevented the 1st Tank Brigade's over-optimization for Liddell Hart's all-tank raids.

Surprise

For raids, as for offensives, Fuller eschewed a preliminary bombardment, in hope the Germans would not see the raid coming. Upon assault, the field guns would throw smoke in front of the first wave.

Combined Arms

Artillery

The only role for field guns is to throw smoke. Given the speed and depth of the intended assault, the assaulters would soon move out of range of the field guns anyway. Medium machine-guns would bombard the flanks during the assaults.

The 40 mechanized heavy weapons would counter artillery and interdict the bridges by which enemies could escape, but these roles would be brief. Tanks of the first wave would target enemy artillery by direct fire, at which point mechanized heavy artillery could move forward to hit targets deeper in the enemy's rear.

Aircraft

Coincident with the first wave, aircraft would fly forward "to attack enemy guns and enemy communications to the rear." They would continue to do so, through the next two waves, and to interdict any counter-attackers.

Tanks and Infantry

Tanks are allocated to every wave. Infantry are missing from the first wave, although engineers are riding in tanks or variants.

The effective pedestrian infantry (dismounted cavalry) join the second wave, to capture the enemy trenches. Other dismounted cavalry join the third wave, to capture prisoners and to engage the flanking positions.

Tanks and Engineers

Engineers would ride some of the tanks in the first wave, ready to dismount in order to demolish enemy artillery. Engineers ride the second and third waves too, to cut wire that the tanks have crushed, and to bomb enemy bunkers.

Speed

Fuller wanted the raiders to concentrate rapidly and stealthily, to penetrate 4,000 yards (3,658 m) within one assault wave, and to be home within hours. He was utilizing current heavy tanks, with a speed of 4 mph, sufficient to penetrate 4,000 yards in 34 minutes (although he does not specify any time).

Back in November 1916, Martel had prospected light tanks with speeds up to 30 mph, which could have made the 4,000 yards in 4.5 minutes, although he had not required them for raiding. In the 1920s, Martel and Liddell Hart cooperated to market tankettes as replacements for all other AFVs. They promised that tankettes could swarm any defensive position quicker than the defenders could defend themselves, at a cross-country speed of 20 mph (although in fact tankettes are too small and under-powered to traverse a battlefield at this speed).

By the 1930s, Liddell Hart settled on current light tanks, at 30 mph, although they are not much larger and are more prone to pitching (due to increased height), which discourages speed over uneven ground. Liddell Hart never admitted the nuance. He imagined that light tanks are fast enough to avoid defenders, despite days of infiltration, days of raiding in the enemy's rear, and days of exfiltration (Newsome 2024: Chapters 5-6).

Sustainment

Fuller's raiders are well sustained, with an average of 72 tanks in each wave, a total of three waves, to a depth of only 4,000 yards. Given the short duration and depth, no supply tanks are needed, and the field guns do not need to advance.

Again, a comparison with Liddell Hart's all-tank raids is informative. Liddell Hart eschewed supporting arms, and campaigned for fewer and fewer service and support assets, lest their trucks slow down the tanks. Eventually, Liddel Hart thought that light tanks could carry or capture all the supplies and consumables they would need for the duration, even though the duration extended to many days in the enemy's rear, for hundreds of miles a day.

Exploitation

Fuller's first paper on "tank raids" does not specify any exploitation force or exploitation phase, although it does aim to exploit captured assets. Engineers would demolish captured fortifications. The tanks would drag any captured artillery. The dismounted cavalry would drive any prisoners. No pursuit is specified, although enemies in flight could be caught by artillery and aircraft fire on the bridges.

Fuller wanted the attackers to repair to friendly lines, with their booty, before dark. They would retain no more territory than could be consolidated by the frontline infantry. The raiders would retire to the rear to recover, ready to deploy to another part of the front – wherever the enemy would not expect them.

No such day raid was launched in the Great War (although a night raid was launched in 1918: see Chapter 11). The resources were instead earmarked for a surprise attack-cum-raid at Cambrai, which became a full offensive, including an attempt at a breakthrough, the most successful attempt to date, and one that the British tank arm continues to celebrate each year as its defining battle honour.

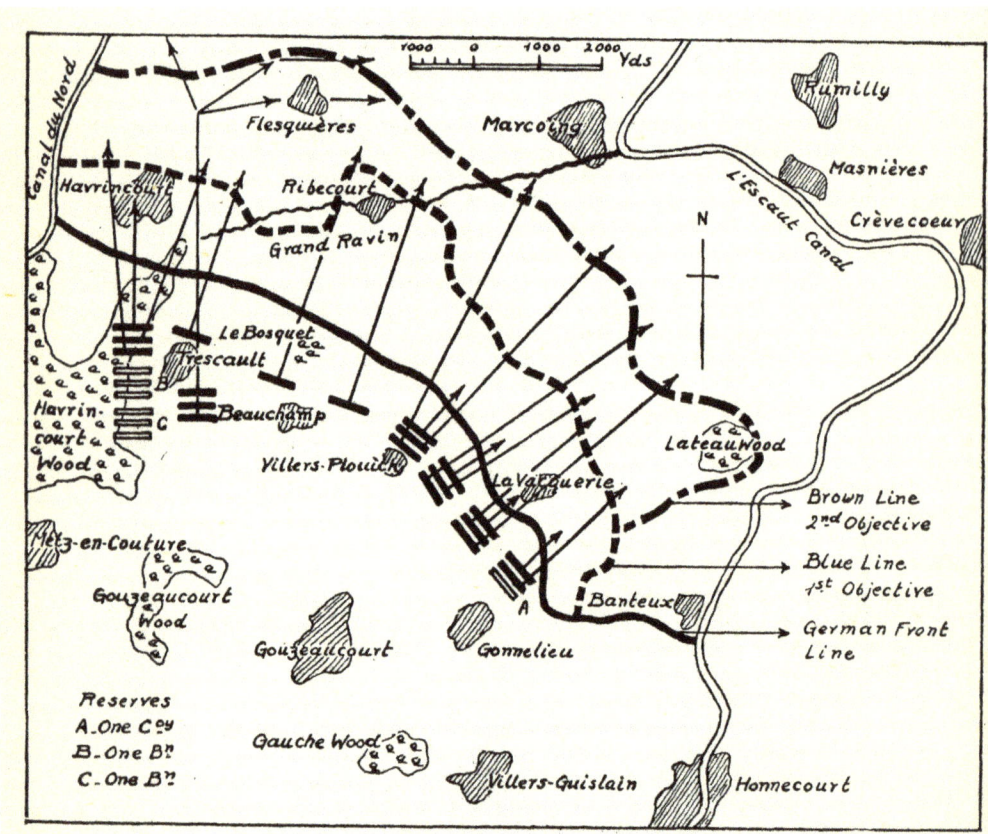

Map 10: The scheme of 29 October 1917 for attacking towards Cambrai (Fuller 1920). The St. Quentin Canal is mislabelled here as the L'Escaut Canal, which does not begin until Cambrai.

9

Cambrai, November 1917

On 8 August 1917, Fuller estimated the capacity to carry out five or six "tank raids" over the next six months, before a decisive offensive in Spring 1918.

However, the offensive at Passchendaele absorbed almost all capacity, from July until October, so the next opportunity for a raid came in November, and this was developed into an offensive – the most successful combined-arms offensive to date.

Terrain

Fuller's paper of 8 August identifies largely dry, undamaged, rolling terrain in the area between two parallel canals, running north-eastwards: Canal du Nord on the left of the British front; Canal de St. Quentin on the right, which connects with the Canal de l'Escaut in Cambrai. Fuller postulated a raid between these canals, followed by an offensive (see Maps 10 and 23).

The Canal de l'Escaut partially interdicted German reserves from reaching the lines. Nearly 6 miles (9.5 km) north of central Cambrai, the Sensee River presents a longer and wider line of interdiction. Fuller wanted the offensive to reach the river. The area contained by the canals and river was termed the "Quadrilateral."

The average distance between the canals was calculated at the time as 10,000 yards (9,144 m). The Germans were using the St. Quentin Canal as a defensive line, but it lay between their reserves and their garrisons of Ribecourt, Crèvecoeur, and Banteux. The area in between is level and open, except for a few villages and woods, and two ridges that run about north-west to south-east, i.e., across the line of advance. The Germans hid forces, particularly artillery, on the reverse slopes. The deadliest ridge for tanks would prove to lay between Flesquières and Havrincourt. The other is further back, known usually as Bourlon Hill, on which is Bourlon Wood (see the panoramas, overleaf). This overlooks the highway running north-west from Cambrai to Arras.

> The ground to be fought over consisted chiefly in open, rolling downland, very lightly shelled, and consequently most suitable to tank movement. The main tactical features were the two canals which practically prohibited the formation of tank offensive flanks and so strategically were a distinct disadvantage to what was meant to be a decisive battle. Between these two canals were two important features: the Flesquières-Havincourt ridge and Bourlon Hill. A third very important feature, known as the Rumilly-Seranvillers ridge, ran parallel to and north of the St. Quentin canal between Crèvecoeur and Marcoing; without the occupation of this ridge a direct attack from the south on Bourlon Hill could only take place under the greatest disadvantage.
>
> The German defences consisted of three main lines of resistance and an outpost line: these lines were the Hindenburg Line, the Hindenburg

These panoramas are of the ridges as seen from the left (western) end of the start line. The originals were drawn by the Tank Corps intelligence staff. Copies were distributed to all units (RACTM Hotblack Box 2).

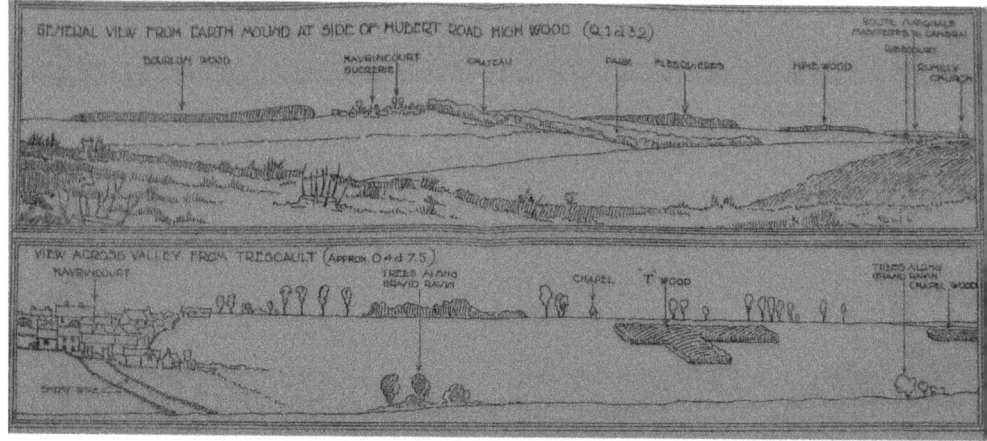

Support Line, and the Beaurevoir-Masnières-Bourlon line, the last being very incomplete. The trenches for the most part were sited on the reverse slopes of the main ridges, and consequently direct artillery observation on them from the British area was impossible. They were protected by immensely thick bands and fields of wire arranged in salient so as to render their destruction most difficult. To have cut these bands by artillery fire would have required several weeks bombardment and scores of thousands of tons of ammunition (Fuller 1920: 144-145).

In order to bypass "bull-headed" Gough, whose 5th Army fronted on this good terrain, Fuller sent copies of the paper to the three key members of the Tank Board: Churchill (recently appointed Minister of Munitions); William Furse (MGO, which was an Army appointment, but then accommodated in the Ministry of Munitions), and Albert Stern (chief of the Ministry's Mechanical Warfare Supply Department).* A copy reached the Prime Minister (David Lloyd George, since December 1916).

Yet time dragged on, and the summer was running out. On 27 August, Fuller lunched with the BCGS (Frank Lyon) of XIX Corps, which partly fronted on the area Fuller had in mind. Lyon agreed that tanks were being wasted in Flanders, and asked whether Fuller had considered "an independent show." Fuller explained his idea for "Tank Raids." Lyon suggested a surprise attack to capture St. Quentin, 23 miles (36 km) to the south of Cambrai. This objective seemed to have been ruled out by GHQ on 4 August, because St. Quentin was on the boundary with a French army. Still, on 28 August, Fuller talked it over with Elles, who went to talk to Byng at 3rd Army HQ, who happened to be scheduled to visit 5th Army HQ on the morrow. Since 3rd Army fronted on to Cambrai, near a boundary with 5th Army, Byng's enthusiasm for diversionary attacks around Cambrai might persuade 5th Army to attack to its right. On 30 August, Elles returned to tell Fuller that he was hopeful about a raid, if aimed somewhere other than St. Quentin. On 2 September,

---

* This became the Mechanical Warfare (Overseas and Allied) Department on 29 October.

Elles returned from 3rd Army HQ to confirm that GHQ had ruled out St. Quentin.

Fuller re-focused on the area before Cambrai. Fuller proposed a larger raid than he had proposed on 8 August. Then he had proposed a start at dusk, a duration of 12 hours at most, and an effective divisional group. Now he scheduled a start at dawn, a duration of 24 hours, and up to three divisions. Still, as before, he did not propose to seize ground, rather to damage combatants and to withdraw with prisoners and booty (Fuller 1920: 138-139).

On 5 September, Byng brought the idea to GHQ. GHQ was receptive to a surprise raid, since it wanted to take advantage of a separate proposal, dating from August, to pre-register targets "silently." (Rather than tip off the enemy by bracketing the target with shells, in order to clarify the range and bearing, silent registration uses theodolites and sound-collectors to triangulate enemy firing.) On 7 September, Elles wrote to GHQ to request the withdrawal of five battalions of tanks, for an offensive or raid, from either the 1st Army or the 3rd Army fronts. GHQ authorized the withdrawal of four battalions, for an operation around Lens, on 1st Army's front. Tanks completed their last attack on the Passchendaele front on 9 October. On 15 October, Elles indicated to Fuller that the Tank Corps was being considered for an operation on 3rd Army's front. On 19 October, Elles informed Fuller that an operation was planned for 20 November, south of Cambrai. Elles confirmed the area on 20 October (Fuller 1920: 140; 1936: 179).

On 21 October, Elles and Fuller, without staff tabs and cap bands, visited the area allotted for the Tank Corps' railhead. The next day, they went forward:

> I remember that visit well. We motored to Gouzeaucourt, a large ruined village, and there told the driver to go back and wait for us at Metz-en-Couture. Then we walked to Villers-Guislain, then to Gonnelieu and through Gouzeaucourt Wood back to our car. It was a wonderful sight from a tank point of view, especially after Ypres; the ground was perfect "going," and I, perhaps a little elated, stepped out faster than usual. As the twilight began to close on us we were striding through Gouzeaucourt Wood, I a length or two ahead, and I remember so well Elles calling out: "Boney, for God's sake stop walking!" (Fuller 1936: 179).

GHQ waited until 24 October before authorizing. Elles summoned a conference of brigade commanders for the next day. Now they had less than 27 days to prepare, 82 days after Fuller had first proposed Cambrai, 136 days since he had proposed St. Quentin. Fuller finished his updated proposal on 29 October (see Map 10). Fuller aimed to advance through all the German defensive lines, which had deepened considerably since 1916, to a depth of 10,000 yards (9,144 m). A full 1,000 yards (914 m) separated the two most forward trenches of the respective sides.

The ground received little rain during the ten days before assault. The journalist Gibbs (1919: 30) viewed the battlefield about an hour after assault. "The country in our lines and the enemy's was rolling and green, unpitted by those great craters which make the Flemish battlefields." Elles recalled that "up to the first Cambrai battle [we had been forced] 'to chip in when we could' in conditions entirely unfavourable." Major Clough Williams-Ellis (1920: viii, 23), the new intelligence officer (after Hotblack was wounded), agreed: "It was, therefore, not till the First Battle of Cambrai, when we did adopt other tactics, that tanks came by their own."

Concentration

Fuller's paper of 3 August requires four infantry divisions (two British, two French) and two tank brigades, with five battalions, to assault, and three cavalry divisions "to exploit success or be used dismounted." His doctrine for raids (8 August) requires an effective combined-arms divisions, with six tank battalions, the dismounts from up to two cavalry divisions, mechanized engineers, and mechanized artillery. On 2 September, he expanded the raid to three infantry divisions, in expectation of nine tank battalions. (The extra battalions were filling with equipment in France, after enshipping from England.) On 25 October, 3rd Army HQ issued an operational plan for two corps, six infantry divisions, nine tank units, and 1,000 artillery pieces in the assault (see Table 6). The 3rd Army correctly estimated two infantry divisions and 34 artillery pieces in the enemy front opposite (Fuller 1920: 144; Fuller, 1936: 211; Neiberg 2005: 276). Tank Corps HQ conferred with the brigade commanders that evening.

> [T]he operation was in no sense a raid, but instead a decisive battle. When I realized this I was aghast, because, on August 4, I had selected this area of attack on account of it being advantageous to a raiding operation, and disadvantageous to one of decisive intention. Further, from where were our reserves to come? (Fuller 1936: 182-183).

The 3rd Army's orders of 2 November allocate 324 fighting tanks and 36 wire-grappling tanks. The Tank Corps assembled 376* fighting tanks, 98 tracked variants (a total of 474 tracked vehicles), 690 officers, and 3,500 other ranks. (The whole Tank Corps in France held only 8,840 men, all ranks, on 20 November.)

Each of three tank brigades held three battalions. The 2nd Brigade held 124 fighting tanks, while the 1st and 3rd each held 126. All but one battalion held 36 fighting tanks across the three companies, 6 spare fighting tanks, one wireless radio tank, two supply tanks, and three or four wire-grappling tanks. The H Battalion, which had most recently arrived, held 40 instead of 42 fighting tanks.

The offensive front was 10 miles (16,093 m) long. A tank was available for every 47 yards (43 m) of front. Fuller's training note of 27 October specifies "one tank to every 100 to 200 yards of front," although he expects formation commanders to adjust distributions by objectives. Either way, the Tank Corps was concentrated at better than doctrinal specification, for the first time (see Table 7).

The 3rd Army allocated 1,003 artillery pieces, i.e., one artillery piece for every 18 yards.

---

* Fuller once reported 432 tanks "used" at Cambrai, which is perhaps the total committed through the many days of battle, perhaps including tanks that were recycled into action ("Tanks as Time and Man[-]Savers," 12 December 1917: 4, RACTM E1980.18). Fuller's (1920: 144-147, 153; 1936: 185-187) first history gives a total of 378 fighting tanks, plus a list of unit allocations that sum to 378, but the total and list were corrected to 376 tanks in his memoirs. Liddell Hart (1959: I, 134) reported 378. In both 1920 and 1936, Fuller reported 98 converted tank variants; adding these in 1920 had got him to 476 vehicles; in 1936, adding them got him to 474. Of these, 127 were repaired or overhauled by Tank Corps Central Workshops after final withdrawal from the Passchendaele operation on 10 October.

Corps	III Corps				IV Corps		Cavalry Corps
Divisions	6th	29th	12th	20th	51st	62nd	1st, 2nd, 3rd Cavalry
Tank Brigade	2nd				3rd		1st	-
Tank battalion	B, H	A (one company only)	C, F	A (less a company), I	D, E (less a company)	G, E (one company only)	
1st Phase missions	Establish defensive positions on the right flank along the ridge Gonnelieu-Bonavis-Crèvecoeur; Capture the crossings over the Canal de l'Escaut at Masnières and Marcoing, and (to the east) the line Masnières-Beaurevoir				Occupy the ridge Flesquières to Havrincourt		-
2nd Phase (Z+150 minutes) missions	-				Seize Bourlon Wood and Hill		Pass cavalry through the gap to isolate Cambrai, and to seize the crossings over the River Sensée
3rd Phase missions	Advance the right flank northwards				-		Clear Cambrai and up to the line Valenciennes-Douai, in order to block the escape of German troops Havrincourt and the River Sensée

Table 6: The 3rd Army's plan, by formations, objectives, and phases, as of 28 October, before changes in November (Fuller 1936: 182-185).

Corps	Division	Infantry brigade	Tank brigade	Tank battalion	Tanks (plus mechanical reserves)	Assembly area	Objective	Exploit towards
III[1]	12th	35th	3rd	C	24 (4)	Villers Guislain and Gouzeaucourt	Blue	Crèvecoeur
		37th			12 (2)		Brown	
		36th		F	24 (4)		Blue	Masnières
					12 (2)		Brown	
	20th	61st		I	18 (3)		Vacquerie	Crèvecoeur
					12 (2)		Blue	
		62nd			6 (1)		Brown	
		60th		A	18 (3)		Blue	Canal, Masnières to Marcoing
					6 (1)		Brown	
	29th	-			12 (2)		Rumilly to Nine Wood	
	6th	16th	2nd	B	24 (4)	Dessart wood	Blue	Marcoing
					12 (2)		Brown	
		71st		H	24 (2)[2]		Blue	Nine wood
					12 (2)		Brown	
IV	51st	152nd	1st	D	42	Havrincourt wood	Blue	Fontaine
		153rd		E	28		Flesquières	Bourlon wood, Bapaume-Cambria road
	62nd	186th			14		Brown	
		185th		G	42		Havrincourt	Bourlon, Graincourt
TOTAL	6	12	3	9	376			

Table 7: final force structure for 20 November (Fuller 1920: 146; 1936: 186).

[1] Fuller's book of 1920 misreported IV Corps as the main corps, but corrected this in his memoirs.
[2] In 1920, Fuller reported 4 tanks in reserve, but his memoirs of 1936 report 2 tanks.

Surprise

Cambrai achieved more surprise than any prior operation involving tanks, but its surprise was not complete. Surprise was greater in time than space, greatest in force structure and force employment. The subsections below examine the choices by preliminary bombardment, operational security, disinformation, and timing.

Bombardment

In the interests of primarily surprise, and secondarily to avoid damaging the ground, the 3rd Army gave up a preliminary bombardment.

Operational Security

Authorized to surprise in both time and space, Fuller led an unprecedented scheme of operational security. He forbade discussion of the operation over the phone or below brigade staff. All assembly was achieved at night. Before dawn, tank tracks were harrowed, wheel tracks rolled. He chose assembly areas in woods. Tanks were hidden under covers, camouflaged as extensions to houses. Guns were hidden inside haystacks. Ammunition was stacked in the lee of hedgerows. The personnel and equipment were hidden under camouflage netting, and required to remove Tank Corps badges and buttons if moving during daylight.

Personnel of all arms were forbidden from activity around 0900 hours, when a German reconnaissance aeroplane flew over the forward area.

Disinformation

Fuller used the Austro-Hungarian offensive at Caporetto in Italy, which had opened on 24 October, as the foundation for a cover story: that the Tank Corps was preparing to deploy to Italy. Brigade commanders and staff were encouraged to spread the rumour. At 2nd Tank Brigade HQ, Major Foot left a copy of Italian grammar on his desk during the day, and sent a request to battalion commanders for a list of personnel who spoke Italian (Foot 1934: 190-192; Fuller 1936: 181, 183).*

Timing

On 11 November, Kiggell (BEF CGS) confirmed in writing some points that Haig had told Byng the day before. The first paragraph states: "The operation is designed to take advantage of the existing favourable local situation. Surprise and rapidity of action are therefore of the utmost importance."

The 3rd Army HQ issued its orders to the field corps and the Tank Corps early on 13 November, without specifying the start date or time.

On the night of 17-18 November, the Germans raided British trenches near Havrincourt Wood. Some prisoners told of tanks in the wood, but the news was not distributed to the German frontline until just after the assault began.

The tanks and infantry rehearsed their approach march on the night of 18-19 November. The tanks started their movements from the assembly areas to the start lines in the evening of 19 November, at a speed limit of 0.5 mph, obscured by mist and German artillery fire. For most of them, the journey measured less than 2 miles. The move was complete about 2100 hours. The Germans opened fire around midnight, sent up alarm rockets at 0500, and continued to fire occasionally until 0600. The tanks restarted engines at 0605, ready to advance at 0620. The intelligence staff received no evidence that the enemy observed the assembly or approach (Fuller 1920: 147; Fuller 1931: 57; Fuller 1932d: 143; Foot 1934: 194; Hotblack, "The Battle of Cambrai," circa December 1934, RACTM Hotblack Box 2)..

---

* Haig's dispatch of March 1918 claims that the offensive at Cambrai was meant to distract the Germans and Austro-Hungarians from their offensive in Italy of 24 October. When Fuller read this dispatch, he complained to his diary of "a fine invention" (6 March 1918).

The next day, Gibbs (1919: 27-28) reported the "best-kept secret of the war... although during the last 24 hours certain uneasy suspicious seem to have been aroused among troops immediately in front of the attack...It was probable that night sentries had heard the movement of traffic on these quiet, silent nights – the clatter of gunwheels over rough roads, the rumble of transport behind the lines."

Combined Arms

Artillery

In the absence of a preliminary bombardment, no pre-registration of targets by fire was allowed. Instead, all targets were pre-registered silently.

During the assault, Fuller wished for artillery to drop smoke on enemy observation posts, and to fire high-explosive on enemy artillery, effectively preventing any enemy artillery from bombarding the assaulters before consolidation of the objectives. He wished for shrapnel to fall just beyond each objective line – to stop defenders from fleeing, and reinforcements from arriving. Medium machine-guns should bombard the objective itself, to suppress enemy infantry.

The 3rd Army HQ detailed Fuller's wishes. At 0610 hours, the tanks started to advance. At 0620 hours (Z-hour), the field guns* started to fire smoke and high-explosive shells up to 300 yards ahead and to the sides; medium machine-guns bombarded 300 yards further ahead; and 6-inch howitzers fired high-explosive yet another 300 yards further ahead. The field and medium guns fired mostly shrapnel on the defensive lines, although some divisions chose to fire high-explosive. Heavy artillery fired mostly high explosive on enemy batteries,** observation posts, rest billets, and command and control centres.

The barrage jumped three times, until landing on the first objective, at Z+52 minutes, where it lingered for 50 minutes. From Z+102, it made three more jumps, until it arrived on the second objective at Z+188, where it lingered for 27 minutes.

The bombardment had no effect on the bunkers, which British intelligence knew as up to 14 m (45 feet) deep, or the concrete fortifications used to protect artillery guns in anti-tank role (two of the latter were expected per divisional area).

The Germans had narrowed their trenches to reduce exposure to plunging fire, so infantry could stand ready in trenches, rather than be surprised in bunkers.

Smoke was fired to obscure the subsequent attack on Fontaine-Notre-Dame, on 23 November, although wind reduced its effectiveness (Fuller 1920: 144, 147; 1936: 183, 202; (Major A.G. Barry, "Precis No. 5," 28 December 1934, Cambrai Battlefield Tour 1935, RACTM Hotblack Box 2).

Aircraft

In total, about 400 aircraft supported the attack.

In Fuller's doctrine, aircraft are supposed to attack enemy batteries and transport, beyond the range of friendly artillery, and to suppress enemy aircraft at their

---

* Of the 1,003 artillery pieces, 462 were 18-pounder guns. Each received 360 high-explosive, 360 shrapnel, and 180 smoke rounds.
** The 70 60-pounder guns fired 16,000 rounds of tear gas on enemy batteries, while 8-inch howitzers fired for 15-minutes on priority targets.

airfields. The 3rd Army allocated seven squadrons of single-seater scout planes to these targets. One squadron of two-seater reconnaissance planes would concentrate on the roads and railways around Cambrai. The 1st Army was ordered to provide part of a scout squadron on the day of assault. GHQ detached its own reconnaissance squadron.

From the time of assault, a squadron of two-seater bombers was allocated to bomb enemy airfields, railway junctions at Douai, Denain, Busigny, Le Cateau, and Valenciennes, and enemy headquarters at Caudry and Escadoeuvres. At some point, it was supposed to switch to enemy balloons, artillery, and transport beyond the range of the artillery bombardment. This bombing failed to interfere with the arrival by railway of 13 infantry divisions, in 730 trains, by 29 November ("Air Instructions," and "The Battle of Cambrai," circa December 1934, RACTM Hotblack Box 2; Fuller 1936: 184).

Tanks and Infantry

On 23 August, Fuller turned the lessons from Passchendaele into a doctrinal memorandum entitled "Minor Tank and Infantry Operations Against Strong Points." The tanks lead the infantry, as before. Fuller's main change is to suggest that infantry "scouts" should keep up with the tanks, effectively as liaisons. The context is the terrain: "The route the tank will take is firstly governed by the condition of the ground…Generally speaking, shelled ground is eminently suited for scouting and stalking." The rest of the infantry hang back. As the rifle section moves forward, the Lewis gun stays, ready to give covering fire.* The infantry are effectively using both the tank and "broken ground" for cover (mostly the broken ground). "Their object is to make use of ground for movement."

Fuller reduces their exposure further by starting the sections 50 to 70 yards (46 to 64 m) apart. Implicitly, his allowance for each tank and infantry section to start apart and to choose its own route reduces control and coordination. Fuller suggests that each rifle section should move in "single file" so that individual members are not lost. "The one thing the infantry must avoid is to move forward in lines or waves of skirmishers," at least until they start firing on the move. The narrow gaps through enemy wire (made by tanks, after a little help from the creeping barrage) also encourage the infantry into narrow columns behind the tanks.

Conventional "bounding" or "fire-and-movement" tactics are implied. They are explicit for the Lewis guns, which "should, when possible, work in pairs on the 'Relay System'." In prior doctrine, Fuller had emphasized envelopment. He still expects tanks "to cut off the line of retreat" from "a concrete shelter," for instance, but allows tanks to assault directly "a machine-gun emplacement." He implies that tank crews should not close with or drive over the emplacement: such a manoeuvre would certainly neutralize the position, but increase the chance of the tank ditching or being attacked with grenades.

He specifies three purposes for the tank:
1. To suppress enemy fire;
2. To distract the enemy from the attacking infantry;
3. To suppress any enemy in cover, until infantry could capture.

---

* He does not mention the grenadiers. Perhaps he assumes that the grenadiers are folded into the section. Perhaps he thinks they are best equipped to act as scouts.

The infantry must "kill the enemy" and occupy the objectives.

> Directly the objective is gained, a prearranged party takes charge of the prisoners, the rest move forward, throwing out their scouts as before, and take up positions from which they can open fire against any counter-attack. The attackers are fighters; they have nothing to do with consolidation – this must be left to the local reserves, who dig and wire under cover of the original attackers (in Fuller 1936: 153-154)

The 3rd and 5th Army HQs accepted the doctrine. Fuller sent a copy to GHQ's DCGS (Butler), who passed it to his BGGS for Training (Brigadier Arthur Solly-Flood) – who was reading it when Fuller visited on 29 August.

During planning with 3rd Army, on 27 October, Fuller issued a new training note, to further specify the "drill." The tank section is reduced to three tanks, which advance in triangular formation: one Male advances to the front; two Females (or "Infantry Tanks") follow, as a "main body" (see Map 11).

The duty of the Advanced Tank is to move slightly ahead of the Main Body

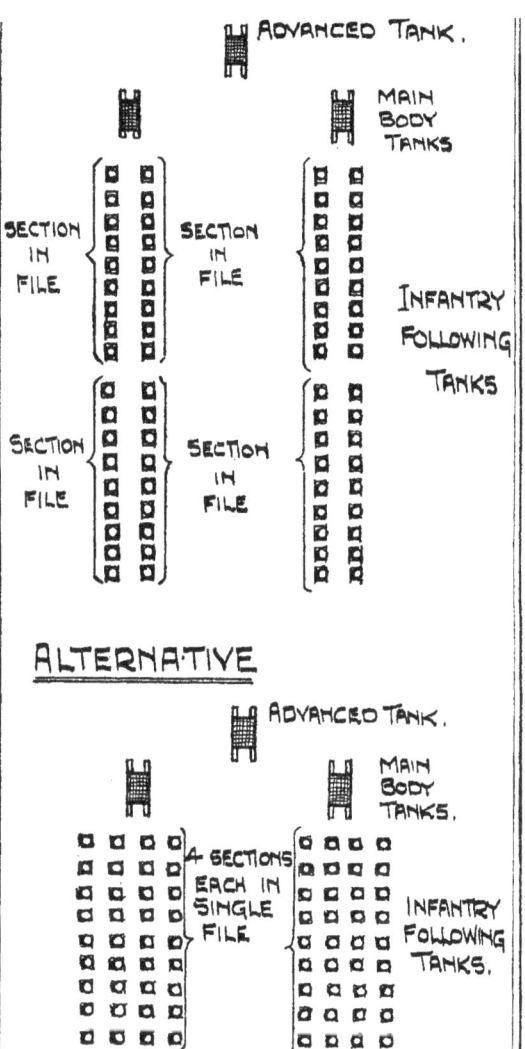

Map 11: Fuller's suggested formations for one section of tanks and two platoons of infantry (The Tank Journal, November 1938: 19).

Tanks in order to keep down the enemy's fire, whilst the Main Body Tanks, followed by the infantry, advance on his wire and trenches. Once this duty is finished the Advanced Tank will come into reserve. The duty of the Main Body Tanks is to place the infantry through the wire and to assist and protect them whilst capturing the area ("Tank and Infantry Operations Without Methodical Artillery Bombardment," S.G. 192, in The Tank Journal, November 1938: 18).

In February, Fuller had prescribed at least two, ideally three, infantry waves or echelons. In the new training note, the first wave ("moppers up," mostly grenadiers) become "trench clearers" or "trench cleaners."

He adds a new second wave, called "trench stops." They have two main tasks. First, they flag the ways through enemy wire. Second, they picket the junctions between the captured defensive line and the communication trenches (which lead to the next defensive line), in order to interdict reinforcements or counter-attackers.

The "trench supports" hold the captured fortifications, as before, and are required to "form an infantry advanced guard on the far side of the trench so as to cover the advance of the next echelon." In other words, they provide fire support for the next assault.

The "next echelon" is either the "trench cleaners" or the first wave of the reserve.

Fuller urges the infantry's self-reliance.

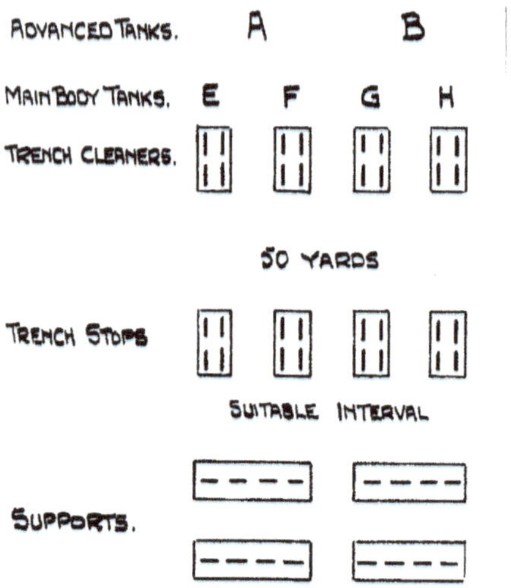

> The section single files must not move in parade orders; they must open out to considerable intervals between files on a staggered frontage, and advance by short bounds. If fired on, each platoon has a Lewis gun of its own to assist it. The infantry have got to realise that their safety and success depend up using their rifles and Lewis guns; that is, fighting with the tanks and not simply in following them. This is what is meant by co-operation, and training will be based upon that principle (in 1936:197).

Map 12: Two sections of tanks lead a battalion of infantry. Each box represents a platoon, each line a section.

Further, Fuller urges the infantry to press on even if all tanks break down.

The 3rd Army's MGGS (Major-General L.R. Vaughan) issued Fuller's training note to all infantry formation and unit HQs, but allowed infantry commanders to choose their own methods. On 1 November, Fuller wrote to all three tank brigade training officers, urging tank personnel to allow time for the infantry to learn at their own pace – otherwise they might lose confidence. On 13 November, the 3rd Army HQ issued orders to the corps: "Tanks will normally operate in sections of 3 tanks," one section per objective. However, this statement allows for lower echelons to choose a different structure. The 51st "Highland" Division, which was assigned to attack Flesquières Ridge, with 70 tanks (19 percent of all tanks assigned), chose its own doctrine, with tragic consequences, as explained below, under "Outcomes."

Tanks and Engineers

For the Tank Corps, the remaining challenges were technical.

> Not only did we know that the whole attack was an experiment for which there was no precedent, but that our tanks could not span the Hindenburg trenches, and therefore could not cross them! Nevertheless, we promised to cross the very largest; we promised to crush paths through the enormous wirefields for the infantry; we promised to remove large sections of those same fields for the cavalry; we promised to haul forward quantities of material to bridge the St. Quentin Canal; we promised to

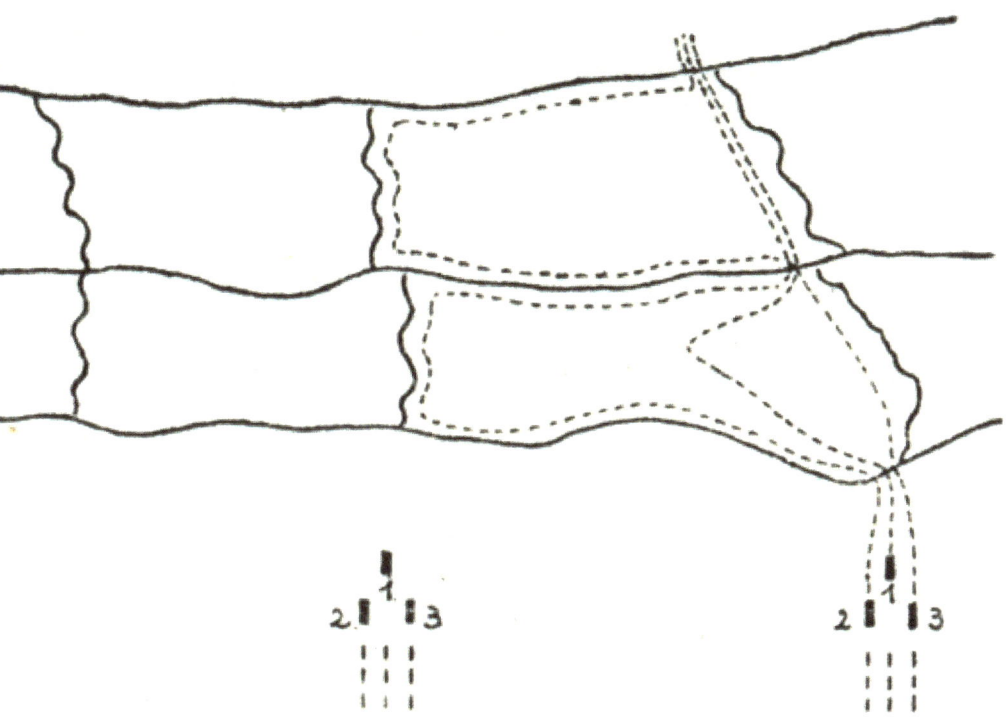

Map 13: Fuller's own drawing of a typical tank attack at Cambrai: The 1st tank drops a fascine into the first trench; the 2nd and 3rd tanks cross the fascine; the 2nd moves left, with infantry following, except the "trench stopping party"; the 3rd tank continues ahead to drop a fascine in the second trench; the 1st and 2nd tanks cross that fascine; the 2nd tank proceeds to drop its fascine into the third trench (Fuller 1932b: 110).

supply ourselves across country with 378 tons of petrol, ammunition, etc., because lorries could not do so; we promised to establish mobile wireless stations, to lay miles of cable, to devise a new tactic and to train the infantry to have confidence in it. In short, every objection and difficulty which GHQ raised, we promised to overcome ("Cambrai to El Alamein," Evening Standard, 20 November 1942: 6).

A total of 98 tanks or gun carriers were converted to specialized variants: 54 supply tanks, two bridging carriers, one signals carrier, nine wireless radio tanks, and 32 wire-grappling tanks. The fighting tanks were adapted to carry fascines.

Fascines

The heavy tanks could cross trenches 10 feet (3 m) wide, but faced anti-tank trenches 12 feet (3.7 m) wide on the Hindenburg Line. The Tank Corps Chief Mechanical Engineer (Lieutenant-Colonel Frank Searle) developed a "fascine" – a bundle of brushwood, 10 feet long, 4.5 feet in diameter, 1.5 tons in weight. This was carried on the front of the tank, secured by chains. The fascine was released by operation of a lever inside the tank. One fascine could half fill the trench, sufficient for a tank to cross. All three fascines from a tank section would fill the trench to the brim. On 24 October, orders went out for 400 tank fascines. Some 400 long tons (406 metric; 448 short) of brushwood was cut in the Forest of Crécy. More than 2,000 fathoms (12,000 feet; 3,658 meters) of chain were acquired from Britain. The brushwood was bound with natural materials into 21,500 portable fascines, of which 75 at a time were chained together to form one 1.5-ton fascine. A total of 286 1.5-ton fascines were produced (Fuller 1920: 129, 140-141; 1936: 180).

Doctrinally, the "Advanced Guard Tank" crushes the wire, before turning left so that its righthand six-pounder gun can fire into the enemy trench. The first "Infantry Tank" would approach the trench, drop its fascine, cross the trench, and turn left, firing into the trench from its rear. The second "Infantry Tank" would cross, and advance on the enemy's support trench, where it would drop its fascine, cross, turn left, and sweep the trench with fire. Once the infantry cross the captured trench, the Advanced Guard would cross the first fascine. Its fascine is a spare, in case one fascine per trench were insufficient (Fuller 1920: 141-142; 1936: 194-196).

Wire-Grapples

In the wake of the second wave, wire-grappling tanks (often mistermed "wire-cutters") were supposed to come forward to clear gaps along the cavalry's routes of advance. They were required at the rate of about one per tank company (12 tanks). The Hindenburg Line featured belts of wire up to 40 yards (37 m) deep (as conventional), but thicker than ever: a broom handle could not be inserted. Tanks flattened the belt to a depth of 3 inches (76 mm), to a width as wide as the tank, sufficient for infantrymen to pick their way through, but not for cavalry to charge through. Specialized tanks were needed to pull entanglements out of the way with towed grapnels.* The idea had been developed by Swinton's force in Summer 1916, and by the Tank Training Centre, Wool, in Summer 1917, although Fuller credits himself (operations officer) and Searle (chief engineer) for the idea.

> We sent back to England for ships' anchors and anchor chains. We fixed these into 32 tanks, and this is how they worked. Once the wire-sweeping tank entered the wirefield it cast its anchors – two in number – and then by moving forward tore the strands asunder, and when nearly through swung right and rolled the entanglement up as if it were a carpet (Fuller, "Cambrai to El Alamein," Evening Standard, 20 November 1942: 6).

One vehicle could clear a gap 50 to 60 yards** wide within five minutes.

> The first tank passed right through the obstacle, the grapnel catching and breaking all the longitudinal strands in the entanglement, so that a narrow clean cut was made right through the obstacles. The other two tanks now advanced and crossed the obstacle a few yards on either side of this cut. The grapnels gathered up the strands of wire, and just as they reached the far edge of the entanglement the tanks turned outwards and moved parallel to the wire and a few yards away from it. The grapnel behind each of these two tanks now contained all the longitudinal strands which were caught up among the barbs, and as the grapnel was dragged

---

* Each grapnel had four prongs and was almost three feet long.
** Fuller's newspaper article of November 1942 misreports a single tank as clearing a gap "500 to 600 yards wide," although the error is possibly the typesetter's.

in the new direction along the wire these strands rolled over and over like a great cable and every single picket or strand of wire was swept up by this kind of snowball which collected round the grapnel. A hundred yards of the heaviest wire entanglements could be cleared in this way quite easily and in a few minutes, leaving absolutely no trace of wire on the ground. The operation could, of course, be carried out more slowly with two or even one tank if necessary (Martel 1931: 48)

Only one vehicle failed. By 1400 hours, the gaps were complete (Fuller 1920: 165; 1936: 187, 198, 213).

The Tank Corps worried about the Germans placing wire in trenches as antipersonnel barriers, so developed a small bridge carried on the tail of a tank, rated for a gap of 10 feet, but it was never needed (Martel 1931: 123-124).

Speed

The German front was 1,000 yards (914 m) from the start line. This distance would take 8.5 minutes for the tanks to cross at their maximum speed, which was expected on the good going, although their speed was still expected to halve (to 2mph) once they start crossing trenches and firing pits.

The final objective line, 9,000 yards (8,230 m) away, could be reached in another 153 minutes, assuming a speed of 2 mph. Thus, theoretically, the assaulters could advance 10,000 yards (9,144 m) in 161.5 minutes (2 hours 41.5 minutes).

On 20 November, they would have nine hours of full daylight, or less than 11 hours from zero-hour to sunset. The German rearward zone was consolidated by 1100 hours, i.e., about 4.5 hours after zero hour, after a straight-line advance of about 6,000 yards (5,486 m) – a speed of 22 yards per minute or 0.75 mph. The final objective line was mostly consolidated by the end of the day.

Sustainment

The plan fulfilled Fuller's expectations in concentration of tanks, but was too heavy in the assault, too light in the reserves, although supply tanks, signal tanks, and mobile field artillery guns were satisfactory in number.

Reserves

At the start of Fuller's planning, the defenders held two infantry divisions and 34 artillery guns, with four divisions in reserve. He always preached that some force should be reserved, with elements from all arms. On 28 October, the 3rd Army HQ sent word that it had reserved three tank companies. The next day, Elles and Fuller visited 3rd Army's chief of staff (Major-General L.R. Vaughan), who complained that the divisional commanders wanted all tanks in the assault. Fuller emphasized that, given surprise, fewer tanks would be needed in the assault. He suggested the reservation of three tank battalions on the left, one tank company on the right, to surround Cambrai, once the assaulters capture the approaches.

Nevertheless, by 2 November the 3rd Army HQ returned to the assumption that cavalry would break through on the first day, so released the three tank companies back into the assault force. The 3rd Army's orders of the day specify that "each successive echelon of infantry will be accompanied by a fresh echelon of tanks."

At that time, the 3rd Army attached 324 fighting tanks to the field corps. The Tank Corps gathered 376 fighting tanks. Yet 3rd Army reserved none.

A few days before the operation, the French offered to reserve two or three infantry divisions, but Haig refused. BEF GHQ's chief of intelligence (Charteris) assured Haig that the Germans had no reserves in the sector. However, around one week before the attack, Major James Cornwall, a GSO2 for Intelligence, discovered from captured troops and documents that three divisions had just arrived from Russia, in reserve to the same sector. Cornwall showed the documents to Charteris, who replied, "You are mistaken. This is just bluff put up by the Germans to deceive us. I am sure that the units you mention are still on the Russian front; they are not to be shown on our Intelligence map. If the C-in-C were to think that the Germans had reinforced this sector, it might shake his confidence in our success." Cornwall left directly for GHQ's DMO (Davidson) to explain the facts, before declaring that he could no longer serve under Charteris. Davidson told Cornwall to remain in position, but to brief him privately (Marshall-Cornwall 1984: 30).

A reserve of seven divisions is a strong one, in any era. It proved sufficient to prevent Allied exploitation. On 30 November, the Germans launched a counter-offensive with 20 divisions. Charteris' scepticism of any German reserve did not stop GHQ from warning the 3rd Army of German intent to counter-attack on 30 November, and did not stop 3rd Army's staff from expunging from its war diary any record of receipt (Travers 1987: 24-26).

Supply Tanks

As of 12 November, Fuller notified the tank brigades that each brigade's "Rallying Area" should include a "Refilling Point." Each battalion dump was supposed to receive 5,000 gallons (22,730 liters) of petrol, 2,500 pounds (1,134 kg) of grease (for tank tracks and sprockets), and 125,000 rounds of 0.303-inch ammunition.

Once the grapnel tanks opened the gaps in the wire, supply tanks moved up, each sufficient to resupply a company (two tons of supplies internally, five tons on sleds). The 54 supply tanks and 110 sleds offered a capacity of 387 long tons (393 metric; 433 short tons), equivalent to the loads of 21,165 men.

Two supply tanks were dedicated to hauling bridging equipment for the cavalry to get over the canal.

Signals Tanks

Upon assault, each battalion HQ sent forward its radio tank, from the assembly area to whatever cover it could find, where it would park. Runners were supposed to hand over written messages, for despatch to higher formations.

Meanwhile, a variant would lay telephone cable to the village of Marcoing, by 1400 hours.

The surest way for tank crews to communicate with higher echelons remained carrier pigeon. Each tank carried two pigeons: these were issued by, and returned to, the associated infantry division's HQ (Fuller 1920: 144; 1936: 187, 198, 213).

Field Artillery

The field guns were prepared to advance in support of the leading troops, although they did not start as soon as they should have done, due to poor communications. By the second day, most of the assaulters were out of range.

Exploitation

No infantry or tanks were reserved for exploitation. Instead, 3rd Army relied entirely on the mounted Cavalry Corps to surround and capture Cambrai,

In February, Fuller had allowed for horse cavalry to exploit the breach, but not without tanks. In June, when prospecting an offensive by Spring 1918, he required light tanks, armoured cars, and mechanized infantry to cooperate with cavalry in the exploitation. On 3 August, he prospected an immediate offensive, including three cavalry divisions "to exploit success or be used dismounted." On 8 August, he prospected a raid with up to two divisions of dismounted cavalry acting as infantry. By now, the Cavalry Corps held five divisions, after GHQ gave up the two Indian divisions it had reserved. In October, GHQ and the 3rd Army HQ allocated all five cavalry divisions for exploitation (except for detachments to screen III Corps and IV Corps, on the right and left flanks respectively).

On 2 November, 3rd Army allotted 12 tanks to the cavalry corps. Fuller issued the orders on 12 November. The next day, 3rd Army added orders for their use. However, at some point, they were removed. Hotblack resented over-reliance on cavalry, but agreed with the cavalry's separation, if only for want of anything better for exploitation. "Haig's problem was not a choice between horses and armoured fighting vehicles, but between horses and nothing at all for mobile warfare" ("BBC TV programme on tanks," 11 June 1970, RACTM Hotblack Box 1).

On 11 November, Kiggell (BEF CGS) confirmed in writing what Haig had told Byng the day before: cavalry should "be passed forward as soon as possible to seize Cambrai and cover the advance northward and north-eastward of V Corps" (which would be advancing on the Sensee) and to send advance guards across the river.

The 3rd Army decided that the 5th Cavalry Division (formerly the 2nd Indian) should advance from Fins, and join up with the 2nd (coming from Villers-Faucon), towards Belle Etoile, south of Cambrai. The 1st (also coming from Fins) would advance on Bois de Neuf, in cooperation with 51st Infantry Division, so as to isolate Cambrai from Bourlon. Thence, it could attack Bourlon from the north and east. The 3rd Cavalry Division and 4th Cavalry Division (formerly 1st Indian) were to move into Fins, once it had been evacuated by 5th and 1st Cavalry Divisions.

All five cavalry divisions were to be ready to move 150 minutes after the launch of the assault, or upon the infantry's occupation of the line Masnières-Marcoing-Flesquières. On 10 November, Cavalry Corps HQ wrote:

> The order for the forward movement of the cavalry divisions from their forward concentration areas will be issued by Cavalry Corps. This order will be issued as soon as it appears that the situation is favourable and that there is a possibility of a cavalry advance.

The cavalry divisions concentrated on schedule on Grand Ravin, which runs south of Ribecourt and Havrincourt, but there they stayed, awaiting orders from Cavalry Corps HQ, six miles to the rear (Fuller 1936: 190, 210).

Around 1100 hours, Major Stephen Foot of 2nd Tank Brigade and Colonel Edward Bryce of B Battalion climbed the hill west of Marcoing and Premy Chapel.

> [N]o cavalry were in sight. A signal tank was not far off; I sent back a message to Tank Corps Headquarters giving an outline of the situation, so favourable for immediate exploitation. Another hour passed; still no

> sign of any cavalry. The precious moments were slipping by and giving the Germans time to rally in front of Cambrai. I grew desperate. We still had some pigeons; I used three of them to send off a "priority" message to be repeated to corps headquarters and GHQ. It would be dark at five. Unless the cavalry arrived very soon there would be no chance of effecting anything that day (Foot 1934: 196-197).

The 1st Cavalry Division was the most important. It was concentrated at Fins, ready to cooperate with 51st Division in a move via Metz-en-Couture on Ribecourt and thence Bourlon, to the north. Ribecourt had been captured since 0700 hours. It could be reached via less than 7 miles (11 km) of flat, straight, road from Fins. The division received orders at 1100 hours, but its vanguard did not reach Ribecourt until about 1300 hours.

> And what was the cavalry doing? Why, carrying out the regular tactics for advancing by stages into an enemy's country! Troop halted in sunken road behind the village, two scouts sent forward to reconnoitre, one of them returns to report to the officer. No wonder they were late! I was furious with that young cavalry officer (Foot 1934: 197).

Ribecourt is 6 miles (9 km) short of Bourlon, by the most direct road. Only the vanguard ever crossed the canal.

Around 1140 hours, the 5th Cavalry Division received orders to move forward. Two brigades started about 1200 hours, one for Masnieres, one for Marcoing, from where an advanced guard reached the canal at Noyelles. At 1530, the divisional commander decided that too little daylight was left to exploit further. A vanguard of the 1st Cavalry Division linked up there at 1600 hours. By 1800 hours, the cavalry withdrew for the night. A few vanguards lingered without orders, and withdrew after dark, usually with heavy casualties (Fuller 1936: 210).

Outcomes

The most enduring outcome for the Tank Corps was psychological. The 3rd Army had issued its final plan on 18 November. On the morning of 19 November, Elles came into Fuller's office to say, "Everyone has worked so splendidly that I think we ought to issue a Special Order. Will you write one?" Fuller started to write by hand on a sheet of waxed duplicating paper, tore it up, and replied: "No, you write it; you are far better at these things than I am." Elles took Fuller's place, and wrote and signed his sixth Special Order. By the look of the original, Elles wrote it in one go, without correction.

> 1. Tomorrow the Tank Corps will have the chance for which it has been waiting for many months – to operate on good going in the van of the battle.
>
> 2. All that hard work and ingenuity can achieve has been done in the way of preparation.
>
> 3. It remains for unit commanders and for tank crews to complete the work by judgment and pluck in the battle itself.

4.   In the light of past experience I leave the good name of the Corps with great confidence in their hands.

5.   I propose leading the attack of the centre division.

Fuller remonstrated about the last proposition, but Elles persisted. Fuller wrote in his memoirs that the proposition "was to give life and soul to all our preparations – it was spiritually the making of the Tank Corps, and in value it transcended all our work" (Fuller 1936: 201).

Elles left Fuller in operational command, Hardress-Lloyd (3rd Brigade) as his designated successor, Lieutenant-Colonel Edward B. Hankey (7th Battalion) as the successor to command 3rd Brigade, and Baker-Carr (1st Brigade) as senior brigade commander. None of these men would become casualties.

Special order No. 6 was distributed to all tank commanders in starting positions. The least experienced unit was H Battalion, so Major Foot and Lieutenant Cazalet of 2nd Brigade HQ walked with it from Dessart Wood to the start line (in front of Beauchamp and Villers-Plouich). They started at 1700 hours, following white tapes. At a speed limit of 0.5 mph, the journey took four hours.

H Battalion received an additional thrill when they learnt that it was in one of their tanks that General Elles was going to lead the attack. And lead it he did, with his head and shoulders through the manhole in the roof waving the Tank Corps flag. Red, brown, and green were the colours – red for fire, brown for mud, and green for the open country beyond (Foot 1934: 194).

One of the tank commanders was similarly inspired:

> Before Cambrai, the plan of attack was explained to us and rehearsed. It was not just the brilliance of the plan which gave us hope and sublime confidence in its success. There was the General's brief order: "I propose leading the attack of the centre division"…There could be no greater inspiration than the knowledge that the General himself was going to risk his life in the attack

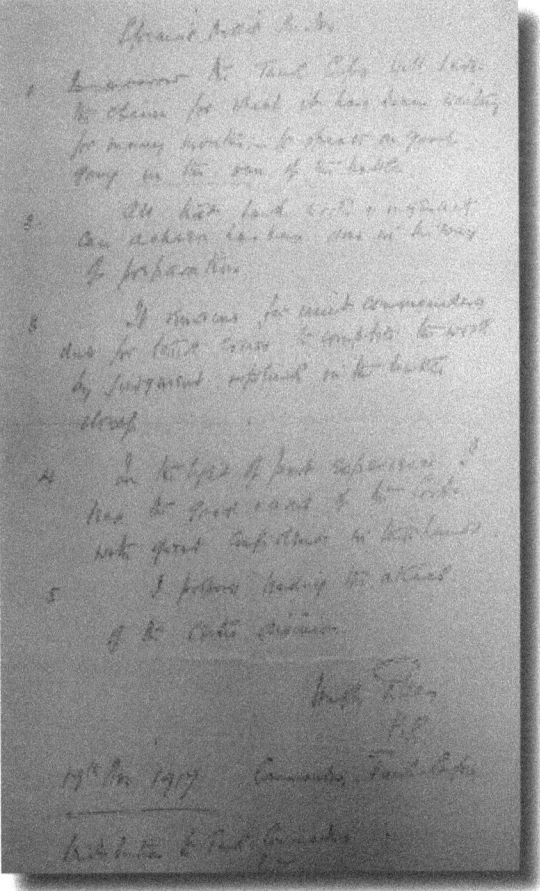

Fuller preserved this duplicate of Elles' Special Order No. 6 (Fuller papers, Box 1).

(D.E.H., "Foreign Doctrines on Tank Employment," The Tank Journal, No. 6, July 1939: 32).

Everywhere except on 51st Division's front, the first objectives were captured within an hour after assault, i.e., by 0720 hours, all forward defensive lines by 0900, and the final line by 1100 (except for Flesquieres). Foot and Cazalet had assembled with H Battalion, but ended up walking behind B Battalion, and the infantrymen who were moving to their second objectives.

> I questioned everybody I met – officers, NCOs, and men. "What did you think of the tanks? Were the gaps in the wire all right? Was the pace too fast or too slow?"
>
> The answers were all the same, "Magnificent," "Couldn't have been better," "Everything just right," "Thumbs up, I do think!"
>
> One infantry company commander told me that he had got to his final objective with only four of his men wounded, and those so lightly that they had refused to leave the ranks. And everywhere there were batches of German prisoners streaming back across the trench system. Victory was in the air; this was something like a battle.
>
> We walked on rapidly towards Marcoing, but before reaching the town we met Colonel Bryce, who was commanding B Battalion. "Come and have lunch," were his first words, and we gratefully accepted the invitation. There on the hillside, right out in the open, Bryce had established his headquarters. Stuck in the ground was the battalion flag, its colour a flaming yellow; and seated [a]round it, with the sun shining overhead, we had our lunch – chicken, pâté de foie gras sandwiches, and champagne, exactly as if we had been at Ascot instead of three miles inside the German lines (Foot 1934: 195-196).

Bryce stuck his flag about 1,200 yards (1,097 m) beyond the German artillery line, about 600 yards (549 m) west of Marcoing. Sixteen of his tanks rallied at the flag, of which 14 tanks (from a company and the Battalion HQ) supported some infantry in the capture of Marcoing at 1130 hours. Days before, the tank officers had planned an attack down to particular firing points. These tanks shot down the German engineers on the bridge before they could complete their electrical firing system. The tanks crossed the bridge and climbed the elevated ground beyond. One tank's right-hand sponson was demolished by a 150-mm (5.9-inch) howitzer shell fired from Lateau Wood, but the tank turned and crushed the howitzer before it could reload. To the left, the company of H Battalion drove the enemy out of Bois de Neuf (Nine Wood), north of Marcoing, before infantry of 51st Division arrived (Fuller 1920: 148).

To the right, the 3rd Company of A Battalion assisted the 29th Division in the capture of all the locks from Masnieres to Marcoing. One section attacked Nine Wood and Noyelles-sur-Escaut. These were then occupied by infantry. In this area, the Fort Garry Horse crossed the canal and exploited towards Rumilly.

With the capture of the Hindenburg rearward area, the heavy tanks were

A bridge over the canal near Marcoing, demolished by the Germans before the "A" Battalion reached it. By the time Fuller saw it, in August 1918, Royal Engineers had pulled aside the broken spans, and constructed a new bridge (Fuller papers).

supposed to rally, except five companies that headed over the Canal de l'Escaut into the defensive line beyond. Furthest right, around midday, nine tanks of the assigned company of F Battalion found cheering civilians and a partially-blown bridge at Masnières. Later, some infantry caught up, and crossed the bridge with fire support from the tanks. Later still, some cavalry crossed. A tank followed, but the bridge collapsed. Thus, tanks could not advance on Rumilly and Seranvillers.

The 51st "Highland" Division had been assigned to attack Flesquières Ridge, with 70 tanks, but chose its own doctrine. Fuller (1936: 198-199) described its commander (Major-General G.M. Harper) as "one of those peculiarly stubborn persons who cannot brook a suggestion or an idea they have not made or conceived." The division chose to structure the tank section with four tanks instead of three. The first tank in each section was designated as the "Wire Crusher." In theory, the other three tanks followed in line, about 75 yards (69 m) behind, the infantry another 200 yards (183 m) behind. In practice, the infantry fell 400 yards (366 m) behind and were pinned by fire. Around the same time, the tanks crested the ridge and came under direct fire from nine enemy artillery batteries (36 105-mm guns, except that a few were probably knocked out by indirect fire). These guns knocked out 27 tanks – a casualty rate of 39 percent.* The infantrymen who reached the gaps in the wire

---

* About 16 German guns (four batteries) were captured in the area. On 21 November, Hotblack observed the tracks of several batteries withdrawn from the firing area, and found German accounts of nine batteries in the line, of which three batteries (one unit) withdrew after dark. Certainly, 16 tanks were knocked out nearby, from three battalions (1933; "The Battle of Cambrai," circa December 1934, RACTM Hotblack Box 2). Haig's official dispatch

The partially-blown steel bridge at Masnières, the Mark V tank that caused its collapse on 20 November, and a wooden bridge constructed by German engineers (RACTM).

were pinned by machine-gun fire from the ruins of Flesquieres. They waited until the morning before the division on the left advanced enough to allow 51st Division to advance out of the valley (Fuller 1936: 209; Fletcher 1994: 79-83; Haworth 1999: 6-7).

Furthest left, a company of G Battalion led 62nd and 36th Divisions into the rear (see Map 14), as far as Graincourt and the Cambrai-Bapaume road, which they crossed in order to reach Anneux and Moeuvres – the deepest penetration of the first day, each of which is 4.2 miles (7,450 yards; 6,812 m) from the opening front, and 9 miles (15,840 yards; 14,484 km) from Fins, in a straight line. The time was close to dusk, and the British had difficulty commanding the heights, so the tanks withdrew to the rally point, followed soon by the infantry (Fuller 1920: 149).

The attack had breached the fourth defensive line in parts. By 1500 hours, Fuller received reports that British troops had captured Gonnelieu, Bois de Lateau, north

---

of March 1918, the British official history, and some tank officers (Hickey 1934: 108), published hearsay that one gunner, of giant size, but unidentified, had knocked out 16 tanks. Fuller read Haig's dispatch on 6 March 1918, when he told his diary that the story of the gunner "is probably a myth" and "will moralize the enemy's artillery." Hotblack judged that one gun could not gain line of fire on all 16 tanks. He found an account of a giant German infantry officer, mortally wounded by a tank's machine-gun while standing in a trench at Flesquieres. He was being carried to the rear by comrades, when they came under fire from machine-guns, and decided to dump him beside a disabled artillery gun, in hope of British aid. Presumably, British hearsay of this officer, alone beside a gun, inspired the myth.

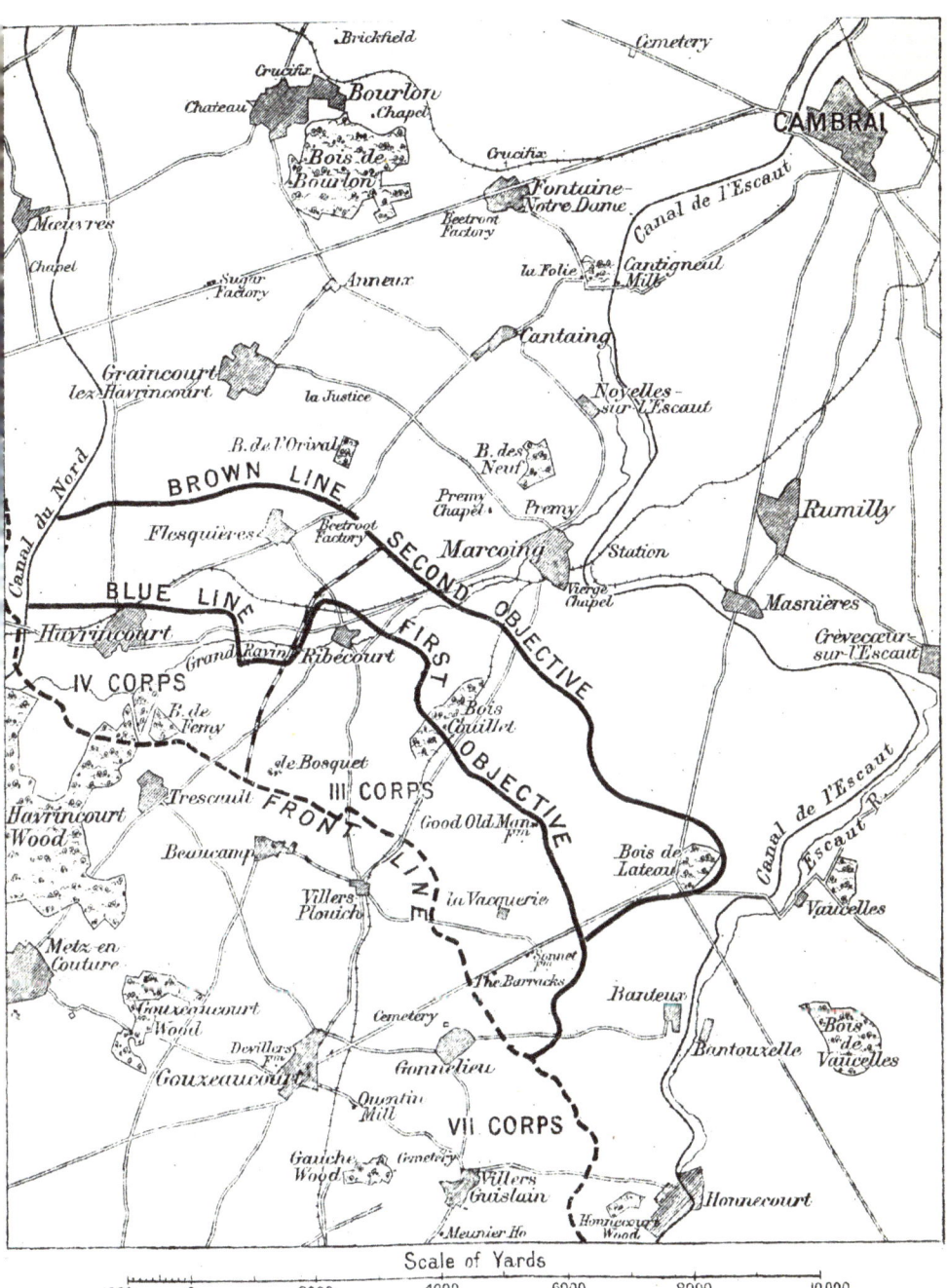

Map 14: The area fought over during the Cambrai campaign (Fuller 1920).

of Masnières, north and east of Marcoing, Bois des Neuf, Flesquières, Canal du Nord, Noyelles, and Graincourt.

Elles returned to Advanced HQ "elated," but Fuller warned that the battle could not be sustained. The whole operation was ruined by 51st Division's failure on

Flesquières Ridge, the collapse of the bridge at Masnières, the cavalry's failure to bridge it in good time, the cavalry's general failure to advance in good time, and the lack of any reserve (Fuller 1936: 207, 211, 213). James Cornwall (GHQ's GSO2 for intelligence) recalled that "the breach in the enemy's defences was not wide enough for cavalry to break through and we were now confronted by the formidably fortified *Siegfried-Stellung*" (Marshall-Cornwall 1984: 31).

By the end of the first day, penetrations extended through up to four defensive lines, up to 4.23 miles (7,450 yards; 6,812 m) deep.* Fuller estimated that the first day of the attack at Cambrai was financially five times cheaper than the first day at Passchendaele, yet was about 60 times quicker to advance.**

The assault front started 13,000 yards (11,887 m) wide, and ended 6,000 yards (5,486 m) wide. The British captured 100 guns and 8,000 prisoners, and lost 4,000 casualties. The Tank Corps lost 36 tanks and 648 men to direct hits (Appendix 1, RACTM E1980.18; Fuller 1920: 152-153; Foot 1934: 198; Marshall-Cornwall 1984: 31).

Given the cavalry's failure on the first day, tanks were ordered into new assaults on the second day. For 21 November, the Tank Corps organized the ready tanks in composite companies, and aimed them at Cantaing, Fontaine, and Bourlon, while cavalry tried to get west of the canal. These arms had never prepared to combine. When tanks took on machine-guns, the infantry went to ground, and the cavalry naturally retreated behind rises or woods. They usually did not re-combine.

The 1st Tank Brigade sent 25 tanks to support 62nd Division against Anneux and Bourlon Wood. The 62nd Division occupied Anneux, but failed to advance north on Bourlon Wood. The 2nd Tank Brigade sent 24 tanks against Cantaing, which is less than 2,900 yards (2,651 m) east of Anneux, and Fontaine-Notre-Dame, which is less than 3,000 yards (2,743 m) east-north-east from Anneux. Noyelles, whose bridge is less than 2,150 yards (1,965 m) south-east from Cantaing, was held.

A full two miles (3.3 km) to the south of Anneux, the cavalry found Flesquieres unoccupied, after marching one mile from Ribecourt. From there, cavalry moved north-eastwards 2.5 miles (4 km) into Cantaing. Medium tanks probably would have exploited to the final objective line, but the cavalry stuck in Cantaing. Infantry marched another 2 miles north into Fontaine-Notre-Dame. They were now up to 6 miles (10,560 yards; 9,656 m) from the previous day's opening front line, but could not occupy the village, and were replaced overnight by German counter-attackers. After two days of fighting, the six infantry divisions had lost 5,167 casualties (Fuller 1920: 141; 1936: 185, 188).

---

* In a speech to the House of Commons on 11 November 1942 Churchill claimed 6,000 yards (3.4 miles), possibly mistaking the ending width for depth (Fuller, "Why Not Dig Up the Mummies?" *The Evening Standard*, 31 March 1943: 4).

** Fuller first released this calculation in a paper ("Notes on Tank Economics") that he produced for the War Secretary in July 1918 (1936: 294). "In the preliminary bombardment which preceded the Battle of Passchendaele 4,282,550 shells, costing some £22,000,000, were fired. In manufacture they represented 176,000,000 man-hours at half a crown the hour. On the first day of the battle of Cambrai 378 fighting tanks were used and 293,149 shells were fired. The tanks cost approximately £5,000 apiece and the shells £5. Though only 48 tanks were hit, I will suppose that all were lost, then the cost of the tanks and shells was, in round figures, £3,350,000, and not £22,000,000. The saving was, therefore, £18,650,000, or 149,000,000 man-hours" (Fuller 1921: 96; "David and Goliath," *The Evening Standard*, 16 December 1942: 6).

In the morning (23 November), the remaining 13 tanks of B Battalion supported the Gordon Highlanders of 51st Division in an attack on Fontaine-Notre-Dame, but the tanks were decimated by field guns, firing directly, some of them along the streets of the village, while the Highlanders were held by machine-guns firing from La Folie Wood on the right.

In the morning of 26 November, German troops entered Bourlon to the northwest. British tanks and infantry again attacked into the outskirts of Bourlon and around Fontaine-Notre-Dame, but eventually turned back.

On 27 November, Byng wrote by hand to Elles with the ruling that the operation had ended.

> To say that the operation without tanks was an impossibility is merely a truism, but to say that the far-reaching success was due to the cooperation of your corps with the infantry and artillery is the point of view I wish you to realise (Fuller papers, Box 1).

On 28 November, at 1930 hours, Fuller issued "Tank Corps Order No. 3," for withdrawal to Fins. However, the Germans realized that the salient was held by just III Corps and IV Corps, without a significant reserve. The repeated attacks on Bourlon Wood had drawn resources from the right (south-eastern) flank. There the Germans attacked at dawn on 30 November, aiming to cut off the III Corps and IV Corps. The German left wing, operating from Honnecourt westwards, quickly captured Villers-Guislain and Gouzeaucourt, which is about 4,000 yards (3,658 m) south of the British starting front line.

> Artillery units were directly attached to the infantry, and the close coordination of the two arms was very successful. The infantry attacked in waves, the first of which went on ahead as far as it could, while the others "mopped up" the isolated centres of resistance that had been left behind. The assault was no longer made in connected lines, but the troops advanced in shock troop formation, effectively supported by the heavier arms which moved forward with them (Foertsch 1940: 95).

The Germans recaptured most of the territory they had lost on 20 November, plus 6,000 prisoners and 158 guns (Marshall-Cornwall 1984: 31).

By 1240 hours, 30 November, 22 tanks were made ready for B Battalion to take forward. Another 14 tanks were made ready for A Battalion. The tanks advanced on Gouzeaucourt, just as the Guards Division recaptured it, so the tanks were pushed forward to defend the approaches. By 1400 hours, H Battalion pushed forward 20 tanks, to drive the Germans across the valley. By the end of the day, the front was stable (Fuller 1920: 151-152; Foot 1943: 200-201).

A counter-attack was arranged for the morning of 1 December with the 2nd Tank Brigade, Guards Division, 4th Cavalry Division, and 5th Cavalry Division, against Villers Guislain and Gauche Wood. About 17 tanks were ready. They cleared the western edge of Gauche Wood, and proceeded through the wood, where the Guards captured 70 machine-guns. Then, they advanced into Villers Guislain, but withdrew under direct artillery fire (Fuller 1920: 152; Foot 1934: 204).

By 5 December, the Germans recaptured almost everything they had lost since 20 November.

That day, Elles visited Kiggell. According to Fuller's diary, Elles related that

Kiggell's "most important utterance was: 'I cannot yet see why cavalry should not be usefully employed in the battlefield'."

Fuller recalled the assault as "a stupendous success" (1920: 148, 150, 152), but complained that "our blow could not be taken advantage of, because the forces which broke through were not powerful enough to cause more than local disorganization" (1920: 97; 1936: 328). The German counter-offensive "was directly attributable to fighting without reserves and had nothing whatever to do with the value of tanks" (1936: 218). At the time, Fuller estimated that the Germans could have caused "disaster" to the whole BEF if they had held 200 tanks ("Anti-Tank Defence," 30 December 1917, RACTM E1980.18).

Foot (1934: 199) recalled "seven days of futile effort, with tired troops and war-worn tanks making ill-prepared attacks against Bourlon Wood, Fontaine village, and similar places. Many lives were lost and little was accomplished beyond extending still further the dangerous bulge in our line that simply invited attack." The official historian also blamed the lack of reserves for the reversal (Miles 1948: 14). For some historians, "this battle ended as yet another draw" (Strohn 2018: 23).

David Lloyd George, then prime minister, later wrote that the "action, though indecisive, if not sterile of result – through no fault of the new arm – will, I think, go down to history as one of the epoch-making events of the war, marking the beginning of a new era in mechanical warfare" (1938: 388).

The Royal Armoured Corps declared it "the pre-birth of the Blitzkrieg" (Owen and Atkins 1944: 9). The first official history of the arm concluded that the "Battle of Cambrai changed the tactical climate of the war – and of warfare" (Liddell Hart 1959: I, 153).

Renault FT light tank. From March 1918, some deliveries were armed with a 37-mm gun, instead of the 8-mm machine-gun.

10

Fuller's First "Plan 1919"

On 10 June 1917, Fuller had started a plan for a decisive offensive in Spring 1918 (see Chapter 7). Within an hour of the assault at Cambrai, on 20 November, Fuller restarted.

> I sat in the GS office gazing at the oiled calico. I was not in the slightest anxious or nervous, for I was certain that the initial attack would be a walk-over – nothing but an act of God could prevent this. I was certain also that the battle would be a limited and in no strategical sense of the word a decisive one, unless another such act were to intervene. As for an hour or two I had nothing to do, I jotted down some notes for a study I had in my head on the use of tanks in 1918 and 1919 (Fuller 1936: 211).

The fight for the salient towards Cambrai, and the recriminations, continued into December. Tank delivery schedules were postponed so far into the future that no combined-arms Allied offensive seemed possible until Summer 1918. On the 14th of December, BEF GHQ issued instructions to switch to the defensive, accompanied by a paper entitled "Memorandum on Defensive Measures." On the 27th, GHQ requested notes on how the Tank Corps could contribute.

On 30 December, Fuller sent a paper on "anti-tank defence." The next day, he sent a paper titled "Defensive and Offensive Use of Tanks 1918" (Fuller's journal, appendices A5 and A4, RACTM E1980.18; 1936: 229-232). The paper expects a German offensive, in Spring, before the Americans could concentrate a decisive expeditionary force. The Germans, Fuller estimated, would attack the French front, in order to persuade the British to reinforce the French, then the Germans would attack the British, with intent to cause such losses or capture so much economically-valuable territory as to force the Allies to sue for peace.

Conventionally, Britain's Spring starts in April, although, given a late end to the cold or wet seasons, an offensive might be postponed into May. Thus, Fuller's raids implicitly would start in March. Nobody on the Allied side yet knew that the German counter-offensive would start on March 21. As of 30 December, Fuller still expected to receive enough Mark V tanks to launch a decisive offensive in August. In the meantime, Fuller wanted to launch "tank raids" to attract German resources away from the French front. Fuller specified each raid with three divisions, lasting one day, as he had proposed on 2 September for a big raid around Cambrai.

On 13 January, GHQ sent a staff officer to discuss Fuller's paper on anti-tank defence. Fuller told his diary that GHQ now doubted the defensive inviolability of rivers and canals. Perhaps somebody was thinking of the Tank Corps' innovations that defeated German trenches at Cambrai. On 15 January, Fuller, in the name of Elles, sent a letter answering the staff officer's questions.* The leading answers are about "objectives":

---

* The letter is not mentioned in Fuller's journal, and is not titled, but is appended between A5 and A6.

1. Strategical localities, i.e., railways, main roads, bridges, defiladed lines of approach, flanking positions, and communication generally.

2. Tactical points, i.e., high ground, villages, woods, and strongly fortified localities.

3. Administrative centres, i.e., headquarters, dumps, billets, wagon parks, aerodromes, signal centres, etc.

Fuller developed a new paper ("Tank Operations Decisive and Preparatory, 1918-1919"), which he submitted on 28 January (Appendix A8, RACTM E1980.18; 1936: 229-232). This proposes a decisive combined-arms offensive in 1919, after combined-arms raids in 1918. The paper foreshadows Fuller's proposal of May 1918 for a similarly configured and scaled offensive in Spring 1919, which became known as "Plan 1919" (see Chapter 13). His paper of January should be known as his first Plan 1919, even though Fuller and subsequent historians ignored the link.

Terrain

After Cambrai, Fuller faced a couple months without enough ready tanks for another operation of the same scale. He lobbied various authorities for increased and accelerated production. His letters and attachments are dominated by hyperbolic assertions of the value of tanks, balanced by compelling quantifications of operational effectiveness. Winston Churchill, as Minister of Munitions, was most receptive, in part because his pose as a current tank enthusiast helped to associate past failures at the Admiralty with current successes. After visiting each other's HQs, Churchill asked Fuller for notes that he could use towards a speech or paper to be delivered to Parliament. Fuller's many arguments in favour of tanks include an analogy to naval warfare, which he would use repeatedly: tracked vehicles enable forces to move across land in all directions, like ships at sea, except with the benefit of elevated ground as cover. "The tank now enables us, without detriment, to add to land warfare many of the advantages of sea warfare; for it can move for long periods independent of communications and yet take all advantage of the accidents of ground" (Fuller to the Minister of Munitions, "Tanks as Time and Man[-]Savers," 12 December 1917, Appendix 2, RACTM E1980.18).

The Tank Corps HQ's letter to GHQ of 15 January lists "the most important" "factors" by which objectives should be selected:

1. Nature of the ground leading up to the objective.

2. Position of the lying up place with relation to the objective [i.e., the assembly area should be inside woods or villages, within 2 miles of the start line, but not in line of sight of the enemy's front].

3. Natural and artificial anti-tank defences protecting the objective.

4. Possibility of obtaining infantry, artillery, and aeroplane co-operation in the attack on the objective [i.e., these arms should be in range or brought in range].

The ground should provide good going. Approaches should not lead through defiles...The nature of the country to be advanced over should provide good cover for the infantry following the tanks.

Fuller's draft manual on "Infantry and Tank Cooperation and Training" (27 January: 1-3, 13, 18)* warns "that the advance of the tank is chiefly limited by the condition of the ground," and that "the chief limitations of the tank are connected with its mobility." The chief "requirement" for the tank in attack is "ground the tank can negotiate." Tanks move at 100 to 120 yards (91 to 110 m) per minute (3.4 to 4 mph) on flat ground, in daylight, 30 to 40 yards (27 to 37 m) per minute (1.0 to 1.4 mph) across trenches or craters in daylight, and 15 yards (14 m) a minute (0.5 mph) at night. The tank will "frequently" bog in wet damaged ground, and "it cannot traverse swamps, thick woods, streams with marshy banks, or deep sunken roads." However, tanks could penetrate into thin woods, in order to get behind enemy positions around the wood's perimeter. Also, tanks "can cross all wire entanglements," a trench 10 feet wide, a step 5 feet tall, and a slope up to 45 degrees.

Fuller does not require certain terrain so much as certain capabilities to overcome all terrain. All tanks "should be able to negotiate hill country." He requires the prospective Heavy Tank Mark VIII (the heaviest and largest of the Western tanks produced in wartime, although too late for action) to cross "artificial obstacles," such as trenches and cuttings. He requires "a submarine or water[-]crossing tank" to pass "rivers and swamps." Since he wrote of the latter in the singular, presumably this type is the same as the pursuit tank or at least a variant. He requires "a small and very mobile tank" to pass through "woods," and to counter enemy tanks, which reminds the reader of the tank "destroyer" or "torpedo" tank that Martel had proposed in November 1916. Indeed, Fuller finishes the section on "tank destroyers" by prospecting their "subsidiary use" as "wood crossers."

Concentration

Fuller's paper of 12 December, for Churchill, promises that by 1919 "one Tank Army, if skilfully directed, will defeat a whole group of armies unequipped with tanks." He specifies 2,000 tanks, 1,000 trucks, and 50,000 men for the tank arm alone. He does not specify a front.

Fuller's papers on "Anti-Tank Defence" (30 December) and on "Defensive and Offensive Use of Tanks" (31 December) warn that "distribution" of tanks in defence delays concentration for attack. He looks forward to a time when more agile types of tank release Mark IVs for dedication to the anti-tank role. As for the offensive, he declares that the offensive at Cambrai proves a front of 10,000 yards (9,144 m) as insufficient. He specifies a front of 25,000 yards (22,860 m), and a force of 1,400 to 1,650 tanks, i.e., one tank every 15 to 18 yards.

His draft manual on tank-infantry cooperation (27 January) repeats the old specification of one tank every 100 to 200 yards. The same manual specifies one tank company per infantry battalion in the assault, with a second infantry battalion ready to lead to the next objective line, and presumably a third battalion in reserve or ready to consolidate (i.e., just 12 tanks per infantry brigade, 36 tanks per infantry division).

---

* Fuller appended to his journal a copy of the original typed draft, as appendix A20.

Fuller's "Tank Operations Decisive and Preparatory, 1918-1919" of 28 January (his first effective Plan 1919) assumes a total front separating German and Western forces of 400 miles (644 km). The paper begins with a demand for the break-in to be widened to at least 100 miles (161 km).

> During the present war several decisive battles have been attempted by us – Loos [September 1915], the Somme [July 1916], Arras [April 1917], Ypres III [July 1917], Cambrai [November 1917]. All have failed, or partially failed, primarily because the grand tactics employed were faulty. These tactics comprised two acts:
>
> 1. The penetration of the enemy's defences.
>
> 2. Exploitation of the success thus gained by pursuit or field [manoeuvre] warfare.
>
> How this pursuit or field warfare was to be developed has always remained a profound mystery.
>
> The grand tactical conception was a faulty one because pursuit or field warfare can only be developed from a gap after the enemy's reserves have been neutralized. In the present war, as in past ones, reserves include not only the forces behind a battle front but also those on the flanks of the decisive attack. These flanking forces must be held taut otherwise they will pinch inwards. Further, for exploitation to follow penetration, the gap created must not be much less than 1/3rd to ¼ of the total battle front (Appendix A8, RACTM E1980.18; 1936: 229-232).

The gap should be widened by enveloping the enemy forces on at least one flank. As the enemy flanks "crumble way," they should be "pursue[d]."

The other 300 miles of front are fixed by "holding attacks." Fuller declares that attacks along 400 miles of front are "probably...impossible" without machines. He requires 5,280 tanks for the break-in front, i.e., one tank for every 33 yards. He requires 3,520 tanks to support the holding attacks on the other 300 miles of front, i.e., one tank every 150 yards.

Counting the "pursuit" tanks gives 7,040 tanks on the front to be penetrated, i.e., one tank per 25 yards of assault front, and a total of 10,560 tanks for all 400 miles of front, i.e., one tank per 66 yards of total front.

Adding in mechanical reserves, Fuller rounds up to 12,000 tanks, i.e., one tank per 59 yards of total front. He requires 200,000 personnel (later amended by hand to 240,000) to crew, service, and support 12,000 tanks. Admitting that Britain could not acquire so many tanks and men, he proposes that the British, French, and US armies should each acquire a third.

The colossal scale of Fuller's ambition appeared to be validated by the German counter-offensive on 21 March, on an assault frontage of 43 miles (69 km). The next day, Fuller wrote in his diary the causes of its success, of which the first is "the large frontage of their attack. The larger the frontage the less chance of minor checks becoming major delays."

Surprise

Fuller's papers of December to January repeat his prior opinions on preliminary bombardment and operational security. They are more talkative about timing.

Preliminary Bombardment

Fuller's paper for Churchill (12 December) reminds the reader that the attack at Cambrai "was a surprise," given "no preliminary artillery bombardment." He would repeat this reminder in most papers of December and January.

The Tank Corps' letter of 15 January allows for a preliminary bombardment, if tanks are reserved for an advance beyond its range. This allowance for a short preliminary bombardment, lasting hours (as specified by Swinton since 1915), was validated by the German preliminary bombardment on 21 March: it lasted five hours, and surprised the Allies.

Operational Security

The Tank Corps' letter to GHQ of 15 January argues that tanks should assemble in woods or villages, within 2 miles (3.2 km) of the start line. "Camouflaging of large numbers of tanks in the open is unsatisfactory, and so are lying[-]up pits dug in the vicinity of the front line." The letter allows for a preliminary bombardment, to cut wire sufficiently for infantry alone to take at least the first line. It reserves tanks for subsequent lines.

Timing

Fuller's papers of December and January allow for assaults and (for the first time) infiltration by tanks at night. His "Defensive and Offensive Use of Tanks" (31 December) expects "tanks to be able to operate at night so as to avoid daylight which is essential to accurate gun fire." He expects the Mark V to operate at night, but does not explain why, except to imply that improved mobility would help.

On 3 January the Tank Corps submitted to London a paper on surprising the enemy by attacking at night.* It requires "a really reliable compass" (magnetic compasses are misled by elementary iron in almost everything that makes up a tank) and "coloured light shells." Fuller remembered that 3rd Army HQ had required illumination shells in Autumn 1916, towards the end of his time on the staff there, and had been turned down, on the ground that new production would interrupt production of current types. (The under-supply of shells, first revealed publicly in Summer 1915, did not abate until after the Somme offensive, at the end of 1916.) By January 1918, Fuller expected no objection to production. He suggested that artillery should fire coloured markers onto objectives, with three different colours to mark respective objectives. He specifies an illumination life of two minutes, and a rate of fire of one marker every few minutes.

The Tank Corps' letter of 15 January does not mention the requirements above, but does allow "small night attacks…if there is a good moon" and "our defences are indifferent." Otherwise, the letter repeats the mantra that the tanks should approach the start line in darkness, and attack "at dawn."

---

* In his diary, Fuller titles the paper as "Mortar Tanks and Coloured Lights." The paper itself has no title. Elles is the signatory according to the typed signature, but Fuller routinely wrote and signed such letters "for" the commander (Appendix A6, RACTM E1980.18).

"Infantry and Tank Cooperation and Training" (27 January) states that tanks and infantry should "usually" assemble at night, and march to starting points with the help of white tape, for an assault around dawn, "at a time which will permit of the tank drivers seeing their way" (8-9). Objectives should be attacked in daylight, except for any second attacks on woods or villages, which should start at dusk (21).

Infiltration

Fuller's "Defensive and Offensive Use of Tanks" (31 December) wants a first wave of Mark Vs to advance, at night, at least 8,000 yards (7,315 m) through the enemy lines, and to the flanks, carrying medium machine-gunners, who would dig in defensively to prevent enemy reinforcements from reaching the front. "The tanks themselves would form a mobile counter-attacking force to this line."

This foreshadows the ambition of his "second" Plan 1919, to pass medium tanks through enemy lines in order to attack enemy HQs, before even the main assault gets going. In both documents, Fuller does not explain how tanks are supposed to pass through an un-assaulted front, except, in the first document, to imply that darkness and improved mobility would be sufficient for Mark V tanks.

Fuller's "first" Plan 1919 (28 January) does not mention surprise, or any activity that would promote surprise. Likely he assumed that readers accept the principle of surprise.

Combined Arms

Artillery: Preliminary

The Tank Corps' letter of 15 January allows for a preliminary bombardment, on condition that infantry capture the first objective line, if not the second, while tanks are reserved for an advance on subsequent objective lines.

Artillery: Assault

The draft of 27 January, on tank-infantry tactics, requires medium machine-guns and 3-inch mortars to fire on the objective during the assault. The paper does not clarify whether the fire is direct or indirect, although it appears to be direct, given the timing.

Meanwhile, indirect artillery fire should lob shrapnel beyond the objective, and lay smoke on the enemy's observation posts. Smoke is required also to obscure any tanks enveloping a wood or village (14, 17).

Artillery: Self-Propelled

Fuller's paper on "Defensive and Offensive Use of Tanks" (31 December) requires, by Autumn 1918, tanks "operating by day to be equipped with a smoke producer and a smoke projector," to obfuscate enemy artillery, and "mortar tanks (tank artillery) to be provided for the destruction of villages." He expects old Mark IV tanks to be fitted with a trench mortar. He expects the Mark V* (a lengthened Mark V) to have capacity to mount both a smoke producer and a smoke projector, without compromising its capacity to carry passengers too.

On 28 January, Fuller requires "a mortar [tank] and possibly an artillery tank," to overcome "villages," presumably by direct fire. He states that the "artillery tank" ideally should be developed from the Mark VIII Heavy Tank, which would have more capacity for a heavy piece than the prior Gun Carriers.

Aircraft

"Anti-Tank Defence" (30 December) expects aircraft to contribute to defensives by machine-gunning enemy infantry, in order to separate them from enemy tanks, which should be destroyed by friendly tanks and artillery. However, he ponders the arming of aircraft with "a light gun" (likely he means the Vickers 1.59-inch (40-mm) breech-loading gun), to attack enemy tanks. Strangely, his other papers do not repeat this specification, or consider its use against artillery, even though its shells could perforate enemy artillery shields where machine-gun bullets would fail.

On 28 January, Fuller repeated his requirement for aircraft to neutralize enemy artillery before a ground assault, although here he frames it a different way. He stresses combined mechanized arms, where "the tank will protect the infantry machine[-]gunners from the enemy's machine[-]gunners, and the aeroplane [will protect] the tank from the enemy's artillery." He requires "bullet-proof...low-flying aeroplanes...[I]n fact, they must become flying tanks."

Tanks and Infantry

On 29 December, Fuller had directed to GHQ a paper on "Training in Cooperation Between Infantry and Tanks."

> Cooperation between infantry and tanks and knowledge of anti-tank tactics are essential if success is to be based on any sounder foundation than a gamble. The principles upon which this cooperation should be founded are as follows:
>
> 1. Knowledge of each other's limitations.
>
> 2. Aptitude to carry out combined manoeuvres.
>
> 3. Comradeship between the two arms.
>
> There are three methods of attaining to these principles:
>
> 1. Explanation: Lectures [to higher commanders and staff on] how work is to be carried out.
>
> 2. Demonstrations: Showing how work is carried out [by two to four companies of tanks at Bray.
>
> 3. Combined Training: Actually carrying out the work.
>
> If perfection is to be gained tank and infantry units must live together for as long periods as possible so that they may grow to understand each other.

Fuller's paper on "Anti-Tank Defence" (30 December) expects combined arms, except that the infantry and aircraft should target enemy infantry, while friendly artillery and tanks should focus on enemy tanks, in order to separate the enemy arms for optimal neutralization.

> Each infantry section must be a fighting group and each section commander must be instructed beforehand what his duties are in the event of a hostile tank attack. As riflemen cannot be expected to produce much effect on tanks they must be taught to fire on the following infantry. They must be brought to realize that if the infantry attackers are destroyed the tanks that have preceded them will have failed to carry out their mission.

Naturally, Fuller urged the training of the arms in such tactics.

His paper on "Defensive and Offensive Use of Tanks" (31 December) specifies "villages" as a particular terrain where more training in combined arms is needed.

> Villages are extremely difficult localities to clear by means of Mark IV Tanks as at present equipped and infantry alone. Cooperation between infantry is frequently lost on account of MG fire proceeding from the village, and tanks have great difficulty in tackling top stories of houses.

The same paper prescribes two echelons of tanks in the assault: advanced guard tanks; and trench-clearing tanks.

The Tank Corps' letter of 15 January 1918 reminds GHQ of the desirability "of obtaining infantry, artillery, and aeroplane cooperation in the attack on the objective." The letter allows infantry to advance alone to the first objective line, given a preliminary bombardment. Whichever objectives that the tanks attack, they should lead. "The advance is almost certain to be followed by infantry, and may possibly be accompanied by aeroplanes and protected by artillery fire."

Fuller's note on "Training in Cooperation Between Infantry and Tanks" (29 December) promises that the Tank Corps is developing a "manual," to be ready in months, and a "training note," to be ready in 10 days. However, the final draft of the training note ("Infantry and Tank Cooperation and Training") waited until 27 January. Some delay is attributable to GHQ. On 2 March, Fuller heard in person, at GHQ, from the staff officer responsible for tanks, that the draft must incorporate "General Staff language" and the principles of war. His diary suggests that the discussion was heated and unresolved that day. Since the men were of the same rank, neither could order the other. He never revised the version of 27 January. On 16 March, 200 copies were issued from the Directorate-General Tanks in London, pending GHQ's version.

The "training note" is practically a manual, with 28 foolscap pages of text, and 11 appended drawings of the tactics. It begins in a similar fashion to Fuller's "Training in Cooperation Between Infantry and Tanks" of 29 December.

> The foundations of cooperation are understanding of each other[']s limitations and joint comradeship, that good fellowship which springs up through close acquaintance…
>
> Not only must there be a common tactics and a full understanding of each other's difficulties, but tank and infantry commanders must get to know each other, understand each other's ways, examine and reconnoitre the ground together and so plot and plan success. Individual friendship as well as collective efficiency plays an important part in war (1, 2).

The training note introduces an unprecedented articulation of respective tactical responsibilities:

> Whatever arm is foremost, that is nearest the enemy, must be cooperated with.
>
> In mass, tanks cooperate with infantry, they reduce the enemy's resistance and cover the approach and reorganization of our own men.
>
> When, however, the working of individual tanks is considered, it is the infantry which will frequently have to cooperate with them. On these occasions the chances created by tanks are fleeting, consequently unless infantry are ready to cooperate at once these chances may be lost (1).

The training note clarifies that tanks should lead until infantry can occupy the objective. However, this early clarification is confused later, where the infantry are urged to "send out scouts in advance," "well out" ahead of the other infantry, and apparently in advance of "the tank" too. "If the ground has been heavily shelled, it will be eminently suited for scouting or stalking." Scouts also "form a link between the tank and infantry, giving confidence to the latter." Unfortunately, this is where the tactics are vaguest (13).

Tanks and infantry should usually "approach" the enemy in single file, although infantry should not advance steadily, but should advance in short rushes between cover, covered by fire from, alternately, the Lewis section and rifle sections. If the Lewis section (two light machine-guns) is without covering fire, it can send forward one machine-gun at a time. "Simply following a tank is not cooperating with it, but fighting their way forwards under its protection is." The infantry must negotiate each tank-track through the wire in single file, but "attack" in line. Even then, the assaulters should not be evenly distributed in a continuous line. Each tank section should aim at a different "tactical point" for entering the enemy's defences (4, 11).

> Given the objective to be attacked, the first thing to do is to divide it into a series of Tank Section Attack Areas. These areas should generally include a tactical point, for if those are captured, it should not be difficult to clear up the trenches between them. If the objective is part of a system of trenches, the area selected should, if possible, be free from communication trenches, for if these are deep and broad the tank may experience trouble in crossing them (5).

The training note is clear about how to structure the assaulters by objectives: ideally, one tank company (12 tanks; 4 sections) per objective (see Map 15).
- One tank per section is advanced ahead of the other two tanks;
- One infantry platoon follows each tank in the "main body" echelon, i.e., 8 infantry platoons, roled as "trench clearers";
- "Trench clearers" are followed at 50 yards by 8 "trench stops" platoons;
- "Trench stops" are followed at 50 yards by 8 "support" platoons.
- The "supports" are followed, "whenever possible," by Stokes 3-inch (76-mm) mortars, "to assist in the attack."

A second battalion may follow the same tank company to the next objective line (see Map 15).

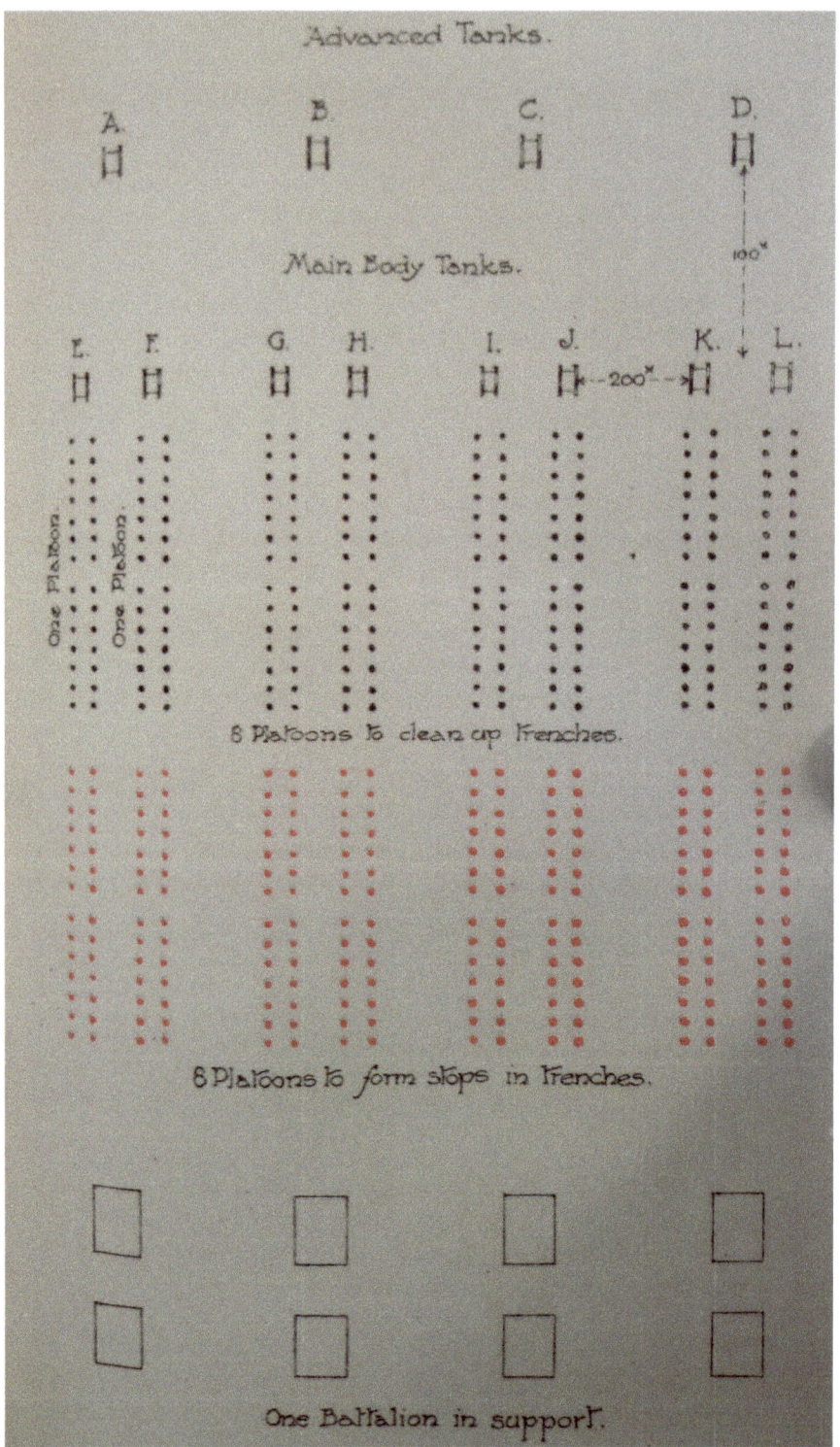

Map 15: The formation to be adopted by one company of tanks and two battalions of infantry, according to "Infantry and Tank Cooperation and Training," 27 January 1918 (Fuller's journal, Appendix A20).

The infantry platoons should be roled as one of three alternatives:
1. Of the "Trench clearers," one section of grenadiers enters the trench, three sections of riflemen move with the tank alongside the trench;
2. "Trench stops" mark paths through the wire, picket trench junctions, and prepare ladders for the clearers to exit the trench in order to advance on the next objective.
3. "Supports" provide fire support to the clearers and stops, and take positions beyond the trench to support the next advance (see Map 16).

A tank should advance on an enemy machine-gun frontally, but should move to the rear of a concrete fortification, to cut off its garrison. Similarly, tanks should envelop a wood or village, to demoralize the garrison by threatening to cut it off, while other tanks approach frontally. Tanks on the flanks are meant to intercept counter-attackers. Preferably, forces at the enemy's rear enter first. Otherwise, tanks penetrate from front to rear, followed by infantry to clear each building (see Map 17). "Main entrances should be avoided as they may be defended by pits and anti-tank guns. The tanks must break in through walls, outhouses[,] and orchards, threatening the enemy, disorganizing him and drawing his fire." The responsibility for entering the objective should be clear to all beforehand, so that friendly forces do not fire on each other. As in open ground, tanks should lead the infantry into villages or woods, except where the terrain is too close (13, 17-22).

Tanks and Engineers

"Infantry and Tank Cooperation and Training" (27 January: 2, 10, 11) declares that one tank can "crush down two paths through [enemy wire] which are passable by two single files of infantry." All three tanks of the tank section should crush the same paths, or divert at least 50 yards away (so as not to tension the wire in the pass). Infantry should keep at least 25 paces from the tank, in case of trailing wires. Up to four platoons could use the same pass, one section at a time, covered by the platoon's other three sections. "Hurried crossings must, however, be avoided, for if

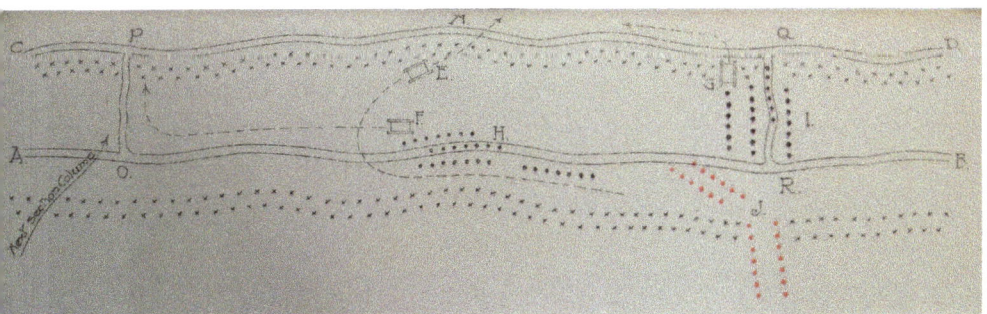

Map 16: The Advanced Tank (E) is first to cross the wire. It turns left to enfilade the fire trench (A-B). The next tank (F) crosses the trench to enfilade from the other side. Once the grenadier section, of the trench cleaner platoon, is in the trench, E proceeds to envelop the support trench (C-D), opposite the third tank (G) and its trench cleaner platoon (I). A trench stop platoon (J) follows F to the junctions at O and P. The next trench stop platoon will follow G to junctions R and Q. Once the fire trench is clear, the trench clearers and the Advanced Tank move into reserve behind the Main Body.

Map 17: The formation for a frontal attack on a village by tanks and infantry.

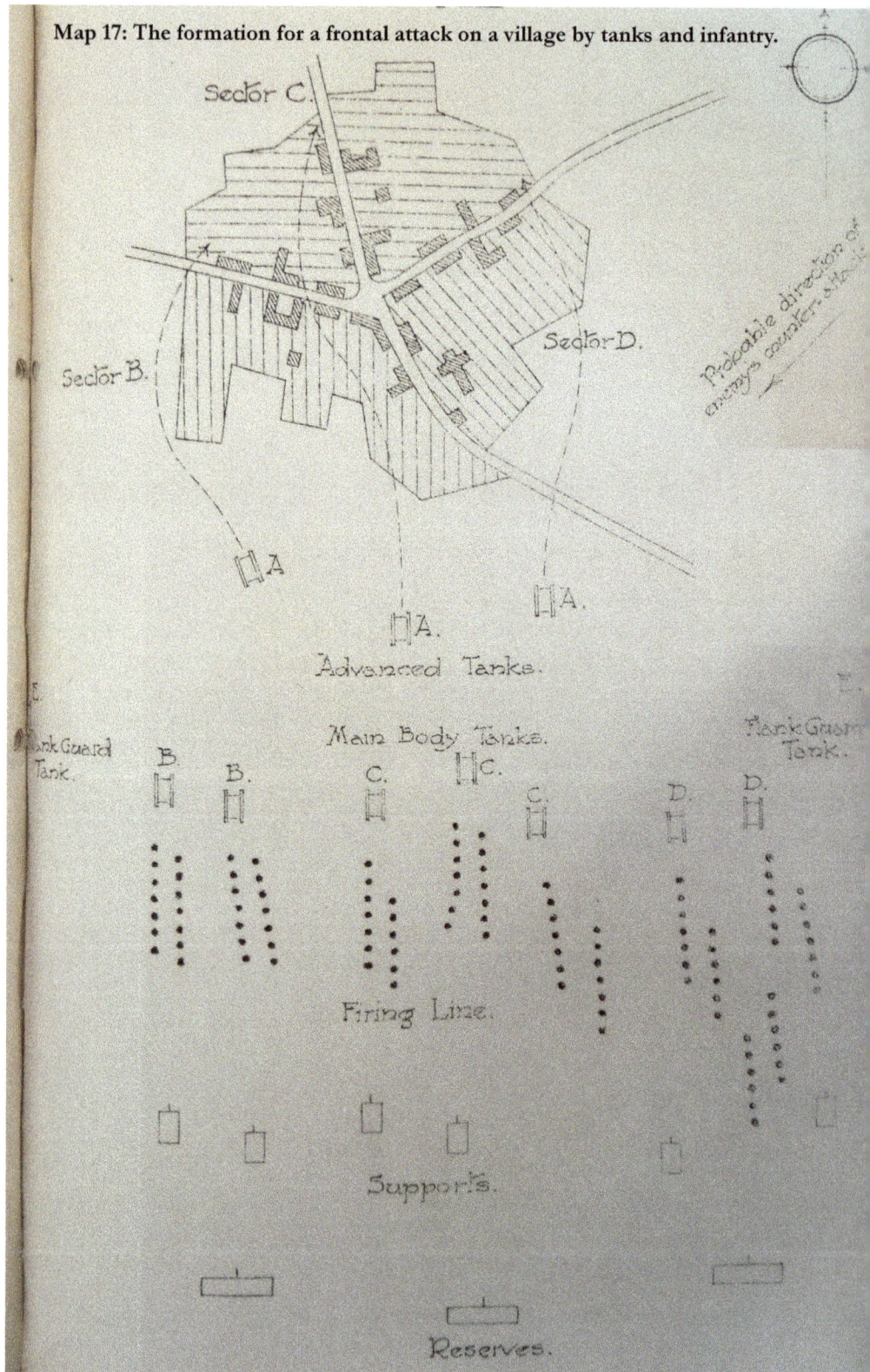

the leading men catch their feet in the crushed[-]down wire and pull it up, delay to those in rear will result."

On 28 January, Fuller requires "a lock bridge[-]laying and pontoon[-]hauling tank," to cross canals, ideally as a variant of the Mark VIII.

Tanks versus Tanks

In case of enemy tank attack, the Tank Corps' letter of 15 January prefers for Male tanks to "be held in rear" of the trenches, ahead of the static anti-tank guns, in order to add to the fire on the leading wave of tanks frontally, and to catch them from the flank, before turning against the next wave. The letter states that the same tanks should act "as counter-attacking units," but emphasizes stationary positions, and does not mention any movement.

If "fixed anti-tank defences" are inadequate, the Tank Corps allows for tanks to be used as "a means of anti-tank defence," either as "individual…mobile batteries," like "mobile field guns," in "cooperation with the fixed and mobile defences," or in cooperation with friendly infantry against an enemy combined infantry-tank attack.

The letter prospects the dedication of Male Mark IV tanks to "anti-tank groups," once enough later models have arrived to fill the tank units, and prospects a specialized "tank destroyer," "an extremely mobile and lightly armoured tank equipped with a pivot high velocity gun or pom-pom [40-mm automatic cannon] with all round fire."

Speed

The "training note" of 27 January contains a section on "mobility." It identifies three tank "characteristics," which are also "principles" of operations in general and of "an infantry and tank operation" in particular: "mobility," "security," and "offensive power" (in their original order). (As categorical capabilities, the normal terms today are "mobility," "survivability," and "lethality.")

As before, the operational principles of mobility and appropriate terrain are conflated. The capability of tanks to move is explicitly applied to other principles, primarily combined arms, sustainment, and exploitation. In the context of "an infantry and tank operation," Fuller emphasizes "quick initiative" and "quick movement" (2, 5).

Sustainment

Fuller's paper on "Anti-Tank Defence" (30 December) specifies a depth of 10,000 yards (9,144 m) for defence against enemy tanks, which conforms with expectations in his other papers that attackers must penetrate 10,000 yards to break through.

> If the last line of our defences, our anti-tank line, lies outside 12 hours marching and fighting endurance of the attackers a complete penetration of our defences is not likely to be effected in one day.

Fuller's "Defensive and Offensive Use of Tanks" (31 December) declares that the offensive at Cambrai has proven that infantrymen can sustain an advance of 10,000 yards at most. He specifies a lower bound of 8,000 yards (7,315 m) and requires fighting tanks and carriers to carry machine-gunners and some infantry beyond that distance. In a hypothetical application, he expects Mark V* variants to carry medium machine-gunners at least 8,000 yards through enemy lines, in darkness, so that the machine-gunners can dig in defensively against any enemy reinforcements trying to reach the frontline. The Mark V* tanks prepare to counter-attack those reinforcements. This penetration is supposed to occur before other Mark V* tanks and pedestrian infantry assault in twilight or moonlight, to occupy the defensive lines. A third wave (Mark V tanks and pedestrian infantry) "would mop up all the enemy's trench garrisons and guns to a depth of 8,000 yards. A fourth wave (Mark V tanks) would reinforce the medium machine-gunners, while infantry carriers bring infantry to consolidate the final objective line. This paper (31 December) expects a total advance of 16,000 yards (14,630 m) in 24 hours. However, his papers of January specify 10,000 yards (9,144 m) as the ideal depth of penetration by an offensive, and require sustainment to this depth within 12 hours of daylight.

"Infantry and Tank Cooperation and Training" (27 January) warns: "tank crews must understand that the advance of infantry is limited by their physical endurance and the enemy's fire, and infantry must equally understand that the advance of the tank is chiefly limited by the condition of the ground." It estimates the tank's penetrative range as 8 to 10 miles (13 to 16 km),* the crew's "endurance" as 8 to 12 hours, and requires "local reserves" to follow the assaulters, "carrying picks and shovels and wire" (1, 3, 14).

Exploitation

"Defensive and Offensive Use of Tanks" (31 December) reminds GHQ of a lesson from Cambrai: "A reserve of tanks must be held in hand for exploitation, possibly independently."

Additionally, "exploiting tanks,"** combined with either cavalrymen mounted on horses or infantrymen mounted in carriers, should be held as a final wave.

His paper of 28 January requires 1,440 heavy tanks in mechanical reserve, and 1,760 exploitation tanks, on an assault front of 100 miles (161 km).

Fuller's papers from December through January, like his second Plan 1919 (of May), are remarkably inattentive to exploitation, perhaps because Fuller was already thinking that medium tanks could infiltrate the enemy's front before the main assault, and act as exploiters concurrently, without the need for tanks roled as exploiters alone (as explained in Chapter 12).

---

* The current Mark IVs were rated for an operating range of 35 miles (56 km), the incoming Mark Vs for 45 miles (72 km).
** Fuller states that Medium B tanks, then still in design, would fulfill this requirement, although in February he would receive an estimate of their speed as only 4 mph (6.4 kmh).

11

Tank Raids, January to June 1918

By December, Fuller accepted that the Tank Corps would remain short of the resources needed for a decisive offensive until Spring 1919. Fuller prescribes many short raids in 1918, on alternating parts of the front. His "Defensive and Offensive Use of Tanks" (31 December) states: "passive defence, for tanks, would be, under almost all conditions, an absurdity." Thus, tanks should "forestall a hostile attack by a raid," or stand by to counter-attack any enemy attack. (His paper on "Anti-Tank Defence," of the previous day, allows for Male tanks to be distributed as anti-tank batteries, but his papers prefer to reserve tanks for raids.) He estimates that one raid on an enemy assembly area would delay an enemy offensive for a month. "Several" raids would prevent an enemy offensive until the offensive season runs out. He accepts a loss rate of 25 percent of tanks per raid, and estimates personnel casualties, across all raids, of 1,500 men, from three divisions.

His paper of 28 January ("Tank Operations Decisive and Preparatory, 1918-1919," which I have identified as his first Plan 1919) initially refers to "preparatory operations." These are intended to attrit the enemy and to improve the front before a decisive combined-arms offensive in 1919. The paper justifies mechanization of both preparatory and offensive operations, on the premise "that when the attacker is armed with a new or improved type of weapon, the defender's losses are the greater." Attackers would suffer most if using the same weapons as the defenders. He wishes for "infantry machine[-]gunners to hold our line," and "tanks and aeroplanes to raid the enemy's line." Here, his paper revives the term "tank raids."

Instead, GHQ kept the Tank Corps in the defensive line. The Germans took the offensive in March 1918. Defending against the German offensive further denuded the Tank Corps. This incapacity had the unforeseen effect of encouraging the first "tank raid," in June, before the Tank Corps was ready for an offensive.

This chapter examines Fuller's proposals of January for tank raids, and the tank raid of June, in terms of the seven principles identified in earlier chapters.

Terrain

On 8 August, Fuller had specified a front for "tank raids" just 8,000 yards (7,315 m) long. On 28 January, he specifies a front of 20,000 yards (18,300 m) for a "deep raid" (10,000 yards or 9,150 m deep), 50,000 yards (45,700 m) long for a "shallow raid" (2,500 yards or 2,290 m deep – insufficient to reach the second line). These

Depth of penetration→		10,000 yards ("deep")		2,500 yards ("shallow")	
Organization	Tanks	Width of front		Equivalent current front	Expected prisoners
		"narrow"	"broad"		
Lower	576 Heavy 410 Medium	20,000 yards	50,000 yards	Arras to Armentieres	15,000-30,000
Higher	864 Heavy 610 Medium	30,000 yards	75,000 yards	Vimy to St. Quentin	22,500-45,000

Table 8: Fuller's expectations for "tank raids," by size of the Tank Corps and depth of penetration, 28 January 1918 (Appendices A1 and A8, RACTM E1980.18; 1936: 236).

specifications are for the currently authorized (but not completed) Tank Corps ("lower organization"). Given authorization of a larger Tank Corps ("higher organization"), the fronts could lengthen by 50 percent (see Table 8).

No specification of the front for the raid at Bucquoy on 22-23 June survives, although it cannot have been much longer than 1,000 yards, since it was meant to neutralize some strongpoints around Bucquoy. The terrain here is flat and slightly elevated above the Somme's flood plain, but was heavily fortified at the time.

Concentration

On 8 August, Fuller specified a raid, with all three current tank brigades, at a concentration of 1 tank per 37 yards. On 31 December, he talks of a similar "one day raid," implicitly with all three legacy brigades. On 28 January, he specifies fronts by organization, which allows us to work out his current standards for concentration: 1 heavy tank per 35 yards of narrow deep front, or 87 yards of broad shallow front. (He applies the same standards to both lower and higher organizations.) Adding in the exploitation tanks gives a concentration of 1 tank per 20 yards of deep narrow front, or 51 yards of shallow broad front.

In the paper of 8 August, the artillery density works out at one divisional piece per 91 yards, given two dismounted cavalry divisions. By 31 December, he requires "three divisions" (the phrase implies infantry divisions), with a density of one divisional piece per 139 yards of deep narrow front, or 347 yards of shallow broad front. Surely, Fuller assumed that higher formations would add artillery.

Since Cambrai, the Tank Corps had grown little in tanks, more in cadres. It now held in France five brigades and 13 units. One unit held medium tanks. The other 12 units averaged less than 27 tanks each, or about half of authorized fill (Fuller 1920: 172-173). Still, Fuller (1936: 267-268) estimated that from January to February the 12 heavy units could have launched at least two raids of 200 tanks each, which would have delayed the German offensive for weeks, if not forever.

> I will repeat it again, there was no reason why, with the 12 battalions of [heavy] tanks we had, we should not have carried out several such raids between January 1st and the middle of March. And had we done so, there can be little doubt that the entire German spring offensive on the Western Front would have been upset; that is, in all probability, there would have been no Second Battle of the Somme, no Battle of the Lys, and no Third Battle of the Aisne; that the moral[e] of our Armies, sapped by the passive defensive, would have been raised by each raid (Fuller 1936: 290).

On 4 February, GHQ's CGS (Kiggell) returned Fuller's paper of 28 January, without comment. In February, the Tank Corps took up the defensive positions that GHQ had ordered a month earlier. The distribution was vast: 320 Mark IV Heavy and 50 Medium A Tanks were allocated to a front 60 miles (97 km) long – one tank for every 285 yards. Fuller agitated for concentration. On 2 March, Haig, citing a recent visit to Gough at 5th Army, confirmed to Elles that he agreed with Kiggell's distribution. Fuller angrily complained to his diary: "D.H. [is] a very stupid man, this only accentuates it. Imagine turning a mobile weapon into a Martello Tower." In the same conference, Ivor Maxse (XVIII Corps) suggested bunkers on reverse slopes, widely distributed, from which tanks could emerge to surprise attackers.

Maxse referred to "Trap Door Spider Tactics" and the "Tactics of the Ferocious Rabbit." Fuller wrote in his diary: "If only these old gentlemen would come and look at a Mark IV Tank they would understand what rot they talk." The argument continued through 3 March, when staff visited Tank Corps HQ, and the next day, when Elles returned to GHQ. That evening, back at Tank Corps HQ, Elles reported to Fuller that Haig "has decided on Martello Tower tactics." Still, on 5 March, Elles visited the DMO (Davidson), seeking authorization for some combined-arms raids.

The Germans attacked on 21 March. The next day, Fuller noted that one of the explanations for the rapid German advance was "our cordon system of defence – strong nowhere. Reserves strung out all down our front." The cordon system was exacerbated by poor command at GHQ, corps, and divisions.

> During the earlier part of our disastrous defeat in March 1918, all [Tank Corps GSOs] went forward, and many of the administrative staff as well. In this particular battle, the Second Battle of the Somme, I was convinced by personal observation on the spot that had other corps acted as the Tank Corps acted, that is to say had their generals and the staffs gone forward in place of backwards, the enemy could have been halted on the Somme in place of being allowed to approach to within cannon-shot of Amiens (Fuller 1936a: 21).

Thus, most reserves were not concentrated where and when needed. Only 180 tanks countered the attackers. The rest were occupied in relocating, marching, and counter-marching. Even where tanks were near the action, their small packets discouraged use. Even where tanks joined the action, GHQ did not intend them to counter-attack so much as to bolster the infantry in defence. For Fuller (1920: 177, 199), GHQ's use of tanks was less efficient and effective than his proposed raids.

On the night of 22-23 June, just five Female tanks led just five platoons of infantry, which suggests a concentration of one tank per 200 yards (183 m).

Surprise

Fuller's writings of January on "tank raids" do not specify any methods for achieving surprise, but appear to assume the same measures as taken at Cambrai: no preliminary bombardment; secret assembly, disguises, and restricted activities (operational security); disinformation; and an overnight approach to the start line.

Surprisingly, these writings on "tank raids" do not include the allowances in coincident papers for assaults at night. Fuller's "Defensive and Offensive Use of Tanks" (31 December) expects "tanks to be able to operate at night…" On 3 January the Tank Corps submitted to London a paper on surprising the enemy by attacking at night. The Tank Corps letter to GHQ of 15 January allows "small night attacks… if there is a good moon" and "our defences are indifferent." However, "Infantry and Tank Cooperation and Training" (27 January) states that tanks and infantry should "usually" assemble at night, and march to starting points with the help of white tape, for an assault around dawn." His paper of 28 January ignores timing.

Yet the raid of 22 to 23 June started and ended in darkness. It started at 2325 hours, and completed within hours. Fuller left no explanation for the choice. After the fact, he (1920: 204) suggested that darkness is net advantageous to tanks, given that enemy artillerymen could not see them. However, he does not explain why more night raids were not launched. Implicitly, he knew that the Germans could adapt, by pushing artillery forward and equipping gunners with flares and searchlights. Explicitly, the Tank Corps was rushing to get ready for the next offensive.

Combined Arms

Aircraft

In the context of "tank raids," Fuller's paper of 28 January expects artillery and aircraft to attack enemy artillery.

Artillery

The same paper expects mortar tanks or artillery tanks to fire smoke.

No artillery were used on the night of 22 to 23 June. Rather, the raid was scheduled within the hours of darkness, when neither side could observe indirect fire.

Tanks and Infantry

Fuller's paper of 28 January expects the infantry garrisoning the frontline to cooperate with tanks in a raid, an expectation that implicitly fulfils his claims for "economy" (i.e., no infantry are reserved behind the front as raiders).

On 22-23 June, the five infantry platoons were stopped by trench mortars and machine-guns before a hamlet nicknamed the Doll's House. Despite reinforcements, there the infantry stayed. The tanks continued, although they soon faced pedestrian enemies. One tank crew defended itself with revolvers, and went on to rescue a wounded platoon commander. All tanks returned without damage.

Speed

In August, Fuller wanted the raiders to penetrate 4,000 yards (3,658 m) within one assault wave, and be home within hours. Current heavy tanks could penetrate 4,000 yards in 34 minutes. He required no medium tanks in August, but by January the first Medium As were available. These were later rated for 7.25 mph (12 kmh) on level ground, although in January Fuller did not specify any expectations. In any case, he expected penetration and withdrawal within about 12 hours, i.e., a round-trip journey at least 22,000 yards (including the advance from the assembly area), at an average speed of at least 1,833 yards per hour (more than 1 mph).

Sustainment

In August, Fuller had prospected raids to a depth of 4,000 yards, with about 200 tanks. On 28 January, he prospects a "deep" raid to 10,000 yards, with at least 576 heavy tanks. Since he already expects tanks to sustain an attack for 10,000 yards in a day, and carriers to carry pedestrians as far, a raid to that depth does not need to be sustained, because the raiders are supposed to return to friendly lines at dusk.

Exploitation

In August, Fuller had not allocated any raiders to exploitation. In January, he allocates hundreds of medium tanks, but their role remains unclear. Presumably they were meant to raid like the heavy tanks, just at more depth and speed.

12

Foot's Plan 1919

From February, Major Stephen Foot, formerly a tank brigade major, served as GSO2 at the Directorate-General Tank Corps (DGTC), where he detailed the Tank Corps' requirements, for authorization by the War Office, and for fulfilment by the Ministry of Munitions. DGTC's work was interrupted by the German offensive in March 1918, when the priority was to restructure the Tank Corps in France to meet the onslaught, including as pedestrian machine-gunners. By April, the Ministry's periodical forecasts of production confirmed that insufficient tanks would be available for a decisive offensive until Spring 1919. German counter-offensives continued through April – indeed the last would not be officially terminated until 29 April, although by then the Allies were planning for their own offensive, to take advantage of German overstretch. On 24 April, Foot added a document titled "A Mobile Army," which proposes suitable terrain, concentration, surprise, combined arms, speed, sustainment, and exploitation for an offensive around May 1919.

Terrain

Foot suggested that the formations should be prepared from October 1918 to April 1919, when the winter weather favours defenders. Foot prescribed separate British, American, and French offensives by May. Within each of the British, American, and French offensives, Foot wanted multiple armies to assault, each to break through on a front at least 30 miles (48 km).

In August 1916, Townshend had theorized that attackers need to penetrate only 5 miles (8,800 yards; 8,046 m) through the defensive lines before a comparatively uninterrupted advance into Germany. Since then, the Germans had deepened their defences, primarily against artillery fire, but also to buy time to attrit the attackers and to organize counter-attackers. The Germans had also constructed new lines to which they could withdraw from their most forward defensive lines. Still, each series of defended lines rarely reached more than 5 miles deep, never more than 6 miles (10,560 yards; 9,656 m), although the attackers might face as many miles again before they hit the next series of defended lines. The Allies had already demonstrated (at Cambrai, in November 1917) that they could penetrate 6 miles of defences, with tanks. The unproven challenge was to penetrate 6 miles of defences quicker than the defenders could withdraw to the next series of defended lines.

Foot required tanks that could move quicker and range deeper, more replacement tanks, and more supply variants, even before he specified the exploitation force.

> The object of this paper is to discuss the question of whether it will be possible for the Allies to obtain a decisive victory in the year 1919.
>
> 1. Victory by penetration: I assume that the victory, if obtained, will be by a deep penetration of the enemy's defensive system, for the following reasons.

a. A deep penetration, if it can be effected, provides the surest method of driving the enemy out of the captured portions of France and Belgium.

b. A deep and swift penetration is necessary if the enemy is to be prevented from the possibility of a slow retirement, accompanied by a methodical destruction, from the result of which it would take several generations for France and Belgium to recover (in Foot 1934: 345).

That last clause evokes a virtuous cycle: penetrate quicker, so that the enemy has less opportunity to damage terrain, then you can penetrate quicker.

Foot promised a penetration of 60 miles (97 km), over six days. Such a distance would take the British front from Passchendaele to Antwerp or Brussels. A second penetration would take the British from either Antwerp or Brussels into Germany.

Foot specifies that the area where the "Mobile Army" is expected to advance should be open country and good going for automobiles. "Special training in open warfare would be a necessity."

Concentration

At the rate that had been standardized in 1916, but rarely achieved, of one tank per 100 yards of front, a 30-mile (48 km) front of assault requires 528 heavy tanks, equivalent to 11 tank units (48 tanks per unit). Three brigade HQs are required: (Foot was planning on four units per brigade, a rate which GHQ had specified back in September 1916, even though most brigades never held more than three.)

Foot implies a slightly denser concentration for the reserved army that would take over the most promising front. Foot terms this a "Mobile Army," meaning a mechanized force. It would hold 12 mechanized infantry divisions and 3 heavy tank brigades (one tank unit per division), enough for one tank every 92 yards (84 m), even excluding brigade reserves or mechanical replacements.

Likely, Foot did not expect the Mobile Army to be spread across all 30 miles (48 km) of a front that an assault army has pushed forward already. If the Mobile Army takes over 15 miles (24 km) of front, equivalent to the widest of the fronts involving tanks during the war (Arras in April; Cambrai in November), then one heavy tank would be available for every 46 yards (42 m) of front.

The "Mobile Army" includes three light tank brigades, which could help to develop the breakthrough. Counting all six brigades, one tank would be available every 46 yards (42 m) of a 30-mile front, or every 23 yards (21 m) of a 15-mile front.

Surprise

For surprise, Foot eschews a preliminary bombardment, and emphasizes the speed of assembly and penetration.

Combined Arms

Foot specifies each "Mobile Army" with 200,000 men, 12 mechanized infantry divisions, 3 heavy tank brigades, 3 light tank brigades, and some aircraft (presumably three groups). Foot did not exclude any arms, except cavalry.

Foot's "Mobile Army" holds three corps. Each corps holds four mechanized infantry divisions, a brigade of heavy tanks, supply variants to sustain the infantry and tanks, and tractors to pull forward the artillery. Aircraft would fly forward of the assaulters to find targets of opportunity, and to provide close support to the arms as they catch up. Like Fuller, Foot emphasizes the capacity of direct fire from tanks and aircraft to replace some of the indirect fire from artillery.

The light tank force was to be held ready to develop and exploit the breakthrough, independently of other arms, except that aircraft would still be flying ahead, and mechanized infantry, heavy tanks, and artillery would be following to consolidate captured objectives.

Speed

Foot emphasizes speed of assembly, if the enemy is not to realize the place and time of assault. Further, "a deep and swift penetration is necessary," to prevent the enemy from a destructive withdrawal. Foot prospected an advance of 60 miles (97 km) in six days, i.e., 10 miles (16 km) per day. Assuming a 12-hour fighting day, the speed of advance would average 0.8 mph (1.3 kmh).

Sustainment

Tracked armoured supply carriers would carry supplies, tracked tractors would tow the artillery, and "infantry carrier tanks" (prospective Mark IX Heavy Tanks) would carry infantry, sufficient to sustain the advance for 60 miles and six days, without the need to capture roads, railways, or their strongpoints.

In theory, this distance could be sustained in three operations, according to current capabilities. As of May 1918, the Mark IX Tank (carrier) – the slowest and shortest-ranging of the vehicles in the production programme for Spring 1919 – was expected to range for 24 miles of level ground, at a speed of 4.5 mph (7.2 kmh), with capacity for 3 crewmen and at least 24 passengers (sometimes 30 were specified) or 12 long tons (12.2 metric; 13.4 short) of supplies.

Foot wanted multiple assault forces, each to break through a front at least 30 miles (48 km) wide. A "Mobile Army" (mechanized force) would be reserved, ready to exploit the best breakthrough. The 12 mechanized infantry divisions and 3 heavy tank brigades would take over the front from the assaulting formations, and effectively act as a fresh wave of assaulters.

Exploitation

The Mobile Army HQ would hold 3 brigades of "light fighting tanks" (formed as a light tank division, for the divisional sustainment assets), ready to "to push ahead as rapidly as possible, avoiding any centres of enemy resistance, but outflanking them, cutting off their communications, supplies, etc., and leaving them to be dealt with by the heavy tanks and main body coming on behind."

Foot's use of the "light tank" class was not meant to evoke the current French light tank, except perhaps in size. He wanted something quicker than the British medium tanks, which were currently not much quicker than the latest heavy tanks.

Note that Foot excluded horsed cavalry, although Fuller would allow for horsed cavalry in the "pursuit" phase.

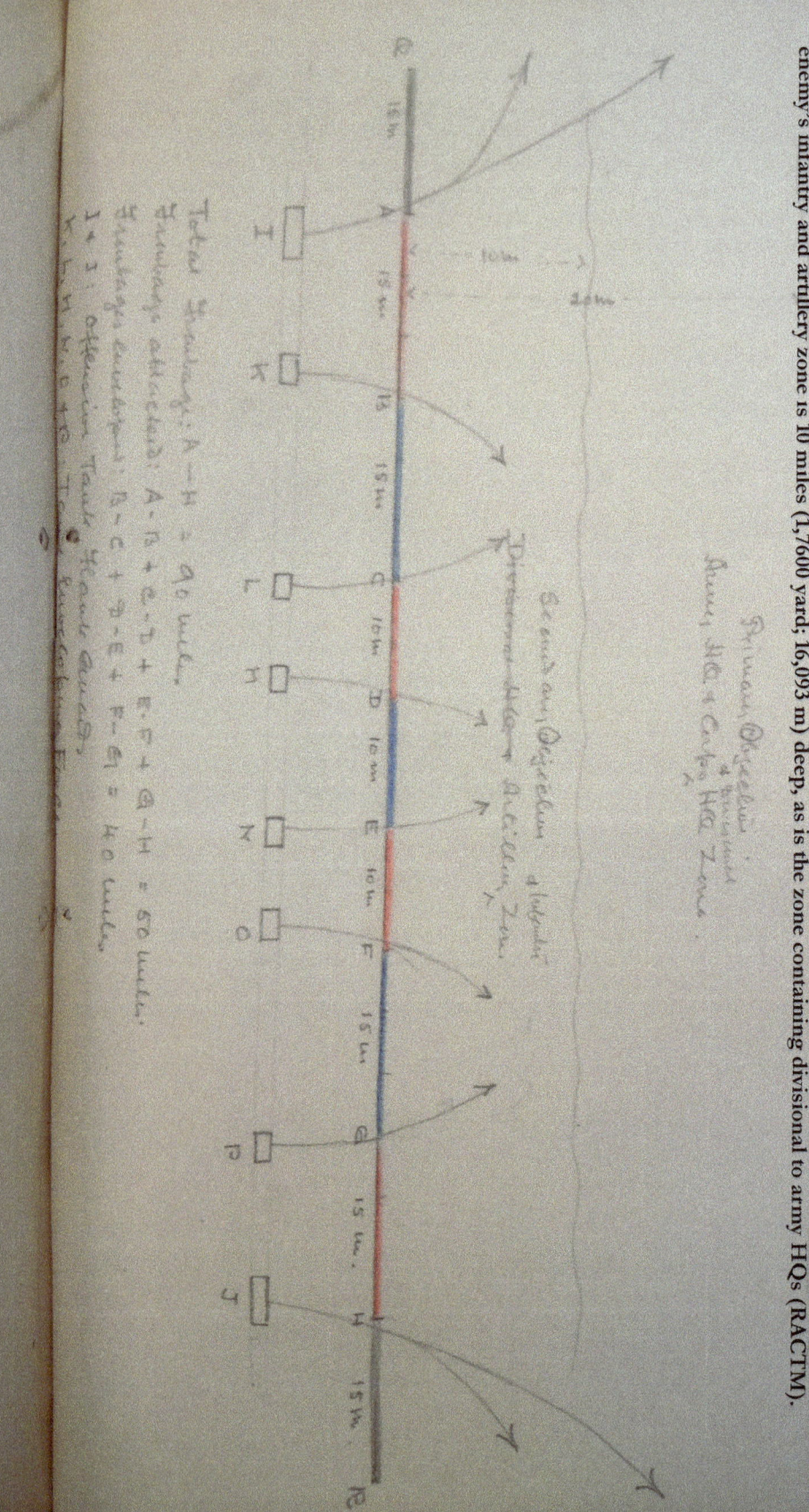

Map 18: Fuller's own sketch, within his draft of what would become "Plan 1919," to illustrate the section he titled "The Morcellated Front of Attack." Each unfilled box represents a tank force, breaking through the enemy's front on the flanks of the red parts of the front. The enemy's infantry and artillery zone is 10 miles (1,7600 yard; 16,093 m) deep, as is the zone containing divisional to army HQs (RACTM).

13

Fuller's Second Plan 1919

Foot and Fuller never clarified how their proposals influenced each other. In June 1917, Fuller had proposed a decisive offensive in Spring 1918, although in smaller scale than what Foot would propose in February 1918. Fuller proposed an assault front of 20 miles (32 km) – still 5 miles (8 km) longer than anything the BEF had yet achieved. He required 750 "light tanks" to exploit it. Foot might not have seen Fuller's proposal of June 1917 (what I have termed "Plan 1918"), but must have heard about it while administering Central Workshops.

On 31 December, Fuller wrote a proposal to launch an offensive in August 1918, in expectation of enough Mark V tanks and enough time to prepare new infantry in cooperation with these tanks. He hoped to win the war before the winter. Otherwise, the Allies must wait until Spring 1919. By January, production schedules fell so far behind as to make any decisive offensive in 1918 seem unlikely. That month, Fuller finished three papers proposing "raids" in 1918, pending a decisive offensive in 1919 (what I have termed his "first Plan 1919"). From February, at DGTC, Foot detailed the Tank Corps' structures and requirements through Spring 1919.

February was the month when Fuller realized that current light and medium tanks could not satisfy his doctrine. So began the long but poorly-documented (and poorly-told) genesis of his most famous doctrinal paper, which he liked to publicize as "Plan 1919," but which I have identified as his "second Plan 1919." Counting his first Plan 1919, the genesis of the second starts in January. Either way, the second was not finished until late May. Its genesis from February to May is told in this chapter's first section, before sections on implications for the principles of terrain, concentration, surprise, combined arms, speed, sustainment, and exploitation.

Genesis of Fuller's Second Plan 1919

An explicit stimulus for Fuller's second Plan 1919 was his dissatisfaction with current medium tanks. The requirement preceded the establishment of the tank arm.* Fuller agreed with the requirement for an exploitation tank, but had not been around to specify Mediums A, B, or C, which perhaps contributed to his scepticism.

Fuller first viewed the pilot Medium A on 5 February, along with other pilot tanks, which he collectively described as "very successful" in his diary. However, he was handed a paper describing Medium A's cross-country speed as only 4 mph (6.4 kmh), the prospective Medium B's as the same, and the prospective Medium

---

* On 3 October 1916, following almost two months of experience with the Heavy Tank Mark I in France, the Tank Supply Department (Albert Stern) of the Ministry of Munitions held a conference on how to improve the tank. The lead civilian designer, William Tritton, wanted to improve power and agility by using two engines, which he had specified for the Flying Elephant super heavy tank. Now he suggested the same arrangement in a "chaser" tank, which he prospected as a high-speed, lightly-armed tank for "chasing" the enemy after the heavier tanks break through. On 25 November, the Ministry of Munitions agreed to authorize the engines and other resources, so Tritton was ordered to build a pilot tank.

C's as 10 mph (16.1 kmh). The same document prospects the production of 1,100 Mark V tanks and variants, and perhaps half as many mediums, by November – of sufficient scale to fulfil his Plan 1918, but not soon enough for a decisive offensive in 1918. This disappointing schedule surely helped to push Fuller's prospect for decisiveness into Spring 1919, with new types of his own specification.

Perhaps the greatest revelation of 5 February was the inadequacy of the light tank by Renault of France. The hand-out of the day describes it as "very handy and easy to conceal," but specifies the same speed across country as for the Medium A, half as many crewmen (two men), and the "disadvantages [that it] must be helped over obstacles and shelled ground by infantry." During the demonstration, the tank crossed a bridge that had been towed over the trench by a heavy tank. Surely this is when Fuller resolved on medium tanks, having required "light tanks" in June 1917.

On 14 February, Fuller viewed the mock-up of Medium C, coincident with a Tank Committee meeting in Lincoln. He was unimpressed, despite its improved lethality and mobility over Medium A.

> When asked by [Vice-]Admiral [Archibald Gordon] Moore [controller of the MWD since October] what I thought of it, I answered "What is it for?" He could not tell me. So much for our designers at home. The Committee meeting was a complete farce. Whatever was suggested "would stop production" so point after point was decided without discussion!

The requirement for Medium D surely started here, but its genesis is confused. Fuller's memoirs credit Searle (Chief Engineer) for demonstrating a Medium A with alternative automotive parts in February, at a speed of 20 mph. It inspired their specification of the same speed for Medium D in March or April (1936: 281). However, Fuller's diary does not mention the fast Medium A. Searle never left papers. Major Philip Johnson reported to Searle as Chief Experimental Officer. Johnson claimed to lead the trial of this tank, and portrayed the Medium D as an incorporation of his inventions (Johnson, "Medium D Machine – Statement of Responsibility for Design," circa 1921, RACTM E1979.53).[*]

The demonstration occurred in February, yet both Johnson and Fuller agree

---

[*] Johnson has been privileged by historians. By the 1950s, he passed papers to Basil Liddell Hart, who was spinning himself as the inventor of mechanized combined-arms warfare, and pretending that Fuller preferred all-tank warfare. Liddell Hart shared these papers with Richard Ogorkiewicz, a younger historian. Ogorkiewicz met with Johnson shortly before the latter's death in 1965, at the age of 88 years, but never tried to speak with Fuller (who died in 1966, aged 87 years) or to access Fuller's papers (which Fuller sent to an American college). Ogorkiewicz was in correspondence with Martel from the 1940s, but Martel fell out with both Liddell Hart and Ogorkiewicz by the late 1950s. In Ogorkiewicz' histories (1960; 1968; 1970), Johnson is the initiator and leader, but Johnson never claimed so. Liddell Hart died in 1970, leaving his papers to the LHCMA. However, Ogorkiewicz held other papers by Johnson, which he eventually donated to the RACTM. The RACTM already held a few official documents authored by Johnson, and donated by other people. The archiving of these papers was not complete until the end of 2016! Unsurprisingly, Ogorkiewicz's histories are inaccurate. For instance, he mistakenly states that Medium D's speed inspired Fuller's doctrine, but this is the wrong way around. Ogorkiewicz (1968: 29) states also that the first Medium D was amphibious, but none was specified as amphibious until December 1918, and none was developed as amphibious until the Medium D** of 1920 (which sank).

that no consensus emerged for a new medium tank, with a speed of 20 mph,* for at least another month. In Johnson's account, the consensus emerges slowly from November until late March, when intelligence confirmed the German A7V tank.

> About March 1918 it was finally realized that the highest possible obtainable speed must be an essential feature of the tank. The vulnerability of the slow-moving Mark IV Tank was specially noticeable at the Battle of Cambrai on 20 Nov[embe]r 1917. The good results obtained by the Medium Mark "A" early in 1918 emphasized the value of speed very clearly – it being appreciably faster than the other types of tank. Further, the appearance of enemy tanks in March 1918 emphasized the value of speed as a protective measure (Johnson to A5, War Office, 23 February 1920, RACTM Medium D).

Fuller's diary does not indicate any slow emerging consensus for a fast tank. Rather, his diary and papers for the month are dominated by tank supplies. On 14 March, Fuller visited Capper in London, who shared a draft of the production programme for 1919, which Capper was escalating through the CIGS, for escalation to the Ministry of Munitions. This is one of the papers Foot must have co-written, although Fuller's diary does not mention Foot, and the paper itself is missing from Fuller's appendices, even though Fuller's diary cross-references it. On 16 March, Fuller returned, to be informed that the CIGS had accepted "Programme A" in principle, except that the War Department could not budget the men, yet. Fuller expected the men to be supplied too late to train them satisfactorily.

In Fuller's memoir, the ideas for Medium D and Plan 1919 come at the same time. The stimulus is not Foot, Capper, Searle, Johnson, the production schedule, or any prior medium tank (although the experimental speedier version of Medium A would inspire his specification of Medium D's speed). Rather, sufficient stimulus was the German counter-offensive that started on 21 March. Fuller decided that fast tanks should aim at enemy commanders and staff, more than the enemy artillery.

> Though of slow development, this idea suddenly flashed across my mind during our debacle in March. What did I then see? Tens of thousands of our men being pulled back by their panic-stricken headquarters. I saw army headquarters retiring, then corps, next divisional, and lastly brigade. I saw the intimate connection between will and action, and that action without will loses all co-ordination: that without an active and directive brain, the army is reduced to a mob. Then I realized that if this idea could be rationalized – by which I mean taken out of the realms of chaos and digested scientifically – a new tactics could be evolved, which would enable a comparatively small tank army to produce this result (1936: 321-322).**

Still, Fuller recorded no such idea in his diary in March or even April. To be fair,

---

* Johnson misrecalled or mistyped the fast Medium A's speed as 30 mph, while he recorded a smaller derivative (Light Infantry Tank) as being first to reach 30 mph – in 1921 ("Medium D Machine – Statement of Responsibility for Design," circa 1921, RACTM E1979.53).
** Fuller re-used this text in a magazine article ("War with the Mind Instead of the Muscles," *Newsweek*, 21 August 1944), and revised it for a later book (1961: 242-243).

Fuller needed a break from administering defensive operations before writing up his idea, although he had opportunities while traveling. Fuller visited Capper on 5 April, "about various tank questions, mostly of a minor nature," according to his diary. The only paper handed over that day is a compilation of battle reports. In the next couple weeks, Fuller was preoccupied with an agenda for the first Inter-Allied Tank Committee. On 21 April, he finished it, at 110 pages!

Foot claimed to finish "Mobile Army" on 24 April, when he handed it to his GSO1 (chief of staff). Two days later, Foot could not contain his impatience, and visited again. The GSO1 took the document out of his drawer, and replaced it, saying: "Some of the ideas aren't bad, but it wouldn't work. I'll have a talk to you about it some time." After lunch, Foot decided to take a copy to Capper. Thirty minutes later, Capper came into Foot's office, buttoning his coat, and saying: "Well, Foot, you will be interested to know that I'm taking your paper across to show it to the DCIGS." (At that time, the Directorate-General was in temporary offices over the street from the War Office.) A few days later, the War Office called a conference on the paper, with the DMO, Director of Organization, Director of Supply and Transport, Director of Artillery, Capper, and Foot.

> [F]rom these beginnings was evolved the whole plan of campaign for 1919. The idea, moreover, was adopted by the French and the Americans, and if the Armistice had not intervened we should have had an immense "Mobile Army" equipped with cross-country tractors instead of horses. A dozen other officers may have sent in similar schemes; I do not know and probably I never shall (Foot 1934: 218).

Meanwhile, on 28 April, Elles, Fuller, Martel, the GSO2 for Training (Major H. Boyd-Rochfort), two GSO3s (Captains A.G. Pearson and Ian M. Stewart), and Searle met with the sole purpose of discussing a future tank, with a speed of 20 mph and an operating range of 200 miles. Surely the meeting followed weeks of unrecorded discussion and consideration: Searle brought sketches and specifications of a future tank, and probably called the meeting. Another stimulus might have been Elles' letter to GHQ of 26 April, praising the performance of seven Medium As two days earlier, although both the praise and the requirement for Medium As is as counter-attackers, while Searle's requirement is for a "chaser." The minutes relate:

> Lieut.-Colonel Searle...pointed out that high speed would only be achieved if every effort was made to keep the weight as low as possible.
>
> The question of armament was discussed under two headings:
>
> a. The subordination of armament to speed.
>
> b. The possibility of destroying enemy's tanks.
>
> The committee agreed that the possibility of producing a machine combining high speed and tank[-]destroying power should first be considered. If the production of such a machine was found to be impossible, then two types should be built, a male and [a] female machine.

Foot and Johnson were not present, and do not mention the meeting in their accounts. Fuller's diary does not mention it until 2 May, when he wrote, with no context, that "the new Chaser tank I think will be a great success." He referenced a copy of the typed version of the minutes from 28 April, which he pasted into his journal (Appendix B46). Perhaps he received the copy that day. Perhaps he had reflected on the performance of the seven Medium As on 24 April, except that the Medium As do not meet his requirements for exploitation. As of May, the Tank Corps rated Medium A's speed on level ground as just 7.25 mph. The Medium B was rated at only 5 mph, the Medium C at 7 mph. At the same time, the Tank Corps (over-)estimated a recently captured German A7V heavy tank at 10 mph.

Another opportunity for Fuller to hear about Foot's paper came on 4 May, when Capper visited Tank Corps HQ, although the meeting had been scheduled to discuss Capper taking over Fuller's role on the Inter-Allied Tank Committee.

On 24 May, about a month after Foot finished his paper, Fuller finished his most famous doctrinal paper, which came to be known as "Plan 1919" (when accepted as the basis for an offensive in Spring 1919), but which I have identified as his "second Plan 1919."* In his diary, he records:

> Write out a forecast of the employment of the Medium D machine. Here is a solution to our difficulties[,] an absolute means of victory if we can only get our military pedants and manufacturers to move.

He appended a hand-written paper, with many edits and insertions, which was never accessed by most historians of the Great War, and remains difficult to read.

---

* Fuller's paper was known by at least three titles. It went though rounds of development, including as an offensive plan. The earliest surviving draft is pasted into his journal. It ends with the date 24 May 1918, although it paraphrases some content from his paper of 28 January, and has been amended by his hand. It contains instructions to the typist, and is the last surviving handwritten draft. The original title of Fuller's draft of May 1918 is: "The Tactics of the Attack as affected by the Speed and Circuit of the Medium D Tank." Fuller later wrote below this title: "Original draft upon which Foch based his plan for 1919" (RACTM E1980.18). His paper was developed through July 1918 with the British General Staff, who escalated to the Allied Commander (French Marshal Ferdinand Foch). Fuller repeatedly claimed that his submission and its title did not change until after 6 August 1918, when Foch wrote to the CIGS (Henry Wilson) to accept his proposal as the basis for an offensive in Spring 1919, for which it was renamed "Plan 1919." A year after the last handwritten draft, Fuller published it as an article in Tank Corps HQ's *Weekly Tank Notes,* entitled "Strategical Paralysis as the Object of the Decisive Attack." Fuller reprinted the whole document in a book (appropriately titled *On Future War*) in 1928. Parts appeared in his memoirs in 1936, and later publications that copied from his memoirs (1923: 118; 1928: 83; "They Now Move Tanks By Numbers," *Evening Standard,* 28 August 1934: 7; 1936: 340; 1955: III, 380; 1961: 243). However, in 1940 he lost most of his papers to a German bomb while they were stored in London, although the original journal survived with family. Fuller seems to have remained unaware of its survival when he donated his papers to Rutgers University, in the early 1960s, with an inventory by his own hand. He died in February 1966. In 1967, his widow donated the journal to the Royal Green Jackets Museum, which took responsibility for the archives of the Oxfordshire & Buckinghamshire Light Infantry Regiment, in which Fuller had been commissioned. In 1980, the Royal Green Jackets Museum loaned Fuller's journal to the Tank Museum. In 2011, this loan became a donation. Most of Fuller's biographers and the war's historians never visited any of the archives described above. One biographer wrongly describes Fuller's memoir as the only surviving source for Plan 1919 (Reid 1998: 49).

It starts as a musing on how the prospective Medium D tank would affect tactics. It ends with a promise of "a decisive victory next year," if enough Medium Ds could be acquired (1, 19). He expects the first to be ready by February 1919, although a sufficient number would take months to build up. The next day, Fuller worried that decisiveness would be delayed until 1920 by the decision, by the commander (General John J. Pershing) of the American Expeditionary Force, that US units should not be attached to Allied units.* On 10 June, Fuller was further dismayed by an admission from Major-General G.P. Dawnay (BEF MGGS), during a visit, that he did not know whether to invest in biolocomotive or mechanical platforms. By then, Fuller was worried that insufficient Medium Ds would be delivered to enable an offensive until July 1919. Within days, the schedule shifted to August 1919.

On 28 May, the CIGS (Henry Wilson) approved a schedule for an offensive on 1 June 1919. That same day, Fuller received a letter from Foot, intimating that the War Office was "agreeable" to tanks becoming the solution to the stalemate. At noon, Fuller left Bermicourt for London, to discuss production. That evening, he met with Foot, who said that the CIGS, DCIGS (Harington), and DMO (Percy de B. Radcliffe) were keen on tanks. Foot showed to Fuller the DGTC's scheme for an expanded tank force. Fuller did not tell Foot what he would write in his diary: the scheme "contains my ideas of a year back, [but] these are now obsolete." In memoirs, he describes his "Plan 1919" of 24 May as "more surprising and economical."

The next day, Fuller met Capper and Sir Arthur Duckham (Deputy Controller of Munitions Supply), who promised to send a copy of Fuller's paper to Churchill. On 30 May (Fuller's memoirs misrecall the day as 29 May), Fuller met Stern (then in charge of the Mark VIII Heavy Tank). On 31 May, he met Harington:

> He told me that when first he came to the War Office he could not find a solitary soul who knew anything about tanks. He then wrote to GHQ for their policy; but they had none, nor had they the time to formulate one. Then he asked me to prepare a paper on the entire reorganization of the Tank Corps, on lines which would enable the War Office to control it. Finally he asked me whether I would be willing to come to the War Office and assist him. This came as a surprise to me, and though I had every personal reason for saying "No," I felt, in the circumstances, that it was my duty to the Tank Corps to say "Yes." This I did; then I left with him a copy of "Plan 1919," as I wanted him to assimilate it at his leisure (1936: 292-283).

Fuller returned to France on 1 June. His "Plan 1919" continued to be detailed, authorized, and budgeted from June to August 1918, when it was routinely known as "Plan 1919" for short. In July, Fuller repeatedly visited the War Office, as the Tank Corps' highest representative (SD7) in the General Staff, although he still lacked a replacement at Tank Corps HQ. On 15 July, Fuller visited the Director of Staff Duties (Arthur Lynden-Bell) to arrange for Foot to be his deputy, and for the appointment of another seven staff officers. He started full-time in the War Office on 1 August.

Fuller and Foot must have known about their respective Plan 1919s by then, if not months earlier. Yet none of their publications mentions the other's Plan 1919.

---

* The US tank commander, Brigadier-General Samuel Rockenbach, relayed this decision.

Terrain

Fuller's second Plan 1919 does not specify terrain, although his doctrinal papers of December and January had specified suitable ground. Like Foot, Fuller implies, from the first page, that most terrain is suitable, given more tracked vehicles.

> Today the introduction of a cross-country petrol-driven machine, tank, or tractor, has expanded communications to include at least 75 percent of the entire terrain of the theatre of war…At the present moment, he who grasps the full meaning of the change, namely, that the earth has now become as easily traversable* as the sea, multiplies his chances of victory to an almost unlimited degree."** Every principle of war becomes easy of application if movement can be accelerated[,] and accelerated at the expense of the opposing side. Today to pit an overland mechanically moving army against one relying on roads, rails, and muscular energy is to pit a fleet of modern battleships*** against one of wind-driven three-deckers (1-2).

He repeats the implication within a page, when he pleads for a new "theory."

> The facts upon which our tactical theory has been based are now rapidly changing[,] and unless our present theory changes with them we shall not be exploiting to the full the prowess of this new machine,**** i.e., the possibility of moving rapidly in all directions with comparative impunity to small arms' fire (3).

The final page clarifies Fuller's prospect.

> The possibility of applying naval tactics to land warfare is an entirely new application of the strategic principles which endows the side which can apply them with at present an incalculable power…Formerly strategy depended on communications, now communications will become universal and though roads and rails will not cease to exist they will become but lines of least resistance (19).

Fuller specified "a frontage of attack of some 100 miles" (11). This is a reduction from the 400 miles he had specified on 28 January (although he had allocated 100 miles to the mechanized assault). The reduction almost conforms with Foot's paper. Foot had specified a front of 30 miles for each army in the assault, which implies a BEF offensive front of 90 miles (145 km). (The BEF had resourced three armies at most for simultaneous offensives.) Indeed, Fuller would later amend "hundred" to read "90." Two pages later, 90 miles are specified without amendment, although here such a front is for the "disorganizing" phase, by medium tanks and aircraft.

> A continuous front of attack of 90 miles may seem too extended to be practicable. By a simple tank manoeuvre [morcellation] this front may be reduced as far as the attackers are concerned to 50 miles without reducing the total 90 miles to be disorganized (13).

---

* After the word "traversable," the words "in all directions" are struck out.
** The words "to an almost unlimited degree" replace the words "many fold."
*** The word "Dreadnoughts" is struck out and replaced by "battleships."
**** The clause "prowess…" replaces "fundamental characteristic of the tank."

By date	Mark V	Mark V*	Mark V**	Mark VII	Mark VIII (UK only)	Mark VIII (Fr. only)	Mark IX, carrier	Medium A	Medium B	Medium C	TOTAL
May 1918	138	80					31	50			299
June 1918	133	180		12			30	39	36		430
July 1918		160		24	15	?	30	29	62	10	330
August 1918		110	90	24	30	?	30		85	20	389
September 1918		80	80	14	70	?	30		84	20	378
October 1918		80	80		116	?	30		85	20	411
November 1918		10	50		244	?	19		46	30	399
December 1918					344	?			13	40	397
TOTAL	271	700	300	74	819	?	200	118	411	140	3,033
Current ORDERS	400	700	300	74	2,046	?	200	200	430	200	4,580

Table 9: Future deliveries of British tanks, as estimated by the Ministry of Munitions in April 1918, before Fuller's second Plan 1919 (Appendix 51, Fuller's journal, RACTM).

This page specifies a 50-mile (80-km) front for the breaking-in forces (heavy tanks and infantry). Presumably the tank-less forces on the other 50 miles (likely 25 miles each side of the breaking-in front) would be advancing just to protect the flanks of the breaking-in forces. The great length of the front proposed by Fuller is a function of his ambition to attack four or five field army headquarters at once (with medium tanks, as detailed below in the section on surprise).

Britain's great effort on the Somme in July 1916 had advanced on a front 16 miles long. The longest front of assault using tanks to date had measured 15 miles (Cambrai, November 1917). None would be longer in 1918. Appropriately, Fuller wished to concentrate tanks on much narrower fronts of penetration.

Concentration

On 9 January 1918, the British, French, and Italian army chiefs had asked the Supreme War Council to determine tank policy. On 21 January, Capper handed to the CIGS a paper titled "Proposals for use of Tanks in the Campaign of 1919," which suggests a British-French force of 8,308 tanks and 110,550 men. However, as of April, the Ministry of Munitions had placed orders for only 4,580 tanks (see Table 9). Fuller seems to have adjusted his requirements to a few hundred more. On 24 May, Fuller acknowledges that "many thousands"* of tanks would be required to defeat the enemy using current strategy, although he does not expect to receive many thousands by 1919, so he recommends that fewer, more capable tanks should aim at the enemy's HQs. The paper itself does not specify the number of heavy tanks. It ends with a requirement for 1,500 Medium Ds by May 1919, which he later amended to 2,000. He appended requirements (see Table 10) for 2,592 heavy tanks, 2,000 Medium D tanks, and 400 Medium C tanks by May 1919, i.e., 4,992 heavy and medium tanks (24 May 1918: 5-6, 20; 1919: 94; 1936: 319, 325, 334).

Across the breaking-in front (50 miles; 80 km), Fuller requires one heavy tank per 100 yards in the first assault wave. Counting all three waves and the reserve gives a concentration of one heavy tank per 34 yards (31 m) of breaking-in front, or one heavy tank per 68 yards (62 m) of total offensive front. Counting both heavy and medium tanks almost halves the frontage per tank.

The tanks would be concentrated on narrower fronts of attack. Fuller suggests a "morcellated front of attack" of 50 miles (see Map 18), instead of a "continuous front of attack." The morcellated front, in his notional example, is composed of four

---

* He had replaced "12,000 to 18,000" with "many thousands."

fronts of assault (two are 10 miles long each, two 15 miles each), although tanks are attacking on only the flanks. Fuller regards a morcellated front as efficient: a few narrow penetrations (eight in the notional example) contrast to typical break-ins across miles of front, separated by weeks of preparations.

Capper helped to persuade the Inter-Allied Tank Committee to conclude (on 4 June) "that a large increase in our tank forces will give the best prospects of success in 1919." The forces were specified at 13,000 tanks and 125,000 tank personnel, of which the British would form 3,300 tanks and 45,000 personnel – short of Fuller's operational requirement (Fuller 1936: 275, 321). On 5 June, he wrote to Central Workshops urging prioritization of Medium D, whose design was being led by Central Workshops. "If erection could start in February and be maintained at the rate of 150 machines for 20 weeks this would give a total of 3,000 machines ready for operations by July 1st." The subsequent paper (undated and unaddressed) in Fuller's journal expects just 2,700 deliveries by 1 August. Only about six weeks would be left in the summer to deploy and use these tanks. Otherwise, a decisive offensive would wait until Spring 1920. Later in June, the Ministry of Munitions estimated only 1,582 deliveries for the year through June 1919 (see Table 11).

On 22 June, the DCIGS (Harington) summoned a conference at the War Office. Elles left for England on 24 June, Fuller on 25 June, carrying an agenda. At 1500 hours, 26 June, the conference opened, with Churchill, John "Jack" Seely (Deputy Minister of Munitions), Harington, Arthur Lynden-Bell (DSD), Radcliffe (DMO&I), William Furse (MGO), Capper (DGTC), Dawnay (BEF MGGS), Elles, Fuller, and others.

> General Harington, who was in the chair, opened by saying that it was necessary to lay down definitely what our future tank policy was to be. He then went on to discuss the question of expansion, and pointed out that, though our present tank personnel numbered some 17,000 in all, we must prepare plans to increase this to 45,000 or 50,000. To this Mr. Churchill said, that if the War Office could find the men, he would supply the machines, and that what he wanted was the military plans and

Force	Mission	Concentration	Heavy tanks	Medium D tanks	Medium C tanks	Service, support	TOTAL
Breaking (front of 50 miles, 88,000 yards, 80,467 m)	1st wave	1 tank per 100 yards	880				880
	2nd wave	1 tank per 100 yards	880				880
	3rd wave	1 tank per 150 yards	587				587
	Reserve	1 tank per 360 yards	245				245
	Envelop flanks	1 tank per 340 yards		260			260
	Protect flanks	1 tank per 677 yards		130			130
Disorganizing (front of 100 miles, although each penetration would be narrow)	Army HQs (4)	20 tanks per HQ		80			80
	Corps HQs (16)	20 tanks per HQ		320			320
	Divisional HQs (70)	5 tanks per HQ		350			350
	Army group HQs (2)	20 tanks per HQ		40			40
Pursuing	Pursuit	1 tank per 144 yards		820	400		1,220
TOTAL tanks			2,592	2,000	400		4,992
TOTAL battalions			54	30	6		90
		TOTAL British battalions	27	7	2		36
		TOTAL French battalions	13	13			26
		TOTAL US battalions	14	14			28
TOTAL brigades			18	10	2		30
TOTAL personnel			51,840	20,000	4,000	14,460	90,300

Table 10: Fuller's force requirements, missions, and concentrations for a decisive offensive in May 1919, as appended to his second Plan 1919, in May 1918 (1936: 334-335).

By date	Mark V*	Mark V**	Mark VII	Mark VIII (UK only)	Mark VIII (Fr. only)	Mark IX, carrier	Medium A	Medium B	Medium C	TOTAL
July 1918	36		1			4	4	37		82
August 1918	48		3	15	20	4	1	35		126
September 1918	37		3	40	50	5		16	3	154
October 1918		30	3	36	70	6		16	3	164
November 1918		40	3	50	80	6		16	5	200
December 1918		40	3	50	90	6		10	5	204
January 1919		40	2	48	50	6			5	151
February 1919		40		50		6			5	101
March 1919		27		87		5			5	124
April 1919				87					5	92
May 1919				87					5	92
June 1919				87					5	92
TOTAL for year	121	217	18	637	360	48	5	130	46	1,582
Orders	700	900	74	1,555	1,500	200	100	450	125	5,604

Table 11: Future deliveries of British tanks, as estimated by the Ministry of Munitions in June 1918 (RACTM Tank Design and Dev. 51-66).

requirements to carry them out. The question of reorganization was then discussed, and also the preparation of a concrete scheme to put before our allies with reference to the tank policy of the future, the part we proposed to play and the parts they should play.

On the whole, little was actually decided upon outside the establishment of a tank department [SD7] in the War Office, which was to come under my direction (Fuller 1936: 286-287).

Fuller's paper of 24 May, and its appendix, were passed to the General Staff for detailing, producing requirements for 12,516 tanks and 121,000 men across all three allies.[*] On 1 July, Capper presented these requirements in a paper titled "Armoured Striking Force for 1919." On 3 July, the General Staff prepared a letter for Wilson's signature, authorizing the numerical requirements, plus a statement that it was "not necessary to consider the actual method of attack" (the doctrine and the plan). These were never signed, because on 4 July the BEF started its offensive at Hamel, which proved the capacity of the tank force (Fuller 1936: 336).

On 5 July, the War Secretary (Lord Milner) visited the Tank Corps HQ in France. The next day, tanks were demonstrated: "he took the keenest possible interest in everything. He would ride in each type of tank we had, and I can still see him scrambling into a Mark V so excitedly that he sat down in a puddle of oil and never noticed it." Milner asked for a paper specifying Fuller's claims that a tank force is most efficient, which Fuller delivered as "Notes on Tank Economics" (1936: 291).

On 6 July, the General Staff conferred again, this time under Wilson. Wilson credited tanks for victory at Hamel, and said that the Supreme Allied Commander (Foch) was in favour of a decisive tank offensive in 1919. Wilson asked Harington (DCIGS) and Radcliffe (DMO) to prepare a paper for the Cabinet (1936: 336).

Fuller was unaware of these meetings and correspondences until days later. He was in France, administering operations at Hamel. He wrote a report on Hamel, which he sent to Harington. Harington replied by hand, seeking Fuller's help.

This attack has happened at a most useful moment for us. CIGS tells me

---

[*] The Germans got the misimpression that 25,000 tanks were planned for deployment in 1919. The Germans planned to deploy 800 tanks (Foertsch 1940: 157).

that Maj-Gen. Foch is strongly in favour of tanks now so I hope we shall get on and the outline of our proposals for next year will go to him in a few days with a private letter from CIGS. Now when can you come over [to SD7] – genuine? you shall have Foot? I want to consult you regarding the disposal of the other officers. Those that have not been helpful must go. The reorganization of WO has passed mil. members [of the Army Council] and will be approved by AC [the full Army Council, including the War Secretary and other ministers] tomorrow – we can then get on – so glad SofS [Milner] went to see you (9 July 1918, in Harington 1940: 82).

The Cabinet meeting included the Dominion premiers, Milner, Wilson, and Harington. The General Staff's requirement for 12,516 tanks and 121,000 men across all three allies was scheduled as the fifth item, but Lloyd George opened with it. He asked Harington: "You wrote this, didn't you?" Harington explained his role. Lloyd George asked: "What's it going to cost?" Harington replied that he had no idea, thinking that the prime minister was referring to financial costs. Lloyd George said: "You are just like all these soldiers, you never think about men's lives." In private, Wilson soothed Harington by explaining that Lloyd George had chosen to bully Harington to impress the Dominion premiers (Harington 1940: 82).

On 14 July, Fuller travelled to London. On 15 July, Fuller met with Harington, to emphasize that Foch should agree to a minimum number of tanks to make viable a decisive offensive in 1919. On 19 July, the Military Members of the Army Council met to prepare a letter to Foch. The letter was signed by Wilson on 20 July. Next, the General Staff developed Capper's paper of 1 July into requirements for 10,500 tanks and 7,296 tracked carriers for the British force alone, i.e., 2.1 times as many tanks as Fuller had required in May (Fuller 1936: 339).

Letter and memorandum were copied to Foch, who sent visitors to Tank Corps HQ, culminating on 25 July with a visit by Wilson's liaison to Foch (General Charles Grant). Haig received copies on 27 July, and replied on 28 July; he objected to the plan to reduce the cavalry in order to increase the Tank Corps. Nevertheless, on 6 August, Foch wrote to Wilson to accept the scheme as the basis for an offensive in Spring 1919, for which it was renamed "Plan 1919." Indeed, Foch wanted the programme hastened (Fuller 1923: 118; 1928: 83; "They Now Move Tanks By Numbers," *Evening Standard*, 28 August 1934: 7; 1936: 340; 1955: III, 380).

In July, British authorizations stood at 34 tank battalions, 6,000 heavy tanks, and 2,000 medium tanks, to be ready by Spring 1919 (Fuller 1920: 65-66).* Meanwhile, the planned deliveries of 1,500 Mark VIII heavy tanks had fallen behind schedule. (The type was named "International," because Britain and America agreed to produce major sub-assemblies, for final assembly in France, but the French assembly plant was never completed.) Capper complained that Stern (in charge of the British parts of the Mark VIII) was a micro-manager, and urged the Ministry to reduce the MWD's activities to only "those concerned with the arrangement necessary for the

---

* Fuller (1926: 79) later wrote that 6,000 to 8,000 tanks were ordered, most of them to be ready by summer 1919. Later still, he recalled that 8,000 tanks were authorized for 1919, presumably including 6,000 heavy tanks and the 2,000 Medium D tanks, which he had required in May 1918 and were authorized in July ("Where are Our Tanks?" *Sunday Pictorial*, 30 January 1944). Robert Larson (1984: 119) misreported 6,000 tanks authorized for 1919.

assembly of the 1,500 [Mark VIII] Tanks, a work of considerable magnitude, which should suffice to absorb all its energies" (Capper to J.E.B. Seely, Deputy Minister of Munitions, 16 July 1918, UKNA WO 158/859). However, Capper's position was abolished at the end of the month, and he went to command an infantry division.

Fuller arrived in the War Office on 31 July, to start his new job (SD7) on the morrow. He expected to programme an expanded Tank Corps for 1919. "What did I find? That men could not be had, because the cavalry would not release them, and that on the War Office priority list tanks took the nineteenth place, the eighteenth being filled by cable railways!" ("Wanted – A Super-General Staff," *The Evening Standard*, 8 January 1942). Fuller was most concerned about the supply of personnel and accommodation. "I did not doubt, under Mr. Churchill's drastic dictatorship, that the machines would be forthcoming." To lower the risks, Fuller persuaded the Tank Board to expand the orders for Mark V Heavy Tanks as a hedge against the failure of the Mark VIII, and to programme the production of Medium C, rather than pass over it in favour of the Medium D. Whenever Medium D would be ready for production, it could replace Medium C (Fuller 1936: 349).

On 1 August, Churchill chaired the Ministry of Munitions Council Committee, which heard that deliveries of tanks in July reached only a third of the estimate given in March, due to shortages of drawings, components, and labour (blamed on conscription and influenza) ("Production of Tanks," 1 August 1918, UKNA MUN 4/6400). On 21 August, Wilson (CIGS) wrote to Haig: "I wish to goodness we had 4000 or 5000 more tanks to give you now as we ought to have[,] had we looked into the future" (in Jeffery 1985: 50). On 9 September, Churchill told the Prime Minister that although the output of tanks was half that of expected, "Elles tells me that the tanks they have will see out the tank men this year." The Great War ended on 11 November 1918. Most of the production orders were cancelled within days.

Thus, we are left with widely varied estimates of the number of tanks the Allies could have deployed by Spring 1919. As estimated in September (see Table 12), about 1,800 tanks and carriers of the required types would be delivered from May 1918 to 4 May 1919. About 1,000 had been delivered from May to September (all were Mark V and Mark V* tanks). If production had fallen to one-third of plan, as was true in July, the Tank Corps would receive less than 1,300 tanks in the 12 months to May 1919. If production continued at one-half of plan, as Churchill had reported in September, the number would grow to about 1,400. If production were to fulfil current estimates, the Tank Corps could expect about 1,800 tanks in the year since Fuller authored his second Plan 1919 (about one-third of Fuller's requirement for 4,992 heavies and mediums). Only 355 mediums were expected by May, only 871 by September; Fuller required 2,000. Plan 1919 would have become Plan 1920, unless planners would accept a much smaller offensive in May 1919.

Surprise

Surprise is another complex principle. The subsections below address choices about preliminary bombardment, operational security, infiltration, and timing.

Preliminary Bombardment

In May 1918, as in December 1917, Fuller does not allow for any preparatory bombardment, except for counter-battery fire.

By date	Mark V* Male	Mark V** Male	Mark V** Female	Mark VII Male	Mark VIII Male	Mark IX carrier	Mark X Male	Mark X Female	Medium B Female	Medium C or D Male	Medium C or D Female	TOTAL
5 October 1918	27					1			4			32
4 November 1918	25					2			16			43
6 December 1918	18					4			23			45
5 January 1919		10	2	0.6	7	4			23	2	5	53.6
4 February 1919		13	2	.6	12	4			23	17	20	91.6
4 March 1919		15	2	.6	20	4	16	16	5	22	26	126.6
4 April 1919		15	3	.6	22	4	17	17	5	26	32	141.6
4 May 1919		15	3	.6	35	4	19	19	5	45	56	201.6
4 June 1919		15	3	.6	50	4	19	19	5	54	70	239.6
5 July 1919		15	3	.6	60	5	19	19	5	54	70	250.6
6 August 1919		15	3	.6	80	5	19	19	5	54	70	270.6
4 September 1919		15	3	.6	80	5	20	20	5	54	70	272.6
TOTAL for year	70	128	24	5.4	366	46	129	129	124	328	419	1768.4
Orders	297	524	108	35	1,500	187	535	535	495	1,355	1,700	6,271

Table 12: Future deliveries of British tanks, as estimated by the Ministry of Munitions in September 1918 (RACTM Tank Design and Dev. 51-66).

Operational Security

Fuller eschews surprise in space, at least on the front as a whole: he wants the preparations to be discoverable by the enemy, in order to attract enemy reserves onto the front, so that more enemy forces will be disorganized.

Still, since the front is 100 miles wide, one could expect surprise locally in space, wherever the first assaults are planned. Fuller himself specified several narrow, concentrated assaults. The launch of the medium tanks would be on even narrower parts of the front, so surprise in space and time should be easier to achieve in the disorganizing than the breaking phase.

Infiltration

The main surprise would be attacks on enemy HQs before the main assault.

> As our present theory is to destroy "personnel" so should our new theory be to destroy "command and supply," not after the enemy's personnel has been disorganized but before it has been attacked, so that it may be found in a complete state of disorganization when attacked. Here we have the highest application of the "Principle of Surprise" – the surprise by novelty of action (24 May 1918: 6).

Fuller's paper opposes the tradition of "wear[ing] down the enemy's fighting strength" (its "body"). He focuses on the commanders and staff at the HQs of the divisions, corps, and armies (the enemy's "brains"). "The decisive point of attack is the brain of the opposing army." Tanks are the means to avoid the body in order to strike at the brain. Rather than "wearing down" or "dissipating" the "body," his preference is "rendering inoperative of his power of command" with "a shot through the brain" ("brain warfare"), followed by a "shot through the stomach," to "dislocate the enemy's supply" (4-5; 1919: 85-88).

Fuller conceptualizes a three-phase offensive: "disorganizing"; "breaking"; and "pursuing." In the "disorganizing" phase, medium tanks would aim at division, corps, and army HQs.

> [C]ould we suddenly remove these from an extensive sector of the German front the total collapse of the fighting personnel which they control would be but a matter of hours (5).

The disorganizing phase remains the vaguest and most optimistic part of Plan

1919. Fuller was always airy about how tanks, without other arms, could infiltrate a front that has not been broken. On this, he had form. His paper on "Defensive and Offensive Use of Tanks," of 31 December 1917, expects Mark V Heavy Tanks to advance at least 8,000 yards through enemy lines, in the dark, before the assault at dawn, in order to deposit medium machine-gunners, who would dig in defensively to prevent enemy reinforcements from reaching the front.

On 24 May, Fuller suggests that enemy reserves could be attracted away by a mock concentration or assault elsewhere. To confuse the suggestion, he refers to "a combination of these two ideas: (a) to force the enemy to mass his reserves in a given sector; (b) to disorganize these reserves before we break through them" (9).

> Once the preparations are well in hand, without any tactical preparation whatsoever, fleets of Medium D tanks should proceed, at top speed, by day or possibly by night directly onto the various headquarters allotted as their objectives (12).

He seems to assume that future mediums would be so fast as to assemble and penetrate quicker than the enemy could counter them. He writes about them attacking "without any tactical warning," as if surprise would help infiltration, as was true for the first day of the German counter-offensive on 21 March. He writes about attacking at "top speed," as if they could race through defences before the defences react. Any surprise surely would be lost beyond the first defensive line, which would warn the lines to its rear. Further, by this stage of the war, the enemy deployed artillery in the second defensive line as direct anti-tank weapons. The medium tanks would need to infiltrate several defensive lines, effectively running the gauntlet of direct and indirect fire, and anti-tank obstacles, without getting sucked into battles for which the heavy tanks are optimized, so that they can reach enemy HQs as quickly as possible (5).

Implicitly, the mediums are infiltrating an intact front, but Fuller does not make infiltration explicit. To help their implicit infiltration, he allows that they could attack "possibly at night." He already prescribes smoke or twilight for the breaking phase, but not for the disorganizing phase. Probably he did not want medium tanks to attack in smoke and darkness given that the mediums would need to navigate for dozens of miles, without other arms, through many lines of defences, towards HQs that occupy less space than a unit. His paper does not specify navigation, except to aim at coloured markers dropped from aircraft or fired from artillery (smoke at day, "lights" or flares at night). The markers sound useful, except that he does not explain how aircraft are supposed to find enemy HQs or why the HQs would linger once marked. In dark hours to date, tanks had navigated by compass bearings, pre-laid tapes, and pedestrian guides, but the latter two aids are incompatible with the depth and speed he had in mind (12).

To be fair, Fuller perhaps saw no point in specifying how the medium tanks would infiltrate until the lines of infiltration would be selected (five or six such lines, given five or six HQs to be targeted).

Attacks on HQs are most viable in the pursuit phase. On 21 July, when planning for the offensive at Amiens, Fuller proposed that both battalions of Medium As should follow the break in, east-south-eastwards, before turning southwards through the German artillery and services facing French 1st Army. Fuller cannot be blamed for lack of specificity then. The 4th Army commander (Henry Rawlinson) set the suggestion aside, and tied the medium tanks to the cavalry, which did not break through. The sole battalion of armoured cars had been attached to Australian Corps, which ordered them to advance towards an area where divisional and corps HQs were located: some cars surprised a corps HQ, transport, another corps HQ, and infantry retreating from the frontline (Fuller 1936: 298-299, 308-309).

These good outcomes did not persuade Fuller to schedule attacks on enemy HQs during the pursuit phase. To the end of life, Fuller repeatedly clarified that he wanted the disorganizing phase to precede the breaking phase, yet he did not add anything about how medium tanks are supposed to penetrate an unbroken front.*

Timing

Although the space of assault might not be a surprise, the timing could be. The General Staff's final version, as proposed to the Allied Supreme Command in July 1918, specifies an assault in the twilight before dawn, under cover of smoke. The plan conflates Fuller's disorganizing and breaking phases. Heavy tanks, medium tanks, infantry, and ground-attack aircraft would assault. Meanwhile, mediums would race ahead towards the enemy's division, corps, and army HQs, destroying

---

* Later, Fuller summarized the plan to send fast tanks – covered by smoke or darkness – "through the enemy's fighting body and, making for all Divisional, Corps, and Army Headquarters, paralyse these brain and nerve centers by direct attack; simultaneously, other fast machines were to attack all railheads, supply, and signal centers, and reduce the personnel at these points to a state of panic." Upon enemy panic, heavier tanks would assault the enemy's frontline, followed by the infantry (1923: 118; 1926b: 78). Later still, he summarized the plan as "suddenly, under cover of night and smoke, to pass a large number of tanks through the enemy's front and attack his command headquarters and supply centers" (1932a: 267); "to pass a fleet of long high-powered machines right through the entrenched belt and attack the enemy's headquarters in rear of it, whilst his front was being attacked by tanks and infantry" (1932b: 111); "to pass a tank army unhindered by infantry through the German front with the object of attacking the command and supply system behind it, and so completely disorganize and demoralize the front itself" ("They Now Move Tanks By Numbers," *Evening Standard*, 28 August 1934: 7); and "to attack the enemy's rear before attacking his front, so that the foundations of his front might be knocked silly when the time came to assault his front." ("The Ideal Tank for Our Attack," *Evening Standard*, 3 March 1943). He recalled that his paper of 24 May advocates a surprise attack by a "breaking force" of heavy tanks and infantry, and a "disorganizing force" of faster Medium D tanks, which would attack command centers and thereby "disorganize" and "paralyse" the enemy, The "pursuing force" would utilize all types of fast tank ("War with the Mind Instead of the Muscles," *Newsweek*, 21 August 1944). He wrote that the final plan was "to launch it [the initial attack] against his rear – his command and supply system – by suddenly and without warning passing powerful tank forces, covered by aircraft, through his front. Next, directly paralyzation of his rear had disorganized his front, to launch a strong tank and infantry attack of the Cambrai pattern against that front" (1945: 140). Penultimately, he summarized the plan as "to use fast-moving tanks, supported by aircraft, …to break through selected points in the German front and make straight for divisional, corps and army headquarters and supply centers," to be followed by the traditional arms in a normal attack (1955: III, 380). "The means proposed were a sudden eruption of squadrons of fast-moving tanks, which unheralded would proceed to the various enemy headquarters, and either round them up or scatter them. Meanwhile every available bombing machine was to concentrate on the supply and road centers. Only after these operations had been given time to mature was the enemy's front to be attack in the normal way, and directly penetration was effected, pursuit was to follow" (1961: 243).

telegraph and telephone communications along the way, and occupying bridges. The pursuit would continue as soon as follow-on forces arrive (Fuller 1936: 339).

Combined Arms

Artillery: Towed

Fuller's second Plan 1919 requires artillery to counter enemy batteries, deliver a creeping barrage, and fire on targets on demand.

Fuller expects the defenders to be too disorganized to cause trouble between the "breaking" fronts. "If this is not thought likely then flank attacks can be supplanted by massed frontal artillery fire, or by weak infantry attacks protected by heavy barrages on the old lines" (14).

Artillery: Self-Propelled

In January, Fuller had required mortar tanks for delivering plunging fire behind fortifications. On 5 February, he saw a demonstration of a Mark IV with a 3-inch Stokes mortar, firing (unfuzed) shells while it advanced. The coincident handout notes that the same mortar could be fired from a towed sledge. No mortar-tank or -sledge was mass-produced before the end of the Great War. Fuller's second Plan 1919 does not mention self-propelled artillery. Instead, it relies on tanks for the heavy fire support, and requires tracked tractors for the artillery, at a time when the word "tractors" was often used to mean carriers too.

> The heavy artillery will disappear as a mobile arm after the first days['] advance and will be relegated to its original position in the siege train, and the field artillery, if still horse drawn, will be unable to keep up with the fighting after the second or third day's advance. Field artillery horses must therefore be replaced by tractors (16).

Aircraft

Fuller lists aircraft and tanks as the "two types of weapons" that can "penetrate or avoid this belt of resistance," meaning the first 18 miles (29 km) of defended territory, short of enemy army HQs (7-8).

> Meanwhile, every available bombing machine should concentrate on the various supply and road centres. The signal communications should not be destroyed, for it is important that the confusion resulting from the dual attack carried out by the Medium D Tanks and the aeroplanes should be made known to all as soon as possible (12).

Other aircraft would drop coloured markers on enemy HQs to help the medium tanks to navigate. At times, he allows the mediums to continue to enemy GHQ, but on one page he allows that it "might be dealt with by dropping several hundred tons of explosives" (13).

During the assault, Fuller expects aircraft to attack enemy artillery, to act as "an advanced guard," to guide tanks onto their objectives, to carry messages between tanks and Tank Corps HQ, to carry tank brigade commanders for observation of their units, to attack enemy's headquarters, and to supply the advanced tanks (15).

Tanks and Infantry

In the "disorganizing" phase, the arms are not combined. Only medium tanks and aircraft are involved, and they are operating independently, except that some aircraft are dropping markers on HQs to help the tanks to navigate.

For the "breaking" phase, Fuller combines heavy tanks, infantry, and artillery. He writes that once the Medium D tanks and aircraft have caused "confusion," and time has elapsed to allow the confusion to become "epidemic," he would launch "a carefully mounted [heavy] tank, infantry, and artillery attack" into the enemy's artillery zone (12).

Fuller allows for infantry to move on foot up to the secondary objective line, to act independently "in areas unsuited to tanks," and to "garrison" objectives seized by the tanks. Beyond the secondary line, he requires infantry to be mechanized, as "a mobile protective base" behind the medium tanks.

> [I]nfantry as at present equipped and known will become first a subsidiary and later a useless* arm on all ground over which tanks can operate... Except for the gaining of the secondary zone, infantry on their feet will be next to useless. They will have to be carried forward by mechanical means if they are ever to keep up with the pursuit of the Medium D Tank (4, 15).

Tanks and Engineers

Fuller does not specify engineering tanks in May 1918, although he surely assumes the same capabilities as executed at Cambrai in November 1917. Radically, he reserves engineers for the sustainment of the advance.

> The duties of the Royal Engineer and Pioneer units will be considerably enlarged. Their work will be chiefly confined to the improvement of communications – roads and rails and the building of bridges; all defence works [at the objectives] will be relegated to the infantry (17).

Most of this engineering work seems to benefit the heavy tanks. Fuller specifies the mediums as "sufficiently light to cross ordinary road, river, and canal bridges." He forgets his specification of January 1918 for amphibious pursuit tanks.

Speed

Fuller's first Plan 1919 (of January) had separated a principle of speed, although he subsumed it under the official principle of "mobility." His second Plan 1919 (of May) does the same. Additionally, speed is introduced as useful to the principle of surprise too.

> The tactics of the Medium D Tank will be mainly based on the Principles of Movement and Surprise. The whole objective of its action being to accentuate surprise by movement not only rapid but unexpected (8).

His expectations of great gains in mobility and surprise seem over-ambitious, given that he specifies the speed of the Medium D at 20 mph (32 kmh). Even when

---

* Fuller had written "a useless arm" before adding "first a subsidiary and later..."

Fuller specified a Medium E (on 15 June), he stuck with a speed of 20 mph. In November 1916, Martel had specified destroyer, engineering, and signals tanks at 20 mph, "torpedo tanks" at 30 mph (48 kmh). In May 1918, the Tank Corps rated the Medium A's speed at 7.25 mph (12 kmh) on level ground, and estimated the speed of a captured A7V heavy tank at 10 mph (16 kmh). The cavalry could charge at more than 13 mph (22 kmh), for minutes, and could sustain an average speed of 5 to 6 mph (8 to 10 kmh) for hours, i.e., beyond the daily speed (20 miles per day) that Fuller requires for the mediums. Fuller expects tanks to keep going through fire that would stop cavalry, and specifies Medium D with a speed 2.5 times the sustained speed of cavalry. He expects mediums to leave infantry further behind.

> Strategically the leading characteristic* of the Medium D Tank is that it is a time-saver, on account of its high speed, its extensive radius of action, and its power of moving in all directions. In battle, compared to infantry, its speed is 10 times greater and radius of action 25 times greater. Its protection power is beyond comparison.
>
> The saving of time in battle means the saving of time in manufacture, consequently the reduction of man power required for manufacture (19).

The speeds of a fighting advance are much slower than a vehicle's maximum speed. Fuller specifies that enemy field army HQs would be reached in 3 to 4 hours, i.e., at 4.5 to 6.0 mph (7.2 to 9.7 kmh). He specifies a sustained advance of 20 miles (32 km) per day, which, assuming a fighting day of 12 hours, implies a speed of 1.7 mph (2.7 kmh) – pretty much the cross-country speed of heavy tanks. All in all, he does not seem justified to promise that Medium D would be fast (and survivable) enough to penetrate enemy defenses without resistance, or to surprise enemy headquarters before the same headquarters receive warnings (9).

Sustainment

Fuller expects the mediums to be self-sustaining, the heaviess and other arms to be sustained by carriers, including the Mark IX. The subsections below break down the sustainment challenges by the disorganizing and breaking phases.

Disorganizing Phase

Fuller expects the mediums to find the enemy's division and corps HQs 10 miles (16 km) from no-man's land, field army headquarters 18 miles (29 km), army group headquarters 45 miles (72 km), and Western GHQ 100 miles (161 km). Fighting at an average speed of 10 mph (16 kmh), a maximum of 20 mph (32 kmh), an army headquarters could be reached within 2 hours.

By May, in northern France, the attackers could count on at least 12 hours of daylight, which implies a penetration of 120 miles (193 km), given a fighting speed of 10 mph. One would expect Fuller to urge the medium tanks to try to reach the enemy GHQ in one day, otherwise GHQ might escape before the medium tanks reach it (7-8, 12-13). However, on one page he leaves it to bombers: "this, at least, would neutralize clear thinking" (13).

---

* "leading characteristic" replaces "chief advantage."

Fuller specifies an "advance to a minimum depth of 20 miles a day." In six days, the advance would reach at least 120 miles (193 km). "[B]y the end of the 7th day the enemy, after a pursuit of 150 miles (241 km), will be reduced to a non-fighting condition" (15-16). In eight days (the upper range of his schedule), the advance could reach at least 160 miles (257 km), although he aimed at 150 miles in total. Such an advance would get the Allies into Germany, from their current front.

This strategy would be more efficient, he argued, despite more ambitious depth than previous proposals. Foot provided for a penetration of 60 miles in 6 days. On 28 April, Tank Corps staff had discussed a tank with a range of 200 miles. On 24 May, Fuller specifies a pursuit of 150 miles in 7 days, and a Medium D with a range of 150 to 200 miles. After the war, he raised its range to 200 to 300 miles.

Breaking Phase

After the Medium D tanks and aircraft have disorganized enemy HQs, miles to the rear of the enemy's front line, the main assault starts, on a front 50 miles wide. Fuller reserved 245 of the 2,592 heavy tanks, either to reinforce the third wave or to restart attacks on objectives that previous waves might have failed to secure.

Fuller expects the heavy tanks and pedestrian infantry to reach only 10,000 yards (9,144 m) deep, up to the artillery zone, on the first day (like Townshend's paper of August 1916, and Foot's paper of April 1918). Here is where he specifies that the infantry "will have to be carried forward in mechanical transport if they are ever to keep up with the pursuit of the Medium D tank." He does not specify supply tanks, but probably takes the Tank Corps' use as ongoing. Explicitly, he requires cross-country lorries for the Army's transportation branch.

> The mobility of the Army Service Corps will be taxed to the utmost. Horses will disappear and road lorries will have to be supplemented by field lorries, if the troops are to be adequately supplied. All road lorries should be easily convertible into field lorries by some simple wheel attachment which will enable them to traverse grass and plough[ed] land (17).

On 28 May 1918, Wilson approved the schedule for an offensive on 1 June 1919. The supply tanks would carry the infantry on to the first objectives, before turning back to fetch supplies, while pedestrian infantry reinforce the first objectives. Given supplies and pedestrians on the first objectives, the tanks and mechanized infantry could proceed to the next (Fuller 1936: 320).

In July, the General Staff detailed requirements for 10,500 tanks and 7,296 tracked carriers for the British force alone – a rate of about 1.4 tanks per carrier (Fuller 1936: 339). Likely, these requirements would not have been fulfilled, even if the war had continued into 1919. If the Ministry had delivered the 4,992 tanks that Fuller required, then, at the same rate, he could expect less than 3,500 carriers. Most of these carriers would be conversions from tanks. According to the production schedule released in September 1918 (see Table 12), only 27 products of the Mark IX type would be delivered by May.

Exploitation

After heavy tanks, infantry, and artillery have broken through to the artillery zone, the "pursuing" could begin.

[T]he pursuing force consist[s] of all medium tanks available and lorry[-]carried infantry. To render this force doubly effective it should be preceded by squadrons of Medium D Tanks which will secure all centres of communication, break up hostile army group headquarters[,] and disperse all formed bodies of troops met with (13).

The pursuit incorporates mediums previously used to disorganize HQs, up to army echelon, on the first day. Fuller expects the mediums to advance to army group HQs by the third day, and to reach as far as enemy GHQ within seven days. Clearly the disorganizing phase and pursuit overlap for at least six days, although Fuller does not admit the overlap.

The pursuers could envelop forces that are too disorganized to escape. Indeed, Fuller uses the semantics of envelopment, as he had since February 1917.

Aircraft also are involved, scouting and attacking in advance of medium tanks. Cavalry are not required: "Aeroplanes will bear to tanks a similar relationship as cavalry to infantry." By 1919, "draught horses will disappear and by degrees riding horses." Fuller disarmingly allows that "if cavalry have sufficient endurance to keep up a pursuit of at least 20 miles a day for a period of 5 to 7 days,* their tactical value will be considerable, for they will be able to form mobile mounted skirmishing lines between the groups of Medium D Tanks" (15-17).

Outcomes

Fuller concluded on 24 May 1918 by promising "every prospect of ending the war" in May 1919. However, Germany agreed an armistice in November 1918, when the tank "was on the point of revolutionizing tactics" (1923: 115). He later claimed that Plan 1919 "would have ended the war with a stupendous drama, the only satisfactory way to win a war" (to Liddell Hart, 26 July 1919, LH 1/302/177). Lloyd George (1938: 388) agreed: "had the advance of the Allies in 1919 taken place, it would have been a devastating march of hordes of mechanical caterpillars."

Fuller prospected "even more startling results than they [the Germans] did in 1939-1940" (1945: 141). He claimed that his Plan 1919 was applied in 1939 in a "modified" form that "became known as *Blitzkrieg*" (1961: 244). In person, Fuller convinced Luvaas (1964: 344) that Plan 1919 "embodied many of the concepts later developed in the German *Blitzkrieg*." Fuller's first biographer described "Plan 1919" as "a most remarkable document" (Trythall 1977: 74). One historian described it as "a blueprint of *Blitzkrieg*" (Terraine 1978: 125), another as an argument "for a fully mechanized army...setting in motion a process which would revolutionise armies" (Macksey 1983: 39).

Unfortunately, most historians of "Plan 1919" never read it. They preferred to consult Liddell Hart more than Fuller, who was discredited by a longer period of advocacy for fascism. Even historians too young to have met either man tend to be students of Liddell Hart's mentees. Further, they tend to be anchored in Liddell Hart's imperative to "counter the orthodoxy." Most lack the military experience to interpret Fuller's sketchy papers and the official discourse. This helps to explain why Fuller's second biographer misdescribed "Plan 1919" as a "misnomer," "not

---

* The number 7 replaces the number 10.

a plan," rather "a conceptual document," just because its title changed. He seems unaware of the detailing of the plan from June to August (Reid 1998: 49).

> [I]t was a hazardous undertaking involving prodigious difficulties, not least the co-ordination and control of an expensive and untried weapon. There was a real danger that numbers of tanks might be trapped and destroyed piecemeal behind the German lines beyond the aid of supporting infantry. When all this is said, it might still be replied that the plan had a chance of working so long as German morale continued to decline (Reid 1987: 54).

Hew Strachan (1983: 155-156) dismissed the doctrine's chances just because the Medium D did not exist until 1923, ignoring the facts that it would have existed by 1919 under wartime programmes of production, and that the offensive would have gone ahead with Medium C, if Medium D had not been ready.

Strachan criticized Fuller's doctrine with two counter-factual claims: "Fuller's projected success for the tank still rested on the assumption that the enemy troops remained ill-trained conscripts prey to moral forces;" and "he did not reckon with the application of the machine to the defence in the shape of the anti-tank gun." Neither of Strachan's claims is true.

A.J. Smithers (1989: 19) judged that Plan 1919 "could not have reached the expectations held in some quarters of a great swarm of modern tanks sweeping everything before them." J.P. Harris (1991: 166-167, 188) wrote that it "has often been treated with greater reverence than it really deserves," "was not even particularly good of its kind," "could at no time have been implemented with hope of success," and "was an ill-thought-out fantasy, the great celebrity of which is largely unmerited."

Similarly, David Stevenson (2011: 220) declared that Plan 1919 "has attracted too much attention." Like Smithers and Harris, Stevenson betrays ignorance by characterizing it as only "an enormous long-range force that could pierce the enemy lines and roam at will...beyond the capabilities of the era." None of these historians studied Plan 1919 as Fuller wrote it, or as the Ministry of Munitions programmed it.

Plan 1919 was viable, except for Fuller's vague hope that medium tanks could infiltrate the enemy's front before the assault, which the General Staff properly finessed in July 1918 by conflating the assault and disorganizing phases.

Map 19: This map of the battlefield was issued to all officers involved operationally. It is marked with tank assembly areas (black-edged rectangles), approach routes to each "Starting Point" ("S.P."), routes to the start line ("taped line"), the nearest fall of the creeping barrage before its first jump ("artillery start line"), the nearest fall of the creeping barrage after its final jump ("artillery halt line"), the final objective line, and the "operating areas" of the tanks and infantry (yellow). Each grid represents a 1,000-yard box. The original scale is 1:20,000 ("Operations by the Australian Corps Against Hamel, Bois de Hamel, and Bois de Vaire, 4th of July, 1918," S.S. 218, July 1918: 1, Fuller Papers).

14

Hamel, July 1918

The BEF's defensive period lasted through May. By then, the Allies did not expect to win before the winter, but they did want to return to the offensive, in order to keep the Germans from building reserves towards another counter-offensive as great as the one they had launched in March. Indeed, by June, GHQ's Director of Military Operations (John "Tavish" Davidson) said he felt in his "fingers" that the Germans would attack at Ypres.* GHQ still hoped that German morale was close to breaking, which indeed would be borne out within months.

As of June, the Tank Corps was building towards offensive readiness by August. However, the 4th Army (Henry Rawlinson) saw an opportunity to cut off a German salient near Hamel. GHQ demanded some tanks for a full combined-arms offensive on 4 July. In scale, this operation is equivalent to Fuller's "tank raid" proposal of January. Its secondary intents, to damage enemy material and morale, and bolster Allied morale, particularly Australian morale, also conform with Fuller's "tank raid" proposal. Rawlinson assigned it to the Australian Corps (Lieutenant General John Monash), who shared a reputation as an innovator. Unfortunately, historians have become mired in a dispute about whether Rawlinson or Monash deserves credit, with ugly nationalist undertones on each side. Fuller repeatedly credited Rawlinson, without mentioning Monash, for seeing the opportunity for attack, and for being better disposed towards tanks. The 4th Australian Division had suffered a costly experience with tanks at Bullecourt on 11 April 1917, and needed "tactful persuasion" to accept any tanks (1920: 305; 1936: 287).

Terrain

In January, Fuller had proposed "tank raids" on a front of at least 20,000 yards (18,288 m), with the currently authorized Tank Corps, and a "deep" final objective line, 10,000 yards (9,144 m) from the start. The latter is also the depth Fuller had recommended on 30 December for anti-tank defences.

The offensive at Hamel was less ambitious. It started 6,000 yards (5,500 m) wide, from opposite Le Hamel, down to the River Somme. The first objective line runs from Hamel through Hamel Wood ("pear-shaped wood") to Vaire Wood. The final objective line lay up to 2,500 yards (2,300 m) to the east of the start line, on a front 7,500 yards (6,900 m) long, on higher ground, with line of sight towards the south-east, north-east, and east (over the River Somme).

The subsoil is chalk, and was well-drained and little damaged at the time. The weather remained fine for the operation.

After the battle, GHQ stressed "the local and special conditions, especially the high moral[e] of the infantry, the fact that there was not much wire, that the ground was suitable for the action of tanks, and that the objective was strictly limited and within the effective fire of the field and heavy artillery as sited for the attack."

---

* Edward Cox (GHQ's BGGS for Intelligence) told Fuller this hearsay on 11 June 1918.

Tank wave	Australian Brigade	Australian battalions	Tank Battalion	Tank Company	Tank Section	Tanks	Objective
1st	11th	1	13th	C	11th and 12th	6	Northern end of Final Line
		0.5	8th	C	9th	3	North of Hamel, to Final Line
		1	8th	C	10th and 11th	6	Hamel Village
		0.5	8th	C	12th	3	South of Hamel, to Final Line
	4th and 11th	0.5	8th	A	2nd	3	Pear Shaped Trench
			8th	A	1st, 3rd, 4th	9	Liaisons between 4th and 11th brigades
	4th	1	8th	B	10th, 11th	6	Hamel and Vaire Woods
		1			9th	3	North of woods, to Final Line
		1			12th	3	South of woods, to Final Line
	6th	1	13th	C	9th and 10th	6	Southern end of Final Line
2nd	4th	1	13th	B	5th and 6th	6	Close support, final wave
	11th	1			7th and 8th	6	Close support, final wave
TOTAL: 2	3	10	2	5	20	60	5

Table 13: Force structure on 4 July 1918 at Hamel, ordered from north (top) to south (bottom) of the assault front (ignoring flanking divisions) ("Operations by the Australian Corps Against Hamel, Bois de Hamel, and Bois de Vaire, 4th of July, 1918," S.S. 218, July 1918: 8; Fuller 1920: 205).

Concentration

Fuller sent his paper of 28 January to GHQ, with a cover letter suggesting that 20 infantry divisions should be kept out of the lines in order to train with tanks, tank variants, and aircraft. Fuller had read the production and recruitment schedules to mean that the force would be sufficient by August.

By March, the Tank Corps in France had grown from 9 to 14 battalions,[*] and from 3 brigades to 5. However, the 3rd Brigade was still converting to medium tanks, and the 5th had formed in March, with just one unit, which still waited for tanks. Another unit was waiting for armoured cars. Thus, the Tank Corps in France counted three ready heavy brigades (1st, 2nd, and 4th, of which the 4th had been formed in December), nine ready heavy battalions – with 324 tanks, one unready heavy battalion, and three medium battalions – with 50 tanks. As of 16 April, the units in France (including service, support, schools, experimentation) were authorized to hold just 12,603 men – fewer than an infantry division. Holdings fell short by some thousands. Units in England were authorized with 4,881 men.[**]

The German counter-offensive delayed readiness for months. The 5th Brigade was disbanded; the 4th was converted to pedestrian light machine-gunners.

The Germans restarted in April, which kept the struggle active into May. As of 7 May, the fighting units in France held 434 tanks (293 Mark IVs – including 67 supply variants; 86 Mark Vs; 55 Mediums; 26 Gun Carriers). Counting vehicles in salvage, repair, experimentation, or training, the Tank Corps in France held 716 tanks (505 Mark IVs – including 118 supply variants; 129 Mark Vs; 82 Mediums; 43 Gun Carriers). By mid-May, the units held 598 tanks (387 Mark IVs; 129 Mark Vs; 82 Medium As), but the Germans had not finished with their offensives. The first three brigades were re-equipped with tanks of the latest type, Mark V, in June, the 4th Brigade in July. As of 1 June, the Tank Corps in France held just 10,479 men. By July, the BEF was still short of the infantry and tanks for the great offensive that Fuller had expected to launch in August.

Rawlinson initially committed three divisions, effectively fulfilling the scale of Fuller's proposed raids, except that these formations held about two-thirds of the

---

[*] The alphabetical designations of the battalions were now changed to numerical.
[**] These data can be found in appendices to Fuller's journal.

personnel they should have held. The American Expeditionary Force was keen to contribute, although in the end its contribution was reduced to four companies of infantry.* Fuller persuaded Rawlinson to allocate more tanks (5 companies, with 60 Mark V tanks, all from 5th Tank Brigade) and less infantry (10 battalions, across three Australian brigades, from three divisions). The assault infantry took over the front the night before the attack, replacing two brigades from the commanding division (4th).** On each flank, an Australian division was obliged to launch diversionary attacks, which were not considered parts of the assault.

On an assault front of 6,000 yards (5,500 m), the concentration works out at one tank per 100 yards (91 m), and one artillery piece every 9.5 yards (8.7 m).

Surprise

Surprise was achieved with an unusual mix of measures: an unusually short and wide preliminary bombardment, disinformation, operational security, an early Z-hour, and obfuscation.

Preliminary Bombardment

Fuller's paper of 31 December eschews a preliminary bombardment for both raids and offensives. The German counter-offensive of 21 March was preceded by a preliminary bombardment lasting five hours, which was short by British standards, but much denser: 1,100,000 shells were fired. Fuller knew the duration but not the density. The next day, Fuller told his dairy that the second cause of the German success was "the shortness of their artillery bombardment."

Given that the enemy's wire belts at Hamel were under-developed, the preliminary bombardment lasted just seven minutes, and focused on enemy trenches.

Some surprise was achieved in space, by bombarding a wider front than just the assault front. Some surprise was achieved in time, by scheduling seven minutes of bombardment, at the same time, on several mornings up to the assault.

Disinformation

Allied disinformation was helped by the despatch, in June, of a Tank Brigade commander (Hardress-Lloyd) to accompany the CIGS to Italy, starting rumours of a move to Italy, as spread before the offensive at Cambrai in Autumn 1917.

Reinforcements were told that they were concentrating defensively against a prospective enemy attack.

Operational Security

The 4th Army forbade any movement of troops, ammunition, or divisional stores during daylight, and ordered each corps to maintain a scout plane overhead to observe compliance. The infantry were withdrawn from the front before being told of the assault. Planning was largely verbal, in person, at Australian Corps HQ, until orders were distributed three days before assault.

---

* This was the AEF's first combat experience except under French command. The AEF had gained its first battle honors on 28 May. The AEF sent ten companies to Australian Corps. Australian Corps retained four companies from the US Army's 33rd Division.
** The 6th Brigade (2nd Division) held only two battalions. The 4th Brigade (4th Division) and 11th Brigade (3rd Division) incorporated platoons from the four companies of the US 33rd Division. They rotated with 12th and 13th Brigades (both 4th Division).

Fuller did not inform tankies of the offensive until then. He ordered them to assemble at night, obscure vehicle tracks, and camouflage the tanks and themselves in ruined houses. They assembled in the villages of Hamelot and Fouilloy on the night of 2-3 July, without enemy interference. The hour of assault was not fixed until 3 July. At 2230 hours that night, the tanks moved forward to the final assembly area, while aircraft flew along the front to obscure their noise, as they had on prior nights. These movements were to complete by 0100 hours. At 0259 hours 4 July, the tanks re-started engines, while aircraft flew overhead.

Timing

On 4 July, at 0302 hours, the daily seven-minute bombardment restarted. The tanks advanced over the final 1,000 yards (914 m) to the start line, during which the creeping bombardment started. They were given 12 minutes, until 0314 hours, before the infantry were supposed to advance. They advanced in twilight, about 1.5 hours before sunrise, with visibility of 15 to 20 yards (14 to 18 m).

GHQ quickly distributed its conclusion that "[t]he success of these operations was largely due to the secrecy with which they were prepared." Yet it warned that "zero hour should be chosen so that there may be sufficient light to enable the tanks to see their way, and to use their weapons effectively, otherwise they are apt to miss their direction and to be drawn off their objective" (BEF GHQ, "Operations by the Australian Corps Against Hamel, Bois de Hamel, and Bois de Vaire, 4th of July, 1918," S.S. 218, July 1918).

Obfuscation

Fuller wanted artillery to bombard the defences with mostly smoke, during the assault, to obscure the advance. On 5 February, he had seen a Mark IV converted to produce smoke,[*] and wanted some tanks to be adapted as smoke-producers (also known as smoke-layers) or smoke-throwers (smoke mortars). He also wanted some capability to fight at night. These capabilities would not be acquired in 1918, but he continued to specify them in hope they would be available by Spring 1919.

The daily seven-minute bombardment mixed smoke, gas, high-explosive, and shrapnel shells, until the day of assault, when no gas was used. The HE blew the dry soil into clouds of dust that worked almost as well as smoke.

Additionally, a company of RE generated smoke on the right flank, and used 4-inch mortars to build smoke in front of the high ground north of the Somme. (The shells were fuzed as air bursts to build the highest edge of the screen.)

Combined Arms

Artillery: Preliminary Bombardment

Fuller's paper of 31 December eschews a preliminary bombardment, as had his earlier papers. The seven-minute bombardment was meant to confuse rather than degrade the enemy, although naturally its mix of high-explosive, shrapnel, and smoke degraded the recipients – psychologically, at least.

---

[*] The accompanying handout notes that one 40-pound (18-kg) cylinder could produce smoke for 2 hours. The note does not indicate how many cylinders were on the tank.

Artillery: Creeping

Upon assault, the field guns opened counter-battery fire and a creeping barrage. The 4th Army received and gathered 302 heavy howitzers (102 4.5-inch, 80 6-inch, and 20 8-inch, 9.2-inch, and 12-inch), 326 18-pounder field guns, and 111 medium machine-guns in indirect-fire role, excluding the 46 medium machine-guns that accompanied the advance. The artillery fired about 200,000 rounds in the first days, while the indirect machine-guns fired nearly 400,000 rounds.

Fuller required artillery and aircraft to focus on enemy artillery. For the first time during preliminary bombardment, two-thirds of the artillery, including all heavy guns, were directed against all known enemy artillery, including on the flanks.* Even the French army on the right fired against artillery within range of the Australians. Most indirect machine-gun fire was directed to the flanks. The enemy artillery on the assault front were silenced for hours, except one 77-mm battery.

From 0302 hours,** the creeping barrage started. The 18-pounder shells were supposed to drop 200 yards (183 m) in front of the infantry's start line (with 60 percent shrapnel, 30 percent HE, 10 percent smoke), the 4.5-inch shells another 200 yards ahead (90 percent HE, 10 percent smoke), the 6-inch shells another 200 yards further ahead. The barrage paused from 0309 to 0310, when it bombarded the frontline for 4 minutes. At 0314 hours, the infantry advanced, and the bombardment jumped ahead 100 yards (91 m) every 3 minutes (1.1 mph; 1.8 kmh) up to the first objective line, and 100 yards every 4 minutes (0.9 mph; 1.4 kmh) from the first objective line to the artillery halt line. Assaulters were urged to keep close to the barrage. Some infantrymen and two tanks were knocked out by friendly fire.

Once the final objective was gained, a standing barrage interdicted any German reinforcements and counter-attackers, for 30 minutes. However, the 4th Army HQ decided afterwards that it should have lasted longer, given that some infantrymen reached the final line late, and that it should have crept forward and back, so as to confuse the enemy as to location.

Aircraft

The Tank Corps had been working for months on cooperation with aircraft. On 24 February, aircraft demonstrated low flight over 2nd Tank Brigade at Bray. Fuller recorded the event in his diary, but no follow-up. One explanation is absorption of the RFC (an arm of the army) by the RAF (an independent service) on 1 April.

In the two weeks before assault, Allied aircraft achieved air dominance. Upon assault, most air effort was directed to ensuring that dominance. A few Allied aircraft were roled as bombers. On the night before assault, they dropped 350 25-pound (11-kg) bombs on targets between the River Somme and the road from Amiens to St. Quentin. At Zero+30 minutes, aircraft dropped 1,100 25-pound bombs and 58 112-pound (51-kg) bombs on enemy headquarters and horse lines.

Tanks and Infantry

The Tank Corps had been training infantry in cooperation with tanks for

---

* The 20 8-inch, 9.2-inch, and 12-inch howitzers were directed against enemy communications too. The proportion of effort allocated to communications is not recorded.
** Fuller and thence many historians misreport this time as 0320 hours, and thus calculate subsequent timings wrongly.

months. On 7 February, it started a series of demonstrations for infantry officers, although the defensive period interrupted this. The Australian Corps did not get to send officers to this series, and thus remained anchored in its disappointing operational experience of 11 April 1917.

This battle included the first use of the Mark V Heavy Tank. Compared to the Mark IV, it offers improved power, transmission, steering, armour, splash plates, and felt linings. From the crew's perspective, the two main advantages are easier steering and more survivability.

The Mark IV could be penetrated by German armour-piercing and reversed "ball" bullets, of standard calibre. The 14-mm armour plates on the front of the Mark V are proof against this calibre (7.92 mm). Mark Vs were used just after the Germans introduced anti-tank rifles of larger calibre (13 mm), of which the British captured their first on the first day of the offensive. It could perforate 14-mm of armour, from 100 yards away. However, Fuller considered it "too conspicuous and too slow a weapon to be really effective against tanks," and of such great recoil as to discourage use. He later estimated that only 1 per cent of all captured anti-tank rifles had been used (Fuller 1920: 262-263).

Artillery remained the greatest threat. A hit from an explosive shell would usually start a fire, perhaps an explosive fire, given the flammable liquids routinely leaking from the engine's lubrication and fuel systems. The Mark V was a little less flammable than the Mark IV, thanks to an improved fuel system.

The Mark IV needs four men to steer. The driver can change the two speed gears directly, but the gears to the final drives are controlled by a gearsman on each side. To steer, the driver signals (by banging the engine casing and holding up a fist) that a gearsman on one side should engage neutral gear, after which the driver locks the differential. The commander would brake the track on that side. Meanwhile, the driver signals (with fingers of the other hand) that the other gearsman should engage one of the two secondary gears, by operating a lever on a sliding pinion. While changing gear, the tank soon comes to a stop, for 5 to 15 seconds, until gears mesh. A stuck gear would take minutes to unstick. The Mark V could be steered by one man, with less chance of a stuck gear. Since the tank could not usually survive an artillery shell, its main defence against artillery, other than retaliatory fire, was to drive a "jinking" route. Thus, improved steering contributed to survivability (Captain H.B.M. Groves, "Precis," 18 December 1934, Cambrai Battlefield Tour 1935, RACTM Hotblack Box 2). On 5 February, the Tank Corps had demonstrated a Mark IV and a pilot Mark V, side by side, both undertaking "a zig-zag advance to escape direct hostile artillery fire," according to the accompanying handout. Second, the two tanks advanced uphill, as if "to close as quickly as possible with enemy on lifting of bombardment or smoke cloud." Finally, the Mark V was demonstrated alone, to "show pace and ease of manoeuvre and control by one man." Rawlinson was not there. Still, likely Fuller cited the demonstration in his argument to Rawlinson. After Mark Vs arrived in April, he could also cite the Tank Corps estimates of its speed on level ground at 5 mph (8 kmh), next to the Mark IV's 3.5 mph.

> When the question of using tanks first arose, General Rawlinson's idea was that they should play an entirely subordinate part. I remember talking this question over with him, and though I could not get him to

agree to allow tanks to lead the van, that is to precede the infantry into battle, I think I convinced him that the Mark V tank would play a more decisive part than he at first imagined (Fuller 1936: 287).

On 12 June, Fuller sent to GHQ a training note on the use of Mark V tanks. The Australians were allowed to arrange their own training with 5th Tank Brigade:

> This was so successful that, days before the battle was launched, the closest comradeship was established between the two formations, each Australian unit training with the tanks which would eventually co-operate with it (1936: 288).

> The co-operation between the infantry and tanks was as near perfect as it could be; all ranks of the tank crews operating were impressed by the superb moral[e] of the Australian troops, who never considered that the presence of the tanks exonerated them from fighting, and who took instant advantage of any opportunity created by the tanks (1920: 207).

The 4th Army's General Staff confirms: "Thanks to the preliminary practice with tanks, the cooperation between them and the infantry was excellent" ("Operations by the Australian Corps Against Hamel...": 4).

The infantry were structured in four waves, initially within touching distance, in order to stay close to the creeping barrage, after which they opened gaps of 50 yards (46 m). Lewis light machine-gunners and rifle-grenadiers were instructed to fire from the hip as soon as fire is received.

Rawlinson insisted on the infantry starting 1,200 yards (1,097 m) ahead. At the pace of the creeping barrage, the tanks were supposed to take 12 minutes to cover the 1,000 yards (914 m) to the start line, but they tended to make it within a few minutes, and to overtake the infantry within a few more minutes.

Speed

The speed of previous operations had been curbed by both bad going and the creeping barrage. At Hamel, the only excuse was the creeping barrage. It moved 100 yards every 3 minutes (1.1 mph; 1.8 kmh) up to the first objective line, and 100 yards every 4 minutes (0.9 mph; 1.4 kmh) from the first objective line to the artillery halt line. The 4th Army conceded that the tanks could have kept a pace of 100 yards every 2 minutes (1.7 mph; 2.7 kmh).

The creeping barrage reached its halt line in about 35 minutes. The tanks could have reached it in about 17 minutes, at their conventionally specified cross-country speed of 2 mph (3.2 kmh). The Mark V was expected to be faster: the Tank Corps currently rated it at 5 mph (8 kmh) maximum, i.e., 1.5 mph (2.4 kmh) or 44 yards (40 m) per minute faster than the Mark IV. This suggests that Mark Vs could have reached the artillery halt line in less than 10 minutes.

The final objective line was up to 2,500 yards (2,286 m) from the start, which the Mark IVs could have been covered in 43 minutes, the Mark Vs in 24 minutes.

The infantry were scheduled to advance at 0314 hours. At 0500 hours, Australian Corps Rear HQ heard from an advanced observation post that Australians were consolidating the final objective line. The interval of time is 106 minutes, suggesting a speed of almost 24 yards (22 m) per minute or 0.8 mph (1.3 kmh). Monash ruled that all objectives were consolidated within 93 minutes, suggesting a speed of almost 27 yards (25 m) per minute or 0.9 mph (1.4 kmh).

Sustainment

Infantry Carriers

Fuller's paper on "Defensive and Offensive Use of Tanks" (31 December) requires some fighting tanks and carriers to carry medium machine-gunners and some infantry 8,000 yards from the start line. For fighting tanks, he had in mind the prospective Mark V* (Mark Five Star), which he currently expected to carry "at least two complete Vickers gun teams." He expected too an "Infantry Carrier Tank" (also the "Infantry Supply Tank," eventually the "Mark IX Tank") to carry either five Vickers medium machine-gun teams or an infantry platoon.

Fuller liked the lengthened Mark IV that was demonstrated on 5 February, when its capacity was given as 15 men and 5 medium machine-guns, or 6 to 10 tons of stores. It was demonstrated as a prospective Mark V*, to be assembled at home, but none would be available until August.

Supply Tanks

Supply tanks were running short. The first had been converted from Mark I and Mark II tanks that were now two years old. The enshipment of Mark V tanks (from April) allowed some Mark IV tanks to be converted into "tenders," but some of these tanks were a year old. On 7 May, units held 67 Mark IV Tenders; another 48 were in salvage or repair (excluding the lengthened version and three in schools).

At that time, the Tank Corps in France held 43 Gun Carriers, although only 26 were with units. In June, the two Gun Carrier Companies were converted to the supply mission. (They were attached to respectively 3rd and 5th Brigades.)

The Gun Carriers and the Mark IV Tenders could not operate as far as the Mark V Tanks. In effect, the range of the supply tanks restrained the advance. Marks I to IV tanks and tenders were rated by the Tank Corps, as of May, for a range of 10 to 12 miles (17,600 to 21,120 yards; 16,093 to 19,312 m), while the Mark V was rated for 20 miles (35,200 yards; 32,187 m), and the Medium A was rated for 35 miles (61,600 yards; 56,327 m). These ratings are straight-line distances on level ground. With tactical manoeuvering and broken ground, the range might halve, so Mark IVs could not achieve the 10,000 yards that Fuller currently wanted to penetrate in one day.

At Hamel, the final objective line was set only 2,500 yards from the start, at most, which is well within the Mark IV's range. Still, the Gun Carriers were preferred, for superior load capacity and lower mileage. Four Gun Carriers (6 men each) were used as supply tanks on 4 July, to carry about 50,000 pounds (22.3 long tons; 22.7 metric tons; 25 short tons) of engineering stores,* ammunition,** and 426 gallons (1,937 litres) of drinking water, equivalent to the loads of 1,250 men. Each vehicle's load averaged about 12,500 pounds (5.670 kg), compared to a pedestrian load of 40 pounds (18 kg). The deliveries were completed within 500 yards (457 m) of the final objective and within 30 minutes of its capture.

---

* For fortifying the line: 464 coils of barbed wire, 1,140 short and 550 long screw picquets for the wire, 153 sheets of corrugated iron.
** 600 3-inch Trench Mortar shells, 240 Mills hand grenades, 40,000 0.303-inch rounds.

All 60 fighting tanks started the day with ammunition and water for infantry (150 3-inch shells for Stokes trench mortars; 10,000 rounds of small-arms ammunition; and 100 gallons of drinking water).

Aircraft dropped by parachute 114,000 rounds of small-arms ammunition and some medical supplies on to the medium machine-gun sections, each of which laid out a white V-shaped cloth (each arm being 6 feet long) as a target.

Signals

No radio tanks or cable-burying tanks were employed, partly because the field guns were not needed to move. Each tank company carried two message-carrying rockets, two SOS rockets, and 18 ground flares to mark positions in emergency.

Exploitation

No forces were reserved for exploitation, given the shallow objectives.

Outcomes

All 60 tanks reached the first defensive line on time; 58 reached final objectives; the other two had been disabled by the creeping barrage. Fifty-five tanks returned to their rallying points on 4 July. The other five tanks were salvaged by the night of 6-7 July. The Tank Corps lost 13 wounded (Fuller 1920: 206-207; 1936: 289).

The Australians lost 775 men killed and wounded, the Americans 134. They captured 1,472 German soldiers, 171 machine-guns, 26 trench mortars, two 77-mm guns, and two 13-mm anti-tank rifles.

On 22 July, the German Army's Chief of Staff (General Erich Ludendorff), who had previously belittled the infantry's "tank fear" (*Tankschrecken*), issued a memo.

> The utmost attention must now be paid to combatting tanks. Our earliest successes against tanks led to a certain contempt for this weapon of warfare. We must, however, now reckon with more dangerous tanks (in Fuller 1920: 263; Hotblack 1920: 701).

GHQ concluded:

> The value of tanks in assisting the advance of the infantry was conclusively proved.

GHQ gave two causes of success:

> 1. The care and skill as regards every detail with which the plan was drawn up by the corps, division, brigade, and battalion staffs.

> 2. The excellent cooperation between the infantry, machine-gunners, artillery, tanks, and RAF (BEF GHQ, in "Operations by the Australian Corps Against Hamel...": 1).

Monash credited "the perfection of team work." "No battle within my previous experience passed off so smoothly, so exactly in timetable, or was so free of any kind of hitch." On the day, Fuller wrote in his diary: "Most successful operation with 4th Australian. This – at last! cancels the Bullecourt incident months ago." In memoirs, he ranked Hamel as more impressive than Cambrai. "In rapidity, brevity, and completeness of success no battle of the war can compare with Hamel." He argued that it had more psychological impact on higher commanders, and thus was necessary to their agreement to the operation towards Amiens – 11 miles (17 km) further on, on 8 August (1920: 305; 1936: 287, 289; Terraine 1978: 70).

> [It was] the turning point…if only for two reasons: (1) it was fought exactly to plan, and (2) not a single tank man was killed in it…[F]rom that day onwards tank-mindedness grew and grew. The Australians became ardent tank enthusiasts, so did Sir Henry Rawlinson, Commander-in-Chief of the 4th Army, and even GHQ began to unfreeze (Fuller, "This Battle Ranks with Waterloo," Evening Standard, 9 August 1943: 6).

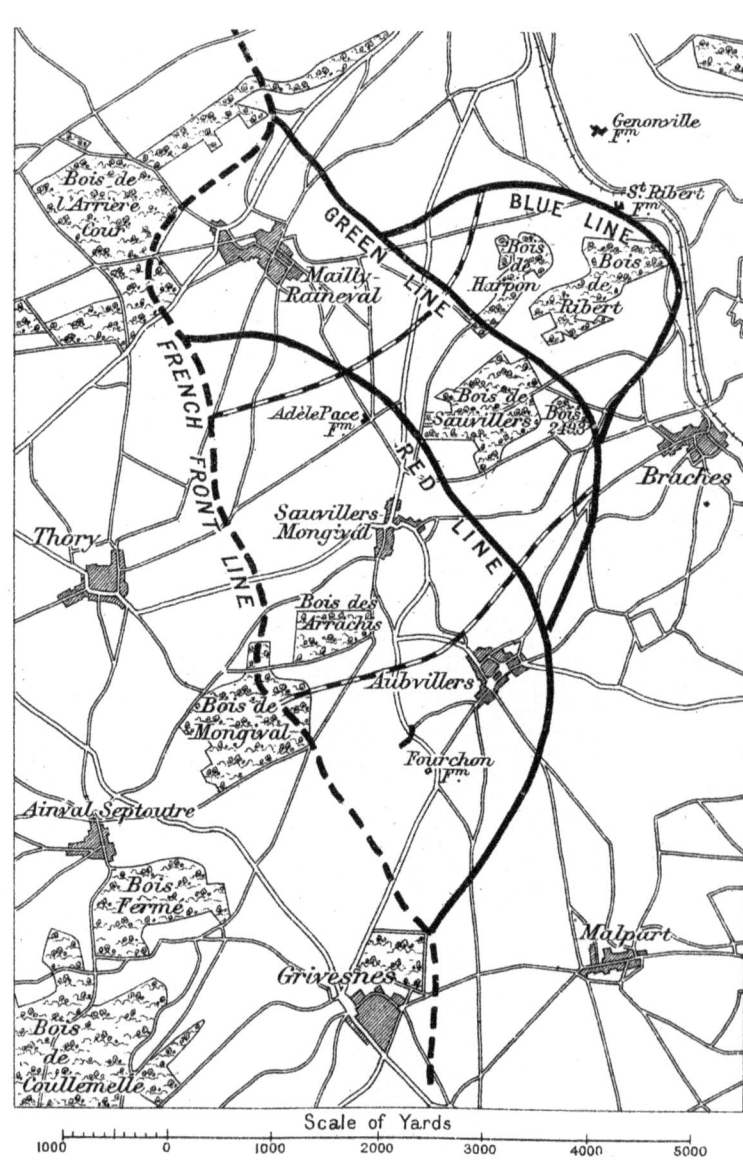

Map 20: The British-French offensive towards Sauvillers, 23 July 1918 (Fuller 1920).

15

Sauvillers-Mongival, July 1918

On 23 July, the British Tank Corps carried out its largest offensive in support of the French, although this was a minor operation by comparison with most Allied offensives. Still, it demonstrates increasing deference to Tank Corps preferences.

Terrain

The French infantry were supposed to advance eastwards to capture the village of Sauvillers-Mongival, and occupy the woods beyond, bypassing Mailly-Raineval to the north (see Map 20). Behind them, French field batteries would take positions to fire on the ridge on the west bank of the River Avre. (Since the front here is south of the much larger urban area of Moreuil, the battle is often named after Moreuil, even though Moreuil was never attacked.)

The terrain is largely unspoilt and rolling. The only obstacles to tanks are woods and villages. The ground was dry until the day of assault, when heavy rain fell.

Concentration

The French 1st Army ordered its IX Corps to commit three divisions: the 3rd was the main assault division; the 15th protected its left flank, the 152nd its right,.

At 1430 hours, 17 July, the 5th Tank Brigade, using 9th Battalion from 3rd Tank Brigade, was ordered to support French 3rd Division. On 18 July, the 9th Battalion moved 16,000 yards (14,630 m) across country from Bus lès Artois to the railhead at Rosel. Meanwhile, its commander (Lieutenant-Colonel H.K. Woods) brought his reconnaissance officers to meet the commander of 3rd Division (Nayal de Bourgon). The next day, these officers reconnoitred the ground.

The rest of the battalion moved across country, from Conty to Bois de Quemetot (4,000 yards; 3,658 m) on the night of 19-20 July, to Bois de Rampont (9,000 yards;

Division (French)	Battalions (French)	Tanks (British)	Front (m)	Depth (m)	Objectives	Casualties (men)
15th	4	0	800	2,000	To keep in line with 3rd Division	15 officers and 500 other ranks
3rd	4	12	2,000	1,000	RED LINE: Bois des Arrachis, Sauvillers-Mongival, Adelpare farm, Ouvrage des Trois Bouqueteaux	French: 26 officers and 680 other ranks; British 54 officers and other ranks
	4	24		2,000	GREEN LINE: the plateau south of Mailly-Raineval around the Bois de Sauvillers to the south-west corner of Bois de Harpon	
	Above plus 8 platoons in reserve	Above plus 6 tanks in reserve		max. 3,000	BLUE LINE: Bois de Harpon; Bois de Ribert	
152nd	4	0	950	2,000	To keep in line with 3rd Division	20 officers and 650 other ranks
TOTAL:3	16	42	3,750	3,000	9	1,891 French; 54 British

Table 14: Force structure on 23 July 1918, ordered from north to south and by objective line (Fuller 1920: 208-209).

8,230 m) on the night of 20-21 July, and to Bois de Hure and Bois du Fay (7,000 yards; 6,401 m) on the night of 21-22 July.

On 22 July, the plans were finalized, communications settled, supplies dumped, and rally-points fixed.

On the night of 22-23 July, the 9th Battalion moved from Bois de Hure and Bois du Fay to the startline. Forty-two tanks had started these moves; 35 were ready to join the assault. The front was unusually narrow: 4,100 yards (3,749 m). Thus, one tank was allocated for every 98 yards (90 m) of front. One tank crossed the start line for every 117 yards (101 m) (see Table 14).

Surprise

The preliminary bombardment was reduced to one hour, immediately before assault. The assault started at 0530 hours, a full 20 minutes after sunrise, although it was obscured by heavy rain on the day.

Combined Arms

Artillery

One hour before the assault, French artillery fired upon German artillery and wire. Upon the assault, the artillery fired a creeping barrage of HE and smoke shells, at the rate of 200 meters (219 yards) every six minutes, up to the first objective line, and 200 meters every eight minutes beyond.

Tanks and Infantry

On 15 May, Fuller had met with the commander of the French 10th Army to discuss training French infantry with British tanks, given changes in the front. That training began on 23 May. From 19 through 21 July, the 5th Tank Brigade Driving School received French infantry for combined-arms training.

The tanks were structured in sections, each of three tanks, of which two would lead the third. A platoon was supposed to follow behind each tank.

Speed

The creeping barrage moved at 200 meters every six minutes (2 kmh; 1.2 mph) up to the first objective, and 200 meters every eight minutes (1.5 kmh; 0.9 mph) thereafter. The first objective line was only 1,000 m (1,094 yards) from the start, the final objective line only 3,000 m (3,280 yards), so the creep would reach the final line at Z+110 minutes (0720 hours), at an average speed of 1.6 km (1 mph). The second objective line was captured around two hours after the start, suggesting an average advance speed of 1 kmh (0.6 mph). The final objective line was contested around four hours in, suggesting an average advance speed of 0.75 kmh (0.5 mph).

Sustainment

Six tanks and 8 infantry platoons were nominally reserved to complete the third wave. Four supply tanks resupplied the infantry on the final objective.

Since the final objective line was only 3,000 m (3,280 yards) deep, it remained within field artillery range, so no artillery were moved during the assault.

Exploitation

No forces were reserved for exploitation.

Outcomes

The tanks cleared Arrachis wood and Sauvillers village, 15 minutes before the infantry arrived. Similarly, the tanks overran light resistance at Adelpare Farm and Les Trois Bouqueteaux.

Two hours into the assault (0730 hours), the tanks advanced from Sauvillers village, by skirting around Sauvillers Wood. The nearest tanks fired six-pounders broadside into the tree line, while other tanks moved on, effectively capturing the second objective line (Green Line). However, most of the infantry loitered for two hours under artillery fire, instead of pushing on to the third objective (Blue) line. "They simply did not understand heavy tanks," complained Fuller (1936: 300).

The B Company persuaded a French battalion from 51st Regiment to attack Harpon wood. The infantry followed close behind the tanks, and took the wood quickly. Other tanks advanced on Bois de St. Ribert without infantry, until six were knocked out by a German battery to the south of the wood. The time was then about 0930 hours. With no French infantry, the tanks withdrew.

Twenty-one tanks rallied. Six were recovered later. The British lost 15 tanks to direct hits, 11 men killed, and 43 wounded. The French lost 1,891 men; the 3rd Division had committed and fought most, but did not lose many more men than the other two divisions. They captured 1,858 German prisoners, 5 artillery guns, 45 trench mortars, and 275 machine-guns (Fuller 1920: 210-211).

One of the first nine A7Vs, this one named "Siegfried," in March 1918.

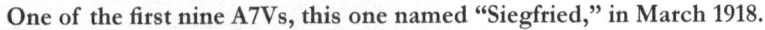

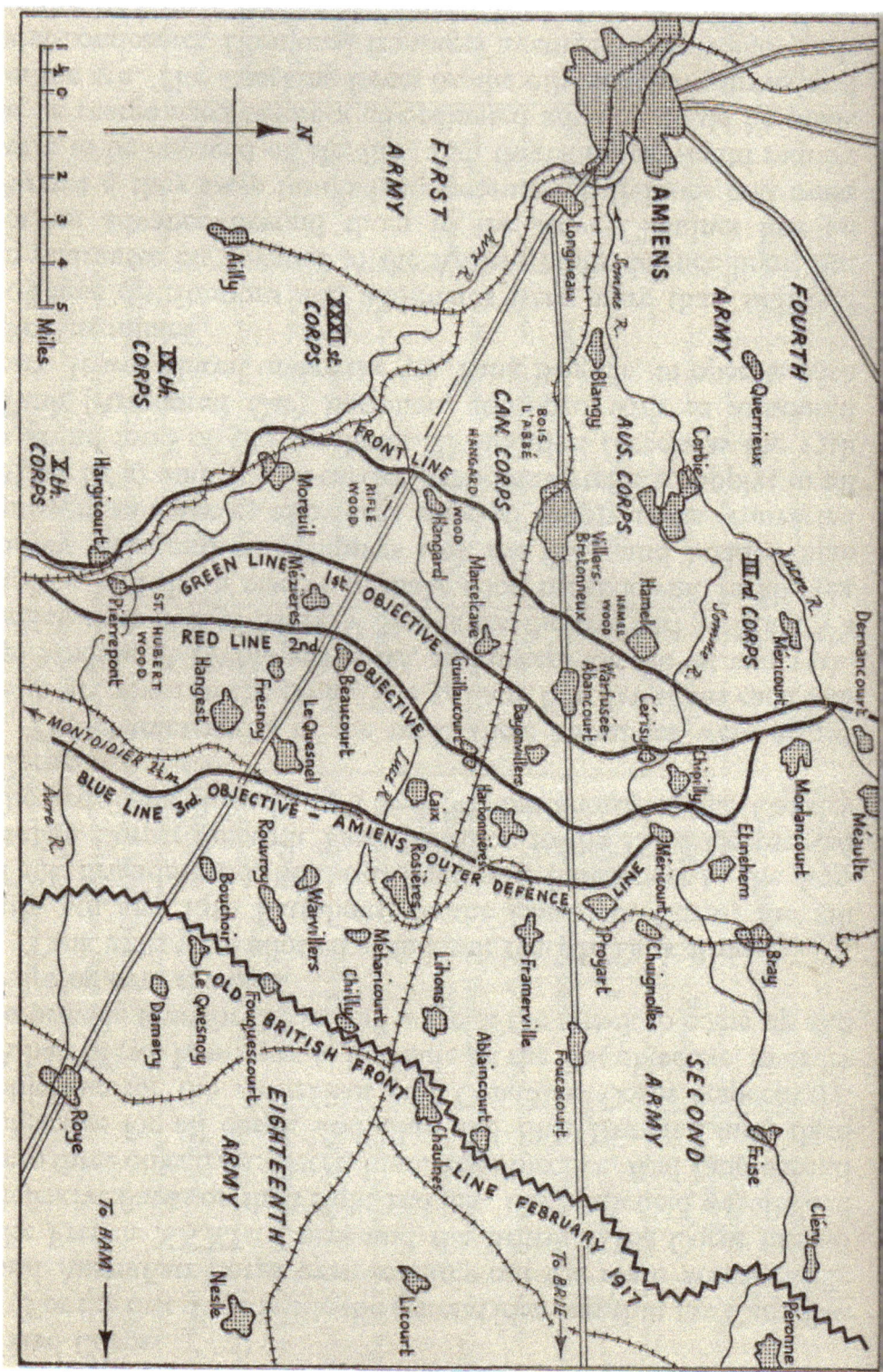

Map 21: The offensive towards Amiens, 8 August 1918 (Fuller 1956: III).

16

Amiens, August 1918

The success of tanks on 4 July at Hamel encouraged a larger combined-arms offensive. The 1st Army proposed to attack the Merville salient, the 2nd Army proposed to attack Kemmel Hill, the 3rd Army Bucquoy and Bapaume, and the 4th Army the salient around Amiens. On 13 July, Haig asked 4th Army to consider a bigger version of the scheme used against Hamel. This would become the most successful use of tanks in the Great War.

Terrain

The 4th Army staff realized the terrain around Amiens as mostly dry and unbroken by artillery fire, and assessed the defences as denuded by reinforcements to other fronts. On 17 July, Rawlinson submitted a plan to capture the defence line running from Le Quesnel through Caix to Méricourt, in order to push German artillery out of range of Amiens, and to gain elevated ground from which to direct Allied artillery on to the next defensive line (see Map 21). Additionally, the salient's neutralization would straighten and shorten the Allied front.

During the same day, Fuller returned to France from London, having met with the Deputy Chief of the Imperial General Staff (DCIGS) and Director of Staff Duties (DSD) to arrange his future position as the General Staff officer for the Tank Corps (SD7). Elles left for London on 19 July.

> On the 21st I was sitting in my office at Bermicourt when the telephone bell rang. It was 4th Army Headquarters calling, and General A[rchibald] A. Montgomery, the MGGS, wanted to speak to Elles, and as Elles was away, he asked me to come down to Flexicourt and see him.
>
> As I put the receiver down, the idea flashed through my head that this meant that General Rawlinson was considering an attack, and it was not exactly an intuition, because almost daily I had gazed at the map of our front which covered one wall in my hut. On it were three pronounced bulges: one pointing towards Hazebrouck, one towards Amiens, and one towards Chateau Thierry. The last had been attacked by the French only three days before and had collapsed; the second had long appeared to us as a gift, if only tanks could be launched against it east of Amiens and north of Compiègne.
>
> I was so certain this call meant an attack that, as I entered General Montgomery's office, I exclaimed: "It's a sitter!" to which he replied: "What is?" And I answered: "The attack you are contemplating." He seemed a little taken aback until I explained to him that we had been thinking about it for weeks. I then discovered that what I was wanted for was to attend a conference which was then in process of assembling, for as I was talking car after car drew up outside the chateau (1936: 296-7).

Rawlinson presided over a discussion with the commanders and staff officers of the Australian Corps (John Monash), Canadian Corps (Arthur Currie), III Corps (Richard Butler, since February 1918), and Cavalry Corps (Charles Kavanagh), plus a liaison from the RAF, and Fuller from the Tank Corps.

> I said: "If the greater part of the Tank Corps is to be used, why not make the attack less limited, that is, more decisive?" And, as I did so, General Monash looked and exclaimed: "Yes, I have been thinking of that myself" (Fuller 1936: 289).

Fuller wanted heavy tanks to break in. To exploit the break-in, he proposed to replace the Cavalry Corps with both battalions of Medium A tanks. He proposed to send them east-south-eastwards from Villers-Bretonneux to Rosières-en-Santerre, then right and southwards through the German artillery and services facing the French 1st Army, ending south-east of Montdidier. Note that this use of mediums to get at enemy artillery and services overlaps part of his proposal for a decisive offensive in Spring 1919 (see Chapter 13).

> Though I realised that such an operation was a risky one, I held, and still do, that it was feasible and would have proved decisive. Anyhow, General Rawlinson set it aside, probably on account of its risks, but I think also because he did not trust the French to make good what the tanks might render possible (Fuller 1936: 299).

At 0800 hours on 22 July, the CIGS (Henry Wilson) visited Rawlinson, who said that he wanted Haig to release five to six divisions for the advance from Villers-Bretonneux (Callwell 1927: II, 117). On 24 July, Davidson (GHQ DMO) told Fuller that the offensive would start in about three weeks, i.e., about 14 August, although this schedule would soon be accelerated by a week. On 29 July, GHQ extended the 4th Army's objectives to the line from Hangest and Le Quesnel to Harbonnières and Méricourt and thence Chaulnes (5 miles or 8 km east of Rosières-en-Santerre, by road), while the French would advance towards Roye (8.5 miles or 13.6 km directly south of Chaulnes, in a straight line).

> The country between our front line and the line Roye-Frise [17 miles or 27 km long] was in every respect suitable to tank movement. East of the Roye-Frise line began the French portion of the old Somme battlefield; the ground here in places had been heavily shelled, but was quite negotiable by heavy tanks. The flanks of the attack were the two difficult points. Neither permitted of the use of offensive wings and both offered good defensive positions for the enemy's machine-gunners (1920: 223).

GHQ's Special Order of 29 July mentions Ham (see Map 23), on the other side of the Somme – 20 miles (33 km) east of Rosières-en-Santerre, and 13 miles from each of Chaulnes and Roye, but is not clear whether Ham is an objective for this or a subsequent operation. On 5 August, GHQ set the final objective line as Chaulnes to Roye to Noyon (12.5 miles or 20 km south-east of Roye) – miles beyond where Fuller had wanted the medium tanks to find enemy artillery and services.

> Though this was strategy of the first order, which my original independent tank manoeuvre would greatly have facilitated, it was now too late

to press for its reconsideration, because the two Medium A battalions had been anchored to the cavalry. The truth is, that the whole plan had grown up anyhow out of a series of independent "brain-waves"; it was in no way co-ordinated by a clear-cut initial plan (Fuller 1936: 305).

Concentration

The 4th Army gathered 800 aircraft, 82 units of field artillery (1,394 guns), 26 units of medium artillery, and 13 batteries of heavy pieces – altogether 2,070 pieces, against 749 German pieces (Fuller 1936: 307; Neiberg 2005: 342).

Fifty-four British infantry divisions now served in France. On 29 July, GHQ committed III Corps (2 divisions) north of the River Somme, Australian Corps (4 divisions) south of the river, and Canadian Corps (4 divisions) furthest south, with the French 1st Army on its right. Three infantry divisions and the Cavalry Corps' three cavalry divisions were allocated to the exploitation phase. Thus, 16 divisions were committed to this offensive, with 257,562 men.

The commitment looks less impressive in net terms: ten attacking divisions against ten defending divisions, and three infantry and three cavalry divisions for exploitation against four German divisions in reserve.

Qualitatively, readiness was patchy. The cavalry were isolated to the rear of the other arms, and demoralized by operational inactivity and under-performance. The Canadian Corps was fatigued by its move to this front and the many deceptions involved. The III Corps was disorganized by a German attack in divisional strength on 6 August, its own counter-attack on 7 August, and German artillery fire, including gas shells, on the night of 7 to 8 August, when it was moving into starting positions. The Australian Corps was best rested, and most recently experienced with tanks (Montgomery 1919: 27-28).

Tanks would make the difference. In July, the Tank Corps peaked at 13,336 men, of which about 7,200 men and 500 replacements were in France. By August, the government had authorized 26 tank battalions, but prepared only 22, of which four remained in England (one was ready in personnel, but would not enship until tanks were ready in France; two were unready in personnel; and one was used just to train officers). Eighteen battalions had been sent to France or were in transit, of which one operated only armoured cars (17th), two operated medium tanks (3rd and 6th), three (with 1st Tank Brigade) awaited conversion from Mark IV to Mark V tanks (expected in mid-August), one (9th) was recovering from its operation with the French (22-23 July), and one (16th) was short of men and tanks (it had been cannibalized to provide reinforcements in April). Thus, only 12 tank battalions and one armoured car unit were considered ready (see Table 15).

Rawlinson's initial attack plan included 8 tank battalions. Fuller suggested at least 11, and up to 14 (if adding the 1st Brigade, with Mark IV tanks) (see Table 16). Rawlinson agreed to 11, rationalizing that tanks release infantry for clearing and occupying, rather than assaulting and carrying. Adding a heavy unit in mechanical reserve and the armoured car unit gets the commitment to 13 units (see Table 17).

The attack started on 8 August with three tank Brigades (3rd, 4th, 5th), nine heavy battalions (1st, 2nd, 4th, 5th, 8th, 10th, 13th, 14th, 15th), two medium (3rd and 6th), and one car (17th, attached to Cavalry Corps), excluding one heavy unit (9th) in mechanical reserve. Each tank unit was authorized at 48 fighting vehicles,

Battalion	Mark V tanks	Mark V* tanks	Medium tanks	Armoured Cars	Concentration dates	Concentration area
1st		36			31 July to 5 August	Poulainville, Saleux, Prouzel, Vignacourt
2nd	42				31 July to 5 August	Vaux, followed by Hospice Fouilly
3rd			48		Nights 2-3, 6-7 August	Naours, Boulevard Pont Noyelles in Amiens
4th	42				31 July to 5 August	Poulainville, Saleux, Prouzel, Vignacourt
5th	42				31 July to 5 August	Poulainville, Saleux, Prouzel, Vignacourt
6th			48		Nights 2-3, 6-7 August	Naours, Boulevard Pont Noyelles in Amiens
7th	Converting				Unused	
8th	42				31 July to 5 August	Vaux, followed by Hospice Fouilly
9th	Recovering				days after assault	
10th	42				31 July to 5 August	Poulainville, Saleux, Prouzel, Vignacourt
11th	Converting				Unused	
12th	Converting				Unused	
13th	42				31 July to 5 August	Vaux, followed by Hospice Fouilly
14th	42				31 July to 5 August	Poulainville, Saleux, Prouzel, Vignacourt
15th		36			31 July to 5 August	Poulainville, Saleux, Prouzel, Vignacourt
16th	Unready				Unready	
17th				127	31 July to 5 August	Australian Corps
18th	Unready				Unready	
TOTAL:18	294	72	96	127	-	-

Table 15: Tank units in France, as of 8 August 1918 (Fuller 1920: 219).

but only the two medium units each held 48. Seven units each held 42 Mark Vs (36 in companies, plus a reserve of six). The 1st and 15th each held 36 Mark V* tanks.

As of 30 July, the units held 366 heavy tanks, 96 medium tanks, 127 armoured cars, and 120 supply tanks (of which 18 were lost by 7 August). The fighting tanks add up to 462,* the tanks and variants to 580.** The Tank Corps reserved 42 Mark V tanks as mechanical replacements. Thus, 420*** fighting tanks were with units, of which 415 went into action in the first assault. Over the four days of battle, given reserves and replacements, 688 tanks were used (Fuller 1920: 228, 227).

As finally planned, the starting front was 22,500 yards (20,574 m) long. The final objective line was 30,000 yards (27,432 m) long. The front for each of ten attacking divisions varied from 2,250 to 3,000 yards (2,057 to 2,743 m). Counting the weapons allocated to the first day of assault, one tank was available for every 54 yards (49 m), one aircraft per 28 yards (26 m), one artillery piece per 11 yards (10 m).

Surprise

Preliminary Bombardment

The 4th Army eschewed a preliminary bombardment. The French chose a preliminary bombardment in lieu of tanks, but their assault started 45 minutes later.

Disinformation

While the Canadians were moving to 4th Army, two battalions and more signal

---

* The 4th Army reported 456 fighting tanks, including 96 medium (Montgomery 1919: 23).
** Fuller later misreported 570 gathered for the start, but under-counted Gun Carriers by ten. He correctly reported 688 tanks involved ("This Battle Ranks with Waterloo," *Evening Standard*, 9 August 1943: 6). Robert Larson (1984: 62) reported 580. Kenneth Macksey (1983: 163-164) reported 604 allied tanks. J.P. Harris (1995: 176) inexplicably reported 552 fighting tanks, supply tanks, and gun carriers.
*** Primary sources agree that 420 tanks were allocated to the first day, of which 415 went into action (Fuller 1920: 223; Army Council 1926: 1; Liddell Hart 1959: I, 177), except for a summary report, which gives 430 tanks: this is presumably a typo for 420 (Elles to GHQ, "Summary of Operations," 29 October 1918, RACTM E2006.515).

Tank Brigade	Units on 30 July	Units by 6 August	Attached to	Attachments
1st	HQ: Estruvalle 7th: Merlimont 11th: Merlimont 12th: Merlimont	(converting from Mark IVs to Mark Vs)	-	-
2nd	HQ: Bois d'Ohlain 10th: Bouvigny 14th: Mont St. Eloi 15th: Simencourt	(broken up to release battalions to other brigades)	-	-
-	-	10th: Bouvigny	III Corps	-
3rd	HQ: Wavrans 3rd: Toutencourt 6th: Merlimont	HQ: Wavrans 3rd: Toutencourt 6th: Merlimont	Cavalry Corps 3rd Division 5th Division	-
4th	HQ: Couturelle 1st: Coullemont 4th: La Cauchie 5th: Bailleulval	HQ: Dury 1st: Coullemont 4th: La Cauchie 5th: Bailleulval 14th: Mont St. Eloi	Canadian Corps 4th Division 1st Division 3rd Division 2nd Division	4th Tank Supply Company 3rd Tank Supply Company; 2nd Tank Supply Company; 3 forward wireless stations 1 back receiving station
-	-	17th	Australian Corps	section of Medium As
5th	HQ: Vaux 2nd: Querrieu wood 8th: Blangy 13th: St. Gratien 9th: Cavillon	HQ: Hospice Fouilly 2nd: Querrieu wood 8th: Blangy 13th: St. Gratien 15th: Simencourt	Australian Corps 2nd and 5th Divisions 4th Division 3rd Division 4th and 5th Divisions	5th Tank Supply Company company from 13th 1st Gun Carrier Company; 2 forward wireless stations; 1 back receiving station
TOTAL: 5	15 units	12 ready units	4 corps, 10 divisions	5 companies

Table 16: Formation structure from 30 July to 8 August 1918 (Fuller 1920: 220).

units went to 2nd Army to send radio traffic suggestive of the whole corps. Nevertheless, German intelligence knew that at least two of the four Canadian divisions had moved, although not to where. The Canadians concentrated on a part of the front screened by the Australian Corps, which extended its front southwards.

On 29 July, infantry on Australian Corps' northern or left corner raided near Morlancourt, and captured 238 men and 36 machine-guns. The next day, they moved southwards, while III Corps extended its front southwards. Then III Corps was the victim of an attack on 6 August that regained the ground the Germans had lost on 29 July. German intelligence discovered the presence of the III Corps (in the form of more than 250 prisoners), but not the Canadian Corps, and did not expect any offensive in the immediate term (Terraine 1978: 88-89; Stevenson 2011: 120-121).

Operational Security

Haig and Foch agreed that London should not be informed until the assault began, for political reasons more than operational security. The 4th Army ordered radio silence during the build up, posted warnings to "keep your mouth shut," and restricted reconnaissance of the front line. On 27 July, the day of assault was fixed for 10 August (although on 6 August it was brought forward to 8 August). That day, Tank Corps HQ was permitted to send one officer to reconnoitre the front. Elles was unaware of the plan until he returned to Tank Corps HQ on 28 July (after being away since 17 July). On 30 July, 5th Tank Brigade HQ hosted a conference, at which Rawlinson explained his plan, and permitted movement orders to be issued that evening. On 31 July, the dumping of supplies began. Fuller left for England on 31 July to open his new position (SD7) in the War Office, although he would return on 7 August to help his successor (Lieutenant-Colonel Henry Karslake) (1920: 218).

By 6 August, 4th Army issued 4,500 mosaics of aerial photographs, 37,825 plates, and 1,840 enlargements, and 279,300 maps (Montgomery 1919: 25-26).

Table 17: BEF allocations and missions, as of 24 July, 26 July, 30 July, and 8 August 1918 (Fuller 1920: 221; 1936: 300-303, 306).

	3rd (Northern)	2,500	13,500	One unit	-		1st	36 Mark V*
	3rd (Central)	3,500	13,500	-			-	-
	4th (Southern)	3,500	13,000	One company (medium)	Removed to Cav.		-	-
	(Reserve) (Beyond Final)	-	Sustain and Exploit	Three companies	Returned to units		-	-
Fr.	?	?	?	1st	One company, plus a section	One Returned to units	-	-
	(Reserve) (Beyond final)	?	Sustain and Exploit	One company (medium)	Removed to Cav.		-	-
	3rd (Beyond final)		Exploit	One company (medium)				
Cav.	1st				One unit (Medium)	Added one unit (medium)	3rd 6th	3rd	48 medium
	3rd			3rd			6th	45 medium
	8th	Mechanical reserves	-	-	-	9th	9th	9th	42 Mark V
-	-	(max. 4)	(max. 10,500)	(max. 13,500)	-	-	-	-	120
TOTAL: 5		14			3	12	11	13	13	294 Mark V / 72 Mark V* / 96 medium / 127 cars

186

The First Tank War

Fuller's plan of 24 July

Corps	Division	Objective line	Width (yards)	Depth (yards)	Tank Brigade	Tank Battalions	4th Army's changes 26 July	Tank battalions 30 July	Tank battalions 8 August	Nominal fighting tanks	Supply tanks, 30 July
III	18th	1st (Green)	6,000	4,000	10th		–	10th	10th	18 Mark V	18
III	58th	2nd (Red)	6,000	6,500	10th					18 Mark V	
Aus.	2nd (as Green)	3rd (Final)	10,000	7,500	5th	Two units, less two companies	Removed to Cav. Returned to unit	2nd, 8th, 13th, 15th	2nd plus a company from 13th	(as Green)	48
Aus.	3rd	1st (Green)	7,500	6,000	5th	One unit, less one company			8th	24 Mark V	
Aus.	4th	2nd (Red)	8,000	11,000	5th	One company (One from Green)			15th	24 Mark V	
Aus.	5th	3rd (Blue)	8,000	12,000	5th	One company (medium)			12th	24 Mark V	
Aus.	– (reserve)	(Beyond final)	–	Sustain and Exploit		Three companies				18 Mark V*	
Cdn.	1st	1st (Southern)	3,000	4,000	4th	One unit, less one company			17th	127 cars 3 mediums	–
Cdn.	2nd	1st (Northern)	3,000	6,000	4th	One unit, less one company		1st, 4th, 5th, 14th	14th	36 Mark V	54
Cdn.	3rd	1st (Central)	3,000	6,000	4th	Two companies, less a section			4th	36 Mark V	
Cdn.		2nd (Southern)	3,000	4,000					5th	36 Mark V	
Cdn.		2nd (Northern)	2,500	11,500						36 Mark V	
Cdn.		2nd (Central)	2,500	11,500							
Cdn.	– (reserve)	(as 1st objective line)	3,000	6,000						(as 1st objective line)	

Assemblies were restricted to nighttime. Some units marched to the rear during daylight, and returned at night. For 5 or 6 nights, fighters patrolled the assemblies and drowned the noise of tanks. Lower ranks were briefed on 6 August. That night, tanks moved to preparatory positions. On 7 August, they moved 2-3 miles further to their starting positions, 1,000 yards behind the infantry (Montgomery 1919: 28).

Timing

The final movements to the starting positions began at 0130 hours, 8 August, at dead slow pace, in darkness and mist, guided by white tape and pedestrians with lit cigarettes. For 4th Army's infantry and artillery, the assault started at 0420 hours, about 70 minutes before sunrise. The tanks advanced at 0445. Fuller (1936: 307) recalled the conditions then as "misty and dry, and…still very dark…ideal for an attack." The French started their assault 45 minutes later, still in mist.

Combined Arms

Artillery

Upon assault, two-thirds of the artillery targeted enemy artillery. By then, the British had mapped 504 of the 530 German artillery pieces in the sector of attack. Meanwhile, field guns started a creeping barrage, 200 yards (183 m) ahead of the start line. At the end of the creeping barrage, they prepared to move forward.

Aircraft

The 4th Army was supported by 376 fighters and about 400 other aircraft, against 106 German aircraft. Most of the British aircraft were scouts. Number 8 Squadron (18 two-seater scouts) was ordered to cooperate with tanks, although such cooperation amounted to flying ahead to attack enemy artillery with machine-guns and to drop coloured smoke as a warning to friendly forces.

Some aircraft carried wireless radios, but they signalled to higher formation HQs, which would struggle to relay any message to tanks. Fuller (1936: 307) recalled that most messages received at Tank Corps HQ were dropped by aeroplanes.

Most aircraft were delayed by mist, until 1000 hours. The window lasted two hours, until about midday, when bombers were diverted against the bridges over the Somme, on reports they were crowded with Germans in retreat. However, the German fighters, although outnumbered, concentrated in defence, and shot down 45 aircraft and damaged another 52 so badly that they were written off. The bridges were not disabled (Montgomery 1919: 24, 32, 50; Terraine 1978: 94-95).

On the second day, Allied aircraft concentrated on air defence.

> [A]t Harbonnières [I] ran into an engagement of a peculiar kind. The road was crammed with men and transport, and everyone was firing into the air at a solitary German aeroplane, which was being pursued by 22 of our machines. The fusillade was terrific, and in the middle of it the German suddenly dived so steeply that I was certain he had been hit. Then of a sudden he flattened out, and no more than 300 feet [91 m] above the ground he roared over our heads and sped eastwards. What eventually happened to him I do not know, but I hope he got safely home; he certainly deserved to after such odds against him (Fuller 1936: 311-312).

Infantry and Tanks

The Australian Corps was now the exemplar for combined-arms attacks. On 25 July, 5th Tank Brigade and Australian infantry cooperated in a demonstration to Allied staff, which Fuller's diary describes as "excellent."

As at Hamel, infantry started 25 minutes before the tanks. The tanks started 8 minutes before the bombardment, although most soon overtook the infantry. Their lead was advantageous against machine-guns in the first defensive line, especially as German machine-gunners were primed to withdraw, given their experiences at Hamel against the more agile Mark V tanks. However, the tanks were exposed to artillery beyond. By 1000 hours, the mist and smoke had disappeared, and the tanks attracted indirect and direct fire.

> [On 9 August], I decided to visit the front and see what conditions were actually like. I motored to Amiens and then on to Villers-Bretonneux, Marcelcave, Lamotte, Bayonvillers, Harbonnières, Guillaucourt, Wiencourt and back, visiting the headquarters of the 3rd, 4th, and 5th Tank Brigades on the way. What struck me most was the comparative stillness of the battlefield, that the dead were remarkably few in number, most being Germans, but that many horses had been killed. Near Bayonvillers I came across a tragic row of Mark V* tanks, all of which as they had topped a slight rise had been hit by a battery of field guns, much as at Flesquières (Fuller 1936: 311-312).

Fuller blamed infantry commanders in his report of 11 August.

> The taxi-cab system of using tanks, that is, of whistling them up whenever required, is still constantly used – and it is absolutely wrong...It must be definitely hammered into infantry commanders that the role of the heavy tank is to break through the enemy defences – trenches and wire, and that it is not to lead the infantry attack across extensive areas of open ground. From a tank point of view the enemy's artillery begins to become dangerous only when his trenches have been penetrated. It is after this act has been accomplished that tanks expect to receive protection from the infantry themselves (in Fuller 1936: 313).

Speed

The barrage fell 200 yards ahead of the startline for 3 minutes. It took another 4 minutes to advance 200 yards, and 24 minutes to advance another 800 yards, i.e., 31 minutes to reach 1,200 yards (1,097 m) from the start line (1.3 mph; 2.1 kmh). From there, it advanced at 100 yards per 4 minutes (0.9 mph; 1.4 kmh).

The Australians consolidated their first objective line by 0700 hours, their second by 1030. They advanced to a depth of 11,000 yards (10,058 m) in 6 hours 10 minutes, at an average speed of 30 yards (27 m) per minute (1 mph; 1.6 kmh). The Canadians consolidated by 1200 hours. The Australians occupied all objectives by 1330 hours, except at the junctions with the Canadians on their right and the British on their left. The maximum depth of advance measured about 13,200 yards (12,070 m), which suggests a speed of 31 yards (28 m) per minute (Montgomery 1919: 25, 35).

On the left (north), the III Corps was given the shallowest objectives and fewest tanks, given wooded terrain, and the infantry's fatigue and disorganization due to engagements before the assault. The 58th Division failed to take the Chipilly Spur of the River Somme, from where the Germans enfiladed the left of the Australian Corps for days (Montgomery 1919: 48; Fuller, 1920: 223; Terraine 1978: 91-92).

Sustainment

The Australian Corps was required to advance 3,500 yards (3,200 m) to the first line (Green), 5,000 yards (4,572 m) to the second (Red), and 2,000 yards (1,829 m) to the third (Blue). Exploiters were supposed to advance another 3,000 yards.

Reserves

The Tank Corps reserved 42 Mark V heavy tanks as "mechanical reserve," i.e., to replace tanks that broke down.

Infantry Carriers

Since 1917, Fuller had required a lengthened tank to carry machine-gun teams. The latest variant, designated Mark V* – a lengthened variant of Mark V, was now available. Each Mark V* had been rated in February for 20-25 passengers, although by May this rating was reduced to 15 men. The type was used operationally for the first time in August: 72 vehicles were available, across two battalions, of which one battalion was allocated to each corps, for support of the infantry on to the third objective. They proved under-powered and poorly ventilated, leaving passengers sickened by heat, fumes, and motion. Subsequently, Mark V* tanks were rarely used to carry infantry (Fuller 1936: 131; Fletcher 1994: 156, 173).

A Mark V* Male leads three Mark V* Females, likely on 9 August 1918. Fuller stapled this print into his journal, under the caption: "Long Mark Vs going up" (RACTM).

Company	Allocation, as of 1 August	Allocation on 8 August	Supplies carried
Number 1 Gun Carrier	5th Tank Brigade	5th Tank Brigade	Explosives
Number 2 Gun Carrier	3rd Tank Brigade	Not used	-
Number 1 Tank Supply	1st Tank Brigade	Not used	-
Number 2 Tank Supply	4th Tank Brigade	4th Tank Brigade	Ammunition and fuel for tanks
Number 3 Tank Supply	Blingel Camp	Canadian Corps	Ammunition and water for infantry and (on sledges) bridging equipment
Number 4 Tank Supply	2nd Tank Brigade	4th Tank Brigade	
Number 5 Tank Supply	Blingel Camp	Australian Corps	

Table 18: Allocations of supply companies, by August 1918 (Fuller 1920: 168-169).

Supply Carriers

Fuller's plans of 24 and 30 July allocate 120 supply tanks to sustainment of the first day: 54 were allocated to resupply the tanks, 66 to resupply the infantry. The types included 22 converted Gun Carriers, and 98 converted Mark IV tanks and unconverted Female Mark IV tanks with sleds. However, two supply tanks were de-allocated before assembly on 5 August, and 16 of the Gun Carriers were lost on 7 August (due to sympathetic explosions after a German shell set alight a camouflage net in an orchard to the west of Villers-Bretonneux). Thus, 102 supply vehicles were available on the day (Fuller 1920: 167-169, 206; 1921: 107; 1936: 302).

Those 102 vehicles were restructured so hurriedly that records of their loads do not survive, except in general terms (see Table 18). Presumably their loads were similar to the loads at Cambrai and Hamel.

Signals

Back in November 1917, eight radio tanks had been used, one per battalion, each acting as a relay to formation HQs. Operations since then had been too defensive or too shallow to require them. By August 1918, seven were available. Australian Corps received two forward stations, while Canadian Corps, being more populous, received three. Each Corps received one radio tank as a relay station from forward stations to the formation HQs.

Field Artillery

In January, Fuller had wanted all tanks to be Male, on two grounds. First, the Germans would be deploying German tanks in 1918. Second, Males fire directly with 6-pounder tank guns, in substitution of indirect fire from 18-pounder field guns, which struggle to keep in range of the advancing tanks and infantry.

Once forces advance 4,000 yards beyond the frontline, the 18-pounders could not fire beyond them without relocating. Fuller required tracked tractors to tow artillery, ammunition, and other supplies. He promised that machines save personnel: "a new method of warfare may be inaugurated against which the enemy is at present impotent" (in 1936: 229-230). Still, the Tank Corps held no tracked tractors. Supply tanks were configured to tow, but pitched more dramatically than horses when moving across country, and thus stressed the gun carriages more. In the end, no artillery tractors were required for this operation, because the final objective was so shallow as to remain within the range of the field artillery.

Exploitation

At Amiens, medium tanks and armoured cars were tasked with exploitation for the first time, although subordinated to different corps and arms (see Table 17).

Medium Tanks and Cavalry

On 21 July, Rawlinson said that he planned to exploit the breakthrough with the three available divisions of cavalry and two battalions of Whippet tanks. Fuller pointed out that cavalry, being unarmoured, are not interoperable with armoured vehicles. (Presumably somebody countered that Whippets are not interoperable, given their inferior maximum speed, although Fuller might have countered that the Whippets offer a superior average speed.) Fuller wanted to allocate a company of medium tanks to each corps, to exploit beyond the final objective. Instead, 4th Army ordered both medium battalions to operate under the Cavalry Corps. One company (16 tanks) was allocated to lead each of 1st and 3rd Cavalry Division.

By noon, the infantry and heavy tanks had cleared a sufficiently wide gap for the Cavalry Corps to exploit. The 4th Army's MGGS (Montgomery 1919: 28-29, 44-46) considered Amiens the first offensive of the war when cavalry pursued a broken enemy. Some penetrated the outer defences of Amiens. However, Fuller dwelt on the cavalry's inability to hold any gains, and the fact that under machine-gun fire only the tanks advanced. "Musical Box" (Lieutenant C.B. Arnold, B Company, 6th Battalion) penetrated 14,000 yards (12,802 m), as far as the German horse line.

> [Al]though fantastic reports were received of cavalry attacks in Rosières and in and around Chaulnes, very few crossed the Blue Line on the 8th; yet by lagging behind the infantry they undoubtedly were able to herd together large numbers of prisoners, the "capture" of whom was placed to their credit. Then when, long after dusk, the cavalry retired, and in some cases almost to our original front line, to water their horses, orders were sent to the Whippet tanks to retire with them! From what I heard then and what I saw of the battlefield on the following day, I am convinced that had the 3rd and 6th Tank Battalions been followed by a brigade of infantry mounted in lorries or buses, it would have been possible to have occupied the high ground about Lihons and Chaulnes on the evening of the 8th. Had this been done, the whole of the German railway communications within the salient would have been blocked, and it is certain that with the loss of Chaulnes the German front opposing the 1st French Army would have fallen back (1936: 307-308).

Armoured Cars and Infantry

By contrast, the battalion of armoured cars was attached to the Australian Corps, advanced without cavalry, and did break through.

> Monash…was the first to put into execution a plan which involved the employment of armoured fighting vehicles for an attack upon the rear of the enemy organization, which normally could not be reached, except from the air. Although he had at his disposal only a small number of very inefficient armoured cars for this role, his plan met with a surprising success…General Monash was definite in his instructions that these armoured cars were to avoid, if they possibly could, becoming involved in rendering direct assistance to our leading troops and that they were to withhold their fire, even from the most tempting targets, until they had reached an area of divisional and corps headquarters (Hotblack, "Reorganization of Tank Units," 12 July 1938, LHCMA Lindsay).

The cars advanced from Warfusée-Abancourt, with a section of medium tanks to act as recovery vehicles. Some cleared the long straight road bisecting the battlefield, all three objective lines, and another 4 miles (6.4 km) eastwards, to the enemy headquarters, around Foucaucourt. There they captured four officers of the German LI Corps, some reinforcements, and some supply transport. The northern sections moved on to Proyart, from the outskirts of which they intercepted enemy infantry retreating from the frontlines (Montgomery 1919: 42; Fuller 1936: 308-309; Terraine 1978: 92).

Infantry

The 4th Army reserved three infantry divisions. Fuller wanted to lengthen the front per division to 4,500 yards (4,115 m), per tank to 120 yards (110 m), in order to release another three divisions and two battalions of heavy tanks into reserve. If Rawlinson had followed Fuller's advice, he would have held six infantry divisions for exploitation against four equivalents in the German 2nd Army's reserve.

GHQ had allocated two divisions to General Reserve (British 8th; US 33rd). On 5 August, GHQ allocated another three divisions to General Reserve, and warned other divisions in other armies to prepare to move, so "that in the event of an initial success the battle will develop into one of considerable magnitude." This sounds like intent for a decisive offensive, but behind the scenes GHQ was worried about German assembly for a counter-offensive. The intelligence was ridiculously over-protected. Lieutenant-General John P. Du Cane, the War Office's liaison at Supreme Allied Command HQ, wrote to the CIGS (Henry Wilson) on 8 August that he was hearing of "20 fresh divisions in reserve" on the German side, which might be used in a counter-attack "in a few days time" (Fuller 1936: 307; Jeffery 1985: 49)

Fuller realized that the General Reserve and other armies could not arrive in time to exploit a breakthrough. His first after-action review (11 August) complains:

> On account of the lack of reserves it was found impossible to maintain a sound tactical organization after the first day. With unlimited or distant objectives it is essential, if fighting is to be effective, to keep a strong reserve in hand, so that a continuous roulement of units may be kept up.

Outcomes

On the first day, the 4th Army lost 6,500 casualties, but captured about twice as many men. (The French captured another 3,000.) Canadian Corps lost 3,500 men, and captured 5,023 men, hundreds of machine-guns, and 161 artillery pieces. The Australians lost 2,900 men, and captured 7,925 men, hundreds of machine-guns, and 173 artillery pieces (Montgomery 1919: 43; Terraine 1978: 92).

Of the 420 tanks allocated to the first assault, 415 started (five had broken down on the start line). Another 42 were in the Tank Corps' mechanical reserve. By the end of the day, about 100 tanks had been disabled, mostly by artillery fire from the Chipilly Ridge. Most of the rest needed replenishment and maintenance.

By the end of the first day, the front line ran from the outer defence line at Amiens to Proyart, west of Rainecourt, east of Vauvillers, east of Rosières, east of Méharicourt, east of Rouvroy, and east of Bouchoir. The maximum penetration sustained was about 7.5 miles (13,200 yards; 12,070 m) deep.

Fuller described the first day as a "tremendous physical, and above all, moral blow" to the enemy, "the most decisive fought on the Western Front," as important as the Battle of Waterloo. The chief German military strategist (Erich Ludendorff) declared "the black day of the German Army in the history of the war," although mostly as a comment on German morale. The German official history described it as "the greatest defeat which the German Army had suffered since the beginning of the war" (Fuller 1920: 227; 1936: 316; "This Battles Ranks with Waterloo," *Evening Standard*, 9 August 1943: 6; Terraine 1978: 95; Stevenson 2011: 123-124).

The cavalry did not fulfil Rawlinson's hope of a breakthrough. In the evening, he ordered the advance to continue in the morning, up to the line Roye, Chaulnes, Bray-sur-Somme, and Dernancourt, particularly on the left (III Corps). The 4th Army had not reserved any tanks, so the Tank Corps rushed to send forward its mechanical reserve, to repair tanks locally, and to relocate tanks from further afield. Only 145 tanks assaulted on the second day, of which 39 were hit by enemy fire. North of the Somme, the 10th Battalion put 16 tanks in support of the 12th and 58th Divisions, but the infantry were held up by machine-guns around Chipilly, while the tanks manoeuvred around the woods and slopes, until five were lost. South of the Somme, the 4th and 5th Tank Brigades sent 89 tanks to attack from Framerville to Bouchoir. Around Framerville, only one tank was hit, but five tanks were hit near Lihons. The advance on the second day reached up to 9,000 yards (8,230 m), but the front was patchy: through Bouchoir, Warvillers, Rosières, Framerville, and Mericourt (Montgomery 1919: 51-57; Fuller 1920: 224-225).

Fuller returned from a tour of the front to Advanced HQ, where he suggested that Elles should persuade the 4th Army "to close the battle down, as it was fast developing into a costly clinch." Rawlinson ordered the effort to continue.

For the third day, 85 tanks were ready, of which 30 were hit by fire. The 4th Tank Brigade sent 43 tanks, in support of 4th Division and the (fresh) 32nd Division, against the line from Roye through Hattencourt to Hallu. Due to late orders, the advance started in daylight without smoke: 23 tanks were hit. Elsewhere, seven tanks from 10th Battalion supported two small attacks by 12th Division, north of Morlancourt and along the road Bray-Corbie. Overnight, the 5th Brigade supported a small attack against Proyart. The Whippets and cavalry were ordered to capture Parvillers, but were held up by the broken ground left over from the offensive of July 1917 (Fuller 1920: 226).

For the fourth day, 38 tanks were ready. The Australian Division, assisted by ten tanks from 2nd Battalion, captured Lihons (although nine tanks arrived late, after getting lost in the fog on the way to the start line). Otherwise, the line did not move.

In four days, 4th Army had advanced up to 14,000 yards (8 miles; 12,802 m) on a front 15,000 yards (13,716 m) long. More importantly, it held all the captured territory. By the end of 11 August, 4th Army had lost 27,000 casualties and captured more than 22,000 men and 400 artillery pieces, from six divisions. The German official history agrees, except to raise the German total losses to around 27,000 men. However, Haig had failed to allocate sufficient reserves to sustain 4th Army's advance beyond 11 August. That evening, Haig decided to halt the attack early in order to focus on other fronts (3rd Army and 1st Army to the north). Three heavy tank battalions (10th, 14th, 15th) were transferred to the 3rd Army for the next offensive. The 4th Tank Brigade stayed with III Corps (Elles to GHQ, "Summary of Operations," 29 October 1918, RACTM E2006.515; Montgomery 1919: 62-64; Fuller 1920: 226-227; 1936: 317; Terraine 1978: 95).

From 8 to 11 August, 688* tanks were involved, of which 193 were knocked out, 480 were received by the Salvage Company, and only 15 remained with units. Most were made ready within days. Meanwhile, 250 Mark IVs were reissued, so that 738 tanks were ready for action by 19 August. The closure of this offensive was due less to the availability of tanks than to the shift of focus elsewhere ("Return of Tanks," 19 August 1918, UKNA WO 158/867; Elles to GHQ, "Summary of Operations," 29 October 1918, in RACTM E2006.515; Central Workshops History, RACTM E2006.1703; Williams-Ellis 1919: 346; Fuller 1920: 224).

From 8 to 11 August, 4th Army penetrated up to 12 miles (21,120 yards; 23,097 m). By the 21st, it captured 23,064 prisoners, more than 400 artillery pieces, and hundreds of machine-guns, for the loss of 27,279 men (Montgomery 1919: 68-70).

Fuller (1920: 228), Major-General Frederick Maurice (1929: 155) (DMO until three months before the battle), and a US Army analyst (Willoughby 1939: 99) listed surprise as the first explanation for success, and blamed shortage of reserves for incomplete exploitation.

Fuller complained that too few tanks had been gathered to sustain the attack beyond the first day, heavy tanks need overhaul after three days, supply tanks lack the agility of Mark V tanks, and medium tanks should not be tied to cavalry. Fuller attributed success to "surprise, the moral effect of the tanks, the high morale of our own infantry, the rapid advance of our guns, and the good roads for supplies."

On 16 August, Rawlinson declared the battle a "success," and attributed this success "largely" to the tanks: "The tactical handling of the tanks in action made calls on the skill and physical endurance of the detachments which were met with by a gallantry and devotion beyond all praise." The problems were technological: "The endurance of Heavy Tanks may be at present be pit [put] down to three days, after which Light Tanks must carry on." Before or during presentation to the Tank Board, somebody wrote by hand in the margin "or else a fresh force of Heavy Tanks." Likely Fuller was the source for both propositions ("Notes on Fourth Army Operations," 16 August 1918, UKNA WO 158/867).

Haig's final dispatch (21 December 1918) credits tanks above other weapons.

> Since the opening of our offensive on August 8, tanks have been employed on every battlefield and the importance of the part played by them in break in up the resistance of the German infantry can scarcely be exaggerated. The whole scheme of the attack of August 8 was dependent upon tanks, and ever since that date on numberless occasions, the success of our infantry has been powerfully assisted or confirmed by their timely arrival.

The Army Council (1926: 1) declared: "The Battle of Amiens was the greatest tank battle of the war." Lloyd George (1938: 1874) agreed that tanks "were largely responsible for that notable victory."

---

* In the earliest of three reports, Fuller put the number as 687 (Weekly Tank Notes, Number 21, 4 January 1919, Appendix A, RACTM E19149.127), but in other documents Fuller reports 688 tanks involved from 8 to 11 August inclusive (1920,: 227; 1936: 316; "This Battles Ranks with Waterloo," *Evening Standard*, 9 August 1943: 6).

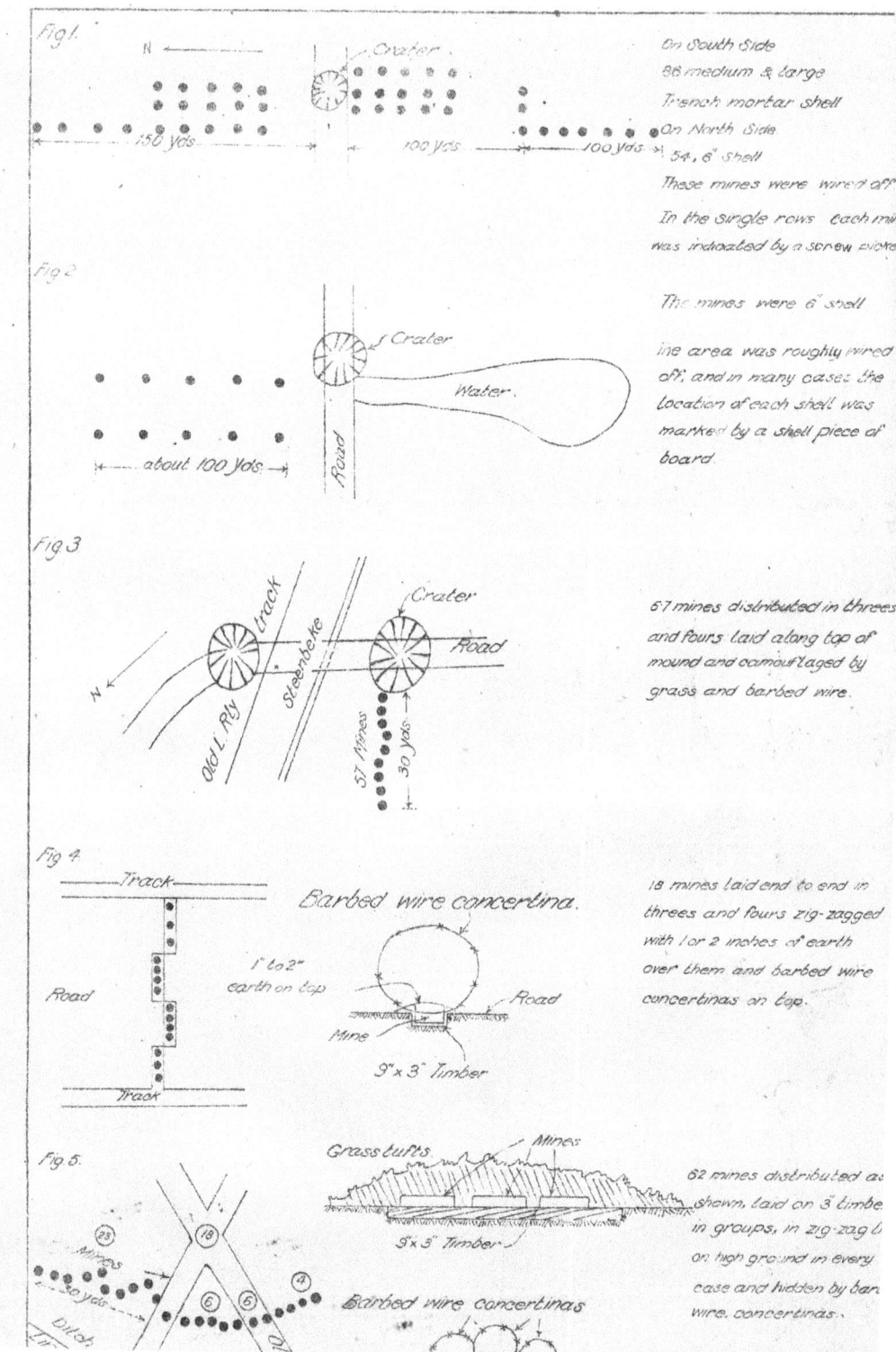

Map 22: German anti-tank minefields encountered from August 1918, as drawn by the Tank Corps intelligence staff (RACTM Hobart).

17

Bapaume and Albert, August 1918

On 10 August, Haig directed that by 11 August some forces, including tanks, should be transferred northwards from 4th Army to 3rd Army, for an offensive through Albert to Bapaume, and to 1st Army, to keep pace, furthest to the north.

Effectively, 11 August was the last day of the offensive at Amiens. Foch pressed Haig to accelerate the next offensive, so Haig agreed to reduce the offensive front to 3rd Army. However, by 14 August, 3rd and 4th Armies persuaded him to postpone, given the strength of the defences, so that artillery could be better prepared. The 3rd Army was scheduled to start on 21 August; if successful, the 4th Army would attack south of the Somme on 22 August.

Terrain

A highway runs straight from Amiens, in 4th Army's area (see Map 21), north-eastwards to Albert, just beyond 3rd Army's front, and in the same direction to Bapaume (less than 12 miles or 19 km from Albert). The 3rd Army's focus was on Bapaume, whose roads radiate out to Arras in the north, Cambrai in the east, Albert to the south-west, and Peronne in the south-east, and whose railways link to Albert and Arras. The 3rd Army planned to attack from the road to Arras, running north-north-east from Albert, on a front 17,000 yards (15,545 m) long, from Beaucourt-sur-Ancre through Bucquoy to Moyenneville. The IV and VI Corps would attack between Bucquoy and Moyenneville. The V Corps would protect the southern flank. They aimed to drive the enemy east of the Arras-Bapaume road and the Arras-Albert railway.

The next day, 4th Army would advance on Albert, on a front of 10,000 yards (9,144 m). The III Corps would attack north of the Somme, on a front running north-eastwards from Bray-sur-Sommes to east of Albert. The Australian Corps would attack south of the Somme, between Herleville and Chuignolles.

Concentration

The 3rd Army held three corps (IV, V, VI). The IV Corps held five divisions (four British, plus New Zealand Division), of which it committed three to assault, two to reserve. The VI Corps committed as many, while V Corps, to the south, committed two, just to protect the right flank, and reserved two.

On 13 August, six tank battalions (3rd, 6th, 9th, 10th, 14th, 15th), of two brigades (2nd, 3rd), were transferred from 4th to 3rd Army. Another three battalions (7th, 11th, 12th), of 1st Tank Brigade, were transferred on 15 August, for a total of nine battalions across three brigades, plus a battalion of armoured cars.

Two brigades, six tank battalions, and the battalion of cars, were allocated across two corps. To the south, the V Corps received none, given unsuitable terrain (see Table 19). Of the 190 tanks, 183 crossed the start line. Not counting V Corps, one tank was available for every 93 yards (85 m).

This is the road from Albert to Bapaume, at Pozières, 4.7 miles (7.5 km) north-east from Albert, 7.6 miles (12.3 km) south-east from Bapaume. Pozières was in German hands on 21 August. The photographer is looking north-north-west towards the 3rd Army's start line. Courcelette is 1.7 miles (2.8 km) directly north-east. The Mark I tank is a relic from the offensive on 15 September 1916. The photo was taken on 11 November 1918 (Fuller 1920).

The 4th Army committed two corps, five divisions, two tank brigades, six tank battalions, and 75 heavy tanks (of which it reserved 15). Of the 60 tanks in assault, one tank was allocated for every 200 yards (183 m) of front (see Table 19).

Surprise

Helping the Allies to maintain surprise was the collapse of German capacity to send scout aircraft over Allied lines, and the remoteness of French spies, who had been developed near the fronts of 1915 to 1917.

The plan eschewed a preliminary bombardment. The assault started at 0455 hours on 21 August, about an hour before sunrise, and was obscured by fog.

Combined Arms

Artillery

The artillery started a creeping barrage and counter-battery fire upon assault, but the Germans had learnt from Amiens, by withdrawing most artillery beyond the range of Allied field artillery – in this case, behind the Albert-Arras railway, which the Allies had set as their third objective line.

Aircraft

Once again, Number 8 Squadron RAF was allocated to cooperate with tanks, although its activities were practically limited to attacking and marking artillery before the tanks arrive, and to dropping written reports on Tank Corps HQ.

Tanks and Infantry

Due to the time consumed in movements, assemblies, and re-organization, no

Army	Corps	Tank Brigade	Tank Battalion	AFV type	AFVs	Formation supported	Objective line
3rd	HQ	1st	17th	Armoured cars	96	3rd Army reserve	Beyond railway
	IV		3rd	Medium A	42	63rd Division	Beyond railway
			7th	Heavy Mark IV	35	37th Division	Second
			10th	Heavy Mark V	24	5th Division	Third (railway)
	VI	2nd	6th	Medium A	27	3rd Division	Beyond railway
			12th	Heavy Mark IV	18	Guards Division	Second
					12	2nd Division	
			15th	Heavy Mark V*	32	3rd Division	Third (railway)
		3rd	9th	Heavy Mark V	(not used until 23 August)		Fourth (ridge
			11th	Heavy Mark V*	(not used until 23 August)		
			14th	Heavy Mark V	(not used until 27 August)		
	V	-	-	-	-	21st and 33rd Divisions	Second
4th	HQ	4th	1st	Heavy Mark V*	15	4th Army reserve	Second
	III		4th	Heavy Mark V	10	12th Division	Second
					4	18th Division	
			5th	Heavy Mark V	10	47th Division	First line
	Aus.	5th	2nd	Heavy Mark V	12	1st Australian Brigade	Second
			8th	Heavy Mark V	12	32nd Division	Second
			13th	Heavy Mark V	12	2nd Australian Brigade	Second
TOTAL:2	5	5	16	5	265 tanks / 96 cars	13 divisions in assault / 4 divisions in reserve	4

Table 19: Forces and objectives for the assaults by 3rd Army towards Bapaume, on 21 August, and by 4th Army towards Albert, 22 August (Fuller 1920: 251-253).

time was available for the tank and infantry units to train together, although some had worked together before. Advanced parties were able to reconnoitre the front, but not to their usual satisfaction, although many tank units had fought in the area in March, and the survivors of the first two companies had fought beyond Albert in September 1916, at Flers, Martinpuich, and Courcelette (Fuller 1920: 251-252).

Speed

As normal, the creeping barrage moved at 100 yards per 4 minutes (0.9 mph; 1.4 kmh). On the first day, the deepest advance reached 2 miles (3.2 km), in five hours, i.e., a speed of less than 12 yards (11 m) per minute or 0.4 mph (0.6 kmh).

Sustainment

The 4th Army reserved 15 heavy tanks, all of them Mark V* tanks, each with capacity for carrying a couple sections of infantry. None was used until the 4th Army's second day of assault (the 3rd Army's third day), when six of these 15 were used for local attacks on objectives not captured on the previous day.

Three supply tanks were allocated to sustain each division in assault. They should add up to 18 on 3rd Army's front, and 12 on 4th Army's front, although records for their use are missing. Some signals tanks too were in use.

Exploitation

The 3rd Army reserved 69 medium tanks, 96 armoured cars, and four infantry divisions for exploitation on the first day. The cars struggled to keep up with the medium tanks across country, so stuck to roads, but the Germans had already mined or cratered these roads at intervals. The tanks loitered, to pull the cars across these craters. None got into the rear of the third line (Ellis and Chamberlain 1972: 17; Fletcher 1994: 164-169, 187-188, 201).

On the second day, the 3rd Army exploited with the same forces to the same objectives as planned for the first day.

Outcomes

The two Mark IV battalions surprised the first objective, and pushed on to the second objective. A battalion of Mark V tanks and a battalion of Mark V* tanks, followed by the two battalions of medium tanks, crossed the second objective on their way to the Arras-Albert railway. By now, the mist had lifted. Of the 190 tanks committed that day, 7 never crossed the start line, and 37 received direct hits. The infantry pushed on with few casualties (Fuller 1920: 253).

The 4th Army started its assault on 22 August. North of the Somme, the infantry of III Corps were pinned down on the start line, but the tanks advanced to a depth of 4,000 yards (3,658 m). By the end of the day, the line ran east of Albert, Meaulte, and Happy Valley, and through the western outskirts of Bray-sur-Somme.

For 23 August, Haig urged both armies to press on, to keep the enemy in retreat. That day, 103 tanks were ready, although fewer were committed. The 3rd Army started at 0400 hours, in moonlight, with 3rd Division, supported by ten Mark IV tanks from 12th Tank Battalion, against the village of Gomiecourt. After its capture, the Guards Division, with four Mark IV tanks, captured Hamelincourt.

At 1100 hours, the VI Corps, with 15 medium tanks, attacked towards Ervillers, Behagnies, and Spignies. By 1200 hours, they were east of the Bapaume-Arras road. At Sapignies, machine-gun fire stopped the infantry, but the Whippets advanced. They captured many prisoners, but not Sapignies and Behagnies. Six Mark V tanks supported 37th Division into Achiet-le-Grand and Bihucourt.

On 4th Army's front, the III Corps, supported by six Mark Vs from the 4th Battalion, captured the hills of Tara and Usna with little resistance. To the south, against greater resistance, the Australian Corps, with 12 Mark Vs from the 8th Battalion, captured the right-hand objective, from where the 2nd and the 13th Tank Battalions, each with 12 tanks, supported the 3rd Australian Brigade north of Chuignolles (Montgomery 1919: 82-83; Fuller 1920: 254-256; Terraine 1978: 106).

The 3rd and 4th Armies took 8,000 prisoners (2,000 were captured by Australian Corps). However, tanks were being shifted to an offensive by 1st Army, at Arras.

Medium A, viewed from its left front. The tower was designed with a machine-gun mounting in four sides, and a driver's position at its right front.

18

Arras, August 1918

The 3rd Army was tasked with the capture of the same objectives that the First Battle of Arras had failed to capture in April 1917: four defensive lines, culminating in the German "Wotan" defensive line – actually multiple belts of wire and two lines of trenches and concrete fortifications, between Drocourt and Quéant.

Terrain

The terrain was still badly damaged from the First Battle of Arras (see Maps 6 and 23), although the ground had recovered in the 14 months since, particularly in the drier weather of recent months. The ground was firm on the first morning (26 August). Light rain fell that morning, but became heavy that night, enough to delay the assembly and the progress of the second day's assault.

Concentration

By 24 August, the 1st, 3rd, and 5th Tank Brigades reported 53 fit tanks between them. In the evening, the 3rd Brigade was transferred from 3rd Army to 1st Army and thence the Canadian Corps. The tanks moved, overnight, 29,000 yards (26,518 m), from Blaireville and Boisleux-au-Mont, through Moyenneville, to Achicourt. With 53 tanks on a front of about 10,600 yards (9,693 m), one tank was available every 200 yards (183 m).

At least six divisions were involved, of which 2nd and 3rd Canadian Divisions bore the brunt in the first assault, on 26 August. (Their assault is known as also the Battle of the Scarpe.)

On their left, the British 51st Division (XVII Corps) kept pace to protect the northern flank, culminating with the capture of Greenland Hill on 30 August.

On 2 September, the 1st and 4th Canadian Divisions assaulted (also known as the Battle of the Drocourt-Quéant Line), with flank support from the British 4th Division (XVII Corps).

Surprise

Given the strength of the defences, the prior decimation of the Canadian Corps, the shortage of tanks, and the urgency of assault, the planners effectively gave up surprise in order to bombard German artillery over several days.

Even so, the first assault mostly failed (26 August), so the final assault on the final defensive line was repeatedly postponed, until 2 September. In between times, effectively the artillery executed a second preliminary bombardment.

The planners continued the norm of a pre-dawn start, but this time in darkness, not twilight. On 26 August, the assault startd at 0300 hours, about 3 hours before sunrise. Rain helped to obscure the noise and sight of the movements. The assault of 2nd September started later, at 0500, with an hour of twilight to go.

Combined Arms

Artillery

On the night of assault, the preliminary bombardment intensified until 0300 hours, when it shifted into a creeping barrage.

Tanks and Infantry

Tank-infantry cooperation may be considered mature by this offensive. No doctrinal changes had been made to tank-infantry cooperation since July, and the Canadians were experienced with tanks since the offensive at Amiens.

Speed

An advance of 3 miles (5,280 yards; 4,828 m) was consolidated in about 4 hours 40 minutes, at an average speed of 19 yards per minute or 0.6 mph (1 kmh).

Sustainment

No supply tanks were allocated, although some fighting tanks carried supplies for the infantry.

Exploitation

Given the shortage of ready tanks, none was reserved for sustainment or exploitation. The medium tanks (about half of all ready tanks) were allocated to assaults instead.

Outcomes

On 26 August, the 2nd and 3rd Canadian Divisions, and 53 tanks from 9th and 11th Battalions, advanced eastwards, with intent to capture all four defensive lines (the final line being the Drocourt-Quéant Line). By 0530 hours, they captured a line running south from Neuville-Vitasse to the Canal de la Scarpe. By 0740, the 2nd Canadian Division captured the villages of Guémappe and Wancourt, while the 3rd Canadian Division took Monchy-le-Preux. Several tanks were knocked out, but their crews joined the infantry in repelling German counter-attacks. One crew returned to their tank, upon hearing that the Germans had occupied it; the crewmen arrived at one sponson door, as the enemy left the other sponson. The advance stuck for the day – on the second line, 3 miles (5 km) ahead of the start line, but only one-third of the way to the final objective line (Fuller 1920: 257).

For 27 August, the 2nd and 3rd Canadian Divisions were ordered to capture the Fresnes-Rouvroy Line (the third line). Without tanks, the infantry could not close, for days. On 31 August, nine Mark IV tanks from 12th Battalion, and four Whippets from 6th Battalion, took the Longatte trench, the Moreuil switch, and the Vraucourt trench. On 1 September, the Whippets supported infantry on to the slopes east of Vaulx-Vraucourt. The Canadians captured the rest of the Fresnes-Rouvroy Line, 3,300 prisoners, 519 machine-guns, and 53 heavy guns.

The assault on the Drocourt-Quéant Line waited until 2 September, although in prior days Allied artillery bombarded the wire. The bombardment switched to the fortifications in the hours before assault. At 0500 hours, the 1st and 4th Canadian Divisions and 3rd Tank Brigade (59 tanks) assaulted, with flank support from the British 4th Division (XVII Corps). Opposition was slighter than expected, although the Germans had concentrated anti-tank rifles at Villers-les-Cagnicourt. By the end of the day, the Canadians had taken the fourth line and the villages to its east (Dury, Cagnicourt, and Villers-les-Cagnicourt).

During the night, the Germans withdrew over the Canal du Nord and destroyed the bridges. On 3 September, the Canadian infantry and Whippet tanks advanced into the empty villages west of the Canal, under indirect fire.

The Canadian Corps suffered 11,000 casualties, captured as many Germans, and probably inflicted as many other casualties. Over the next eight days, German forces withdrew to the Hindenburg Line, giving up the territory they had won in March and April.

Fuller described the Second Battle of Arras as "an overwhelming success," and the month from 8 August as "probably the most decisive month in the whole war." In August, 1,184 tanks had fought, of which Central Workshops received 544, of which 269 had been salvaged, including one tank that had been salvaged three times. From 21 August to 3 September, 511 tanks deployed, and 53,000 prisoners and 470 artillery guns were captured (Return of Tanks, 19 August 1918, UKNA WO 158/867; Elles to GHQ, "Summary of Operations," 29 October 1918, RACTM E2006.515; Central Workshops History, RACTM E2006.1703; Williams-Ellis 1919: 346; Fuller 1920: 259).

Brigade	Unit	AFV type
-	18th Battalion	-
1st	7th Battalion	Heavy Mark IV
	11th Battalion	Heavy Mark V*
	12th Battalion	Heavy Mark IV
	15th Battalion	Heavy Mark V*
2nd	10th Battalion	Heavy Mark V
	14th Battalion	Heavy Mark V
3rd	3rd Battalion	Medium A
	6th Battalion	Medium A
	9th Battalion	Heavy Mark V
	17th Battalion	Armoured cars
4th	1st Battalion	Heavy Mark V
	4th Battalion	Heavy Mark V
	5th Battalion	Heavy Mark V
	US 301st Battalion	Heavy Mark V*
5th	2nd Battalion	Heavy Mark V
	8th Battalion	Heavy Mark V
	13th Battalion	Heavy Mark V

Table 20: British-administered tank formations and units in France, early September 1918 (war diaries; Fuller 1920: 266).

Brigade	Unit or Sub-Unit	AFV type	Count	Location	Formation to which attached	Objective
1st	HQ	-		Bihucourt	3rd Army	
	7th Battalion	Mark IV	16	Bullecourt	Canadian Corps	Second Line
	11th Battalion	Mark V*	12	Barastre	IV Corps	Gouzeaucourt, Trescault
	12th Battalion	Mark IV		West of Ruyaulcourt		
	1st Tank Supply Company	Mark IV supply		South of Velu		
	2nd Gun Carrier Company	Gun Carrier		Bancourt		
2nd	HQ	-		Gomiecourt	3rd Army	
	10th Battalion	Mark V*	11	Gomiecourt		
	14th Battalion	Mark V		Auchy les Hesdin	Army reserve	Final line
	15th Battalion	Mark V*	12	Winnipeg Camp	VI Corps	Flesquieres, Premy south of Bourlon wood
	2nd Tank Supply Company	Mark IV supply	14	Hermies	XVII Corps	
	1st Gun Carrier Company	Gun Carrier		Gomiecourt		
3rd	HQ	-		NW of Vaux-Vraucourt		
	5th Battalion	Mark V		Barleux	IX Corps	
	6th Battalion	Medium A	9	East of Cartigny		
	9th Battalion	Mark V	16	South of Tincourt	32nd Division	Catelet-Nauroy
	3rd Tank Supply Company	Mark IV supply	8	South of Tincourt	32nd Division	Canal Catelet-Nauroy
4th	HQ	-		Templeux-la-Fosse	Australian Corps	
	1st Battalion	Mark V	21	Manancourt	US 30th Division	Bellicourt
	4th Battalion	Mark V	12	South of Manancourt	US 27th Division	Knoll, Guillemont, Quennemont
	US 301st Battalion	Mark V*	39	South of Manancourt	US 27th Division	Bony
	4th Tank Supply Company	Mark IV supply		South of Manancourt		
5th	HQ	-		Bois-de-Buire	Australian Corps	
	2nd Battalion	Mark V	8	Suzanne	5th Aus. Division	Beaurevoir
	3rd Battalion	Medium A	8	South of Roisel	3rd Aus. Division	Beaurevoir
			8		2nd Aus. Division	Serain and Premont
	8th Battalion	Mark V	24	South of Tincourt	5th Aus. Division	Catelet-Nauroy
	13th Battalion	Mark V	12	South of Tincourt	Corps reserve	Beaurevoir
	16th Battalion	Mark V*	24	South of Tincourt	Corps reserve	Beaurevoir
	17th Battalion	Armoured cars	12	Buire	3rd Aus. Division	Catelet-Nauroy
	5th Tank Supply Company	Mark IV supply	89	South of Tincourt	Corps reserve	railway

Table 21: BEF-administered formations and units in France, and assignments, on 27 September 1918 (war diaries; Fuller 1920: 267-268; Montgomery 1919: 155-156).

19

Épehy, September 1918

The 4th Army (Rawlinson) already planned to capture the high ground ahead of the Hindenburg Line, but Haig wanted to replenish, after 180,000 casualties in six weeks. On 12 September, three divisions (under 3rd Army), without tanks, captured Havrincourt, against light resistance, from four demoralized German divisions. The apparent collapse of German capacity persuaded Haig to approve Rawlinson's plan on 13 September, with a D-Day of 18 September.

Terrain

The objective consisted of fortified, elevated ground, 3 miles (5 km) deep, 20 miles (32 km) long. The ground is generally level. It had not been damaged by previous fighting. The ground was dry up to the morning of assault, when rain turned it slippery, such that tanks slipped off embanked roads or into ditches.

Concentration

On 4 September, all five tank brigades were withdrawn into GHQ Reserve for refitting and reorganization before the offensives against the Hindenburg Line (see Table 20). The eighteenth and final tank battalion to enship from Britain to France during the war was enshipped in September, but awaited tanks (Fuller 1920: 162).

On 13 September, BEF GHQ released 2nd Tank Battalion to 4th Army, with just 23 tanks: 8 (A Company) were alloted to III Corps, 9 (B Company) to Australian Corps, and 6 (C Company to IX Corps (Montgomery 1919: 125).

On 17 September, the 3rd and 4th Armies, with French 1st Army co-operating to the south of Holnon, started an offensive at Épehy, without tanks. On the 18th, just 20 tanks assisted III Corps, Australian Corps, and IX Corps, on a front 7,000 yards (6,401 m) long, from Épchy to Villeret – a rate of one tank per 350 yards (320 m). Given 1,488 artillery pieces, one piece was available every 5 yards.

A fourth corps was involved (V Corps of 3rd Army) to protect the left flank. A corps from the French 1st Army was supposed to protect the right flank, although it failed to keep pace with IX Corps, which in turn failed to keep up with Australian Corps. At least eight divisions were involved on the first day, although all were understrength. The two Australian divisions, for instance, held less than 6,800 men between them (Montgomery 1919: 123-124, 130-131; Terraine 1978: 130).

Surprise

The 4th Army eschewed a preliminary bombardment. The tanks assembled secretly (aircraft flew overhead to obscure their engine noise), while the 1st and 4th Australian Divisions deployed dummy tanks on a wider front, to mislead the enemy as to the front of assault, and to demoralize the enemy.

The 4th Army chose an assault time for the start of twilight (0520 hours), about an hour before sunrise, as at Arras. Heavy rain started just before assault. Dark clouds persisted all day, obscuring the attackers (Montgomery 1919: 125).

Combined Arms

Artillery

At zero-hour, 1,488 artillery pieces opened fire: 510 medium and heavy pieces bombarded enemy batteries; 228 4.5-inch howitzers and 750 field guns started a creeping barrage. Additionally, 300 medium machine-guns bombarded the line. In fact, they started early, due to an error in synchronization, making the other arms appreciate a contribution that normally would be lost in the noise of artillery fire (Montgomery 1919: 124; Terraine 1978: 129; Boff 2018: 118).

Aircraft

Aircraft were tasked with obscuring the noise of tank movements, and to drop smoke on the third of 77-mm field guns that had been advanced as anti-tank guns.

Tanks and Infantry

Cooperation was made easier by Australian experience and enthusiasm.

Speed

The creeping barrage moved 100 yards after 2 minutes, and 100 yards every 3 minutes, for a total movement of 1,300 yards (1,189 m) in 38 minutes (1.2 mph; 1.9 kmh). Thereafter, it moved at 100 yards every 4 minutes (0.9 mph; 1.4 kmh), except to dwell for 60 minutes just beyond the first objective line, and for 15 minutes just beyond the second. About 4 hours 25 minutes were allowed to advance 3 miles, a speed of 0.7 mph (1.1 kmh) (Montgomery 1919: 124, 129).

Sustainment

No supply tanks were allocated, although some fighting tanks were assigned to carry supplies for the infantry, in addition to their normal fighting loads.

Some field guns moved forward, while the rest of the 750 field guns delivered the creeping barrage between the first and second objective lines.

Exploitation

No forces were reserved. Instead, assaulters rested two days after the first day.

Outcomes

On the left, III Corps failed to take Épehy and Peizière, until late in the day. On the right, IX Corps failed to take its objectives. In the centre, 1st and 4th Australian Divisions captured Ronssoy and Hargicourt, 4,243 prisoners, 300 machine-guns, 30 trench mortars, and 87 field guns, for the loss of 1,260 Australian casualties. Their advance reached up to 7,000 yards deep, and averaged 5,000 yards deep (Ibid: 130).

On 21 September, nine tanks from 2nd Tank Battalion supported III Corps against the Knoll and Guillemont farm. Two Mark V* tanks carried two platoons, but could not drop them due to machine-gun fire. The forces rested again.

On 24 September, 19 tanks from 13th Battalion supported 1st and 6th Divisions of IX Corps towards Fresnoy-le-Petit and the Quadrilateral. The enemy responded with toxic gas, forcing some crews to wear respirators for two hours.

In the end, the three corps captured 11,750 prisoners and 100 artillery pieces.

20

Canal du Nord, September 1918

The next offensive was planned against the Hindenburg Line. It was reported as 8,000 to 10,000 yards (7,315 to 9,144 m) deep. The BEF fronted on to it for a length of 16 miles (25.8 km). GHQ divided the front into two sectors: northern, between the Sensée river and Gouzeaucourt, to be assaulted by 1st Army, with 3rd Army covering the right flank; southern, to be assaulted by 4th Army.

The offensives started on the same day (27 September), but are complex and vast enough to be considered in separate chapters. This chapter considers the 1st Army's offensive across the Canal du Nord, towards Cambrai (see Map 23). The next Chapter (21) considers the 4th Army's assault on the St. Quentin Canal.

Terrain

Opposite 1st Army, the Germans had incorporated the Canal du Nord into their defences. Beyond were marshes, another defensive line, and elevated ground. To distract from the main assault across the Canal du Nord by Canadian Corps, XXII Corps attacked the Canal du Nord between Sauchy-Lestrée and Palluel, while the remainder of XXII Corps and VII Corps attacked north of the Scarpe River.

The Canadian Corps proposed to attack towards the canal's southern end, where it was dry. At 12 feet (3.7 m) deep and 36 to 50 feet (11 to 15 m) wide, it was effectively an obstacle to all but pedestrians. Where its slopes are gentle, the enemy had cut the bank vertically to a depth of 9 feet (2.7 m). For several hundred yards between Moeuvres and Inchy, they constructed a retaining wall on the eastern side. The dry section measured 2.3 miles (3.7 km) long. Canadian Corps planned to cross a section 2,700 yards (2,469 m) long, between Sains-lès-Marquion and Mœuvres. Most of this section was flooded, but least defended. Most of the troops would cross via wooden bridges, prefabricated by engineers. Some infantry and all 16 tanks would cross a dry part. Once over the canal, Canadian Corps would capture the Marquion Line, including the villages of Marquion and Bourlon, and Bourlon Wood (on Bourlon Hill). From there, it would capture a line of elevated ground, from Fontaine-Notre-Dame to Sauchy-Lestrée, near Cambrai. Upon commitment of a third division, the Canadian Corps planned to occupy a line six miles (9.5 km) long (Fuller 1920: 268-270; Terraine 1978: 137-138).

Concentration

As of 21 September, the brigades held 410 tanks (Weekly Tank State Reports, 14 and 21 September 1918, UKNA WO 158/867). The formations were reorganized on 24 September. Just 65 tanks were engaged on 27 September, in support of at least seven divisions, across four corps (IV, VI, XVII, Canadian), on 1st Army's front, for a density of one tank every 300 yards (274 m), approximately (see Table 21).

In total, 785 artillery pieces supported the Canadian Corps, about as many in the other corps, or one piece every 13 yards.

Surprise

The artillery engaged in days of counter-battery fire before the assault, all along the Hindenburg Line, without indicating the lines of assault. The assault started at 0520 hours, about 80 minutes before sunrise (27 September).

Combined Arms

Artillery

After days of counter-battery fire, the assault and creeping barrages started together, at 0520 hours. The fire initially fell 200 yards (183 m) in front of the start line. After 4 minutes, it jumped 100 yards (91 m). Three minutes hence, it jumped another 100 yards. Three minutes after that, it advanced 100 yards, and continued to jump 100 yards every 4 minutes.

The creeping barrage was unusual in that some gunfire crept backwards while other gunfire jumped forward, so that the German defenders would not know when to emerge from their shelters in order to catch the infantry jumping forward.

Tanks and Infantry

Tank and infantry cooperation was turned on its head in some regards for this operation, because of the reliance on infantry to cross the Canal first, and on engineers to make any steep slopes or sodden areas passable. In this operation, tanks followed the infantry across the canal, and tended to remain followers as the infantry consolidated and coordinated with engineers.

Speed

The creeping barrage advanced mostly at 100 yards every 4 minutes, or less than 0.9 mph (1.4 kmh).

Sustainment

Up to two radio tanks and 10 supply tanks were allocated to sustain each of the divisions in the assault, although the records are incomplete.

Exploitation

No forces were reserved for exploitation. Some medium tanks were used on this front, but for assaulting, not exploitating. Most exploitation forces were allocated to the simultaneous offensive over the St. Quentin Canal, although the assault did not go as planned, so the exploitation also did not go as planned (as explained in the next chapter).

Outcomes

On 27 September, four Canadian battalions, supported by 16 Mark IV tanks from 7th Battalion, crossed the Canal near Moeuvres. One tank was disabled by a mine, which German engineers had buried in a road they had constructed through the dry canal. Two tanks were disabled by artillery near Deligny Hill. The rest remained in high demand, given the failure of field guns to get across the canal in time to help the assault on the second objective line. Field guns first attempted a crossing at 0840, but were driven back. Meanwhile, the infantry of two divisions crossed on foot. With the 13 tanks, they captured Bourlon village and the western edge of Bourlon Wood, by mid-morning. By mid-afternoon, some of the field guns arrived, so some infantry and 11 tanks advanced to the final objective line.

Most of the 65 tanks were supporting the divisions on the flanks, with fewer losses but less glory.

On the second day, Canadian infantry, with six tanks from 7th Battalion, captured Raillencourt and St. Olle, but failed to cross the Marcoing Line, in the face of counter-attacks. They succeeded on September 29, but lost another 2,000 casualties.

By September 30, the 3rd and 4th Divisions reached the outskirts of Cambrai. Unwilling to assault a defended city, the Canadian Corps attempted to encircle it. On 1 October, with the help of artillery that had moved forward during the prior evening, the Canadians advanced only one mile, and dug in.

In five days, they had captured 7,000 prisoners and 205 artillery pieces, but lost 10,000 casualties. On October 8, the Germans counterattacked the three divisions of the 3rd Army to the north, but withdrew from Cambrai that night. Even then, the city remained hazardous with booby traps and unexploded ordnance (Terraine 1978: 167-169).

The St. Quentin Canal was dammed to the north of this bridge to Bellenglise (off frame to right), but dry to its south. The Germans demolished the bridge and wired the banks. By the time Fuller took this photograph, Royal Engineers had constructed a wooden replacement. To avoid the wire, the 46th Division crossed to the north of the dam, from left (west) to right (east).

Men of the 137th Brigade, 46th Division, disperse, after receiving a speech from their commanding officer (Brigadier-General John Vaughan Campbell), who was standing on the Riqueval Bridge, off frame to right. To the south are the wooden rafts and footbridges they had used to cross the St. Quentin Canal, from right (west) to left (east), on 29 September 1918. This photograph was taken on 2 October. The canal curves south-westwards for 1.3 miles (2.1 km) to the dam at Bellenglise. Note the Lewis light machine-gunners at bottom of frame (IWM Q9509).

21

St. Quentin Canal, September 1918

Also on 27 September, the 4th Army assaulted the St. Quentin Canal, which runs north to Cambrai – the ultimate objective for 1st Army. The 3rd Army was protecting the northern flank of the 4th Army, and the southern flank of 1st Army.

Terrain

Opposite 4th Army, the Hindenburg Line took in the St. Quentin Canal, 35 feet (11 m) in width, and ranging from 30 to 50 feet (9 to 15 m) in depth (see Map 23).

At the southern end of the front, the 4th Army aimed at the northern end of the tunnel before Le Tronquoy, which is only 1,100 yards (1,006 m) long, but under a well defended hill. The canal runs mostly north-westwards to Bellenglise. This stretch was dry, but wired on its banks. To the north of the bridge to Bellenglise, the Germans built a dam, which contained 6 to 8 feet (1.8 to 2.4 m) of water. From there, the canal runs for 1.3 miles (2.1 km), through an ever deeper cutting, to Riqueval bridge. North of Riqueval bridge, the canal runs for 0.8 miles (1.3 km) to Bellicourt, where it enters a brick tunnel. This tunnel runs north for 3.5 miles (5.6 km). The Germans used it as a dry shelter, by damming the canal just inside the

The southern entrance to the tunnel at Bellicourt, after the battle. The overlaid vertical black line points to the remains of the wooden screen (Montgomery 1920: 162).

entrance. To defend the interior, they constructed a concrete wall from the dam to the ceiling, with a door and three loopholes for machine-guns. They concealed the dam with a wooden screen at the entrance, and defended the approaches to the entrance with pillboxes. They fortified the ground above most densely, but that is where most of the infantry and tanks would cross.

Concentration

Monash planned for tanks to lead infantry, first to the farms or hamlets known as Knoll, Guillemont, and Quennemont, which enfiladed the northern approach to the Bellicourt tunnel. Once these were captured, he wanted tanks to lead across the tunnel, to a defensive line between Le Catelet (less than 1,400 yards or 1,280 m to the east of the northern entrance to the tunnel) and Nauroy (1,700 yards or 1,554 m to the east of the southern entrance). The straight distance between Le Catelet and Nauroy is 5,800 yards (5,304 m). Confusingly the 4th Army categorized the canal, the intermediate defences, Catelet, and Nauroy as the "first line" (Green Line).

From there, Monash wanted the assaulters to reach the final line, through Beaurevoir, which is another 5,000 yards (4,572 m) east of Le Catelet. Even at most direct, the assaulters would need to advance about 10,000 yards (9,144 m), through the most fortified territory the Australians had yet seen, on an expanding front. The assaulters would need to fight through six lines of trenches and 6,000 yards (5,486 m) of ground, on a front starting and ending 10,000 yards (9,144 m) wide.

Monash wanted everything achieved in one day (27 September). Rawlinson sensibly gave Monash a second day to reach the final line, the first day to reach the Catelet-Nauroy Line. Eventually, they succeeded, although over more days than expected (Fuller 1920: 268-270; Terraine 1978: 142; Stevenson 2011: 138. 140).

Australian Corps was strong in terms of divisions (three) and experience, but not troops, either quantitatively or qualitatively . It had withdrawn out of the line on 25 September, to await replacements. It had suffered one mutinous company on 21 September (which refused to join an attack after being promised relief) and six disobedient battalions thereafter (which refused to be disbanded).

The Corps was reinforced with two US Army divisions (27th, 30th), but these were inexperienced. The Australians properly sent 200 advisers, but these proved insufficient, especially as the American officers did not interrupt their external training courses, and did not substitute the trainees for the assault. (Only 18 officers were with the 12 companies on 27 September.) The imbalance was compounded by Monash's decision to assign the Americans to the first objectives, so that he could save two Australian divisions for the final line, and reserve a third.

The 4th Tank Brigade (1st, 4th, US 301st Battalions) supported the two US Army divisions in Australian Corps. The 5th Tank Brigade (8th, 13th, 16th Battalions) supported the first two Australian divisions (see Table 21).

Even then, the Australian Corps would not have succeeded alone. Fortunately, Rawlinson accepted from IX Corps (Walter Braithwaite) a plan to cross the 1.3-mile (2.1 km) length of canal between Riqueval bridge and Bellenglise, where it was wettest and deepest, but least defended. The 46th Division would establish a bridgehead, and turn south and north to capture Bellenglise and Riqueval respectively. The 32nd Division would pass through to the Catelet-Nauroy Line.

The 3rd Tank Brigade (5th, 6th, 9th Battalions) would follow the assault over the tunnel, and turn south to link up with IX Corps (see Table 21).

Monash under-required tanks, despite his recent good experience with them. Rawlinson more than doubled the requirement, to 201 tanks, suggesting one tank per 50 yards (46 m). However, counting only the 153 tanks allocated to assaults on the first day, the density falls to one tank per 65 yards (59 m) (see Table 21). Given 1,600 artillery pieces, one artillery piece was available every 6.25 yards (5.7 m).

After the failure of the preliminary attack on 27 September, 181 tanks were allocated on 29 September, a density of one tank per 55 yards (50 m). One artillery piece was allocated for every 10 yards (9.1 m) of offensive front.

To the north, the III Corps protected the northern flank, with 12th Division on a front of 3,000 yards, and 18th Division in reserve.

Altogether, the assault employed 40,000 men across nine divisions from three corps, against 35,000 defenders, of which 5,000 were reserved (Fuller 1920: 269; Terraine 1978: 142-143; Stevenson 2011: 139-140).

Surprise

The 4th Army considered that the build-up could not be disguised, and that the wire was of unprecedented scale, so chose a preliminary bombardment. Still, the 4th Army attempted to hide the timing and location of assault by bombarding on a wider front.

The assault started at 0530 hours, 70 minutes before sunrise, in mist and drizzle on 27 September, and in fog on 29 September, behind smoke.

Combined Arms

Artillery

The 4th Army committed 1,000 artillery pieces to support Australian Corps, leaving 600 elsewhere. (Another 5,000 pieces were with the rest of the BEF.)

Counter-battery fire was considerable, mostly by the 600 medium (4.5-inch) and heavy (6-inch) howitzers, before they switched against the wire. Upon assault, the field guns switched to a creeping barrage – 85 percent HE, 15 percent smoke.

After the US failure on 27 September, the main event was re-scheduled for 29 September. The preliminary and creeping barrages added up to the highest British expenditure of artillery ammunition in 24 hours: 943,847 rounds, from noon of the 28th to noon of the 29th. From 26 September to 4 October, 1,299,467 artillery rounds were fired. In addition, 800 medium machine-guns bombarded the first defensive line upon assault (Montgomery 1919: 154; Terraine 1978: 145, 166).

Aircraft

The RAF was less useful to the assault and pursuit than planned. Blaming the weather, it flew on only two days from 9 to 16 October.

Tanks and Infantry

On 27 September, when the 1st Army was assaulting Canal Du Nord, the 4th Army attempted to seize attack positions for its assault on St. Quentin Canal. Two thousand men of the US 106th Regiment, 27th Division, supported by 12 Mark V tanks from 4th Battalion, advanced on a two-mile front, behind a creeping barrage, for almost a mile. Their objectives were the fortified farms or hamlets known as Knoll, Guillemont, and Quennemont, and the trenches in between, from which they sent back 250 prisoners. However, resistance and counter-attacks drove them back, although this was not clear until the morning. The regiment lost 1,540 casualties (Fuller 1920: 269; Terraine 1978: 147-148).

With most US soldiers still missing, a new assault could not be mounted on 28 September. On 29 September, the other three regiments of 27th Division assaulted behind a creeping barrage, this time 1,000 yards (914 m) behind, in an attempt to lower risk. In dense fog and smoke, the US infantry stumbled into unsuppressed defenders, went to ground, or got lost. The 3rd Australian Division started on time, but soon ran into Americans and Germans. The Australians were under orders to ignore the US objectives, in order to exploit beyond, but the objectives had not been taken. By the end of the day, the Americans lost 3,500 casualties, the Australians 1,000, on this front alone.

To the south, US 30th Division assaulted, followed by 5th Australian Division, with similar results: the Americans lost 1,881 casualties, the Australians 1,500.

The US 301st Tank Battalion was supposed to help the infantry to capture the trenches east of Bony. It started at 0550 hours (30 minutes after the infantry). The tanks were supposed to navigate via the Knoll and thence Guillemont Farm to Quennemont Farm, whose hill was allocated as the start line for the attack, but the enemy still defended these strongpoints. Eight tanks detonated British mines, which had been laid in February, west of Guillemont Farm. Each mine, made from 2-inch trench-mortar bombs, each containing 50 pounds of ammonal, destroyed the floor of the tank and the crew (Fuller 1920: 271). Twelve were knocked out by field guns, nine ditched during evasion. Seven were knocked out as they appeared out of the mist, 100 yards from German anti-tank rifles in Guillemont Farm (Montgomery 1919: 163). Fuller toured the battlefield on 4 October.

> Around Guillemont Farm the ground was literally covered with American dead, all clean killed by machine-gun fire. At the time burial parties were collecting them in long rows – most must have been magnificent men. Apparently, from what I could learn, the attack of the 27th American Division had been shockingly planned, prepared, and executed. The infantry advanced some 1,500 yards behind their artillery barrage, which was placed 300 yards behind the German position! The result was slaughter, and the 301st American Tank Battalion which supported this attack, never having been warned of the existence of a minefield laid by the 5th Army in February, floundered into it and was blown to pieces. Of the 39 tanks which took part in this massacre, only 10 rallied. This attack was a complete fiasco and a disgrace (Fuller 1936: 356).

Most of the 5th Brigade (8th, 13th, 16th Battalions) was reserved for sustainment or exploitation. Hotblack, restored as GSO2 for intelligence, after convalescence, took forward two Mark V* tanks from 16th Battalion to clear the enemy from the hill around Quennemont Farm, which enfiladed any advance over the tunnel. The tanks came under machine-gun fire, while enemy riflemen and grenadiers worked closer. Hotblack shot his revolver through loopholes, until knocked out by a shell.

In the confused struggle which followed we were able to keep the enemy off the top of the hill. [The] British tanks were hit and I was wounded in the head. I was just able to drag, by their shoulder straps, our wounded to comparative safety down the hill (undated, RACTM Hotblack 2).

For this, he earned a bar to his Military Cross, but also a second head injury, which blinded him for the rest of the war.

Meanwhile, 3rd Tank Brigade sent 24 Mark Vs (9th Battalion) and 9 mediums over the tunnel and southwards. Sixteen Mark Vs were to assist 46th Division in the bridgehead. The other 8 Mark Vs and the 9 mediums were to assist the 32nd Division to the second line. However, all came under direct fire from artillery. Of the 141 tanks sent over the tunnel, 75 were disabled (Montgomery 1919: 155).

At 0550 hours, the 46th Division had started to cross the canal south of the tunnel, with 3,000 French life-belts and improvised rafts, pulled across by life-lines secured on the other side. They carried ladders to help their climb over the wire and up the steep bank, while engineers constructed bridges. In the fog, and close to the creeping barrage, the leading brigade overran the defensive line on schedule (by 0830 hours), and took 2,000 prisoners, for the loss of less than 600 men. The next two brigades passed through to seize the second defensive line. There they met some friendly tanks, 6,000 yards beyond their start line. The 46th Division captured 4,200 of the 5,300 prisoners taken by 4th Army that day, plus 70 of the 90 artillery pieces, for the cost of fewer than 800 casualties. In the afternoon 32nd Division took over, seized the final objective line by 1530 hours, and pursued the enemy (Montgomery 1919: 161-162; Terraine 1978: 151-153).

Speed

The creeping barrage advanced 100 yards every 4 minutes, or less than 0.9 mph (1.4 kmh). The fastest advance was achieved by IX Corps, to the assigned depth of 6,000 yards (5,486 m) in 3.5 hours, at about 30 yards per minute or 1 mph (1.6 kmh).

Sustainment

As in the crossing of the Canal Du Nord, up to two radio tanks and 10 supply tanks were allocated to sustain any infantry division in the assault.

Exploitation

On 17 September, GHQ practised a pursuit by cavalry, embussed infantry and engineers, aircraft, and field guns. Haig was most critical of the cavalry, who "must not make direct charges at enemy defensive strongpoints." On 25 September, Wilson (CIGS) received a letter from Haig asking for "yeomanry, cyclists, motor machine-guns, lorries – anything to make him [Haig] more mobile in the coming great attack" (Wilson, diary, 25 September 1918, in Callwell 1927: 127).

The 2nd Australian Division, 5th Cavalry Brigade, 24 heavy tanks, 16 medium tanks, and 20 armoured cars were reserved for exploitation. Although the heavy tanks and infantry were expected to reinforce the assault on the final line, mediums were expected to penetrate beyond. The 5th Cavalry Brigade, 20 cars, and eight mediums (3rd Battalion), were expected to advance to Serain and Premont (the latter is 4 miles or 6.4 km east-north-east from Beaurevoir). From there, the cars would continue for at least another 2.2 miles (3.5 km) eastwards to cut the railway running north-south. GHQ held on to the rest of the Cavalry Corps, uncertain whether to send it to 3rd Army or 4th Army. The failure of the assault on 27 September provoked a new plan, to be executed on 29 September, which essentially conflated a new assault with exploitation. On 28 September, the Cavalry Corps was allocated to 4th Army, generally to operate on the boundary with 1st Army. The next day, the cars and tanks got only as far as Bony, where German fire knocked out four cars and four Whippets, before the rest withdrew (Montgomery 1919: 156-157, 167). Fuller (1920: 275) estimated that two brigades of mediums could have prevented enemy withdrawal and won the war.

Outcomes

In August and September, the German Army in France lost 464,000 casualties. By the end of 30 September, 30 miles (48 km) of the Hindenburg Line was in Allied hands. By 3 October, only the Beaurevoir Line remained. This was overrun by 5 October (Montgomery 1919: 188-189; Stevenson 2011: 140-141, 162).

Enemy withdrawal from Cambrai on 8 October was part of the abandonment of the Hindenburg Line. On 9 October, 3rd Cavalry Division, 66th Division, and seven armoured cars started in pursuit. When infantry were held up by fire from Clary and Gattigny Wood, the two cars with 6th Cavalry Brigade (the third had broken an axle) scattered the defenders of the crossroads to the south of the Wood, and captured 10 machine-guns. They proceeded to clear the railway cutting and wood near Honnechy, and continued to the bridge over the cutting at Maurois. One car crossed before it was blown. This car engaged the defenders of Maurois, Honnechy, its station, and its bridge, where the second got across. They reunited in Busigny, where they dispersed a team of trench mortars, before rallying.

Meanwhile, Canadian Cavalry Brigade charged across a mile of open ground against a rearguard near Clary, forcing it to flee. Now over-confident, it charged the southern half of Gattigny Wood and Honnechy, but lost 58 men and 401 horses dead, and 348 men wounded, for the gain of 400 prisoners, 60 machine-guns, and 10 field guns. This was its last action of the war. Infantry cleared the wood after 1100 hours, and took 200 prisoners, 40 machine-guns, and a 150-mm howitzer. On the right, 6th Cavalry Brigade took Honnechy and 100 prisoners, and linked with the Canadians, for the loss of 16 men killed, 145 men wounded, and 255 horses disabled. That evening, 7th Cavalry Brigade and two cars (it started with four) passed through, and entered Le Cateau, but withdrew against resistance. The next day, the Cavalry Corps was withdrawn (Montgomery 1919: 199-200; Terraine 1978: 170-171).

The Allies captured 48,000 men and 630 artillery pieces in 14 days. However, from 8 August to 10 October, the tank units transferred 819 vehicles to the Salvage Company, and lost 550 officers and 2,557 other ranks, out of 9,500 authorized combatants (Williams-Ellis 1920: 261). For the Corps, the offensive ended on 11 October, with 5 Mark V tanks from 5th Battalion helping 6th Division to advance 1,500 yards towards Andigny-les-Fermés. Since 8 October, the 4th Army front had moved 10.5 miles (17 km) on average. To the north, 5th Army entered Lille, recently abandoned.

Rawlinson judged the crossing of the canal "a crushing defeat on the enemy." Fuller declared a victory over the Hindenburg Line, but complained of inadequate exploitation (1920: 275-276).

22

Selle, October 1918

Following the break-through of the Hindenburg Line, the Germans retired to a new line on the east side of the River Selle (see Map 23). The BEF advanced to the west bank by 10 October. The 4th Army and French 1st Army prepared to attack on 17 October, the 3rd Army on 20 October.

Terrain

The Selle valley (see Map 23) is up to 200 feet (61 m) deep, with steep sides. The river was normally 3 to 4 feet (0.9 to 1.2 m) deep, and 15 feet (4.6 m) wide, with a maximum width of 20 feet (6.1 m), at Le Cateau, where the banks are retained by brick walls. The lowland is marshy, 100 to 200 yards (91 to 183 m) either side. The river was in "No Man's Land," so tank officers went forward at night to discover potential fords, over which they laid tapes. They discovered that the river had been dammed at the south end of Le Cateau, at Saint-Benin (2 miles or 3.3 km directly south-west of Le Cateau), and at Saint-Crépin (another mile south). The flood was already too wide to cross without new bridges, which would be costly to construct under direct fire. However, just 0.4 miles (0.6 km) further south, at Saint-Souplet, the river was 8 feet (2.4 m) wide, 4 feet (1.2 m) deep. A crossing-front of 500 yards was chosen. Since Rawlinson wanted 50th Division of XIII Corps to assault, the XIII Corps took over 2,000 yards of front held by US II Corps to its south. Its front then measured 8,000 yards (7,315 m), from north of Saint-Souplet to a mile north of Le Cateau, near Montay. The US II Corps was left with 4,000 yards (3,658 m) of front, from Saint-Souplet to north of Vaux-Andigny. The IX Corps held 7,000 yards (6,401 m), from Vaux-Andigny to the road between Bohain and Aisonville, and south of the head of the Selle.

The western approaches to the Selle are open, but the eastern side is enclosed by hedges and orchards. The terrain was undamaged, although often marshy from rain and flooding.

On 14 October, the weather cleared enough for reconnaissance planes to confirm that the Germans had not completed two defensive lines shown on a German map that had been captured on 13 October, apart from some wire and trenches. The first line ran along the Selle between Le Cateau and Vaux-Andigny, to the north of 4th Army's furthest advance on 11 October. The straight distance between these towns is 10,000 yards (5.7 miles; 9.2 km). The other line ran along the Canal de la Sambre à l'Oise, at least 5 miles (8 km) to the east of the Selle. (Both are oriented north-south in general.) Moreover, aircraft reported forces withdrawing over the Canal.

The 4th Army's front ran for 10.8 miles (17.4 km), although most of the effort would be on the 4.5 miles (7.3 km) held by XIII Corps. This Corps was ordered to capture the ground south of Montay and the Richemont stream, which runs eastwards from Montay, and south-eastwards to Bazuel (2.2 miles or 3.5 km to the east-south-east of Le Cateau by a straight road), and on a line south from Bazuel for 3 miles (4.8 km) through Mazinghien, and another 2 miles (4 km) to Wassigny. The

French would advance to protect the southern end. This third line measures at least 9.5 miles (15.2 km), including the stream. If the enemy were to collapse, the same troops were supposed to advance south-eastwards astride the roads from Bazuel and Mazinghien to respectively Catillon and La Laurette, both on the Canal de la Sambre à l'Oise. The road journey from Bazuel to the bridge at Catillon measures 2.9 miles (4.6 km). The road journey from Mazinghien to the lock near La Laurette measures 2.2 miles (3.6 km). The canal between the lock and the bridge measures the same (Montgomery 1919: 204-206, 221; Fuller 1920: 283).

Concentration

Eight divisions (six British, two American) were committed to the 4th Army's assault on 17 October. Intelligence expected four fresh and two exhausted enemy divisions, although prisoners would be captured from eight divisions on the first day. The 3rd Army used as many on 20 October. The BEF used 24 divisions by the end of the offensive on 24 October.

By 30 September, the Tank Corps held 12,698 men – less than its peak of 13,336 in July. Most were not in France, where the average battalion was left with 24 crews and fewer tanks. On 12 October, most tank battalions were withdrawn into GHQ reserve for refitting. Only 4th Brigade remained with the 4th Army. It held six depleted battalions (1st, 5th, 6th, 10th, 16th, US 301st). The 1st Battalion supported XIII Corps on the left, 301st supported US II Corps in the centre. Initially, the 5th Battalion supported IX Corps on the right. The IX Corps reserved the 6th (medium tanks) and 10th and 16th (Mark Vs), but, after the restructuring of the front, the 5th and 10th were withdrawn (Montgomery 1919: 203-204, 207, 225).

For 17 October, 48 heavy tanks were allocated, one per 396 yards of front. Adding the 12 mediums would improve the allocation to one tank per 317 yards. With 1,320 artillery pieces committed, one piece was available for every 13 yards (Fuller 1920: 283; Stevenson 2011: 166).

Only four tanks (11th Battalion) were used by 3rd Army on 20 October.

Surprise

An assault over the Selle seemed inevitable to both sides, so 4th Army opted for six days of preliminary bombardment. The assault was scheduled for 0520 hours, about 50 minutes before sunrise. Fog blanketed the area.

At the southern end of the front, a brigade gathered dummy tanks and men, and fired a barrage through Riqerval Wood, which provoked an enemy bombardment of the brigade's outpost line. Meanwhile, the rest of 46th Division assaulted across the open ground between the wood and Vaux-Andigny (Montgomery 1919: 210).

Combined Arms

Artillery

The 4th Army expended 17 million pounds (7,589 long tons; 8,500 US tons) of ammunition in six days of bombardment, although not all 1,320 artillery pieces were in position until the final two days. The 6-inch guns shelled bridges over the Sambre & Oise Canal, and the approaches. Other guns shelled artillery, wire, and strongpoints. The final 48 hours (from 0800 hours, 15 October) focused on defensive lines. Upon assault, medium machine-guns bombarded the reverse slopes of the enemy defences. The creeping barrage crept for 4,000 yards (3,658 m), after which the artillery were supposed to advance (Montgomery 1919: 204, 207).

Aircraft

Aircraft were not available during the offensive, due to fog and rain.

Tanks and Infantry

As at the St. Quentin Canal, tanks followed the infantry over the River Selle. In the fog, cooperation was difficult. Even infantry sub-units lost each other.

Just three Mark Vs from 16th Battalion supported 46th Division south of Vaux-Andigny, and south of the head of the Selle. These three were supposed to deal with the first strongpoint and first trenches, but thereafter one was supposed to peel south into Riqerval Wood, while the other two mopped up the villages of Regnicourt and Andigny-les-Fermés. Such missions, without dedicated infantry, and in fog, are unusually risky. At least two were knocked out.

To the north, three Mark Vs of 16th Battalion were attached to each of the two assault brigades of 6th Division. They got lost, to their advantage, in that their objectives were generally secure by the time they arrived.

The final three heavies of 16th Battalion supported 1st Division on its bound to the second line, of which at least one was knocked out. Five of the 12 tanks rallied, including two that had ditched (war diaries; Montgomery 1919: 210-211).

North of IX Corps, US II Corps faced a front almost half as long. It put two weak divisions (27th, 30th) into the assault, each with 12 tanks (all from US 301st Battalion), although only 20 tanks reached the start line. One bogged in the Selle. The others got lost, lagged, or ditched, and do not seem to have contributed much. Eleven rallied. The infantry were enfiladed by fire from Saint-Martin-Rivière and the railway embankment a few hundred yards beyond the river (their first objective line). Towards the south, some infantry of 30th Division crossed this line and got almost as far as Ribeauville. The 27th Division was slower: assaulters reached their second objective line (the road north from L'Arbre de Guise to Le Cateau), only to be thrown back by a counter-attack; they did not return until close to dusk.

North of II Corps, the XIII Corps sent two divisions into assault (50th and 66th), and reserved the 25th. The 50th was supported by 12 Mark Vs from 1st Battalion, of which 11 reached the crossing point. Beyond, they split into sections: four to the left, three in the center, four to the right. On the right, one bogged, but three mopped up the first objective. In the centre, one crew was overcome by toxic gas, and one tank was knocked out by direct artillery fire. On the left, three tanks bogged, but the fourth overran two machine-guns, two field guns, and two trench mortars, before returning to Saint-Souplet (war diaries; Montgomery 1919: 210-224).

Tanks and Engineers

On 17 October, each tank carried a crib to drop into the Selle, except on 46th Division's front, south of the riverhead. For XIII Corps, Royal Engineers assembled 12 pedestrian bridges north of Saint-Souplet, and four more at Saint-Benin, within three minutes of Zero-Hour, obscured by smoke and fog. Feints at bridging were launched around Le Cateau. On 20 October, four tanks crossed an under-water bridge, which had been constructed overnight.

Speed

The creeping barrage advanced 100 yards every 3 minutes up to the first line, up to 2,000 yards (1,829 m) from the start, i.e., a speed of 1.1 mph (1.8 kmh). Here it would dwell for 30 minutes, before proceeding at the same speed to the second line, for up to 2,000 yards again. Altogether, the 4,000 yards would be covered in 150 minutes, i.e., a speed of 0.9 mph (1.4 kmh).

On the southern front (IX Corps), the assaulters fell behind the barrage, due to enemy resistance, or got lost in the fog. The 1st Division held most of the second line by midday, i.e., 6 hours 40 minutes after the assault divisions had started, which suggests a speed of 600 yards per hour or less than 0.4 mph (0.6 kmh). The advance to the third line was delayed until 1715 hours, so that artillery could be organized. It was rebuffed, partly by toxic gas. The US II Corps penetrated 3,500 yards, at most, beyond the Selle. The gap between the river and the second line narrows as the railway runs north-westwards, but was not consolidated until 1630 hours. The XIII Corps reached it at the same time (Montgomery 1919: 207, 215-217).

Sustainment

Artillery (both heavy and field) were supposed to move forward once assaulters pass the second objective line, i.e., after an advance of up to 4,000 yards.

Supply tanks were in use, at the normal rate of 3 per division, at least for some divisions: 18 were required across six divisions.

The IX Corps committed two divisions (6th and 46th) to capture the first line, plus one (16th) to capture the second and third. No forces were reserved to sustain the advance. Rather, 4th Army ordered assaulters to keep going to the Canal, given intelligence that enemy morale was about to crack (Montgomery 1919: 207).

Exploitation

The 4th Army reserved 5th Cavalry Brigade (one battalion per corps) and 12 medium tanks for exploitation. They never exploited, due to the slow advance. At 1000 hours, four mediums were ordered to help the infantry of 1st Division to reach the second line, but three were knocked out by a field gun.

One cavalry squadron was attached to each of the two assaulting divisions in US II Corps, which reserved a third squadron, but these were not used on the first day.

Outcomes

On IX Corps' front, 7 in 12 tanks were lost (58 percent). On II Corps front, 9 in 20 were lost (45 percent; or 54 percent counting the four that did not make the start). Only one of 11 tanks that started with XIII Corps was knocked out, but three stayed bogged. The 4th Army captured 4,500 prisoners and 20 artillery pieces that day. It restarted at 0530, without tanks. Overnight, 18-19 October, most defenders withdrew over the Canal. The 4th Army captured its third objective line, but was repelled by fire from villages before the Canal. In three days, 4th Army captured 5,139 men and 60 artillery pieces (Montgomery 1919: 225, 229).

On 20 October, 3rd Army crossed the river, supported by four Mark V* tanks from 11th Battalion, towards Neuvilly and Amervalles. Two supported the 17th Division: one broke down, the other took a shell in a track. Two others helped 38th Division to capture the first objective, then bogged.

23

Mormal Forest, October 1918

Most soldiers expected to fight into 1919. The CIGS warned that the German "Army is not beaten. It has been roughly handled and is sore and tired, but it is still well able to extricate itself from awkward angles and corners and to fall back in continuous and unbroken line to the [River] Lys, to the Scheldt, to the Meuse." Wilson hoped for more Allied success over the Austro-Hungarians in Italy, and the Turks in Syria, to persuade Germany to give up (Terraine 1978: 206; Wilson to Lord Cavan, commander, British forces Italy, 19 October 1918, in Jeffery 1985: 56).

On 23 October, 3rd and 4th Armies launched a wider offensive, as far north as Valenciennes, across a front about 20 miles long.

Terrain

The 3rd Army advanced towards the Forest of Mormal, which then covered 40 square miles (104 square km), except that the Germans had cut timber in patches.

The ground rises to the Forest, and thus is drier. The 4th Army kept pace to the south, on lower, damper and often marshy ground. On both fronts, the terrain is rolling, interdicted by orchards, woods, hedgerows, and villages, so line of sight is short. Most of the tanks were allocated to the flatter, more open ground at the southern end of 4th Army's front, but even here a high proportion of tanks bogged.

Concentration

Each army held four divisons on the front of assault, and four in reserve. On the first day, 4th Army captured prisoners from six divisions.

Four tank units were committed. Under 3rd Army, the 12th Battalion (2 tanks) supported IV Corps, the 11th (6 tanks) supported V Corps. Under 4th Army, the 10th (24 tanks) supported XIII Corps, the 301st (12 tanks) supported IX Corps. These 44 tanks suggest one tank per 800 yards (Montgomery 1919: 230-231).

Surprise

Given a full moon on the night of 22 to 23 October, 4th Army chose to assault at 0120 hours (5 hours before sunrise), in hope of surprising the enemy as to timing. Since the 3rd Army's front bulged furthest eastwards, its V Corps started at 0200 hours, in expectation that the 4th Army's XIII Corps would be advancing in line by then. On 24th October, the assault started at 0400 (Montgomery 1919: 231, 236).

Combined Arms

Artillery

Allied artillery effectively did not cease in the three complete days between the end of the last offensive and the opening of this offensive, except for the movement of guns forward.

Medium machine-guns supplemented the preliminary bombardment, to cover the noise of tanks assembling, and the creeping barrage.

Tanks and Infantry

Furthest south, the US 301st Tank Battalion (12 tanks) supported IX Corps in the capture of the villages of Catillon and Ors on the west side of the Canal. The Germans responded with toxic gas shells, but nine tanks led through the wire and hedges, and on to most of the final objective line, without need for the three tanks in reserve. The infantry took 3,000 prisoners.

The 10th Tank Battalion (24 tanks) supported XIII Corps, of which 16 supported 18th Division, eight supported 25th Division.

Eight tanks (A Company) supported 55th Brigade of 18th Division, except one did not make the start line, and one was immobilized on the start line by an enemy shell, leaving the other two in the same section to support the assigned battalion. Of the four with another battalion, one was knocked out by a field gun while meeting a counter-attack on the first line, and one broke down, but the other two continued to the fourth line and beyond, before rallying.

Four tanks supported 53rd Brigade, except two stayed on the start line, after gas shells harmed the crewmen and damaged a track. The other two were hit on the first objective line.

Four tanks (also from B Company) supported 54th Brigade. One broke a track before the start line, and another was knocked out by a shell just beyond the start line, but the other two supported infantry on to the final line.

Of the eight tanks (C Company) with 25th Division, one broke down on its way to the start line, two between the start line and the first objective. The remaining five crossed the railway embankment, but three bogged down, one was hit twice by shells, and one was left to continue to the final objective line and to rally.

On 24 October, eight tanks from 10th Tank Battalion were sent to support the 18th and 25th Divisions of XIII Corps, to clear the area around Robersart, less than a mile from the Forest's south-west corner. The two attached to 7th Brigade both broke down without reaching the enemy. Four were attached to 55th Brigade, except one tank kept falling behind with engine trouble. The main resistance was at Renuart farm, until a six-pounder shell detonated its ammunition dump. The fourth tank caught up in the evening, and dwelt to mop up, while the other three rallied, and ended up spending the night for want of fuel. Two tanks supported 74th Brigade, except one started late, after fixing a stuck gear. The other supported the infantry on to the first line, even after it broke down. The fixed tank arrived in time to help the infantry on to the final objective, although, during its return, it broke down and was hit by artillery (war diaries; Fuller 1920: 284-285).

Speed

The creeping barrage moved 100 yards (183 m) every 4 minutes, i.e., 0.9 mph (1.4 kmh), apart from special barrages for attacks through woods.

On the right, the 1st Division advanced about 4,000 yards, up to Catillon, by 0800 hours, suggesting a speed of 600 yards per hour (0.3 mph; 0.5 kmh).

To its north, the 25th Division advanced less than 3,000 yards, across the well-defended Richemont stream, to Pommereuil, by 1030, suggesting an average speed of 327 yards per hour (0.19 mph; 0.30 kmh).

Furthest north, the 18th Division, which was keeping pace with 3rd Army, advanced deepest, for 8,000 yards, by 2000 hours, i.e. 429 yards per hour (0.24 mph; 0.39 kmh) (Montgomery 1919: 232-236).

Sustainment

A supply tank and a cable-laying tank were attached to each of the two assaulting brigades of 18th Division, XIII Corps. A radio tank was attached to each of 6th and 25th Division. No supply tanks were allocated to either, but each of the eight Mark V* tanks with 25th Division, and each of the 12, Mark V* tanks with the 6th Division, carried 5,000 rounds of 0.303-inch ammunition for the infantry.

Some 18-pounders and 6-inch howitzers advanced after the creeping barrage.

Exploitation

No forces were reserved for exploitation.

Outcomes

The tanks suffered high rates of break down and bogging in this operation, due to the wooded and marshy terrain and the accurate shell fire. The easiest ground was at the southern end, near the Canal, where all nine of the starting tanks with 301st Battalion reached the final line. From 10th Battalion, only five of 24 tanks reached the final line on 23 October, and only one of eight on 24 October.

By the end of 24 October, the final line was in Allied hands, except Catillon and Ors. The 4th Army captured 1,230 men and 60 artillery pieces. From 17 to 24 October, the three British armies involved had captured 20,000 prisoners and 475 artillery pieces (Montgomery 1919: 237; Terraine 1978: 206).

From September 1917, a dedicated carrier (Mark IX) was developed from the Mark V tank. The Mark IX (below) is unique in the series for flat sides (without sponsons), two oval doors in each side, and a flatter nose. The engine was moved forward, the gearbox rearward, and the outer track frames were deleted, to increase internal volume. Girders were added transversely to stiffen the sides and floor. The vehicle was rated for a load of 10 long tons (10.2 metric; 11.2 short) or 50 soldiers. Mountings for machine-guns were designed at front and rear (Fuller 1920: 109, 166; 1936: 81, 130; Martel 1931: 53).

Map 23: Operations from 17 October 1918 (Montgomery 1919).

24

Sambre, November 1918

Given German organization of a defensive line on the River Meuse (Maas), GHQ ordered (29 October) an offensive by all three armies, to start on 4 November. Some commanders told troops it would be the last offensive, and so it proved.

Terrain

On 1 November, US 1st Army and French 4th Army broke through the Meuse-Argonne front. Later that day, Canadian Corps (3rd Army) reached Valenciennes, while 4th Army advanced to the Canal de la Sambre à l'Oise, except at Catillon and Happegarbes (one mile west of Landrecies) (see Map 23). At 0600 hours on the next day, three Mark Vs from 10th Battalion helped an infantry battalion to advance south of Happegarbes, into a southwards bulge of the Canal that commanded the ground as far as Catillon. After heavy fighting, and 60 prisoners, the position seemed secure. Three hours later, the British were bombarded by high-explosive and toxic gas, before counter-attackers arrived from the north-east. A second wave surrounded battalion HQ, which resisted until nightfall, when it ordered withdrawal. Two tanks rallied; one ditched (war diary; Montgomery 1919: 240-241).

For 4 November, the British planned to advance 15 miles (24 km) eastwards to the cities of Maubeuge and Mons. From Mons, they could advance another 50 miles (80 km) on Namur, where the Meuse turns north-eastwards towards Liege and the German border (see Map 23). The offensive was huge, on a front of 30 miles (48 km), south-westwards from Condé-sur-l'Escaut through Valenciennes, and southwards to the west of Mormal Forest, to the River Oise. The final objective line, from Mons to Mauberge, measures 12 miles (19 km) in a straight line. The French front of assault, to the south, measured another 15 miles (24 km).

The offensive came to be known as the Battle of the Sambre, just because the canalized Sambre River runs north-eastwards to Mauberge from Landrecies. The capture of Landrecies would allow British forces to move south of Mormal Forest, although they would be funnelled between the Rivers Sambre and Oise at Hirson (22 miles or 36 km from Landrecies). The advance cuts across the River Sambre's tributaries. The Canal de la Sambre à l'Oise connects the Sambre at Landrecies to the Oise at La Fère. It is 35 to 40 feet (11 to 12 meters) wide, with embankments 70 feet (21 meters) apart. The Sambre itself is 60 to 70 feet wide (18 to 21 meters) where canalized. The Canal and the river were wider where the Germans had demolished locks and dykes. The tributaries are in deeper valleys.

Concentration

The BEF committed three armies (1st, 3rd, 4th), eight corps, and 17 divisions. The French committed their 1st Army, with three corps and 11 divisions.

The Tank Corps in France was down to its 1st and 2nd Brigades, with about 100 tanks. The other three brigades had been withdrawn for refit. Only 2nd Brigade, 5

Army	Corps	Division	Brigade	Tank battalion	AFVs	Sustainment tanks	Objective
1st	XXII	11th		-	-	-	
		56th		-	-	-	
	Cdn.	3rd		-	-	-	
		4th		-	-	-	
3rd	IV	37th	111th	14th	2 heavies	-	Jolimetz
			112th	14th	3 heavies	-	west of Louvigniers
		NZ	Rifle, 1st	-	-	-	Le Quesnoy
	V	17th	52nd	9th	3 heavies	-	Mormal Forest
		38th	115th	9th	3 heavies	-	Englefontaine
	VI	Guards		-	-	-	
		62nd		-	-	-	
		-	-	6th	12 mediums	-	(reserve)
	XVII	19th		-	-	-	
		24th		-	-	-	
4th	IX	1st	2nd	-	-	-	Lock 1, south of Catillon
			1st	-	-	-	Canal's bend to south
			3rd	10th	3 heavies	1 supply	Catillon
		32nd	14th	-	-	-	south of Ors
			96th	10th	3 heavies	1 supply	north of Ors
		-	-	-	4 heavies	1 supply, 1 radio	(reserve)
	XIII	18th	53rd	14th	6 heavies	1 supply	Hecq
			54th	14th	4 heavies	-	Preux aux Bois
			55th	-	-	1 cable-layer	south, east of Sassegnies
			-	17th	2 cars	-	Mormal Forest
		25th	75th	9th	3 heavies	4 bridging	Landrecies
			7th, 74th	-	-	-	Maroilles
		60th		-	-	-	Final line
		50th	149th	9th	6 heavies	1 supply	southwest Mormal Forest
			150th	9th	5 heavies	-	Mormal Forest
			151st	-	-	1 cable-layer	Final line
			-	17th	2 cars	-	Mormal Forest
		-	-	17th	5 cars	-	(exploit)
TOTAL: 3	8	17	21	5	45 heavies 12 mediums 9 cars	5 supply 4 bridging 2 cable-layer 1 radio	-

Table 22: The BEF's allocations for the offensive on 4 November 1918 (see: war diaries; Montgomery 1919: 247; Fuller 1920: 285; Clayton 2018).

units, 57 tanks,[*] and 9 cars were allocated to the offensive (see Table 22). The tanks were spread across 8 divisions, 5 corps, and 2 armies. Four heavies were reserved by IX Corps, with intent to commit against the final line. The VI Corps reserved twelve mediums for exploitation. Counting only the 41 heavies in the assault, on a front of 15 miles, gives a concentration of one heavy per 644 yards (589 m).

Surprise

Surprise was wanted, so that the enemy would not reinforce the defenders of the waterways. Thus, preliminary bombardment was limited to counter-battery fire, with no change from normal harassing rates.

Assembly was executed on the night of 3-4 November. Start times varied from 0530 to 0615 hours, up to 90 minutes before sunrise. The morning was misty.

Combined Arms

Artillery

Apart from some counter-battery fire, the artillery saved their effort for creeping

---

[*] Fuller's history (1920: 285) reports 37 tanks, likely a typo for 57. Montgomery (1919: 247) reports 42 heavies and no mediums.

and block barrages. Most of the fire was on "blocks" of land, to suppress defenders, while attackers bypassed them. The ammunition mixed HE, shrapnel, thermite, and smoke. The mix was densest in smoke around Ors and Catillon at the southern end, utilizing 4-inch mortars. Medium machine-guns contributed to the bombardment of Catillon itself (Montgomery 1919: 243-246).

Tanks and Infantry

Due to the dense country, most heavy tanks started 300 yards (274 m) behind the infantry. The tanks generally found little work, while the infantry crossed the waterways ahead of the tanks, the engineers built bridges, and (after crossing the waterways) the infantry disappeared into Mormal Forest. Most tank casualties were caused by obstacles, especially soft ground, not enemy fire.

For 3rd Brigade's assault on Catillon, three tanks of 10th Battalion were allotted, although one broke down before the start line. One assisted the infantry into southern Catillon, and one assisted other infantry to the bridge.

Three supply tanks (the fourth had broken down) carried bridging material to the canal, near Landrecies. They found British infantry held up by machine-gun fire. One vehicle was knocked out, but the section commander carried on, with the other vehicle alongside, to shelter the infantry's advance.

Just to the north, three tanks from 9th Battalion helped 25th Division to capture Faubourg Soyeres and the Chateau just short of the south-west corner of the Forest. One was knocked out by indirect fire, and the other two were delayed by obstacles and engine trouble, but they were necessary to the captures.

Ten tanks of 14th Battalion were allocated to support 18th Division to capture Hecq, on the same line to the north, of which only one failed to reach the start. Nine engaged the enemy, although three were knocked out, and four ditched.

To the north, 11 tanks of 9th Battalion helped 50th Division into Mormal Forest, although two foundered before the start line, one was overcome by toxic gas, one bogged after the start line, and one was knocked out, leaving six.

Six tanks from the same battalion supported 17th and 38th Divisions to the northern corner of Mormal Forest, but three ditched before the start line, and one was knocked out just beyond the start line, leaving two with 38th Division, until they two foundered.

Furthest north, five tanks from 14th Battalion supported 37th Division, except all three tanks with the southern of the two brigades. which foundered (war diaries).

Tanks and Engineers

The Canal and river were considered too wide and deep to be made passable by cribs. The Canal's embankments also increased the risks for tanks. Tanks were expected to cross via reconstructed bridges.

Pedestrian assaulters of the canal were issued with lifebelts. The first assaulters from 1st and 32nd Divisions crossed the Canal, each with four floating bridges. Each bridge was fitted with a ladder at the front to help to scale the embankment. Subsequent infantry crossed by single-file bridges, constructed from wood and pushed forward on wheels (1st Division), or from petrol tins lashed together (32nd Division). At Landrecies, the first assaulters from 25th Division paddled and roped themselves across on 80 rafts, each made from 16 petrol tins lashed to a timber frame. The rafts were then lashed together to form a pontoon bridge. Berthon boats were reserved (Montgomery 1919: 246, 252).

Speed

The creeping barrage advanced 100 yards every 4 or 6 minutes (0.6 to 0.9 mph), depending on the ground. By dusk, the depth of the bridgehead ranged from 4,400 yards (2.5 miles; 4 km) to 6,000 yards (3.4 miles; 5.5 km) (in Mormal Forest), and averaged 5,300 yards (3 miles; 4.8 km). This suggests that the fastest advance averaged 545 yards per hour (0.3 mph; 0.5 kmh), the slowest 400 yards per hour (0.2 mph; 0.4 kmh). The 1st Division advanced 4,000 yards by 1715 hours, i.e., in 10.5 hours, a speed of 381 yards per hour (0.2 mph; 0.3 kmh).

Sustainment

The IX Corps reserved 4 heavy tanks, for use as either mechanical replacements or supply tanks. In the end, they were committed against the final line.

Twelve supply variants were used by 4th Army. Four supplied four divisions, one supplied the tank battalion supporting the two divisions of IX Corps, one carried a radio for that same battalion, two laid cable for two divisions of VIII Corps, and four were assigned to carry bridging material for the engineers.

In the 3rd Army, fighting tanks carried other supplies.

Due to the close country, and deep valleys, artillery were pushed close to the front before the offensive, and prepared to advance after the initial assault. At Ors, a bridge was ready to take field guns at 1300 hours. These guns were in action by 1600 hours.

Exploitation

The 3rd Army reserved 12 medium tanks, while the 4th Army reserved 5 cars for exploitation, and assigned 4 cars to recconnoitre Mormal Forest on the first day, and for exploitation on subsequent days.

On 5 November, 6 mediums and 9 cars supported 3rd Guards Brigade north of the Mormal Forest. The ditches and fences of the area tended to hold up infantry, while medium tanks and cars moved ahead to keep up with the retreating enemy. At the end of that day, all tanks and cars were withdrawn for overhaul. This was the last day when tanks were in action during the Great War (Fuller 1920: 286).

Outcomes

On the right (south) of the British line, the 1st and 32nd Divisions of IX Corps lost around 1,150 men in the crossing.

To the north, under 3rd Army, the IV and V Corps, with 11 tanks between them, attacked into Forêt de Mormal, and reached most of their objectives.

By the end of the day, the 3rd and 4th Armies captured a line 2.5 miles (4 km) deep and 15 miles (24 km) long, 4,000 prisoners, and 80 artillery pieces.

The French 1st Army captured Guise and Origny-en-Thiérache, completing an Allied line almost 50 miles (80 km) long.

By 9 November, the tank brigades held 240 tanks, while the Schools held 205 tanks (Weekly Tank State Report, 9 November 1918, UKNA WO 158/867). The Tank Force was withdrawn for reorganization again, which was still incomplete when the armistice came into effect on 11 November.

25

Findings

Since 18 July (when the Allies started an offensive on the Marne), the BEF took 188,700 prisoners, 2,840 artillery pieces, 3,000 trench mortars, and 29,000 machine-guns, the French took 139,000 prisoners and 1,880 artillery pieces, the Americans took 43,000 and 1,421, and the Belgians took 14,500 and 474. These captures suggest that the BEF performed best. Britain's superior doctrine, tanks, artillery guns and fire control, infantry structure, and infantry tactics are among the explanations. Certainly, the BEF deployed the best heavy and medium tanks, and used them most effectively, although the French used the best lights (Newsome 2021a).

Fuller (1921: 95-96) liked to point out that the first day of the offensive on the Somme (1 July 1916) produced 40,000 British casualties, whereas the first day of the offensive at Amiens (8 August 1918) produced 1,000. The necessary difference for Fuller was tanks: more were in action on 8 August than any other day of the war.

Haig's final despatch, in December 1918, concluded: "the importance of the part played by them [tanks] in breaking up the resistance of the German infantry can scarcely be exaggerated…It is no disparagement of the courage of our infantry, or of the skill and devotion of our artillery, to say that the achievements of those essential arms would have fallen short of the full measure of success achieved by our armies had it not been for the very gallant work of the Tank Corps." Lloyd George (1938: 388) criticized the BEF's "slowness to realise" the tanks' potential. "But by the summer of 1918 their value was definitely established." Foot (1934: 225) judged "that the victories of the hundred days were mainly due to the tanks. The German soldiers had not changed since March, the British soldiers were the same; but now we had some really efficient tanks and knew how to use them." Elles recalled that "we were able to look forward to 1919 with a certain knowledge that we had much in hand against any measure of opposition – short of a superior tank – that the enemy could produce" (in Williams Ellis 1920: ix). Fuller (1945: 141) described the tank as second to only the naval blockade in its overall contribution to victory. Given the small size of the Tank Corps relative to other arms, he added: "the moral effect…vastly exceeded the physical damage done." A British engineer agreed that "the slow but certain pressure of sea power, the arrival of large American reinforcements, and the exploitation of success by their tanks…enable[d] the Allies to overcome the enemy" (Portway 1951: 23). A German veteran admitted that "their [tanks'] success was great" (Foertsch 1940: 157).

This chapter assesses the inputs and outputs for 19 offensives involving British tanks, both quantitative, as summarized in Table 23, and qualitative. The findings are organized by the seven principles of mechanized warfare already identified: terrain, concentration, surprise, combined arms, speed, sustainment, exploitation.

Terrain

The first doctrinists required dry, undamaged terrain, but GHQ introduced tanks on the most damaged and waterlogged part of its front, in hope of saving a mistaken offensive (the mistermed Battle of the Somme). Also, it mistakenly wanted to aim tanks at villages and woods, which indirect fire had struggled to neutralize.

The first six offensives to use tanks (ignoring restarts or follow-ups beyond the first day) were on waterlogged terrain, from September 1916, around Flers and Courcelette, to July 1917 at Passchendaele. The first offensive to launch tanks on dry and undamaged terrain was Cambrai, on 20 November 1917.

Including Cambrai, the final 13 offensives in my dataset started on dry ground, except for two start days in heavy rain, and the flooded waterways of the final five offensives. Eight of those last 13 offensives were on ground undamaged by previous offensives. Clearly, GHQ realized the need for suitable terrain by October 1917, to the benefit of the subsequent 13 offensives involving tanks, although the BEF slogged through the self-inflicted marshes of Passchendaele first.

Across the first six offensives, all waterlogged, the deepest penetration was 6,000 yards, with an average of less than 3,900, a median of 4,400 (half of penetrations are below the median, half above). The final 13 offensives, mostly dry, penetrated to a maximum of 13,200 yards, with an average of 5,500, a median of 5,300 yards.

The number of tanks cannot explain the increased penetration in the last 13 offensives: the average concentration was practically the same in the first six (one tank every 252.5 yards) as the final 13 (one tank every 257 yards). The counts of ready tanks per offensive fell in the final three operations, to fewer tanks than had been allocated to the first offensive, and on much longer fronts.

Concentration

The tank arm never concentrated as many tanks for operations as it wanted. The first doctrininists had wanted one tank every 100 yards of front. This was bettered in only 4 of the 19 operations in my dataset. The average assault front per tank is 256 yards, the median is 200 yards, with a range from 47 yards (Cambrai, 20 November 1917) to 800 yards (Mormal Forest, 23 October 1918). The two best penetrations were achieved with the two best concentrations: 7,500 yards deep at Cambrai (47 yards of front per tank); 13,200 yards deep at Amiens (54 yards of front per tank) . The bivariate correlation is in the expected direction (negative, i.e., if the front per tank gets wider, the penetration gets shorter), although weak (-0.1), suggesting that many other factors affect penetration. Indeed, this book has identified concentration as only one of seven principles.

GHQ committed tanks before enough were available to fulfil the doctrinists' desired concentration. Thereafter the supply of tanks fell behind schedule. The government and GHQ always prioritized aircraft and artillery over tanks. Across the 19 offensives in my dataset, one artillery piece was allocated to every 9 yards of front, on average, compared to one tank per 256 yards, on average. In the fiscal year through March 1918, tanks accounted for just 1.4% of expenditure by the Ministry of Munitions. A tank force to Fuller's requirements was not programmed by the government until Summer 1918, for delivery in Summer 1919.

Meanwhile, the Tank Corps usually did not receive enough new tanks or enough time between offensives to make ready enough tanks to break through the enemy's defences. The average number of tanks allotted to the first day of assault is just 98 tanks (the median is more meaningful, at 50 tanks), across 19 offensives in my dataset, with a range from 14 (25 September 1916, at Thiepval) to 420 (8 August

1918, at Amiens). The two offensives with the most tanks were also most successful: November 1917 (Cambrai) and August 1918 (Amiens).

Surprise

Surprise was highly valued but rarely achieved. Surprise was given up in time and space in six offensives, achieved in time but not space in seven, achieved in space but not time in two, and achieved in both time and space in only four. The four offensives included the two most successful: Cambrai, Sauvillers, Amiens, Bapaume. Both Fuller (1920: 228) and Martel (1931: 35) concluded that the primary doctrinal requirement was surprise.

Surprise in time and space was achieved by eschewing a preliminary barrage, disinforming the enemy, securing assembly areas, and advancing before dawn.

Preliminary bombardments were eschewed after the first day of an offensive, by when the defences were expected to be damaged already, starting on the second day (26 September 1916) of attacks at Thiepval. The first time a bombardment was eschewed ahead of the first day of an offensive involving tanks was at Cambrai in November 1917, and this was the first time surprise was achieved in both time and space (although the Germans got wind of an offensive somewhere along the front). Bombardments were fully eschewed before the first days of only 5 of 19 offensives in my dataset, including the two most successful (Cambrai; Amiens). Three assaults started after no more than 60 minutes of bombardment (Ancre, Hamel, Sauvillers). Two assaults started after more than 60 minutes of bombardment, on at least one of many days of bombardment, but the bombardments were directed against enemy artillery only, with intent to appear indistinguishable from normal harassing fire (Canal du Nord; Sambre).

Surprise in time but not space was achieved by firing a barrage at the same time on successive days, without the enemy knowing which of those barrages would be the last bombardment before assault (as first tried at Ancre in November 1916). This innovation was given up for the next offensive with tanks, in part because it was much bigger (April 1917, at Arras), but brought back for the offensive on Messines, in June 1917, only to be abandoned again for Passchendaele in July. Thereafter, preliminary bombardments were reduced to short periods daily, except from Summer 1918: by then, the urgency of Allied offensiveness, and the funnelling of the terrain between obstacles, left little doubt as to when and where the offensive was coming.

The surprise in time was maximized, closer to the enemy's positions, by firing smoke ahead of the tanks (first used at Cambrai in November 1917), by starting the advance in twilight, and by starting in darkness. None of the 19 offensives in my dataset started in full daylight. Sixteen started in twilight. Three started in darkness. Churchill had specified night-fighting capabilities since late 1914, although less for surprise than to terrify the defenders with electric lights. Fuller prescribed night-fighting capabilities from 1917. The first offensive with tanks to start in darkness was at Hamel, in July 1918, although only 2.5 hours before sunrise. This time gap is not far off the conventional twilight gap of 2 hours. The time gap was extended to 4 hours for the offensive at Arras in August. Fuller was involved in the planning of a night-time raid in June 1918, starting a couple hours after dusk, which, he judged, reduced the exposure of the tanks more than the defenders.

Some surprise in space was achieved by crossing obstacles that the Germans had expected to be tank-proof. Tanks were first equipped with fascines to fill trenches in November 1917 (for the offensive at Cambrai). Tanks dropped cribs into the River Selle in October 1918. From September 1918, canals were crossed by the infantry via temporary bridges, rafts, and personal flotation devices, and by tanks via causeways and reconstructed bridges.

In order to achieve surprise in wider and deeper space, doctrinists specified more obstacle-crossing capabilities, and more tracked vehicles for other arms and branches. By November 1916, Martel specified amphibiousness for all tanks, to help them to swim across wider waterways, without waiting for engineers to build bridges or causeways. In 1917, in response to plans to land on Belgium's coast, the Tank Corps developed variants that could be landed from ships, cross soft beaches, breach sea walls, and climb sea walls. In January 1918, Fuller required, by Spring 1919, "a submarine or water[-]crossing tank" to pass "rivers and swamps," although it is absent from his second Plan 1919. These requirements and solutions would be proved correct during the Second World War.

Combined Arms

In the Great War, British tanks always attacked with artillery, aircraft (except in bad weather), infantry (except where tanks got ahead of pinned infantry), and engineers acting as combat engineers (except where tanks adapted for engineering were sufficient). Cavalry were usually assigned to exploit independently. Where cavalry were combined with tanks or armoured cars, they usually separated. Even Fuller's notional "tank raids" combined all arms except cavalry, despite scurrilous retrospective claims (by Martel, Liddel Hart, and disciples) that he wanted to reduce the arms to tanks or to subordinate tanks to the infantry.

Tanks were never the dominant arm. The largest and most used arms were the infantry and artillery. The least used was the cavalry. The tank arm was always the smallest. It tended to complain that the other arms' privileges constrained the tank arm, interfered with combined arms, and curbed operational performance. The tank arm grew slowly. The other arms combined slowly, although infantry and engineers led the way. Fuller complained that combined arms could have been achieved in 1916 if higher commanders had shared the vision of the first tank doctrinists. A German opponent judged that the tank's premature deployment meant "its coordination with the other arms was still imperfect," but, by 1918, "the old question of fire or movement was answered by fire and movement together" (Foertsch 1940: 157). Niall Ferguson (1998: 308) found that "the British merely grafted the new weapons on to their existing unchanging concepts and remained preoccupied with manpower [preponderant numbers and morale]." By contrast, "the Germans shaped tactics around new technology."

Cavalry

For Fuller, the most privileged arms were cavalry and artillery. Cavalry were clipped before artillery. Through 1917, cavalry were allocated to exploit every offensive involving tanks, but never required to combine with tanks. This lack of combination helps to explain their caution even where the going was good and the other arms had broken through, as at Cambrai. Thereafter, cavalry were either excluded from offensives or allocated to exploit with other arms. Their combination with other arms remained nominal, hardly trained, and practically a marriage of convenience, such that cavalry usually stayed behind other arms where they expected resistance, but raced off alone where they did not.

Artillery

The bombardment effort shifted from mostly preliminary to mostly creeping. In 14 of the 19 offensives in my dataset, artillery delivered creeping bombardments. In five of the 14 cases, artillery fired no preliminary bombardment. Preliminary bombardments allocated an increasing proportion of effort to counter-battery fire. Creeping barrages were often simultaneous with counter-battery fire. The efforts benefited from technical improvements, such as silent registration of enemy guns, more responsiveness to assaulters, and readiness to advance during the assault. By April 1917, FOOs were being distributed down to brigade echelon. For Fuller, the war ended in 1918, not 1919, because higher echelons relegated "bombardment" behind "a combination of tanks and infantry, of velocity and stability, of new and old" ("Bomb Mind is the Somme Mind," *Evening Standard*, 8 February 1943: 6).

Still, no artillery guns or FOOs were dedicated to support tanks. The tank arm was never satisfied with the artillery's neutralization of enemy artillery in the anti-tank role, particularly as the Germans advanced and fortified them. Fulfillment of the tank arm's requirements for self-propelled artillery would have helped. The artillery could have helped by combining at least FOOs if not tractor-drawn guns.

Aircraft

Aircraft helped. Certainly the main tasks of aircraft during the assault became the discovery and engagement of enemy artillery. However, few British aircraft were sufficiently armed to neutralize artillery. They mostly discovered, marked, reported, and moved on. Only one squadron was routinely tasked with assisting tanks, and it held no aircraft specialized for the purpose. The RFC was at fault for turning down suggestions, dating back to 1916, to acquire specialized close-support aircraft and interoperable communications.

Infantry

The arms that combined most intimately and routinely were tanks and infantry. Infantry responded with profound changes in structure and tactics, at least at lower echelons. Still, issues remained, epitomized by the question of which arm should lead. The tank doctrinists wanted tanks to lead, in order to suppress defenders (particular machine-gunners) before infantry arrive. In the first seven offensives, tanks did lead. In the seventh, at Cambrai, the question was finessed by Fuller, by allocating some infantry (inaccurately termed "scouts") to liaise with tanks, and to scout sometimes ahead. Still, in two of the next three subsequent operations, some commanders insisted on infantry leading, usually with tragic consequences. In the final five operations, infantry led, but to establish bridgeheads over waterways.

Infantry-tank combination was curbed by the over-commitment and shortage of tanks. The tank arm's first doctrine required 30 tanks per division in the assault. At first use, in September 1916, less than 5 tanks were allocated per division. The rate fell steadily in 1916, to just 1.9 tanks per division at Ancre on 13 November. Fortunately, this proved to be the minimum for the war, but, still, the rate did not reach doctrinal requirements until Cambrai in November 1917, when 63 tanks per assault division were allocated – practically the number Fuller had required in his proposal of August for a "surprise attack" around Cambrai. This was the peak rate for the war. The rate fell, until a second high of 42 tanks per division at Amiens in August 1918, after which the rate generally fell, to 2.4 tanks per division in the final operation of the war. Across all 19 offensives in my dataset, the allocation of tanks per infantry division works out at 14 on average, 7 as a median.

Engineers

From the start of the tank arm, Royal Engineers were attached to develop its doctrine and training. Helpfully, many tank personnel had started their careers with the RE, including Swinton. When tanks deployed, Engineers were detailed to develop training areas in France too. From the first operation, Engineers improved assembly areas, lines of march, and starting positions, and followed up to correct obstacles, and sometimes advanced with assaulters to breach obstacles (primarily wire) under fire. The combination of tanks and engineers was most intimate and routine before the assault, but we should not underestimate the use of the RE, and allied equivalents, in the assault.

The tank arm helped by developing engineering solutions. Swinton and his staff developed solutions to wire from the start, including grapnels and hawsers, although GHQ hardly encouraged innovations, partly because it under-estimated the challenges on the battlefield. The shortage of tanks for fighting requirements curbed the arm's development of variants. Supply tanks were used to carry RE stores when supply tanks were first used in action in April 1917, at Arras. The first time tanks used grapnels and fascines in action was in November, at Cambrai (32 tanks). The arm had developed towed pedestrian bridges, and used supply tanks to carry bridging equipment. By January 1918, Fuller required bridging tanks. Tanks carried cribs to drop into the Selle in October 1918. Tanks could not cross wider waterways on cribs, so relied on engineers to assemble bridges. Still, where the waterway was in captured territory, tanks carried or towed the equipment.

Speed

Urgency of advance is explicit in Ernest Swinton's doctrine of February 1916, lest enemy artillery fire or counter-attackers hit the objectives before assaulters consolidate them. Swinton and his staff officers proved a speed for tanks of 2 mph across fortified ground – half the maximum speed. However, the first operations, and most operations, were slowed by the creeping barrage, to 1.7 mph. Advances for the day were usually slower, due to long pauses in the barrage, and delays in capturing, consolidating, reorganizing, and resupplying. Across 19 operations, the speed of advance ranges from 0.25 to 1.7 mph (0.4 to 2.7 kmh), with an average of 0.96 mph (1.5 kmh), a median of 0.90 mph (1.4 kmh).

The first tanks could surpass these speeds without resistance, but also needed to fight through resistance, so could not be built just for speed. They were optimized for lethality, survivability, and obstacle-crossing over speed. Still, the first tanks were fast enough to combine with pedestrian infantry, and better at crossing obstacles than most tanks today. The main shortfall in mobility was along the dimension of agility, which has implications for lethality and survivability. Agility improved dramatically with the Mark V, which was the dominant type by mid-1918.

Faster speed helps tanks to surprise objectives, avoid fights, intercept enemies, and catch enemies in flight. Mediums were faster, at the expense of lethality, survivability, and obstacle-crossing. Still, their speeds were not great by today's standards. Medium A was deployed with a rating of 7.5 mph, which was often downgraded. Nevertheless, its speed was sufficient, over defended, fortified, or damaged ground, to outpace cavalry, given superior obstacle-crossing, lethality, and survivability.

In August 1917, Fuller developed a raiding strategy that expects an advance into, and withdrawal from, the enemy's rear within hours. By Spring 1918, Fuller prospected medium tanks that could strike enemy headquarters before assaulters break into the enemy's frontline. In April, Fuller and colleagues specified Medium D at 20 mph. Nevertheless, in May, Fuller wrote his second Plan 1919 with a daily rate of advance of 20 miles, which implies an average daytime speed of 1.7 mph, i.e., the speed of the typical creeping barrage.

Sustainment

The arm generally lacked enough tanks, crews, and supply tanks to sustain its advances into the rear of the German defended lines. By sustained advances, I mean advances that are held beyond the first day. Tanks sometimes penetrated beyond the sustained advance line, such as Dinnaken at Flers in September 1916, and Musical Box at Amiens in August 1918. Across the 19 offensives in my dataset, the sustained penetration averages 5,000 yards, with a median of 5,300 yards, a maximum of 13,200, a minimum of 1,000. In only one offensive, the penetration surpassed the 10,000 yards that Fuller and some peers set as the threshold between the fortified zone and the exploitable rear. This was at Amiens. The next deepest advance was at Cambrai: it reached 7,500 yards on the first day, and 10,500 yards on the second, which was considered a breakthrough, although it would be let down by insufficient reserves to prevent counter-attackers.

To explain the tank's contribution to these varied advances, subsections below measure sustainment as tank availability, crew availability, reserves, reliability of tanks, repairability of tanks, and availability of supply tanks.

Tank Availability

Certainly, unreliability contributes to unreadiness, but generals and historians routinely bemoan the unreliability of tanks without mentioning the under-supply of tanks, still less of crews. Improving the reliability of current tanks, or the speed of repairs, would take a lot of development, with diminishing returns. The most effective immediate solution would have been more replacement vehicles, but supplies always ran behind schedule. Most of the units were short of tanks most of the time. The first companies were committed without any replacements or reserves. In most subsequent operations, no replacements were available, except those in repair.

Yes, reliability and repair capacity contribute to readiness rates, on which more in a moment. Here, the point is that the Tank Corps never received tanks to fill units at the same speed at which it readied personnel for those units. The Army Council agreed by the 1920s (when Fuller was most influential on the General Staff): "tanks were used on every possible occasion, but their numbers were totally insufficient to meet the demands made on them. They had become essential to the infantry attack and an infantry attack unsupported by these machines was always costly, and frequently ineffective" (1926: 1). Two artillerymen found an "impression remained among infantrymen that tanks were decisive in set-piece battles but only a useful auxiliary in the extended fighting that followed." Still, they did not doubt that more numerous or reliable tanks would have sustained the fighting (Bidwell and Graham 1982: 138). The German opponent agreed that "experiments with only a few units cannot be entirely avoided…But the elements of success were there. Economies of men and of material could be effected…Really decisive tactical successes could once more be achieved; if they were not operatively followed up, that was another matter" (Foertsch 1940: 157). Brian Pedersen (2007: 58) fairly judged that tanks "contributed to the Allied breakthrough at Arras," but, "with the rapidly changing nature of the war, and continued shortfalls of the tank as a complete combat system, the Tank Corps never achieved truly decisive results." Two key findings are implied in the quotes above: sufficient reserves would have allowed for sustained penetration; and that even without a sustained penetration, tanks contribute to more efficient and effective penetrations.

However, some historians skip these implications. T.L.H. Butterfield (1966: 160) stated that although "the tank had established itself in assault, its value as a mobile weapon, capable of carrying out a sustained drive, was not proven." John Terraine (1978: 98) reviewed numbers at Amiens before declaring "that both mechanically and humanly, the tank of 1918 was not a war-winning weapon." David Stevenson (2011: 122, 163, 212-220) appears to concur. Robin Prior and Trevor Williams (2002: 17) emphasize that the tank "was decidedly vulnerable to established weapons," by which they mean artillery and hand-grenades at short range. They imagine that unless these weapons "had already been severely dealt with by other means – no great number of tanks was likely to get as far as the enemy trenches." (Here they make combined arms a reason to rebut one arm!) Robert Kershaw (2008: 30) could not see beyond the high rate of tank losses per day of battle. "Clearly the tank was not a war-winning wonder weapon." More fairly, Jonathan Boff (2018: 118) wrote: "tanks were neither in fact nor potentially the war-winning weapon…But neither were they an irrelevance." The Tank Corps needed more tanks – and crews.

Crew Availability

The tank arm usually lacked enough crews for its ready tanks. Fuller always required more crews than tanks, and continued to do so after the Great War. Fuller judged that a tank crew cannot fight effectively in a tank much beyond 12 hours, so prescribed three crews for every tank, in order to sustain fighting over a week. The British tank arm has never enjoyed three times as many crews as tanks.

The government never recruited enough crewmen to fulfill the Tank Corps' ambitions (except when programming for a decisive offensive in Spring 1919). The Tank Corps in France employed thousands fewer personnel than a single infantry division or the Cavalry Corps, even at their smallest.* The British Army mobilized

---

* An infantry division was authorized at 19,000 men. The Cavalry Corps was authorized at nearly 30,000. The Tank Corps peaked at 13,336 men in July. About 21,000 men (including Americans, Canadians, Australians, and New Zealanders) were trained by the Tank Corps Training Centre, of which 14,000 were issued to units there, and 7,000 were enshipped as individual replacements. By the end of the war, about 16,000 personnel were being adminis-

75 infantry and 8 cavalry or mounted divisions during the Great War, of which the BEF used 59 infantry and 5 cavalry divisions in 1918 alone. Only the first 17 tank battalions saw action. Few saw action fully equipped.*

Even though the Tank Corps was the smallest arm, it did not consume more personnel per gun, and did not suffer as many casualties as other arms. A tank unit required 3.07 men per gun, compared to 6.2 in a trench mortar battery, 14.5 in a machine-gun battalion, and 32.6 in an artillery unit. The Tank Corps suffered a lower rate of casualties than the other arms (about half the rate of cavalrymen).** Of the 908,000 British and imperial military personnel who died during the war, only 1,319 (less than 0.15%) died in the Tank Corps.

One would expect the proportion to be smaller than the other arms if only because the tank arm was latest to form. Still, the operational tempo for the tank arm was higher than the cavalry in the final two years of war, and increased in the final eight months, given the German counter-offensives and the urgent offensives meant to take advantage of German incapacity. Operational tempo (and shortage of personnel) peaked in the last 96 days of war, from the offensive at Amiens on 8 August. In these last three months or so, 598 officers and 2,826 other ranks became casualties, a rate of about 25 percent. This high proportion can be explained by the increased use of crews, more than any change in doctrine. In the last 96 days, the Tank Corps could not crew all its tanks. It fought on 39 of those 96 days. Some crews fought 15 or 16 actions, with six days between actions on average (Fuller 1920: 228; 1936: 380-381; "Tank Against Tank," *Evening Standard*, 29 November 1941: 11; "Some statistics re. tanks in the war," circa 1926, RACTM Hobart Box 1).

Reserves

The under-supply of tanks, the premature deployment of tanks, the attrition of tanks, and the under-supply of crewmen prevented the tank arm from building mechanical reserves at conventional rates (at least 10 percent of unit fill). No tanks were reserved by an assaulting corps or army until Arras (9 April 1917), i.e., nearly seven months after first use. The reserve proved insufficient (12 tanks, 9 divisions), and was meant to sustain the final wave rather than to replace casualties.

Mechanical reserves were available in only three offensives in my dataset (Hamel, 14 July 1918; Amiens, 8 August; Sambre, 4 November). Across 19 offensives in my dataset, heavy tanks were reserved in seven assaults, an average of 13 tanks per operation. Across the seven assaults with reserved heavy tanks, the average is 44 tanks, with a range from 4 (Sambre) to 96 (Passchendaele).

Reliability

The readiness of tanks reflects the operational tempo, supply of new tanks, their reliability, and capacity to repair tanks. In the final 96 days, 1,993 tanks and cars were used, with a peak (Amiens, 8 August) of 462 fighting tanks allocated, of

---

tered by the Training Centre (Fuller 1923: 164).
* The 18th Battalion landed in France in September 1918. Another 8 British and 1 Canadian battalions had been raised in England since August but never enshipped (Fuller 1920: 162).
** Fuller (1921: 95-96) calculated the rate as 12.58% for tankies, 17.27% in the Machine-Gun Corps, 19.96% in the infantry, 20.35% for engineers, 20.37% for artillerymen, 23.33% for cavalrymen, and 27.39% for other branches.

which 415 went into action in the first assault. This suggests that most vehicles were unready most of the time. To improve readiness requires a reduced operational tempo, more reliable vehicles, more repair assets, or more replacements.

Historians tend to complain about unreliability of tanks, without quantifying. Fuller reported the mean distance between "overhauls" as 70 miles (110 km), until the Mark V, when the standard rose to 100 miles (160 km). Given their slow speeds and short advances, these "overhaul" rates are to be expected: tanks operated for days between overhauls. Fuller observed that each tank needs maintenance at the end of a day's fighting (still true today) and that most heavy tanks need overhaul at the end of three days (still true today, although suppliers and procurers do not like to admit as much). Most of the work on the tanks was maintenance, not repair, even though "overhaul" implies stripping the engine.

Fuller repeatedly specified improved reliability and operating range in future tanks, and sometimes required more reliable versions of current tanks over new platforms. On 31 December 1917, he admitted that "the Mark IV Tank…should have revolutionized the entire tactical outlook of this war…[but] is not sufficiently perfect a machine." He expected enough Mark Vs by August to revolutionize tactics ("Defensive and Offensive Use of Tanks 1918," Appendix A4, RACTM E1980.18). On 5 June, he urged that Medium D's "engine, radiator, transmission, control feed, etc., must be tested and proved experimentally and in advance of the general design, as is being done with the tracks and spring gear." On 15 June, he specified Medium E with a distance between part-replacement of 500 miles. In August, he persuaded the Tank Board to order more Mark V tanks at the expense of the prospective Mark VIII tanks, which are more capable, but, he suspected, given their heavier weight and novel parts, less reliable. At the same time, he also urged production of Medium C tanks, rather than skip over the Medium C in favour of the more capable but risky Medium D.

Repairability

Like reliability, repairability is a routine subject of complaint without quantification. Few tanks were ever broken beyond repair. They were usually repaired within days. In the final 96 days, units passed 887 tanks and armoured cars to the Salvage Company, which struck off only 15. It escalated 313 to Central Workshops, which struck off or cannibalized 109, and repaired 204 in time for reissue before the end of the war (Fuller 1920: 286; "Bomb Mind is the Somme Mind," *Evening Standard*, 8 February 1943: 6). The write-off rate here is only 14 percent.

A larger Corps could have repaired quicker. Tank designers can help. Fuller was mindful by 15 June 1918, when he specified Medium E with parts easy to access.

Supply Tanks

The final aspect of sustainment is resupply of assaulters with consumables. No supply tanks were used until Messines (7 June 1917). Supply tanks then became normative: they were used in 12 of the 19 offensives in my dataset. In three of the later offensives, supply tanks were unavailable, but fighting tanks carried supplies. The average advance was 5,800 yards (5,304 m) with supply tanks, 3,900 yards (3,566 m) without, although other factors contribute to this discrepancy.

At most, 102 supply tanks were used in an offensive (Amiens, August 1918). At minimum, none was used, the next lowest number being four. Across 19 offensives, an average of 16 supply tanks were used, a median of 12. Ignoring offensives when no supply tanks were available at all, the average number of supply tanks per division was 3.75, enough to supply the infantry, but not the tanks as well. At first, supply tanks had been used to replenish fighting tanks, but in most operations they were used to resupply infantry, while tanks rallied to the rear. However, Martel, Fuller, and Foot required supply tanks for a fully mechanized force.

Exploitation

Until 1918, GHQ hoped that cavalry alone could exploit breakthroughs, and that the mostly equine transport could sustain those arms. The offensive on the Somme should have persuaded GHQ otherwise, before tanks arrived in August 1916, but GHQ still assigned exploitation to cavalry alone. Indeed, at least three cavalry divisions were assigned to exploit in the first seven offensives involving tanks. In the fourth and fifth offensives, GHQ added infantry divisions. Tanks were first reserved in a way that allowed for use during exploitation in the fourth offensive involving tanks (at Arras, April 1917). This reserve was ambiguous. In the event, the tanks were used for sustainment, not exploitation. At Passchendaele (the sixth of the series), in June 1917, the only exploitation force was again the Cavalry Corps. At Cambrai in November, it grew to five cavalry divisions, but they proved too cautious and vulnerable to exploit the breakthrough. For the eighth and ninth offensives, the ambition was reduced in depth, and no exploiters were reserved.

The next offensive to aim for breakthrough was at Amiens in August 1918, when 3 cavalry divisions, 3 infantry divisions, 96 medium tanks, and 127 armoured cars were reserved to exploit. This was the largest British exploitation force of the war.

The cavalry again disappointed. For the next offensive, at Bapaume, they dropped out of the exploitation force, while infantry, medium tanks, and armoured cars stayed in. The next four offensives were smaller and less ambitious, without any exploiters reserved. By September, Haig was experimenting with motorized combined-arms exploiters, and expressing most disappointment in the cavalry. In subsequent operations, a few cavalry, medium tanks, and cars were mixed as exploiters, but automobiles were short.

The acquirers of the first heavy tank had foreseen the requirement for an exploitation tank in 1916. They developed what would be designated Medium A, but the Medium A was delayed by GHQ's disinterest. The first mediums were in France by January 1918, but were first used in March, to counter German attackers. They were first used to exploit at Amiens in August, as epitomized by "Musical Box" getting beyond where the salient eventually settled. Thereafter, they were kept out of less ambitious offensives, such that they were allocated to only five of the last ten offensives, and often used to assault.

Across the five offensives where mediums were reserved for exploitation, the advance averaged 6,760 yards (6,181 m), compared to 4,700 yards (4,298 m) in the other offensives. For the first seven offensives, when only cavalry were allocated for exploitation, the advance averages just 500 yards (457 m).

The tank arm was necessary to victory in 1918, and established seven principles of mechanized warfare that still apply today.

(overleaf) **Table 23: British doctrines and operations of the Great War, by geography, inputs, and outputs, in chronological order, 1915 to 1918.**

Date	Region	Place	Terrain	Doctrinist or Planner	Yards of assault front	Divisions in assault first day	Yards per division	Tanks allocated to assault	Assault tanks per division	Yards per assault tank	Yards per artillery
January 1915	-	-	-	Churchill	-	-	-	40-50	-	-	-
June 1915	-	-	-	Swinton	5,000	-	-	50	-	100	-
December 1915	-	-	-	Churchill	-	-	-	60	-	-	-
February 1916	-	-	Dry, open	Swinton	9,000	3	3,000	90	30	100	-
August 1916	Somme	-	villages, woods, forts	BEF GHQ	6,000	2	3,000	60	30	100	-
August 1916	-	-	-	Townshend	-	-	-	-	-	-	-
15 September 1916	Somme	Flers	Water-logged	GHQ, 4th Army, Reserve (5th) Army	6,160	11	560	54	4.9	114	6
25 September 1916	Somme	Thiepval	"		1,500	4	375	13	3,25	115	2
26 September 1916	Somme	Thiepval	"		1,500	4	375	14	3.5	107	2
13 November 1916	Somme	Ancre	"	GHQ, Reserve Army	4,000	8	500	15	1.9	267	2.9
November 1916	--	-	-	Martel	-	(no infantry)	-	(1,864 tracked vehicles)	-	-	-
February 1917	-	-	-	Fuller	-	-	-	-	-	100	-
9 April 1917	Pas-de-Calais	Arras	Water-logged to dry	GHQ, 1st, Army, 3rd Army, 5th Army	26,400	14	1,886	48	3.4	550	5
10 April 1917	Pas-de-Calais	Arras			1,000	1	1,000	12	12	83	-
11 April 1917	Pas-de-Calais	Arras			1,500	1	1,500	12	12	125	-
7 June 1917	West Flanders	Messines Ridge		GHQ, 2nd Army	15,840	12	1,320	48	4	330	20
10 June 1917 (Plan 1918)	-	-	Un-damaged	Fuller	35,200	-	-	1,000	-	35	-
31 July 1917	West Flanders	Passchendaele	Marsh	GHQ, 5th Army	17,600	13	1,354	120	9.2	147	5.5
3 August 1917 ("surprise attack")	Picardy	Cambrai to St. Quentin	Dry and un-damaged	Fuller	26,400	4	6,600	240	60	110	-
8 August 1917 ("Tank Raids")	-	-		Fuller	8,000	1-2	4,000-8,000	216	108-216	37	91-125
20 November 1917	Picardy	Cambrai		Fuller, GHQ, 3rd Army, 5th Army	17,600	6	2,933	376	62.7	47	18
January 1918 ("Tank Operations Decisive…")	100 miles of 400-mile front	-		Fuller	176,000	?	?	5,280	(36, as of 27 January)	33	?
"Tank Raids," lower organization	Where enemy concentrates				20,000 or 50,000	3	6,667 or 16,667	576	192	35 or 87	139 or 347
…higher organization					30,000 or 75,000	4.5?	10,000 or 25,000	864	192	35 or 87	139 or 347
4 July 1918	Somme	Hamel	Dry but cratered	Fuller, 4th Army	7,000	3	2,333	60	20	100	9.5
23 July 1918	Somme	Sauvillers	Dry until D-Day, un-damaged	Fuller, French 1st Army	4,100	3	587	42	14	98	20
8 August 1918	Picardy	Amiens	Dry but cratered	GHQ, 4th Army	22,500	10	2,250	420	42	54	11
21 August 1918	Pas-de-Calais	Bapaume	Dry but cratered	GHQ, 3rd Army	17,000	6	2,833	190	32	93	10
22 August 1918	Sommes	Albert	Dry but cratered	GHQ, 4th Army	10,000	4	2,500	50	12.5	200	10
26 August 1918	Pas-de-Calais	Arras	Dry until D-Day, damaged	GHQ, 3rd Army	10,600	6	1,767	53	8.8	200	10
18 September 1918	Somme	Épehy	Dry and un-damaged	GHQ, 4th Army	7,000	8	875	20	2.5	350	5
27 September 1918	Picardy	Canal du Nord	Dry to flooded	GHQ, 1st Army	19,500	13	1,500	65	5	300	13
27 September 1918	Picardy	St. Quentin Canal	Dry to flooded	GHQ, 4th Army	10,000	8	1,250	153	16	65	6.25
17 October 1918	Nord	Selle	Wet to marshy	GHQ, 1st Army	19,000	8	2,375	48	6	396	13
23 October 1918	Nord	Mormal Forest	Dry to flooded	GHQ, 3rd Army, 4th Army	35,200	16	2,200	44	2.75	800	5
4 November 1918	Nord	Sambre	Wet to flooded	GHQ, 1st Army, 3rd Army, 4th Army	26,400	17	1,552	41	2.4	644	5

The First Tank War

Time of assault	Preliminary bombardment	Assault bombardment	Attack aircraft targets...	Leading arm	Speed of advance (mph)	Reserved assault tanks	Supply tanks	Exploitation forces: Cavalry divisions	Exploitation forces: Infantry divisions	Exploitation forces: Medium tanks	Exploitation forces: Cars	Sustained penetration (yards)
Night	Days	-	-	Infantry carriers	-							c.2,200 (2nd line)
Dawn	Hours	Counter-battery	-	Tanks	-							3,000 (3rd line)
Night	0	-	-		-							c.1,100 (1st line)
Dawn, with smoke	Hours	Counter-battery	Artillery	Tanks	2.0							4,000 (Artillery line)
Dawn	Days	Creeping	Artillery	Infantry	2.0							8,800
-	-	-	-	Tanks								8,800
Twilight	3 days	Creeping	-	Tanks	1.7			3				3,500
Twilight	3 days	Creeping	-	Tanks	1.7			3				1,000
Twilight	0	Creeping	-	Tanks	1.7			3				2,000
Twilight	1 hour, each of 7 days	Creeping	Artillery	Tanks	0.5			3				2,200
-	-	Self-propelled	-	(Tracked vehicles only)								-
Twilight	2 days	FOOs on objectives	Artillery (directly and via FOOs)	Tanks								8,800
Twilight	21 days	Creeping; FOOs down to some brigades		Tanks	1.7	12		3	9			6,000
Twilight	0			Tanks								0
Twilight	0			Tanks								0
Twilight	11 days	Creeping		Tanks	1.7	24	16	3	3			5,300
Twilight	0	Creeping; self-propelled direct-fire	Artillery	Tanks								4,000
Twilight	26 days	Creeping	Artillery	Tanks	1.7	96	36	3				5,300
Twilight	0	Creeping	Artillery	Tanks								8,800
Dusk, with smoke	0	Counter-battery and bridges	Artillery, comms, counter-attackers	Tanks								4,000
Twilight, with smoke	0	Counter-battery; Creeping	Artillery, comms, HQs, transport	Tanks and infantry scouts	0.75		66	5				7,500
Night for Mark V* tanks carrying machine-gunners; dawn for rest	-	Creeping; mortar tanks and artillery tanks	Artillery	Tanks	1.7							16,000
					1.0							10,000
					1.0							
Night, with smoke	7 minutes each day	Counter-battery; Creeping	Artillery, comms, HQs, transport	Infantry	0.9	60	4					2,500
Twilight	1 hour	Creeping	-	Tanks	0.75		4					3,300
Twilight	0	Counter-battery; Creeping	Artillery, bridges	Infantry	1.0	42	102	3	3	96	127	13,200
Twilight	0	Counter-battery; Creeping	Artillery	Tanks	0.4		18		4	69	96	4,000
Twilight	0	Counter-battery; Creeping	Artillery	Tanks	0.4	15	12					4,000
Night	3 days	Creeping	Artillery	Tanks	0.6							5,300
Twilight	0	Creeping	Artillery	Tanks	1.7							5,300
Twilight	5 days counter-battery	Creeping	Artillery	Infantry	0.9		12					5,300
Twilight	5 days	Creeping	Artillery	Infantry	1.0	76		0.3	1	16	20	6,000
Twilight	2 days	Creeping	Artillery	Infantry	0.4	0	12	0.3		12		5,300
Night	3 days	Creeping	Artillery	Infantry	0.2-0.3	0	12					4,000
Twilight	5 days counter-battery	Creeping	Artillery	Infantry	0.2-0.3	4	12			12	9	5,300

References

Baker-Carr, Christopher d'Arcy (1930). From Chauffeur to Brigadier. London: Ernest Benn Limited.
Bidwell, Reginald George Shelford, and Dominick Graham (1982). Fire Power: British Army Weapons and Theories of War, 1904-1945, London: Harper Collins.
Boff, Jonathan (2018). "The British Army in 1918," in Matthias Strohn, ed., 1918: Winning the War, Losing the War, Oxford: Osprey: 97-127.
Butterfield, T.L.H. (1966). "Design and Development of Fighting Tanks," Proceedings of the Institution of Mechanical Engineers, 180/5: 159-189.
Callwell, C.E. (1927). Field-Marshal Sir Henry Wilson: His Life and Diaries, 2 volumes, London: Cassell.
Cavaleri, David P. (1995). "The Premature Debut," Armor, 104/6: 24-28.
Charteris, John (1929). Field-Marshal Earl Haig, New York: Charles Scribner's Sons.
Churchill, Winston S. (1923). The World Crisis, Volume II, 1915, London: Thornton Butterworth.
- (1927). The World Crisis, Volume III, 1916-1918, Part 1, London: Thornton Butterworth.
Clayton, Derek (2018). Decisive Victory: The Battle of the Sambre: 4 November 1918, Solihull, England: Helion.
Cockburn, Claud (1967). I Claud: An Autobiography, London: Harmondsworth.
Faulkner, Richard (1995). "Flers-Courcelette: The First Tank Battle," Armor, 104/2: 33-37.
Ferguson, Niall (1998). The Pity of War: Explaining World War I, New York: Basic.
Fletcher, David J., ed. (1994). Tanks and Trenches: First Hand Accounts of Tank Warfare in the First World War, Stroud, England: Alan Sutton.
Foertsch, Hermann (1940). The Art of Modern Warfare, translated by Theodore W. Knauth, New York: Veritas Press, .
Foley, J. (1963). The Boilerplate War, London: Frederick Muller.
Foot, Stephen H. (1934). Three Lives: An Autobiography. London: Heinemann.
- (1935). Life Began Yesterday. London: Harper & Brothers.
- (1937). Three Lives – and Now: An Autobiography. London: Heinemann.
Forty, George (1989). The Royal Tank Regiment, London: Guild.
Fuller, J.F.C. (1913) Hints on Training Territorial Infantry, London: Gale & Polden.
- (1914a). "The Procedure of the Infantry Attack: A Synthesis from a Psychological Standpoint," RUSI Journal, 59/6: 63-74.
- (1914b). Training Soldiers for War, London: Hugh Rees.
- (1914c). "The Tactics of Penetration: A Counterblast to German Numerical Superiority," RUSI Journal,, 59/438: 378-389.
- (1916). "The Principles of War with Reference to the Campaigns of 1914-1915," Journal of the Royal United Services Institution, 61/441: 1-40.
- (27 October 1917). "Tank and Infantry Operations Without Methodical Artillery Bombardment," S.G. 192, in The Tank Journal, November 1938: 18
- (1919) "Strategical Paralysis as the Object of the Decisive Attack," in Weekly Tank Notes, 31 May and 7 June 1919, in Fuller 1928: 83-105.
- (1920). Tanks in the Great War, 1914-1918, London: John Murray.

- (1921). "Tanks in Future Warfare," Nineteenth Century and After, 90/533: 93-108.
- (1923). The Reformation of War, London: Hutchinson.
- (1926a). The Foundations of the Science of War, London: Hutchinson.
- (1926b). "The Tactics of Penetration," The Journal of the Royal Artillery, in Fuller 1928: 38-82.
- (1928). On Future Warfare, London: Sifton Praed & Company.
- (1931). Lectures on F.S.R. II, London: Sifton Praed & Company.
- (1932a). The Dragon's Teeth: A Study of War and Peace, London: Constable.
- (1932b). Lectures on F.S.R. III (Operations Between Mechanized Forces), London: Sifton, Praed.
- (1936). Memoirs of an Unconventional Soldier, London: Ivor Nicholson .
- (1945). Armament and History: A Study of the Influence of Armament on History from the Dawn of Classical Warfare to the Second World War, London: Eyre & Spottiswoode.
- (1955). A Military History of the Western World, III, From the American Civil War to the End of World War II, New York: Funk & Wagnalls.
- (1961). The Conduct of War, 1789-1961: A Study of the Impact of the French, Industrial, and Russian Revolutions on War and its Conduct, London: Eyre & Spottiswoode.

Gat, Azar (1998). Fascist and Liberal Visions of War: Fuller, Liddell Hart, Douhet, and Other Modernists, Oxford, England: Clarendon Press

Gibbs, Philip (1919). Open Warfare: The Way to Victory, London: Heinemann.

D.E.H. (1939). "Foreign Doctrines on Tank Employment," The Tank Journal, 10/6: 31-41.

Harington, Charles (1940). Tim Harington Looks Back, London: John Murray.

Harris, J. Paul, (1995). Men, Ideas, and Tanks: British Military Thought and Armoured Forces, 1903-1939, Manchester University Press.

Hochschild, Adam (2011). To End All Wars: A Story of Loyalty and Rebellion, 1914-1918, Boston: Houghton Mifflin Harcourt.

Hotblack, F. Elliot, "Tanks – and the National Genius," The National Review, January 1920: 697-703.
- (1933). "Cambrai Myth?" The Royal Tank Corps Journal: 285-286.

Jeffery, Keith (1985). The Military Correspondence of Field Marshal Sir Henry Wilson, 1918-1922, London: The Bodley Head for the Army Records Society.

Kershaw, Robert (2008). Tank Men: The Human Story of Tanks at War, London: Hodder & Stoughton.

Larson, Robert H. (1984). The British Army and the Theory of Armored Warfare, 1918-40, Newark, N.J.: University of Delaware Press.

Liddell Hart, Basil (1959). The Tanks: The History of the Royal Tank Regiment and its Predecessors Heavy Branch Machine-Gun Corps Tank Corps and Royal Tank Corps, 1914-1945, 2 volumes, London: Cassell.

Lloyd George, David (1938). War Memoirs of David Lloyd George, 2 Volumes, London: Odhams Press.

Luvaas, Jay (1964). The Education of an Army: British Military Thought, 1815-1940, Chicago University Press.

Macksey, Kenneth (1983). A History of the Royal Armoured Corps and its Predecessors, 1914-1975, Beaminster, England: Newtown Publications.

Marshall-Cornwall, James H. (1984). Wars and Rumours of Wars: A Memoir, London: Leo Cooper, Secker & Warburg.
Martel, Giffard (1931). In the Wake of the Tank: The First Fifteen Years of Mechanization in the British Army, London: Sifton Praed and Co.
- (1945). Our Armoured Forces, London: Faber & Faber.
- (1946). "The Development of Mechanization 1933 to 1939," Journal of the Royal United Services Institution, 91/564: 577-583.
- (1949). An Outspoken Soldier: His Views and Memoirs, London: Sifton Praed.
Miles, Wilfrid (1948). History of the Great War: Military Operations: France and Belgium, 1917, Volume III, The Battle of Cambrai, London: His Majesty's Stationery Offive.
Montgomery, Archibald (1919). The Story of the 4th Army in the Battles of the Hundred Days, August 8th to November 11th 1918, London: Hodder & Stoughton.
Neiberg, Michael S. (2005). Fighting the Great War: A Global History, Cambridge: Harvard University Press.
Newsome, Bruce Oliver (2021a). The Rise and Fall of Western Tanks, I, 1855-1939, Coronado, California: Tank Archives Press.
- (2021b). The Rise and Fall of Western Tanks, II, 1939-1955, Coronado, California: Tank Archives Press.
- (2024). Sir Basil Liddell Hart and Tanks, Coronado, California: Perseublishing.
- (2025). Sir Basil Liddell Hart: Life, Thought, Legacy, Coronado: Perseublishing.
Ogorkiewicz, Richard (1960). Armour: The Development of Mechanised Forces and their Equipment, London: Stevens & Sons and Atlantic Books.
- (1968). Design and Development of Fighting Vehicles, London: Macdonald.
- (1970). Armoured Forces: A History of Armoured Forces and their Vehicles, New York: Arco.
Owen, Frank (1955). Tempestuous Journey: Lloyd George: His Life and Times, New York: Macgraw-Hill.
Owen, Frank, and HW Atkins (1944). The First Official Account of The Royal Armoured Corps: Through Mud and Blood to the Green Fields Beyond, London: His Majesty's Stationery Office.
Pedersen, Brian A. (2007). "What Kept the Tank from Being the Decisive Weapon of World War One?" Masters thesis, Command and General Staff College, Fort Leavenworth, Kansas.
Pidgeon, Trevor (1995). Tanks at Flers: An Account of the First Use of Tanks in War at the Battle of Flers-Courcelette, the Somme, 15 September 1916, Cobham, England: Fairmile Books.
Portway, Donald (1951). Military Science Today, 3rd ed., Oxford University Press.
Prior, Robin (2014). "1916: Impasse," in The Cambridge History of the First World War, Volume 1, Global War, Cambridge University Press: 89-109.
Prior, Robin, and Trevor Wilson (2002). Passchendaele: The Untold Story, 2nd ed., New Haven: Yale University Press.
Reid, Brian Holden (1987). J.F.C. Fuller: Military Thinker, London: Macmillan Press.
- (1998). Studies in British Military Thought: Debates with Fuller and Liddell Hart, Lincoln: University of Nebraska.
Short, Neil (2004). Germany's West Wall: The Siegfried Line, Fortress 15, Oxford, England: Osprey.

Smithers, A.J. (1989). Rude Mechanicals: An Account of Tank Maturity During the Second World War, London: Grafton.
Stern, Albert G. (1919). Tanks, 1914-1918: Logbook of a Pioneer, London: Hodder & Stoughton.
Stevenson, David (2011). With Our Backs to the Wall: Victory and Defeat in 1918, Cambridge, MA: Belknap.
Strachan, Hew (1983). European Armies and the Conduct of War, London: George Allen & Unwin.
Strohn, Matthias (2018). "1918: The Final Year of World War I and its Long Shadow of History," in Matthias Strohn, ed., 1918: Winning the War, Losing the War, Oxford: Osprey: 22-37.
Swinton, Ernest Dunlop (1932). Eyewitness: Being Personal Reminiscences of Certain Phases of the Great War, including the Genesis of the Tank, London: Hodder & Stoughton.
Terraine, John A. (1978). To Win a War: 1918, The Year of Victory, London: Sidgwick & Jackson.
Travers, Tim (1987). The Killing Ground: The British Army, the Western Front, and the Emergence of Modern Warfare, 1900-1918, London: Allen & Unwin.
Trythall, Anthony John (1977). "Boney" Fuller: Soldier, Strategist, and Writer, 1878-1966, New Brunswick, NJ: Rutgers University Press.
United Kingdom, Ministry of Defence (2025). Glossary of Terms and Definitions, https://assets.publishing.service.gov.uk/media/5a7cb41b40f0b6629523b496/glossary-of-terms-and-abbreviations.pdf
United Kingdom, War Office (1909; amended 1913). Field Service Regulations, Part 2, Organization and Administration, London: His Majesty's Stationery Office.
United Kingdom, Army Council (1926). Demonstration of Tanks and Other Cross-Country Vehicles, 13 November 1926, London: War Office.
United States, Department of Defense (2021). Dictionary of Military and Associated Terms, Joint Publication 1-02, Washington DC: Government Printing Office. https://irp.fas.org/doddir/dod/dictionary.pdf
USMA (United States Military Academy) (1950). A Short Military History of World War I: Atlas, West Point, NY.
Williams-Ellis, Clough, and A. Williams-Ellis (1920). The Tank Corps, London: Country Life and George Newnes.
Zabecki, David T. (2018). "The German Army in 1918," in Matthias Strohn, ed., 1918: Winning the War, Losing the War, Oxford: Osprey: 38-68.

Index

Achicourt, 201
Achiet-le-Grand, 200
Admiralty, 13, 14, 16, 18, 25, 27, 38, 54, 124
Aircraft, 9, 11, 19, 32, 34, 45, 64, 74, 79, 86, 95-98, 105-106, 129-130, 140, 142-143, 151, 158-161, 163-164, 168, 170-171, 175, 183, 184, 188, 198, 205-206, 213, 215, 217, 219, 230, 232, 233
Aisne River, 138
Albert, 49, 197-200, 224
All-tank operations, 62, 67, 95-97, 146n
Allenby, Edmund, 73
Allnatt, J.C., 84
Alsonville, 217
American Expeditionary Force, 150, 169
Amervalles, 220
Amiens, 12, 139, 158, 171, 176, 180, 181, 189, 191-195, 197, 198, 202, 229-231, 234-239
Amphibiousness, 11, 67-68, 83, 146n, 161, 232
Ancre, 12, 49, 63, 197, 231, 233
Andigny-les-Fermes, 216, 219
Anley, F. Gore, 53, 71n
Anneux, 118, 120
Anti-tank capabilities, 55, 61, 67-68, 93, 105, 109, 123-125, 129-130, 133, 135, 137, 158, 165, 167, 172, 175, 203, 206, 214, 233
Anti-Tank Defence, by Fuller, December 1917, 122, 123, 125, 129, 130, 135, 137, 167
Antwerp, 13, 142
L'Arbre de Guise, 219
Armour, defined, 8
Armoured car, 159, 183, 191-193, 199, 215-216, 226, 228, 238-239
Arms, 10
Army, 1st, British, 71-72, 101, 106, 180,181, 194, 197, 200-201, 207, 211, 213, 216, 226
Army, 1st, French, 158, 177, 182-183, 192, 205, 217, 225, 228
Army, 1st, US, 225
Army, 2nd, 77, 79, 81, 84, 88, 181, 185, 193
Army, 3rd, 34, 55, 57-59, 64, 71-73, 76, 93, 100-102, 104-108, 111-114, 127, 181, 194, 197, 199-201, 204, 205, 207, 209, 211, 216-218, 220-221, 223, 225, 226, 228
Army, 4th, 23, 27, 28n, 33, 39, 41, 45, 158, 167, 169, 171, 173, 176, 180, 181-186, 192-195, 197-200, 205, 207, 211-218, 220221, 223, 225, 226, 228
Army, 5th, 71-72, 74, 76, 83-87, 93, 100, 107, 138, 214, 216
Army, 10th, French, 178
Army, British, 32, 46, 61-62, 96, 126, 236
Army, French, 58, 126
Army, Reserve, 23, 27, 39, 49, 71, 84
Army, US, 55, 126, 150, 169n, 195, 212
Army Council, 155, 195, 235
Arnold, C.B., 192
Arras, 63, 70, 71, 77, 89, 99, 126, 142, 197-203, 205, 231, 234, 236, 237, 239

Artillery, 11, 13-15, 18-19, 21, 28, 32-39, 41-51, 55, 64, 68, 71-76, 79-81, 85-88, 90-92, 95-100, 102-107, 111, 113, 116-118, 121-122, 124, 127-130, 138, 140-141, 143, 147-148, 158-160, 163, 167, 169-173, 175, 178-179, 181-184, 188-189, 191, 193, 195, 197-199, 201-203, 205-209, 213-216, 218-221, 223, 226, 228, 229-237
Artillery pre-registration, 33, 73, 79, 101, 105,
Atkin-Berry, H.C., 52
Automobiles, defined, 8
Avre River, 177, 180
Baker-Carr, Christopher, 84, 115
Banteux, 94, 98, 99, 119
Bapaume, 45, 118, 181, 197, 200, 231, 239
Battalion, Tank, 1st, 103, 116, 121, 183-187, 199, 203-204, 218-219
Battalion, Tank, 2nd, 84, 103, 114, 116, 121, 183-187, 194, 197, 199, 200, 203-204, 295-206
Battalion, Tank, 3rd, 103, 162, 183-187, 192, 197, 199, 203-204, 215
Battalion, Tank, 4th, 58, 76, 103, 183-187, 199, 200, 203-204, 214
Battalion, Tank, 5th, 103, 183-187, 199, 203,-204 213, 216, 218
Battalion, Tank, 6th, 103, 117, 162, 183-187, 192, 194, 197, 199, 202-204, 213, 218, 226
Battalion, Tank, 7th, 103, 118, 184-187, 197, 199, 203-204, 208-209
Battalion, Tank, 8th, 102, 103, 115-116,121, 183-187, 199, 200, 203-204, 212, 214
Battalion, Tank, 9th, 103, 184-187, 197, 199, 203-204, 213, 222, 226, 227
Battalion, Tank, 10th, 184-187, 194, 197, 199, 203-204, 215, 218, 221, 223, 225-227
Battalion, Tank, 11th, 184-187, 197, 199, 200, 202-204, 218, 220-221
Battalion, Tank, 12th, 184-187, 197, 199, 200, 202-204, 221
Battalion, Tank, 13th, 183-187, 199, 200, 203-204, 206, 212, 214
Battalion, Tank, 14th, 183-187, 194, 197, 199, 203-204, 226, 227
Battalion, Tank, 15th, 183-187, 194, 197, 199, 203
Battalion, Tank, 16th, 184-187, 199, 203, 212, 214, 218-219
Battalion, Tank, 17th, 183-187, 192, 203, 215, 226
Battalion, Tank, 18th, 184, 203, 237n
Battalion, Tank, 19th, 183
Battalion, Tank, 301st, US, 203, 214, 218-219, 221-223
Bayonvillers, 189
Bazuel, 217-218
Beauchamp, 115, 119
Beaucourt-sur-Ancre, 49-51, 197
Beaumont Hamel, 49-51, 60
Beauquesne, 52
Beaurevoir, 100, 103, 204, 212, 216

Behagnies, 200
Belgium, 13, 83, 142, 224, 232
Belle Etoile, 113
Bellenglise, 209, 210-213
Bellicourt, 180, 204, 211-212
Bermicourt, 52, 59, 150, 181
Berthon boats, 227
Big Willie, 17-18, 20, 25, 26, 32, 38, 39
Bihucourt, 200
Bird, Wilkinson D., 17
Blitzkrieg, 11, 122, 164
Boer Wars, 13, 56
Les Boeufs, 23, 27, 46
Bohain, 217
Bois de Gattigny
Bois de Hamel, 166, 168, 170
Bois de Hure, 178
Bois de la Folie, 121
Bois de Lateau, 116, 119
Bois de Neuf, 113, 116-117, 119, 120
Bois de Quemetot, 177
Bois de Rampont, 177
Bois de Riquerval
Bois de Saint-Ribert, 176, 179
Bois de Vaire, 166-168, 170
Bois des Arrachis, 176, 179
Bois du Fay, 178
Bois Lateau, 119
Boisleux-au-Mont, 201
Bonavis, 103
Bony, 204, 214, 216
Bouchoir, 180, 193, 194
Bourlon, 99, 100, 103, 113, 114, 119, 120-122, 204, 207, 209
Bovington Camp, 54, 72
Boyd-Rochfort, H., 148
Braithwaite, Walter, 212
Bray, 129, 171
Bray-sur-Somme, 180, 194, 197, 200
Brigade, 1st, 226
Brigade, 2nd, 226
Brigade, 3rd, 226-227
Brigade, 4th, Australian, 168, 169
Brigade, 6th, Australian, 168, 169
Brigade, 7th, 222, 226
Brigade, 11th, Australian, 168, 169
Brigade, 14th, 226
Brigade, 16th, 103
Brigade, 35th, 103
Brigade, 36th, 103
Brigade, 37th, 103
Brigade, 52nd, 226
Brigade, 53rd, 222
Brigade, 54th, 222
Brigade, 55th, 222
Brigade, 60th, 103
Brigade, 61st, 103
Brigade, 62nd, 103
Brigade, 71st, 103
Brigade, 74th, 222, 226

Brigade, 75th, 226
Brigade, 96th, 226
Brigade, 111st, 226
Brigade, 112th, 226
Brigade, 115th, 226
Brigade, 137th, 210
Brigade, 149th, 226
Brigade, 150th, 226
Brigade, 151st, 226
Brigade, 152nd, 103
Brigade, 153rd, 103
Brigade, 185th, 103
Brigade, 186th, 103
Brigade, Cavalry, 5th, 220
Brigade, Cavalry, 6th, 216
Brigade, Cavalry, 7th, 216
Brigade, Cavalry, Canadian, 117, 216
Brigade, Guards, 3rd, 228
Brigade, Tank, 1st, 72, 83-85, 94, 95-96, 102, 103, 115, 120, 138, 168, 183-185, 191, 197, 199, 201, 203-205, 207, 225, 228
Brigade, Tank, 2nd, 72, 77, 83, 85, 94, 102-104, 114, 115, 120-121, 138, 168, 171, 183-185, 191, 197, 199, 203-205, 207, 225, 228
Brigade, Tank, 3rd, 72, 83, 85, 93, 94, 102, 103, 115, 138, 168, 174, 177, 183-187, 189, 191, 197, 199, 201, 203-205, 207, 213, 215, 225, 228
Brigade, Tank, 4th, 138, 168, 183-187, 189, 191, 194, 199, 203-205, 207, 212, 218, 225, 228
Brigade, Tank, 5th, 138, 168, 169, 173, 174, 177-178, 183-187, 189, 191, 194, 199, 201, 203-205, 207, 212, 214, 225, 228
British Expeditionary Force, 7, 13, 15, 18, 26, 52, 57, 60-61, 71, 81, 94, 104, 112-113, 123, 131, 145, 150-151, 153-154, 159, 167-168, 170, 175, 205, 207, 217-218, 225, 229, 237
Brockbank, S.G., 52
Bruges, 83, 88, 224
Brussels, 142
Bryce, Edward, 114, 116
Bucquoy, 138, 181, 197
Bullecourt, 72, 76, 167, 176
Bullock of Chicago, 14-15, 17
Busigny, 106, 216
Butler, Richard H.K., 71n, 72-73, 93, 107, 182
Butler, R.P., 52
Byng, Julian, 93, 94, 100, 101, 104, 113, 121
Cagnicourt, 203
Caix, 180, 181,
Cambrai, 11-12, 20, 30, 60, 67, 88, 89, 93-95, 98-122, 123-127, 136, 138, 139, 141-142, 147, 152, 159, 161, 169, 172, 176, 191, 197, 207, 209, 211, 216, 224, 230-235, 239
Campbell, John Vaughan, 210
Canal de la Sambre a l'Oise, 217-227
Canal de la Scarpe, 202, 224
Canal de l'Escaut, 99
Canal de St.-Quentin, 95, 99, 207, 208-213, 219, 224
Canal du Nord, 95, 99, 203, 207-209, 213-216, 224, 231

Canal Ypres-Comines, 79, 224
Cantaing, 119, 120
Caporetto, 104
Capper, John, 93, 147-156
Le Cateau, 106, 216-217, 219, 224
Le Catelet, 104, 212, 224
Caterpillars, 16-18, 23, 25, 28, 31,32, 37-38, 43, 164
Catillon, 224, 226
Caudry, 106
Cavalry, 8, 11, 23, 24, 32, 38, 44, 45, 51, 55, 65, 69, 75, 76, 83, 87, 92, 93, 95, 97, 98, 102, 109, 110, 112, 113, 114, 117, 120, 121, 122, 136, 138, 142, 143, 155, 156, 159, 162, 164, 182, 183, 191, 192, 194, 195, 215, 216, 220, 232-233, 235, 236, 237, 239
Central Workshops, 52, 53, 58-59, 77, 86, 91, 102n, 145, 153, 203, 238
Charteris, John, 85, 88, 112
Chaulnes, 182, 192, 194
Chipilly, 180, 190, 193, 194
Chuignolles, 180, 197, 200
Churchill, Winston S., 13-14, 16-18, 21, 23-25, 28-34, 37-38, 41, 43, 47, 54, 63, 100, 120, 124, 125, 127, 150, 153-154, 156, 231
Clapham Junction, 84
Combined arms, defined, 9
Combles, 23, 47
Comines, 79, 224
Command, defined, 9
Committee of Imperial Defence, 25, 34,
Communications, 9
Compasses, 137, 158
Concentration, defined, 8
Control, defined, 9
Cooperation, defined, 9
Corbie, 49, 180, 194
Cordon tactics, 139
Cornwall, James, 112, 120
Corps, II, British, 50, 87, 217, 220
Corps, II, US, 217-220
Corps, III, 27, 46, 103, 113, 119, 121, 182-183, 185, 189, 194, 197, 199, 200, 205-206, 213
Corps, IV, 46, 103, 113, 119, 121, 197, 199, 204, 221, 226, 228
Corps, V, 49, 113, 197, 199, 205, 221, 226, 228
Corps, VI, 70, 72, 197, 199, 200, 204, 226
Corps, VII, 57, 70, 72, 119, 207, 217
Corps, VIII, 228
Corps, IX, British, 80, 204-206, 212-213, 215, 217-222, 226
Corps, IX, French, 177
Corps, XIII, 49, 217-223, 226
Corps, XIV, 27
Corps, XV, 27, 46
Corps, XVII, 70, 72, 201, 203, 204, 226
Corps, XVIII, 88, 139
Corps, XIX, 88, 100
Corps, XXXI, 180
Corps, XXII, 207, 226
Corps, LI, German, 193
Corps, ANZAC, 80
Corps, Australian, 159, 166-170, 172-173, 175, 180, 182-183, 185, 189-192, 197, 199, 200, 204, 205, 212-213
Corps, Canadian, 27, 45, 70, 71, 94, 180, 182-183,, 185, 191, 201, 203, 204, 207, 209, 225, 226
Courage, Anthony, 77
Courcelette, 12, 22-23, 26, 27, 45, 49, 53, 57, 63, 198-199, 230
Cox, Edward, 167
Creeping barrage, 10, 21, 32, 33, 39, 41, 50, 68, 73, 74, 79, 80, 86, 87, 160, 166, 170, 171, 173, 175, 178, 188, 198, 199, 202, 206, 208, 213, 214, 215, 219, 220, 222, 223, 226, 228, 233-235
Crèvecoeur, 94, 99, 204
Crowley, Aleister, 56
Curragh, 56
Currie, Arthur, 182
The Daily Mirror, 63
Dannart wire, 38n
Davidson, John, 93, 94, 112, 139, 167, 182
Dawnay, G.P., 150, 153
Defensive and Offensive Use of Tanks 1918, by Fuller, December 1917, 123, 125, 127-128, 130, 136, 137, 139, 158, 174, 238
Deligny, 208
Delville Wood, 31, 46
Denain, 106, 224
Dernancourt, 194
Dessart, 103, 105
Dinnaken, 43, 46-47, 235
Dismounted, 8
Division, 1st, Australian, 205-206
Division, 1st, British, 219-220, 222, 226-228
Division, 1st, Canadian, 185-187, 203
Division, 2nd, Australian, 169, 185-187, 204, 215
Division, 2nd, British, 50, 169n
Division, 2nd, Canadian, 27, 185-187, 201-202
Division, 3rd, Australian, 169, 185-187, 204, 214
Division, 3rd, British, 50, 169n, 177, 179, 200, 226
Division, 3rd, Canadian, 27, 185-187, 201-202
Division, 3rd, French, 177
Division, 4th, Australian, 76, 167, 169, 185-187, 205-206
Division, 4th, British, 169n, 194, 201, 203, 209, 226
Division, 4th, Canadian, 50, 185-187, 201, 203
Division, 5th, Australian, 185-187, 204, 214
Division, 6th, 27, 46, 103, 206, 216, 223
Division, 8th, 85, 193
Division, 11th, 85, 226
Division, 12th, 103
Division, 14th, 27, 46
Division, 15th, British, 27, 46, 85
Division, 15th, French, 177
Division, 16th, 85
Division, 17th, 220, 226, 227
Division, 18th, 50, 85, 213, 222-223, 226-227
Division, 19th, 50, 226
Division, 20th, 103
Division, 24th, 85, 226
Division, 25th, 85, 219, 222-223, 226-227

Division, 27th, US, 204, 212-215, 219
Division, 29th, 103, 116
Division, 30th, British, 85
Division, 30th, US, 204, 214, 219, 212
Division, 32nd, 194, 204, 212-213, 215, 226-228
Division, 33rd, US, 169n, 193
Division, 36th, 85, 118
Division, 37th, 57, 200, 226-227
Division, 38th, 220, 226-227
Division, 39th, 50, 85
Division, 41st, 27, 46
Division, 46th, 204, 210, 212, 215, 218-219
Division, 47th, 27, 46-47
Division, 48th, 85, 88
Division, 50th, 27, 46, 217, 219, 226
Division, 51st, 50, 85, 103, 108, 113-114, 116-118, 120-121, 201, 227
Division, 55th, 85
Division, 56th, 27, 46, 226
Division, 58th, 190, 194
Division, 60th, 226
Division, 62nd, 103, 120, 226
Division, 63rd, 49-50
Division, 66th, 216, 219
Division, 152nd, French, 177
Division, Cavalry, 1st, British, 51, 76, 87, 102, 103, 113-114, 183, 192
Division, Cavalry, 1st, Indian, see: 4th Cavalry Division
Division, Cavalry, 2nd, British, 51, 76, 87, 102, 103, 113, 183
Division, Cavalry, 2nd, Indian, see: 5th Cavalry Division
Division, Cavalry, 3rd, 51, 76, 87, 102, 103, 113, 183, 185, 192, 216
Division, Cavalry, 4th, 113, 121
Division, Cavalry, 5th, 113-114, 121, 185
Division, Guards, 27, 46, 121-122, 200, 226, 228
Division, New Zealand, 27, 46, 197, 226
Doctrine, defined, 7
Doctrine, German, 41-43
Dolls House, 140
Douai, 103, 106, 224
Drocourt, 201-202
Du Cane, John, 193
Duckham, Arthur, 150
Dundas, R.W., 52
Dury, 203
Elles, Hugh Jamieson, 11, 52-59, 62, 71, 77, 93-94, 100-101, 111, 114-115, 117, 120-123, 127, 138-139, 148, 153, 156, 181, 184-185, 194-195, 203, 229
Elveden, 20, 26, 30, 35, 38-41
Englefontaine, 226
Epehy, 12, 205, 206
Ervillers, 200
Escadoeuvres, 106
Estienne, Jean Baptiste, 71-75
Exploitation, defined, 10
d'Eyncourt, E. Tennyson, 71, 75-76, 85
Fanshawe, Robert, 88

Fascines, 109-110, 232, 234
Female tank, 25
La Fere, 224, 225
La Folie, 121
, 7, 62
Fins, 113, 114, 118, 121
Flares, 140, 158, 175
Flers, France, 22-23, 26, 27, 41, 45-47, 53, 57, 63, 199, 230, 235
Flesquieres, 98, 99, 100, 103, 108, 113, 116, 117, 118, 120, 189, 204
Foch, Ferdinand, 149n, 154, 155, 185, 197
Fontaine-Notre-Dame, 105, 119, 120-122, 207
Foot, Stephen, 11-12, 53, 57-59, 77, 79, 83, 104, 114-116, 122, 141-143, 145, 147-151, 155, 163, 229, 239
Fouilloy, 170
Formation of Emergency Lewis Gun Units, by Fuller, March 1917, 66
Fort Garry Horse, 117
Forward Observation Officer, 33, 34, 64, 233
Foster & Company, 15-16
Framerville, 180, 194
Fresnes, 202
Fresnoy, 180, 206
Freuchy, 76
Frise, 180, 182
Fuller, J.F.C., 10-12, 19, 44, 47, 50, 52-80, 83-85, 87-130, 135-140, 143, 145-164, 167-194, 200, 202-203, 205, 207, 212-216, 226n, 229-239
Furse, WIlliam, 100, 153
Gat, Azar, 67
General Headquarters, 7, 11, 13, 15, 16, 18, 20-21, 23-26, 28-37, 39, 41-42, 44-45, 49-50, 52, 53-55, 57, 62-63, 71-74, 76-77, 79-80, 83-85, 87-88, 93-94, 100-101, 106-107, 109, 112-114, 120, 123-124, 127-130, 136, 139, 142, 148, 150, 160, 162, 164, 167-168, 170, 173, 175-176, 182-184, 193-195, 203, 205, 215-216, 218, 225, 229, 230, 234, 239
Gheluvelt, 63
Gibbs, Philip, 24, 101, 105
Ginchy, 31
Gird Trench, 47
Gomiecourt, 180, 200
Gonnelieu, 98, 101, 103, 119
Gough, Hubert, 49, 76, 83-86, 93, 100, 138
Gouzeaucourt, 98, 101, 103, 119, 121, 207
Graincourt, 118-120
Grand Ravin, 113
Grant, Charles, 155
Grenadiers, 19, 34, 65, 74, 106n, 108, 133
Grivesnes, 176
Guemappe, 202
Gueudecourt, 23, 27, 43, 46
Guillaucourt, 180, 189
Guillemont, 204, 206, 212, 214
Guise, 224, 228
Gun, 1,59-inch, 129
Gun, 6-pounder, 19, 20, 25, 50, 110, 179, 222
Gun, 18-pounder, 75, 77, 91, 92, 95, 96, 105, 171, 175, 188, 191, 206, 209, 213, 215, 223, 228

Gun, 60-pounder, 55, 92, 95, 105n
Gun, 77-mm, 17, 46, 77, 117-118n, 121, 189, 206, 214, 216, 219, 220, 222
Haig, Douglas, 18, 24-26, 29, 39, 53, 58,63, 83-85, 87-88, 93-94, 104, 112-113, 118n, 138-139, 155-156, 181-182, 185, 194-195, 197, 200, 205, 215, 229, 239
Ham, 182, 224
Hamel, 154, 155, 167-176, 180, 181, 189, 191, 231, 237
Hamelot, 170
Hamelincourt, 200
Hangard, 180
Hangest, 180, 182
Hankey, Edward B., 115
Hankey, Maurice, 25, 34
Hansa Line, 50
Happegarbes, 225
Harbonnieres, 180, 182, 188, 189
Hardress-Lloyd, John, 93, 94, 115, 169
Hargicourt, 206
Harington, Charles, H., 77, 150, 153-155
Harper, G.M., 117
Harris, J.P., 69, 165, 184n
Le Havre, 28
Havrincourt, 98, 99, 100, 103, 104, 113, 119, 205
Hazebrouck, 181
Heavy Section Machine-Gun Corps, 20, 25
Hecq, 226
Hendecourt, 76
Henderson, David, 34
Herleville, 197
Hindenburg Line, 63, 76, 99, 108-110, 117, 120, 203, 205, 207-208, 211, 216-217
Hinterzone, 41
Hirson, 224, 225
Hollond, S.E., 64, 73
Holnon, 205
Holt tractors, 12, 13, 15
Honnechy, 216
Honnecourt, 98, 119, 121
Hotblack, F. Elliot, 51, 54, 60, 83, 101, 105-106, 113, 118, 214
Howitzer, 105-mm, 117
Howitzer, 150-mm, 116, 216
Howitzer, 4.5-inch, 92, 171, 206, 213
Howitzer, 6-inch, 55, 92, 95, 105, 171, 213, 218, 223
Howitzer, 8-inch, 105n, 171
Howitzer, 9.2-inch, 171
Howitzer, 12-inch, 171
Inchy, 207
Infantry, 8, 9, 10, 13, 15, 16, 18, 19, 20, 21, 23, 24, 25, 28, 29, 31-39, 40-47, 50-51, 53, 55-57, 62, 64-65, 67-69, 71, 73-75, 79-80, 85-93, 95, 97-98, 102, 104-113, 116-121, 125-131, 133, 135-140, 142-143, 145-147, 149, 156, 159-179, 183, 185, 188-195, 198-200, 202-203, 206-209, 212-223, 225, 227-229, 232-239
Infantry, moppers up, 65, 108
Infantry, scouts, 106-107, 131, 233
Infantry, trench clearers, 108, 131, 133
Infantry, trench stops, 108, 109, 133

Infantry, trench supports, 65, 108, 133
Infantry-tank communications, 36, 86
Infantry and Tank Cooperation and Training, by Tank Corps, 27 January 1918, 9, 23n, 39n, 62, 125, 128, 130-133, 136, 139
Infantry carriers, 13, 90, 92, 143, 174, 190
Inter-Allied Tank Committee, 148, 149, 153
Italy, 104, 169, 221
Joffre, Joseph, 58
Johnson, Philip, 146-147, 149
Jolimetz, 226
Kampffeld, 41
Kavanagh, Charles, 182
Kemmel Hill, 181
Kiggell, Launcelot, 88, 93, 94, 104, 113, 122, 138
Killen-Strait tractor, 17-18, 37
Klerken, 83
Knox, William G., 56
Lamotte, 189
Land Cruiser, 16, 25, 37
Landrecies, 224, 226
Landships, 7, 13, 14, 16, 17, 54
La Laurette, 218
Lens, 101
Les Boeufs, 23, 27, 46
Lihons, 180, 192, 194
Liddell Hart, Basil, 28n, 29, 59n, 67, 95-97, 102n, 146n, 168
Lille, 216, 224
Little Willie, 15-16
Lloyd George, David, 17, 26n, 29, 100, 155, 164, 195,
Logistics, defined, 10
Loos, 24, 126
Louvigniers, 226
Ludendorff, Erich, 175, 194
Luvaas, Jay, 67, 164
Lynden-Bell, Arthur, 150, 153
Lyon, Frank, 100
Lys River, 138, 221, 224
Machine-Gun Corps, 20, 25, 32, 237n
Machine-gun destroyer, 14, 15, 25, 67
Machine-gun, light, Lewis, 66, 74, 106, 108, 131, 173, 210
Machine-gun, medium, Vickers, 33, 92, 96, 105, 120, 128, 136, 158, 171, 174, 175, 206, 213, 219, 222, 227
Mailly-Raineval, 176, 177
Malpart, 176
Manoeuvre, defined, 8
Marcelcave, 189
Marcoing, 94, 98, 99, 102, 103, 113-117, 119, 120, 209, 224
Marne River, 229
Marollies, 226
Marquion, 207, 224
Martel, Giffard, 11, 20, 39, 41, 53-55, 58, 61-62, 67-69, 75, 80, 92, 97, 111, 125, 146n, 148, 162, 231, 232, 239
Martello tactics, 138-139

Martinpuich, 23, 27, 46, 199
Masnieres, 94, 98, 100, 103, 113-114, 117-120
Master-General Ordnance, 59, 100, 153
Mauberge, 224, 225
Maurice, Frederick, 71, 195
Maurois, 216
Maxse, Ivor, 139
Mazinghien, 217-218
Mechanization, defined, 8
Memorandum on Defensive Measures, by GHQ, December 1917, 123
Meharicout, 180, 193,
Mericourt, 180, 181, 182, 194
Merville, 181
Messines, 77-84, 86, 87, 89, 91, 224, 231, 238
Metz-en-Couture, 101, 114, 119
Meuse River, 221, 225
Michel, Henri, 71
Middlesex Volunteers, 56
Milner, Alfred, 154, 155
Ministry of Munitions, 18n, 26n, 31, 37, 55, 61, 71, 85, 100, 141, 145n, 147, 152-156, 165, 230
A Mobile Army, by Foot, April 1918, 141-143, 148
Mobile Army, 142
Mobility, defined, 8
Moeuvres, 118, 207-208
Monash, John, 167, 174, 175, 182, 192, 212, 213
Monchy le Preux, 72, 76, 202
Mons, 224, 225
Montagu, Edwin, 29
Montay, 217
Montdidier, 182
Montgomery, Archibald, 181, 192
Moore, Archibald, 146
Morcellated attack, 144, 152, 153
Moreuil, 177, 180, 202
Morlancourt, 180, 185, 194
Mormal Forest, 12, 221, 224, 225-228, 230
Morse code, 19, 45, 74
Mortar, 2-inch, 214
Mortar, 3-inch, Stokes, 61, 128, 133, 160, 174, 175
Mortar, 4-inch, 170, 227
Mortar, 8-inch, Livens, 61, 68
Mortar Tanks and Coloured Lights, by Fuller, January 1918, 127, 129
Morval, 23, 27, 46
Mother, see: Big Willie
Motor Machine-Gun Service, 26
Mounted, defined, 8
Movable Machine-Gun Cupolas, 16
Moyenneville, 197, 201
The MS in Red Ink, by Townshend, August 1916, 58, 91
Musical Box, 192, 232
Namur, 224, 225
Nauroy, 204, 212
Neuville Vitasse, 76, 202
Neuvilly, 220
Note on the Employment of Tanks, by Swinton, February 1916, 18-19, 24, 28, 30, 32, 34-36, 41, 43, 54

Notes on Tank Economics, by Fuller, July 1918, 120n, 154
Notes on the Use of Tanks and on the General Principles of their Employment as an Adjunct to the Infantry Attack, by GHQ, May 1917, 80
Noyelles-Sur-Escaut, 114, 117, 119, 120
Noyon, 182
Ogorkiewicz, Richard, 146n
Oosttaverne, 80
Origny-en-Thierache, 228
Ors, 222, 226, 228
Ostend, 88, 224
Oxfordshire (and Buckinghamshire) Light Infantry, 56, 149
Palluel, 207
Parvillers, 194
Passchendaele, 82-83, 88, 89, 91, 93, 94, 99, 101, 102n, 106, 120, 142, 224, 230, 231, 237, 239
Pearson, A.G., 148
Pedrail, 14, 17, 37
Peiziere, 206
Peronne, 197, 224
Pershing, John. J., 150
Pigeons, 45, 112, 114
Plan 1918, 11, 89-93, 145-146
Plan 1919, Foot's, 141-143, 151
Plan 1919, Fuller's first, 11-12, 123-126, 137, 145, 161
Plan 1919, Fuller's second, 11-12, 89, 90, 93, 124, 128, 145-156, 160-161, 164-165, 235
Plumer, Herbert, 77, 84
Polygon Wood, 88
Pommereuil, 222
Pozieres, 198
Preliminary bombardment, 15, 16, 18, 21, 24, 26, 29, 32-35, 39, 41, 47, 50, 59, 63-64, 71-74, 76-77, 79, 83-84, 86, 90-91, 93, 95-96, 103-106, 120, 127-128, 130, 139, 142, 156, 169-171, 173, 178, 184, 198, 201-202, 205, 213, 218, 222, 226, 231, 233
Preliminary Notes on the Tactical Employment of Tanks, by GHQ, 16 August 1916, 20, 23, 26, 30-31, 35-36, 41, 44, 80
Premont, 204, 215, 224
Premy, 114, 119, 204
Preux aux Bois, 226
Principles of mechanized warfare, 7-8
Principles of war, 7-8, 61-62, 130
Projected Bases for the Tactical Employment of Tanks in 1918, by Fuller, June 1917, 89
Proyart, 180, 193, 194
Puisieux, 49
Pursuit, 10, 59, 92-93, 98, 125-126, 143, 158-159, 161, 163-164, 213, 215-216
Pushable shield, 13-14, 16, 25
Quadrilateral, 46, 99, 206
Quartermaster, 26, 53-55
Queant, 76, 202
Quennemont, 204, 212, 214
Le Quesnel, 180, 182
Le Quesnoy, 180, 224, 226

Radcliffe, Percy, 150, 153, 154
Radios, 44-45, 92, 102, 109, 112, 185, 188,
Raiding, 10-12, 75, 89, 91, 94-102, 113, 123-124, 137-140, 145, 167-169, 185, 231-232, 235
Raillencourt, 209
Rawlinson, Henry, 39, 158, 167-169, 172-173, 176, 181-183, 185, 192-195, 205, 212-213, 216-217
Redan Ridge, 49
Reincourt, 76
Ribeauville, 219
Ribecourt, 94, 99, 114, 120, 213
Richemont River, 217, 222
Riqueval, 210-213
Robertson, William, 26
Rockenbach, Samuel, 150n
Rocquigny, 45
Ronssoy, 206
Rosieres-en-Santerre, 180, 182, 192-194
Roulers, 83
Rouvroy, 180, , 193, 202
Royal Air Force, 171, 175, 182, 188, 198, 213
Royal Armoured Corps, 122
Royal Engineers, 14, 20, 32, 37-38, 41, 53-55, 57, 59, 67-68, 86-87, 91, 95, 97, 98, 102, 108-110, 133, 146, 161-162, 170, 174, 207-208, 215, 219, 227-229, 232, 234, 237n
Royal Flying Corps, 34, 171, 233
Royal Green Jackets, 149n
Royal Marines, 13
Royal Navy Air Service, 13, 25-26
Roye, 180, 182, 194, 224
Rumilly, 98, 99, 117, 119
Runners, 36, 45, 64, 86, 112
Sains-les-Marquion, 207
Saint-Benin, 217, 219
Saint-Crepin 217
Saint-Julien, 88
Saint-Martin-Riviere, 219
Saint-Olle, 209
Saint-Pierre-Divon, 49
Saint-Quentin, 93, 95, 100-101, 171, 207, 208, 224
Saint-Quentin Canal, 12, 98, 99, 109, 209, 210, 211, 213, 219
Saint-Ribert, 176, 179
Saint-Souplet, 217, 219
Salvage Company, 52, 53, 195, 216, 238
Sambre River, 12, 224, 225, 231, 237
Sandhurst, 56
Sapignies, 200
Le Sars, 45
Sassegnies, 226
Sauchy-Lestree, 207
Sauvillers-Mongival, 177, 179, 231
Scarpe River, 71, 72, 76, 201, 202, 207, 224
Scheldt River, 221, 224
Schulz, Otto, 31
Schwaben Redoubt, 47
Scott-Moncrieff, George, 17
SD7, 150, 154-156, 181, 185
Searchlights, 14, 140

Searle, France, 109-110, 146-148
Seely, John, 153, 156
Sehnenstellung, 80
Selle River, 12, 217-220, 232, 234
Sensee River, 99, 103, 113
Serain, 204, 215
Seranvillers, 99, 117
Serre-les-Puisieux, 49
Siegfriedstellung, 63, 120
Signalling balloons, 19, 36, 45
Signalling flags, 36, 108
Signalling lamps, 34, 61n
Signalling rockets, 19, 36, 104, 175
Smith, H.G., 71
Solly-Flood, Arthur, 107
Somme, 20, 23-26, 33, 41-42, 45, 49, 52-53, 57, 64, 68, 126-127, 138-139, 152, 167, 170-171, 182,
Speed, defined, 9
Spotlight, 14
Staden, 83
Staff College, Army, 56, 57
Stern, Albert, 21, 71, 75, 100, 145n, 150, 156
Stewart, Ian, 149
Stuff Trench, 50
Sueter, Murray, 25
Supreme Allied Command, 154, 159, 193
Supreme War Council, 152
Surprise, defined, 8
Sustainment, defined, 10
Swinton, Ernest, 10, 21, 13-54, 57, 62, 67, 68, 73, 91, 110, 127, 234
Syria, 221
The Tactical Employment of Tanks 1918, by Fuller, August 1917, 89
Tandy, M. O'C., 20, 28-32, 35-36, 38-39, 41, 44
Tank, defined, 7
Tank, A7V, 147, 149, 162
Tank, Ambulance, 54-55
Tank, Artillery, 129, 140
Tank, Battle, 55
Tank, Bridging, 90, 92, 109, 112, 135, 227, 228, 234
Tank, cable-burying, 19, 45, 109, 175, 223, 228
Tank, Destroyer, 55, 125
Tank, dummy, 205, 218
Tank, Engineers, 55, 67
Tank, Female, 25, 29, 34, 47, 51, 91, 107, 139, 148, 190, 191
Tank, Flying Elephant, 145
Tank, Gun Carrier, 55, 92, 95, 109, 129, 168, 174, 184, 191
Tank, Light, 55, 75, 90, 92, 96-97, 113, 142-143, 145-146, 159, 195
Tank, Light, FT, Renault, 75, 92, 146
Tank, Male, 25, 29, 34, 50-51, 68, 76, 91, 107, 135, 137, 148, 190, 191
Tank, Man-Killing, see: Tank, Female
Tank, Mark I, 15-16, 23, 31, 37, 55, 62, 72, 76, 77, 80, 145n, 174, 198
Tank, Mark II, 62, 72, 76, 174
Tank, Mark III, 62

Tank, Mark IV, 61, 62, 72, 75, 77, 80, 88, 93, 125, 129, 130, 135, 136n, 138, 139, 147, 160, 168, 170, 172-174, 183, 191, 195, 200, 202, 208, 238

Tank, Mark V, 118, 123, 127-129, 136, 145-146, 152, 154, 156, 158, 168-169, 172-174, 183-184, 190, 195, 199-200, 214-216, 218-219, 223, 225, 235, 238

Tank, Mark V*, 93, 136, 152, 154, 156, 157, 174, 184, 190, 199-200, 206, 214, 220, 223

Tank, Mark V**, 152, 154, 157

Tank, Mark VII, 152, 154, 157

Tank, Mark VIII, 125, 135, 150, 152, 154, 155-156, 238

Tank, Mark IX, 143, 152, 154, 157, 162-163, 174, 223

Tank, Mark X, 157

Tank, Medium A, 69, 75, 120, 138, 140, 143, 145-149, 152, 154, 158-159, 168, 174, 182-184, 191-193, 195, 199-200, 202, 208, 215-216, 218, 220, 226, 228, 229, 235, 239

Tank, Medium B, 136n, 145, 149, 152, 154, 157

Tank, Medium C, 145-146, 149, 152, 154, 157, 156, 165, 238

Tank, Medium D, 10-11, 128, 146-165, 235, 238

Tank, Medium E, 162, 238

Tank, Mortar, 129, 140, 160

Tank, radio, 19, 45, 90, 92, 102, 109, 112, 175, 191, 208, 215, 223, 228

Tank, Signals, 54-55, 112, 162, 199

Tank, Smoke, 170

Tank, Supply, 10, 44, 55, 69, 77, 79-80, 87, 89, 91, 97, 102, 109, 111-112, 163, 168, 174, 178, 184, 191, 195, 199, 202, 206, 208, 215, 220, 223, 227-228, 234, 235, 238-239

Tank, Torpedo, 55, 61, 68, 125, 162,

Tank, wire-grappling, 18, 38, 91, 102, 109-112, 234

A Tank Army, by Martel, November 1916, 54, 61, 67, 75, 80

Tank Army, 62, 125, 147, 159n

Tank Corps, 9, 10, 12, 20, 23n, 29, 39n, 54, 55, 59, 60, 63, 67, 69, 71, 83-87, 89, 93-94, 101-102, 104, 108, 109, 111, 112, 114, 115, 120, 121, 123, 124, 127, 128, 130, 135, 137-141, 145, 149, 150, 154-156, 160, 162-163, 167-168, 170-175, 177, 181-185, 188, 190-191, 193-194, 198, 218, 225, 229-230, 232, 235-237

Tank Operations Decisive and Preparatory 1918-1919, by Fuller, January 1918, 10, 124, 126, 137

Tank Raids, by Fuller, August 1917, 95-98, 100-101

Tank Raids, Fuller's expectations as of January 1918, 123, 137-140, 145, 167

Tank Supply Committee, 53

Tank Training Note Number 16, by Fuller, February 1917, 61-64, 69, 80

Tank unditching gear, 86

Tankette, 21, 67, 97

Tapper, Michael J., 54

Telegraph, 19, 109, 160

Telephone, 44-45, 112, 160

Terrain, defined, 8

Thetford, 20, 54

Thiepval, 12, 23, 33, 47, 49, 231

Thierry, 181

Thilloy, 45

Thourout, 83

Tourcoing, 224

Tournai, 224

Townshend, F.H.E., 11, 53, 57-60, 91, 141, 163

Training in Cooperation Between Infantry and Tanks, by Fuller, December 1917, 129-130

Trades, 10

Trap Door Spider Tactics, 139

Trescault, 98, 119

Tritton, William, 145n

Le Tronquoy, 211

Uzielli, T.J., 52, 54-55, 59

Valenciennes, 103, 106, 221, 224, 225

Variants of the Offensive, by Churchill, 3 December 1915, 16-18, 24, 28, 30, 32, 37, 41, 43

Vaughan, L.R., 108, 111

Vauvillers, 193

Vaulx-Vraucourt, 202

Vaux-Andigny, 217-219

Villeret, 205

Villers-Bretonneux, 180, 182, 189, 191

Villers-Faucon, 113

Villers-Guislain, 98, 101, 103, 119, 121-122

Villers-les-Cagnicourt, 203

Villers-Plouich, 98, 115, 119

Vorfeldzone, 41

Wagons, horse-drawn, 42, 44, 124

Wancourt, 202

War Department, 13, 15, 26n, 54, 147

War Office, 7, 14, 16, 18n, 20, 24-25, 37, 54, 63, 71, 93, 141, 148, 150, 153, 154, 156, 185, 193

Wareham, 54

Warfusee, 193

Warlencourt, 45

Warvillers, 180, 194

Wassigny, 217

Watson, W.H.L., 76

Western GHQ, 160, 162, 164

Whigham, Robert D., 71

Wiencourt, 189

Wigram, Kenneth, 93

Williams-Ellis, Clough, 101

Wilson, Henry, 149n, 150-156, 163, 182, 193, 215, 221

Wilson, Walter Gordon, 15

Wire obstacles, 10, 15-19, 23-24, 29, 32-41, 44-45, 47, 50, 63-65, 73, 75, 90-92, 97, 100, 106-112, 116-117, 125, 127, 131, 133, 135, 136, 167, 169, 174, 178, 188-189, 201-202, 209, 211, 213, 215, 217, 218, 222, 234

Wood: see Bois

Wotan Line, 201

Yeomanry, 215

Ypres, 79, 82, 83, 101, 126, 167, 224

Yvrench, 58

253

About the author

Bruce Oliver Newsome, Ph.D., is a historian, political scientist, and defence, risk, and security consultant. He held standing faculty positions at University of Texas, University of San Diego, University of California Berkeley, University of Pennsylvania, and the Defence Academy of the United Kingdom. Before teaching, he spent five years at the RAND Corporation, advising national governments on defence and security. He served in the British Army reserves, US Army National Guard, and Texas State Guard.

Other books by this author

Tank Raids and Blitzkrieg: The Development and Misrepresentation of Maneuver Warfare from the Great War to the Second World War, Perseublishing, 2025

Indirect Approach: From Sun Tzu to Liddell Hart, Persublishing, 2025.

Sir Basil Liddell Hart: Life, Thought, Legacy, Perseublishing, 2025.

Sir Basil Liddell Hart and Tanks, Perseublishing, 2024.

A Practical Introduction to Security and Risk Management, Perseublishing, 2023.

Panzer III vs. Valentine Tank, North Africa, 1941-1943, Osprey, 2023.

The Rise and Fall of Western Tanks, Volume I, 1855-1939, and Volume II, 1939-1955, Tank Archives Press, 2021.

A Practical Introduction to Homeland Security and Emergency Management from Home to Abroad, Rowman & Littlefield, 2020. With Jack Jarmon.

The Tiger Tank and Allied Intelligence, 4 volumes, Tank Archives Press, 2020.

Countering New(est) Terrorism: Assessing, Negotiating, and Ending Hostage Crises, Kidnappings, and Active Shootings, CRC Press, Taylor & Francis, 2018.

M1 Abrams Main Battle Tank: Owners' Workshop Manual. Haynes, 2017.

An Introduction to Research, Analysis, and Writing: Practical Skills for Social Science Students, SAGE, 2015.

Made, Not Born: Why Some Soldiers Are Better than Others. Praeger, 2007.

Getting Inside the Terrorist Mind, RAND, 2007.

Breaching the Fortress Wall: Understanding Terrorist Efforts to Overcome Defensive Technologies, RAND, 2007.

www.ingramcontent.com/pod-product-compliance
Lightning Source LLC
Chambersburg PA
CBHW061754070526
44586CB00023B/2610